Institutional Analysis and Praxis

Tara Natarajan · Wolfram Elsner
Scott T. Fullwiler
Editors

Institutional Analysis and Praxis

The Social Fabric Matrix Approach

 Springer

Editors
Tara Natarajan
Saint Michael's College
Winooski Park, Box 234
Colchester, VT 05439
USA

Wolfram Elsner
Institute for Institutional and Innovation Economics-iino
Faculty for Economics and Business Studies
University of Bremen
Hochschulring 4
D-28359 Bremen
Germany

Scott T. Fullwiler
Wartburg College
100 Wartburg Blvd.
Waverly, IA 50677
USA

ISBN 978-0-387-88740-1   e-ISBN 978-0-387-88741-8
DOI 10.1007/978-0-387-88741-8
Springer New York Dordrecht Heidelberg London

Library of Congress Control Number: 2009930640

Printed on acid-free paper

Springer is part of Springer Science+Business Media (www.springer.com)

To Greg and Theresa Hayden

Foreword

There has never been a better time for the social fabric matrix. As this book is being published, the idea that unregulated market capitalism leads to the best of all possible worlds has been thoroughly discredited. A series of economic and social problems have come to the forefront of national discussion and policy debates. There is now widespread acceptance that human activity, particularly the consumption of nonrenewable energy resources, has contributed to global warming. The lack of oversight of the financial industry encouraged reckless practices that endangered the stability of the entire financial system, prompting bailout efforts based on the fragile interdependence of the financial and economic systems. The shortcomings of our health care system are increasingly evident, including the growing number of uninsured citizens, the difficulties for businesses in offering health insurance, and the effects of health and health care on the ability of individuals and families to maintain a decent standard of living. Perhaps the best illustration of a complex system that cries out for coordinated policy-making is in the critical area of energy, where public and private decisions on energy policy not only have direct effects on consumer costs, but also have effects on global warming, local ecosystems, international relations, the health of our citizens, and the sustainability of companies and communities.

In short, there is growing recognition of the interdependence of the economic system with the environment and the broader institutions of society. The social fabric matrix is a critical tool for understanding and mapping this interdependence, looking not only at direct effects but also at the many indirect effects and interactions that occur with almost every economic and policy decision. As the essays in this book make clear, it is highly versatile, with applications to a wide spectrum of public and private decision-making.

I first met Greg Hayden, who designed the social fabric matrix, when I was a college intern in the Nebraska legislature. I was working on a project on energy policy, for which he was an advisor. I was so impressed with Greg's perspective that I chose to come to the University of Nebraska-Lincoln to study with him in graduate school. It was one of the best decisions of my life. He gave me a thorough grounding in institutional economics and excellent training in doing policy-relevant research. His intelligence, wit, and caring were an inspiration to me and many other young scholars. It was clear both then and now that he combines excellent analytical skills with a deep concern about real-world outcomes, reflecting his desire to ensure that social and economic institutions effectively serve society's values.

Greg strongly impressed a candidate in the Nebraska Governor's race, Bob Kerrey, so that when Kerrey was elected he asked Greg to be one of his top aides. I also joined state government at that time and helped Greg design and implement several task forces on economic development. All of our work was based on the principles that he developed in the social fabric matrix, examining the connections among economic activity, technology, public and private policy, social and physical infrastructure, and environmental and community health. Those principles have stayed with me and informed all of my research and policy work.

More than ever, the actions of individuals and organizations can have cascading effects throughout the economic, social, environmental, and political systems. This book will help to spread awareness of the social fabric matrix and show how it is an excellent tool for addressing our mounting economic and social problems in an intelligent and humane way.

Douglas Kruse
Rutgers University

Contents

Contributors

Richard V. Adkisson is Wells Fargo Professor of Economics and International Business at New Mexico State University. He currently serves as editor of the *Journal of Economic Issues*. His research interests include institutional economics, public policy, and economic development. Published papers can be found in the *Journal of Economic Issues, International Trade Journal, Growth and Change, Journal of Borderlands Studies, Social Science Journal*, and *Policy Studies Review*.

Sebastian Berger is an assistant professor at Roanoke College and was awarded the 2008 Helen Potter Award for the most original paper by a promising scholar in the *Review of Social Economy*. Areas of his work are ecological institutional economics and theories of social costs. Berger's work has been published in the *Journal of Economics Issues, Journal of Ecological Economics*, and *Review of Social Economy*. His doctoral thesis was published by Peter Lang Verlag in 2007 as "Europäischer Institutionalismus" and analyzes the role of Circular Cumulative Causation within Evolutionary Economics.

Steven R. Bolduc is Associate Professor of Economics and Director of the Public, Human Service, and Health Administration Graduate Program at Minnesota State University-Moorhead. His areas of research interest include Original Institutional Economics, Microeconomics, Ecological Economics, and Public Policy Analysis. Bolduc received his Ph.D. in Economics from the University of Nebraska under the supervision of F. Gregory Hayden.

Wayne Edwards is Associate Professor of Economics at the University of Alaska Anchorage. His general area of inquiry is at-risk groups of people. In recent years, he has published several articles on the Circumpolar North. His newest work involves indigenous peoples in South Asia.

Wolfram Elsner is Professor of Economics in the Institute for Institutional and Innovation Economics – iino, Faculty of Economics and Business Studies, University of Bremen, Germany. He worked as head of a city development agency and as Director of the Planning Division of the Ministry of Economic Affairs of the State of Bremen, among others, from 1986 to 1995. He has been a member of AFEE since 1985 and a founding member of EAEPE in 1989. He is on the editorial board of several international journals, has edited and co-edited books, edits two book series on institutional economics, and has published in many journals.

Scott T. Fullwiler is Associate Professor of Economics, James A. Leach Chair in Banking and Monetary Economics, and Social Entrepreneurship Program Director at Wartburg College in Waverly, Iowa. He is also a Research Associate at the Center for Full Employment and Price Stability at the University of Missouri-Kansas City. His research focuses on monetary operations, interest rates, fiscal policy, and large macroeconometric models; he has a particular interest in investigating traditional macroeconomic topics using the Social Fabric Matrix Approach. He received his Ph.D. from the University of Nebraska under the supervision of F. Gregory Hayden.

Roderic Gill is a long-term ecological economics researcher, organizer of Australia's inaugural ecological economics conference and author of Australia's first ecological economics research agenda. He has personally supervised over 20 Ph.D. completions in the ecological economics, system dynamics, systems thinking area, and is a former director of the Centre for Ecological Economics and Water Policy Research at the University of New England, Australia.

Matthew Gray completed a Ph.D. at the University of New England, Australia in 2006, after having worked there for 7 years. His research focused specifically on the SFM and its integration with ideas from system dynamics, ecological economics, and environmental management. He currently works as a consultant researcher, a business manager and teaches in the area of sustainability at the Queensland University of Technology, Brisbane.

F. Gregory Hayden is Professor of Economics at the University of Nebraska-Lincoln. His research has been devoted to three areas since receiving his doctorate in economics at the University of Texas-Austin. They are (1) the development of the social fabric matrix, (2) development of a meta policymaking paradigm, and (3) the application of instrumental philosophy to policy analysis. The three areas have been integrated in his institutional economic theory research and public policy analysis. Consequently, his publications are extensive and diverse. He is a recipient of the Veblen-Commons Award.

Jerry L. Hoffman is a labor organizer and bargaining specialist with the Nebraska State Education Association, a state affiliate of the National Education Association. He received his M.A. in Institutional Economics and Public Policy at the University of Nebraska. Mr. Hoffman has nearly 20 years of experience as an education organizer, public education finance activist, public education reformer, community developer, and policy advisor.

Tristan Philip Skrdla Markwell studied economics, mathematics and statistics, and political science at the University of Nebraska-Lincoln. He holds an M.A. in Economics from the University of Nebraska-Lincoln. He is currently a Quality Analyst with Providence Health & Services in Portland, OR.

Tara Natarajan is an Associate Professor of Economics at Saint Michael's College in Vermont. Her primary area of research is development, poverty, and agrarian area studies. She applies institutional economics to study industrialization of agriculture, rural development activism, poverty, and livelihoods related to dry land southern India. More recently, she has also coauthored works on poverty amongst Native Alaskans. She has published in the *Journal of Economic Issues*, *Natives Studies Review*, and *Forum for Social Economics*, amongst others.

Saeed Parto is co-founder and Director of Research at Afghanistan Public Policy Research Organization (APPRO). He holds a Ph.D. in Geography from the University of Waterloo (Ontario, Canada) and specializes in policy and institutional analysis. He is also visiting lecturer at the Faculty of Arts and Social Sciences, Maastricht University (The Netherlands).

Michael J. Radzicki is an Associate Professor of Economics at Worcester Polytechnic Institute in Worcester, Massachusetts. He received his Ph.D. in economics from the University of Notre Dame and his training in system dynamics modeling from the Massachusetts Institute of Technology. His research focuses on using insights from cognitive psychology, Post Keynesian economics, and institutional economics to build system dynamics and agent-based computer simulation models of complex socioeconomic systems. In addition to his work in economics and computational methods, Radzicki is an avid long distance runner, martial artist, golfer, and futures trader. In 2006 he served as president of the System Dynamics Society.

Akshay Regmi was an intern in Political Economy and Governance at the Afghanistan Research and Evaluation Unit at the time of this study.

James I. Sturgeon is professor of economics and department chair at the University of Missouri-Kansas City and an Honorary Fellow at Bremen University. He teaches Institutional Economics and Industrial Organization. He has served as president of the Association for Evolutionary Economics and the Association for Institutional Thought and was a Co-founder of the latter. His research and publishing interest is institutional economic theory.

The Social Fabric Matrix Approach to Policy Analysis: An Introduction

Scott T. Fullwiler, Wolfram Elsner, and Tara Natarajan

Abstract The purpose of this chapter is to introduce the reader to the Social Fabric Matrix approach to policy analysis (SFM-A) as laid out in Hayden (2006). This chapter is better understood as a "how to" chapter rather than as a more traditional summary or discussion of the rest of the contributions in the volume. The chapter describes the foundations of the SFM-A approach in general systems theory and instrumentalist philosophy. It then describes the process of building an SFM, and presents extensions of the SFM-A to normative systems analysis, analysis of time and timeliness, quantitative modeling, and social indicators. The chapter concludes with a brief summary of the rest of the chapters.

Introduction

In *Policymaking for a Good Society: The Social Fabric Matrix Approach to Policy Analysis and Program Evaluation* (hereafter referred to as *Policymaking*), F. Gregory Hayden lays out a rigorous, comprehensive methodology for undertaking policy-relevant research on complex real-world problems. The Social Fabric Matrix Approach (hereafter, SFM-A) and methodology is philosophically and theoretically developed from, and consistent with, the *original evolutionary-institutional economics* (hereafter, OIE – "Original" Institutional Economics) and is one of the most comprehensive, empirical, and policy-relevant methodologies to come out of OIE.

The publication, subsequent discussion, and further applications of *Policymaking* provide an opportunity to further explore and demonstrate the potential for fruitful research, policy analysis, and policy recommendations in the context of the SFM methodology.

This volume is needed and presented because of the relevance of the SFM-A and its influence on scientific methodology and policy analysis. In short, the SFM-A is creating, if not a new school of thought, then a class of applied, empirical, and policy-relevant analyses of complex problems in networked configurations. We basically refer to *complexity* when there are direct interdependencies among many heterogenous agents. As one reviewer of *Policymaking* suggests, the SFM approach

S.T. Fullwiler (✉)
Wartburg College, Waverly, IA, USA

T. Natarajan et al. (eds.), *Institutional Analysis and Praxis*,
DOI 10.1007/978-0-387-88741-8_1, © Springer Science+Business Media, LLC 2009

"in fact may serve as *the* future methodology not only for complex heterodox economic analysis but also for policy evaluation in order to make policy more consistent with the complexity of reality" (Elsner 2007).

Modern society faces a number of already well-documented challenges from ecological destruction; globalization, uneven development, and economic inequality; un(der)employment; financial market shortcomings; power and hierarchical regulations; innovation vs. vested interests; the aging of populations in many societies, and so forth – with other yet unnamed challenges sure to be added. They all reflect, among other things, an increasing complexity (Elsner 2005). Addressing such challenges appropriately will require critical analysis of complex *interrelations* and *incentive structures, ceremonial* and *instrumental* institutional arrangements and values, ideologies and belief systems, (often faulty) public policies, actions, and nonactions – hence, the need for relevant research methodologies.

Hayden (2006a, p.1) writes that, unfortunately, "the understanding we have gained from science and from experiencing the technological society on a day-to-day basis has… yet to produce a good society." Instead,

> people work more hours only to watch their wages and salaries fall; they support more environmental protection endeavors only to learn that pollution levels continue to grow and species continue to be lost; people gain higher levels of education and training only to remain underemployed. Government employees work hard, gather more data than ever, and access greater computer capability, yet productivity problems continue to abound; tax payments to governments and consumer payments to corporations continue to grow, but every day we see infrastructure deteriorating and consumer products becoming shoddier. Production has grown on a global scale and trade has increased among nations, while per capita income in over half of these nations is lower than a decade ago… the resource commitment to health care is massive yet the reality of the American health care system is that it is very sick; and billions of public dollars are poured into farm payments, while … family farms continue to fail. (p.2)

Policymaking explains "an approach to policy analysis and planning that *will* allow us to capture the complexity of the world around us and be consistent with modern science" (p.1; emphasis added). Thus, past and even current ongoing failures notwithstanding,

> the premise here is that we know enough, care enough, and have adequate resources and technology to solve our social, economic, and environmental problems. Or, stated differently, this book is optimistic by current standards of cynicism and pessimism. Our knowledge base is sufficient to do the research to understand our problems, our will is more than adequate, our work ethic is strong, our resources are abundant, and people are sufficiently educated to carry out the tasks in a technological society. (p.2)

The shortcoming heretofore has been that "we have not had the analytical means necessary to meld our will, knowledge, and institutions into a policy paradigm that allows us to obtain success" (p.2).

It is no small feat to design a method with such broad applicability as the SFM-A has already demonstrated, particularly since to do so also requires a significant break from previous dominant analytical paradigms that relied heavily upon reductionism and determinism (i.e., noncomplexity). Instead, Hayden argues that, a new approach, if it is to be successful, must integrate modern science with an instrumentalist philosophy:

> because we no longer believe that life—as structured in an institutional and ecological milieu—is one dimensional, our measures and analytical tools cannot be one dimensional. Because we no longer think that beliefs and values can be ignored, if for example, we want

successful irrigation systems or health care plans, an approach is needed to integrate what sociologists and anthropologists know about beliefs and values with the expertise of engineers, ecologists, agronomists, economists, physicians, and other expertise as needed for the problem at hand. This integration can no longer be the kind that has persons working with different expertise working in isolation, and their independent work then placed under one cover. The analysts need to be guided by a common model, or, to use Einstein's term, a common frame. The engineer's work must be guided by belief criteria, the sociologists' analysis should be consistent with the relevant technology, the economists' models need to be non-equilibrium systems, policymakers' actions are the results of integrated modeling, and so forth. (p. 1)

The editors and contributors to this volume suggest that the SFM-A provides not only a powerful framework for policy research but also a framework that is comprehensive and adaptable to a wide variety of socioeconomic and policy issues. Moreover, policy success obtained *without* such a complexity-reflecting analytical approach will be *coincidental*.

In this chapter, we introduce the SFM-A by first discussing its theoretical underpinnings, then the SFM itself, and finally its larger paradigm for policy analysis.

Instrumentalist Philosophy and the SFM Methodology

Marc Tool writes that "[v]alue premises permeate the whole of social inquiry. If inquiry is purposive—and it must be—it is value laden…. Value assumptions, premises, criteria, are involved in our perception of what is a proper object of inquiry" (1986, p. 57). Nobel Prize winning economist Gunnar Myrdal agreed that "valuations are always with us. Disinterested research there has never been and can never be… Our valuations determine our approach to a problem, the definition of the concepts, the selection of observations, and, … in fact, the whole pursuit of study from beginning to the end" (quoted in Hickerson 1988, p. 167). As mentioned, the SFM-A is based upon the *instrumentalist* approach to inquiry. The instrumentalist approach emphasizes the normative, embedded *process* of research and its influence on experience, the relationship of knowing to the purpose of solving problems, and the need for solutions to evolve with changing and evolving contexts.

Hayden (2006a, Chap. 3) lists three conceptual pillars for applying instrumentalist philosophy in the policy sciences: the transactional approach to science, a problem orientation, and judging actions by their consequences.

Regarding the first of these, Hayden writes, "'trans' means across, and the emphasis is on the reality that there are numerous rules, regulatory criteria, enforcement agencies, laws, institutions, and beliefs across any relationship or transaction; numerous overlapping forces guide the agents and their actions" (p. 25). The argument here is that traditional, interactional approaches – such as neoclassical economics' supply and demand equilibrium analysis – are by themselves overly simplistic to serve as the foundation for real-world policy analysis. For instance, instead of the interactional forces of supply and demand in a mythical "loanable funds" market, the real world of borrowing and lending includes

the Federal Reserve System, the International Group of Seven (G-7), the International Monetary Fund, the World Bank, the international electronic currency system, the local savings and loan (and therefore the Resolution Trust Fund), the Federal Deposit Insurance Corporation (FDIC), the Community Reinvestment Act, state governments, labor union pension funds, the bond market, U. S. Supreme Court decisions, property rights, and so forth. Field of concern, upon field of concern; context overlapped with context; criteria layered upon criteria—that is the transactional world of finance. (p. 27)

More could certainly be added to that list. The *transactional approach* to science thereby calls upon the researcher investigating a given phenomena to "seek complexity and order it" (p. 27).

But, of course, "policy inquiry would be impossible if all connections were pursued" (p. 28). Research in a transactional context thus begins not with the building of a model or a detailing of various interactions within a system, but rather through determination of what information is to be learned and which questions are to be answered. That is, "the solution [to the question of what part of a theory or real-world system to study] is to define the context of inquiry by the problem to be solved" (ibid.); if the problem to be investigated is not defined, "there is no indication of where to start, go, or stop the policy research" (p. 29). Thus, research based upon instrumentalist philosophy begins with the identification of a problem as the subject for analysis and develops the proper methodology to explore and analyze the complex interrelational sets of the problem structure.

The problem-based approach in a transactional context is also a natural fit with OIE. The founders of OIE long ago recognized the nonequilibrium, evolutionary nature of real-world capitalism. Thorstein Veblen, John Commons, Karl Polanyi, and Clarence Ayres (to name but a few) all made significant contributions to current understanding of the legal, sociological, and technological foundations of economic systems, while Wesley Mitchell pioneered efforts to quantify economic indicators and measure the outcomes of a modern capitalist system. More recently, OIE scholars have similarly advanced understanding in policy-relevant areas including the interrelationship between ecological systems and socioeconomic systems and the nature of money, finance, and accounting in a capitalist economy.

Finally, as instrumentalism is an evaluative approach based upon problems in a transactional context, policies should be judged by their consequences: "the purpose of policy analysis is to discover the consequences of particular actions, and to formulate policy so as to secure some consequences and avoid others" (p. 29). *Criteria* used in evaluation are necessarily normative since problems and the nature of inquiry are normative in nature as well. Instrumentalist philosophy thus points to normative, social criteria as *standards of judgment.* As Warren Samuels has explained, the very concept of "efficiency" – in this case, as often proxied in economics research by "output" or like terms – is necessarily normative:

The definition of "output"—of what it is that one is to be efficient about—requires an antecedent normative specification as to the appropriate performance goal for society. Social output (the aggregate well-being of society), consumptive output (the value of goods from the consumer point of view), and productive output (the value of goods from the producer point of view, i.e., profits) are three examples of alternatives that are available.

The recognition of the multiplicity of efficient solutions and the contingency of any given efficient solution on the presumed structure of rights and the definition of output reveals the inherent normative element that is present in efficiency-based decision making. (Samuels 1978, 1981; quoted in Mercuro and Medema 1997, p. 119)

Hayden (1982) suggests three sources of normative criteria for instrumental evaluation of consequences, drawing upon the work of Karl Polanyi, Walter Neale, and Marc Tool. Polanyi's (1957) concept of *sufficiency* was necessary to evaluate consequences (Hayden 2006a, Chap. 9). When a given process is insufficient for a desirable system to be sustained, the process is not instrumentally efficient. Significantly, sufficiency may not be consistent with "optimization" of deliveries. Tool (1979) claims that *participatory democracy* provides a swift feedback to policies and proposed solutions, since affected groups or social interests are able to voice concerns. The increased speed of instrumental valuation of policies enables better refinement and application of normative criteria (Hayden 2006a, Chap. 3). Finally, Neale argues that "a requirement for social processes is that they be *legitimate*" (Neale 1980, p. 393; emphasis in original):

> Legitimacy requires a social moral consensus on norms with regard to the *consequences* of social policy and with regard to the *procedures* which produce those consequences. Therefore, policy analysis for structuring social processes cannot be fruitful unless the social criteria guiding the policy analysis are fair and just. If there is not a social consensus on these criteria, then the resulting policy will be inconsistent with the social consensus. (Neale, cited in Hayden (1982, p. 643)

Given an evolving socioecological–technological context, solutions must be reevaluated for instrumental efficiency against normative criteria, while the criteria must be consistent with the evolving context:

> There is no contextual shift if the problem can be solved by selecting policies that will align and strengthen the bonds of current institutions and beliefs. If, however, the socioeconomic problem is more pronounced, a common situation is for the policy criteria to be consistent with *current* beliefs, thereby selecting policy arrangements that perpetuate the problem or make it worse. Institutions usually need to be changed to solve problems. This means a major task of any policy analysis is to design a set of criteria that will be consistent with the *new* set of beliefs and institutions necessary for solving the problem. (Hayden 2006a, p. 41; emphasis in original)

What Hayden refers to as "contextual shifts" are frequently driven by technological evolution, such as the "information revolution." Technology contributes to faster paces of contextual shift, and "the faster disruptions happen, the less opportunity for the instrumental research process to gain an understanding of the most reasonable policy to be successful" (p. 41). Thus, the evaluation of technology is crucial for instrumental efficiency. By way of contrast, the received view of economists and many policymakers that technological change is self-evidently good constitutes a ceremonial institutional behavior rather than an instrumentally efficient one. However, "If the source of human progress resides in the *process* of instrumental valuing rather than in technology..., then it is the *evaluation of the consequences* of any particular use of [technology] which is progressive. Ceremonialism is a failure to evaluate by testing consequences." (Mayhew 1981, p. 515)

General Systems Analysis

In order to design effective policy solutions, there is a clear need to bring to bear the most current and up-to-date knowledge created by experts in the relevant fields, be they the natural environment, the financial system, physical infrastructure, health policy, and so forth. Such expertise is also required for designing and then interpreting indicators of policy effectiveness. This is all rather straightforward, of course. However, there are some clear "do's" and "don'ts," since "policy relevant knowledge" is what is sought.

Systems theory originated in the natural sciences and has been central to the emerging chaos theory, complex-adaptive systems theory, or self-organizing systems theory literatures. Ludwig von Bertalanffy, one of the most important originators of systems theory similarly noted that the "concepts and principles of systems theory are not limited to material systems, but can be applied to any [whole] consisting of interacting [components]" (quoted in Greene 1991, p. 234). De Greene agreed that "we can speak of a *transportation system, an urban system, a health services system, an anti-crime and violence system,* etc." (De Greene 1973, p. 4; emphasis in original).

Within the economics literature, consideration of a systems-oriented approach is central in the work of several of the founders of OIE. Thorstein Veblen's dichotomy between ceremonial and technological aspects of society emphasized the need to examine interrelationships and conflict from a perspective incorporating both social customs and technical evolution. Polanyi (1957) argued that social systems are instituted processes in which human institutions, technology, and the ecology interact with one another. Commons (1924/1955) founded his analysis of the workings of capitalism on analysis of the codification of social beliefs, customs, and norms into laws and regulations. Each suggested that an appropriate approach to analysis of economic problems embedded economic analysis within an examination of the social fabric relevant to these problems.

The most fundamental point of emphasis within systems methodology is a *holistic*, or "top–down" approach, which "has been viewed by scientists and practitioners as a revolutionary departure from earlier mechanistic, reductionist thinking… [and] … represent[s] a major shift or global reorientation in scientific thinking" (Greene 1991, p. 228). Reductionist thinking is the analysis of individual parts in isolation from the whole, and the whole is then seen as the sum of its parts, or isomorphic. Doyne Farmer, a chaos theorist, states,

> The trend in science… has been toward reductionism, a constant breaking things down into little bitty pieces…. What people are finally realizing is that that process has a dead end to it. Scientists are much more interested in the idea that the whole can be greater than the sum of the parts [or non-isomorphic]. (quoted in Radzicki (1990, p. 57)

Systems analysts will obviously research the parts of a system, as well. However, in contrast to reductionist methods, systems theorists disaggregate the system into subsystems without engaging in reductionism by recognizing that "(a) each of the fractions, in isolation, is capable of being completely understood, and most important, that (b) *any* property of the original system can be reconstructed from the relevant properties of the fractional subsystems" (Hayden 2006a, p. 54).

By taking a holistic approach to analysis, systems analysts have recognized several characteristics of real-world systems (Hayden 2006a, Chap. 4):

1. Real-world systems exhibit *interdependence* and *openness*. Consistent with the holistic viewpoint, systems theory examines parts of a system with respect to their relation-

ship to the whole. Von Bertalanffy defined a system as "a complex of components in mutual interaction" (von Bertalanffy 1974, p. 1,100). The systems approach posits that parts of a system do not act in isolation. For example, the weather influences the yields of agricultural crops, while farming methods ultimately influence the climate, as was visible during the Dust Bowl years of the 1930s (Hayden 2006a, p. 31). In human societies, behaviors influence and are influenced by value systems, government regulations, technologies, societal structures, and so forth. Indeed, it is the interaction and evolution of the components of the system that is under investigation in the systems approach.

Richard Mattessich argues that the insistence by systems researchers "that *every system must be analyzed within the context of its environment* [. . .] constitutes the crux of the modern systems approach" (1978, 21; italics in original). The technological realities of modern society encourage particular activities that would not have been considered in other eras. Banking regulations and monetary policies in Western societies and in Islamic societies will be different due to different perspectives on the morality of debt and interest. In natural systems, Albert Einstein explained that time and motion were concepts that were relative to a particular context. Further, systems overlap in their actions with other systems, such as the interaction of human transportation systems and the effect on environmental systems of the resulting pollution, oil extraction, and highway construction. De Greene uses the term "sociotechnical system" to refer to "the problems of the interaction of technology with society and with patterns of life and work [which have] been with us in force since the Industrial Revolution and even before" (De Greene 1973, 4-5). Hayden (2006a) likewise suggests the terms "socioecological" and "socio-technical-environmental."

Real world systems are *open systems*, having a context within and interdependence with other systems outside themselves. "Open systems are those with a continuous flow of energy, information, or materials from environment to system and return" (De Greene 1973, p. 36). Human systems interact with ecosystems and technological systems, for example:

> The cell receives oxygen from the blood stream; the body similarly takes in oxygen from the air and food from the external world... The functioning personality is heavily dependent upon the continuous inflow of stimulation from the external environment. Similarly, social organizations must also draw renewed supplies of energy from other institutions,... or the material environment. No social structure is self-sufficient or self-contained. (Katz and Kahn 1969, pp. 92–93)

2. Real-world systems, as all complex systems, typically are *nonequilibrium* systems, but at the same time exhibiting the potentials of *self-governance* and *homeostasis*, or rather than short-run, static or stable equilibrium or becoming motionless, the concern within the system is with maintenance of certain system structures and properties of their processes within which evolution and sustainability may coexist. "At the simple level [the steady state] is one of homeostasis over time, [while] at more complex levels [it] becomes one of preserving the character of the system through growth and expansion" (Katz and Kahn 1969, p. 96). Complex systems may respond to changes in the environment in achieving goals and thus may exhibit some *equifinality* in that certain attractors system orbits can be achieved from a number of different points of origination and along a variety of different paths.

Complex systems also may exhibit *control* and *self-regulation* mechanisms. Rules in cellular systems, such as that in DNA, provide "chemical messages from the collections of cells that constrain the detailed genetic expression of individual cells that make up the collection" (Pattee 1973, p. 77). Social systems are continuously influenced in their evolution by evolving technological standards and requirements (De Greene 1973; Hayden 1998, 2006a). Social systems have beliefs, rules, regulations, and requirements that influence the performance of the system (Hayden 1998). Finally, Swaney (1987) explains that ecological systems provide constraints and rules for themselves and for the interaction of ecosystems with sociotechnical systems.

Complex systems typically have *hierarchical arrangements* that can come in many forms. Flows of physical materials and/or information integrate levels of existing system hierarchies and reinforce relations among the system components. "Hierarchical growth [within an entire system] by restructuring to a higher level of organization can occur when subsystems having different properties come into contact" (De Greene 1973, p. 72). Among social systems, "Even egalitarian or the most dysfunctional of systems have hierarchies" (Greene 1991, p. 237). Such hierarchy does not imply statics or authoritarianism. It is some structural property of complex systems rather, subject to evolution and some self-governance, reflecting the state of complexity and entropy of systems and allowing to extend the system's capabilities of self-organization, homeostasis, or equifinality.

Always present in systems is some form of *feedback*. Positive feedback reinforces growth or encourages decay in systems (De Greene 1973, p. 22); it is "fundamental to all growth processes in both living and non-living systems… [including]… fire, organisms, knowledge, capital, fads and fashions, mob violence, and political bandwagons" (p. 22). Negative feedback may sometimes be associated with "self-regulation and goal directions" and can be seen in "oscillations, fluctuations, and periodicities" associated with efforts to restore levels consistent with system sustainability (p. 22).

3. *Sequenced deliveries and flows*, or action–reaction sequences among agents, may integrate hierarchical levels and reinforce interdependent/overlapping components, feedback, and control mechanisms within the system. As sequenced flows, systems exist in *real* or *historical time*, where the flows and deliveries are the actual "clock" for the system that must remain coordinated for the sustainability of the system's functioning. Real time will be discussed further in the description of time and timeliness later.

4. Finally, systems exhibit *differentiation* and *elaboration*, evolving and becoming more complex; parts of social systems and ecosystems become more specialized in their roles. Such activities may enable a system to avoid entropy and preserve the character of the system through growth (see also above on hierarchy):

> Growth [first] calls for supportive subsystems of a specialized character not necessary when the system is smaller. In the second place, there is a point where quantitative changes produce a qualitative difference in the functioning of a system. A small college which triples its size is no longer the same institution in terms of the relation between its administration

and faculty, relations among the various academic departments, or the nature of its instruction. (Katz and Kahn 1969, p. 98)

The properties of differentiation and elaboration imply that the future products or outcomes of system processes are truly uncertain, path-dependent, and *nonergodic* (Arthur 1988; Davidson 1996), since the past record may not be a mirror of the future behavior. More complex combinations within systems produce more possible outcomes. According to De Greene, the "jumps from the Ptolemaic to the Copernican systems in astronomy and from classical mechanics to quantum mechanics, both within two or three decades, represent well known examples" of sociotechnical systems differentiating and becoming more elaborate through self-restructuring (De Greene 1973, p. 72).

In sum, the systems approach emphasizes examination of real-world systems through a holistic "lens" while recognizing the interdependent, homeostatic/self-sustaining potentials of real-world systems. During examination, research focuses upon describing and modeling system structures, processes, orbits, attractors or sustainability thresholds, the paths that the system follows to achieve its outcomes, system control mechanisms, hierarchical arrangements, positive and negative feedback, sequenced flows, and characteristics contributing to differentiation and elaboration, all in an attempt to understand, predict, and generate suggestions for future use by actors, regulators, and policymakers within the system.

The Social Fabric Matrix

To ensure that the approach of the scientist is consistent with the goal of creating research relevant for real-world economic systems, "tools" of analysis must be developed:

> [Researchers] can only operationalize a perspective through tools of analysis, and the tools must exist before the analysis can proceed. The tool kit is not as important as the perspective, but it is imperative for giving the perspective meaning in any applied sense. (Hayden 1982, p. 638)

The SFM is "an influence map or matrix...[which serves as a] systematic attempt to identify the relevant set of influences that shape the behaviour of a system.... It is a picture of a system" (Gill 1996, p. 169). Consistent with the systems approach, the SFM enables a rigorous *way to go about thinking* about a particular problem or issue, from which useful information and efficient solutions can be obtained. The SFM essentially forces the researcher to take a systems perspective and to understand all of the relevant parts of a system and their interrelationships:

> The focus of the SFM is to provide a means to assist in the integration of diverse fields of scientific knowledge, utilize diverse kinds of information in order to describe a system, identify knowledge gaps in a system for future research, analyze crises and opportunities within a system, evaluate policies and programs, and create social indicators for future monitoring. (Hayden 2006a, p. 73)

The context of analysis undertaken is "holistic and transactional" (p. 218), and thus inescapable a priori value judgments of the SFM's design are consistent with the design of an integrated framework for the purpose of bringing holistic, systems-oriented theory and research into the policy arena in an organized and effective manner (Hayden 1993, p. 307).

Once a problem is defined, the next step is to begin to consider the various components of the system within the "SFM taxonomy," which is made up of six component categories: cultural values, social beliefs, personal attitudes, natural environment, technology, and social institutions (Hayden 2006a, pp. 76–85). The categories are drawn from interdisciplinary scholarship in both the social and natural sciences (Hayden 1993, p. 308) and "by tracing the evolution of the [OIE] paradigm" (Hayden 1982, p. 638). There is also a taxonomy of possible deliveries among the six categories, shown in Fig. 1 and for which arrows imply that deliveries are possible between those component categories. The placement of the arrows in the figure is based upon anthropology, social psychology, institutional economics, and natural resource-based literatures, which together indicate that sociotechnical-ecological systems are organized in this manner (Hayden 2006a, p. 75).

Although the component categories are separated for explanatory purposes in the figure, they "are in fact instituted in many interdependent, transdependent, and recurrent ways" (p. 88):

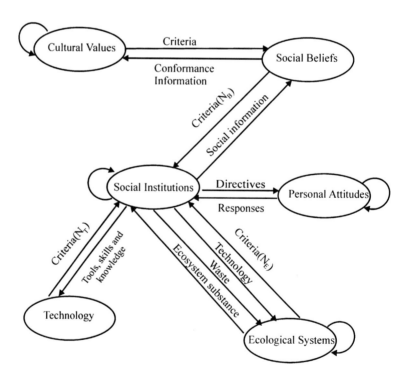

Fig. 1 Transactions for social fabric matrix component categories (*Source*: Hayden 2006a, p. 18)

Receiving Components	Households	Water Aquifer	Goods Producer	Chemical Processor	River	Farmers
Delivering Components	1	2	3	4	5	6
1. Households	0	0	0	0	0	0
2. Water Aquifer	1	0	0	0	0	0
3. Goods Producer	1	0	0	0	0	0
4. Chemical Processor	0	1	1	0	0	0
5. River	0	0	0	0	0	0
6. Farmers	0	0	0	1	1	0

Fig. 2 Simple social fabric matrix (*Source*: Hayden 2006a, p. 93)

> For example, technology does not exist separately from social institutions, and the societal
> relations are in turn structured around a tool base. Likewise, the environment does not exist
> as unmolested nature, that is, there is no natural environment (no natural nature?). Both
> flora and fauna are embedded—sometimes to extinction—in the social and technical
> process. (Hayden 1982, p. 644)

The system's components are listed in the SFM as in a standard input–output matrix
(though deliveries within an input–output matrix would typically make up only a
small percentage of those in a SFM), such as the sample SFM in Fig. 2. The system's
values, beliefs, institutions, and so on – the components – are listed in the first column
of the matrix (one for each row); these are then duplicated in the top row (one for
each column) of the matrix. The components in the first column, listed vertically,
are "delivering entries"; those listed in the first row, horizontally, are "receiving
entries." As the entries in the first column have been repeated in the first row, the
list of receiving entries duplicates the list of receiving entries, meaning that receiving
entries may be deliverers, and vice versa. "What is immediately found with respect
to any problem is that many of the separately listed components affect each other"
(Hayden 2006a, p. 88). For this reason, the same list of components is listed for
matrix rows as are listed across the columns, which means that "a row component
can be followed horizontally across the matrix to discover the direct columns to
which it makes deliveries based upon research available" (p. 88).

The purpose of illustrating deliveries and receipts within the SFM is twofold:
One principle is that *flow levels* are needed to fully describe societal and environmental processes. The flows of goods, services, information, and people through
the network both structure and maintain community relationships. For example, the
flow of investment to particular kinds of cultivation technology will determine the
level of organic matter in the soil. (Hayden 1993, p. 312; emphasis in original)

The other principle is that real-world systems depend on *delivery* among the component parts. Systems deliver bads and disservices as well as goods and services. Natural environments deliver nitrogen-fixing bacteria as well as floods. Factories deliver output as well as pollution. The continuity of a system depends on delivery among components according to social rules and natural principles. For example, income must be delivered to households for the continuance of the economic system, and organic residue and amino acids must be delivered to ammonia-producing bacteria for the continuance of the nitrogen cycle. Problems are created in systems when the delivery among the components is inconsistent with the maintenance of the system (Hayden 1993, p. 312; emphasis in original). The underlying implication is that the process of delivering and receiving is ongoing and the analysis is of a system in motion (Hayden 1989, p. 37).

The SFM is completed as the researcher notes where deliveries between components occur, a process which requires the researcher to articulate the system's component parts as well as the integrated process of the whole. As this is being done,

> the SFM becomes a tool to aid thinking and organize research. As researchers is conducted cell-by-cell across each row, linkages among components and elements will be discovered that otherwise would have been overlooked. This process helps to discover research gaps, identified as particular matrix cells for which there is inadequate information. Furthermore, the process of completing the research for the matrix will job researchers' memories of additional components to be added to the original list. They can quickly be inserted as new row and column entries and their deliveries noted in the cells. (Hayden 2006a, p. 88)

As Gill (1996 p. 173; emphasis added) puts it, "the final configuration of the matrix is less important than the *process underlying its construction*. Through *building* the matrix, the analyst will derive relevant insights into the cause of the problem under investigation."

The character of the delivery is dependent upon the problem and resulting characteristics of the system under investigation. As Hayden (2006a, p. 87) explains, "the SFM is a non-common denominator process matrix."

> For example, it can handle energy, pollution, and dollars as well as water, steel, and belief criteria.... All the information in the rows and columns [therefore] are not summative ([contrary to] an input-output matrix). (Hayden 1989, p. 39)

The information needed for each cell depends upon the context of the delivery and the problem being studied, but the following should be considered: What is delivered? What is the level of delivery? Geographic location of delivery? Time of delivery? Appropriate rule for delivery? For example, Meister's (1990), study on U.S. farm policy included deliveries of rice from the U.S. to wheat importing nations, payments from importing countries to U.S. grain traders, and subsidies to grain traders from government agencies. Hayden and Stephenson (1992, 1993, 1995) illustrated interlocking directorships with the entries into the SFM cells. Hayden and Bolduc (2000) included payment flows and requirements from legal contracts.

Finally, it cannot be emphasized enough that during each step of constructing a SFM – listing components, determining where there are deliveries, determining the nature of the deliveries – the researcher is always consulting and interacting with documents and agents from the real-world system under consideration. For instance, Hayden and Bolduc developed an SFM describing costs and operations of a low-level radioactive waste site that would serve five different states in the following manner:

> The analysis is based on a great deal of personal experience by the authors with the actors and institutions of the network. In addition, numerous primary documents have been consulted. They include the main contracts and agreements, the invoices and accounting systems, meeting minutes, the legal opinions and court decisions, legislative bills, considerable correspondence, the U.S. Security and Exchange Commission (SEC) 10-K reports of the primary corporations, and the Safety Analysis Report (SAR) which is the name given to a multiple volume application submitted for a license to build and operate the CIC radioactive waste facility. (Hayden and Bolduc 2000, p. 238)

Once again, Gill (1996, p. 173) gets at the heart of the matter: "the final product should reflect the thinking of the system's constituency, not just that of the analyst."

Extensions and Uses for the Social Fabric Matrix

Several further uses for the SFM have been demonstrated, and there will surely be more in the future given the increasing interaction and overlap between those familiar with the systems-oriented sciences and those familiar with the SFM approach. This section discusses three uses or extensions presented by Hayden in *Policymaking* or other previously published research: normative systems analysis, system time and timeliness, and quantitative analyses and methods.

Hayden (1998) describes qualitative analysis of the normative details of a social system. The goal is to further detail and thereby understand the purposive actions of actors in a system that contribute to how it achieves its goals and sustains itself. Richard Mattessich describes a duality between purposive actions of actors in a system and "material" representations of a system:

> If a system can be identified with some goal, and thus be looked at from a teleologic point of view, we might be able to catch a glimpse of the norms which determine or dominate this goal. We might also discover that some of these norms are, more or less permanently, incorporated into the system structure while others are, more or less temporarily, imposed from the environment. In other words, the notions of goal, prescription, norm, value judgment, reflection, mind, consciousness and those of related terms, belong to one category, serving to represent the specifically reflective or *mental facet* of *every* system; whereas the notions of datum, fact, description, assertion, empirical judgment etc. belong to an entirely different category, serving to represent the specifically material facet of every system. (Mattessich 1978, p. 17; emphasis in original)

The distinction is not between abstraction and fact, since "all scientific thought is based upon abstraction" (Hayden 1998, p. 90). Mattessich understands that a strict duality that brings the separation of reflective, mental, prescriptive, or *normative* aspects of a system from so-called facts, descriptions, or *positive* knowledge of a system is not useful. Rather, we must recognize that the processes of "being created" (as a system) and of "creating" (e.g. pursuing a specific goal) depict *the connection* between the normative reflective aspect and the positive-material aspect better than do traditional means of representation, because these system processes not only reveal the material aspects but also *the creation, incorporation, mutation and transfer of norms.* (Mattessich 1978, p. 18; emphasis in original)

Thus, understanding the goal-oriented, *normative* character of a system is imperative since it is through such characteristics that the *facts* of the system are "created" or come into being. As Hayden puts it, norms "determine the patterns of institutional activity that give institutions correlative capability and statistical regularity" (Hayden 1998, p. 92), whereas neoclassical economists increasingly combine more sophisticated econometrics with exceptionally thin institutional analysis; the former is not much use without the latter.

OIE researchers have also emphasized the normative nature of systems. Veblen, for example, explained economic behavior through analysis of social beliefs and customs and through their conflicts and interaction with technology. Polanyi developed deontic categories of norms providing prohibitions, obligations, and permissions to influence actions of institutions within a system (Hayden 1998, pp. 91–92). Common's (1924/1955) analysis of capitalism similarly described "working rules" that serve as normative evaluative criteria for duties, liberties, rights, and exposures. Hayden (1998) points out that importance of understanding evolving normative concerns and related deontic categories of norms was at the core of Commons's critique of orthodox economics:

Economic theory, in directing its attention to commodities and feelings, overlooked the significance of property and liberty as those concepts were developed by the courts. Consequently, its definitions of values and cost were fashioned in terms of commodities, or pains and pleasures, instead of terms of persuasion, coercion, command, and obedience. (Commons 1924/1955, p. 379)

As Walter Neale put it, "one may speak of individualism or individual motives, but it is within the constraints and meanings given by institutions that the individual feels and responds and plans" (Neale 1988, p. 229; emphasis in original).

In describing a real-world system, then, one should explain how normative criteria from social beliefs, environmental systems, and technology become articulated to guide institutional behavior. A tool such as the SFM provides a method for uncovering, explaining, and illustrating which components determine, and are influenced within, an evolving social system with regard to a particular problem or context. Further normative analysis as presented in Hayden (1998) can illustrate how norms become operative guides to behavior. To do this, one must describe the relevant rules, regulations, and requirements, as well as the technological and ecological criteria, which *create* the manifestation and operationalization of norms in a social system. To aid in this, Hayden (1998) presents a framework based upon a "turn to deontic logic, the logic of duty and obligation" to enhance qualitative modeling of socio-economic systems. He argues that deontic logic "provides the tools to define the extent of duty and obligation" lying within the existing rules, regulations, requirements and other criteria in a social system (Hayden 1998, p. 90). Mattessich agrees that "the connection between systems analysis and deontic logic becomes more obvious through the insight that norms, value judgments, and imperatives play a particularly important role in systems" (Mattessich 1978, p. 26).

As in the previous discussion of general systems analysis, time within the context of the pursuit of timeliness in policy (Hayden 2006a, Chap. 8). Hayden defines systems as "flows of sequenced deliveries" for which an SFM is an illustration. In order to properly understand how the deliveries are *sequenced* and how to undertake successful planning, time must be properly understood. *Time* is "not a natural phenomenon; rather it is a societal construct. What exists in society are duration clocks and coordination clocks selected by society, and the sequencing of events as scheduled by societal patterns" (Hayden 2006a, p. 146). It is well known that scientists have defined time differently depending upon the nature of that which was being analyzed (Henry and Wray 1998). As a societal construct, different societies also have taken very different perspectives on time, which have become more complex as societies have become more complex.

The integration of science (and the notion of relative time), technology, and holistic science results in another construct: *real time* (Hayden 2006a, pp. 168–169). Real time, or system time, refers to the sequential events of a system, rather than to clock time. In real time, "the system determines the measurement instrument... Real time is defined in a system context that takes account of the appearance, duration, passage, and succession of events as they are interrelated within a system" (Hayden 1987, p. 1,306). In other words, the sequential deliveries themselves are the "clock" with which to measure time in modern sociotechnical processes.

Real-world processes have several characteristics consistent with a real-time perspective. Processes within a system occur at different temporal rates; for example, the very slow pace of the US Court's or Congress's decisions with regard to the function of markets compared to the much more rapid pace of market transactions themselves (p. 180). Real world systems are *polychronic* in that events occur simultaneously (p. 175–178). Succession and evolution in real-world systems, common in both the social sciences and the natural sciences, create alternating as well as new time and durational relationships (pp. 180–181). Real-world processes are nonequilibrium systems since stability is not maintained through achievement of a "point of rest" but rather through maintenance of sufficient levels of sequenced flows (p. 179). In real-world systems there is no duality of dynamic change and stability; since processes are evolutionary in nature, both dynamic change (including influences of legislative, court, or regulatory decisions) and "control are necessary to maintain stability and the re-creation of processes" (p. 179).

Consequently, any uniformly flowing time construct that is independent of a process will be inadequate for analyzing and planning sociotechnical processes in modern societies. Researchers, planners, and policymakers want to be able to effect instrumentally efficient outcomes from a system. In order to do this, Commons (1924/1955), p. 379) explained that we "must know *what, when, how much,* and *how far* to do [a particular activity] at a particular time and place in the flow of events. This we designate the principle of timeliness." In other words, because "policies determine which species are to exist, which children are to go hungry, how soon the ozone cover will be depleted, how high the incidence of cancer will be, how high the flow of income and investment will be, and so forth," Hayden argues,

> the task goes beyond simple coordinating processes; the task is to determine them. With this recognition, we step beyond real time to social time through which societal decision making determines [...] timeliness. (Hayden 2006a, p. 182)

In social time, "the events are not just sequenced by the system, but the socio-technical-environmental system is determined by the conscious temporal concept of timeliness through discretionary social institutions" (Hayden 1987, p. 1,306). Hayden (2006a, pp. 170–171) suggests detailed mapping of processes and system deliveries in order to enable analysis of systems operating in real time. *Digraphs*, for instance, can be made to illustrate different temporal rates, *polychronicity*, nonequilibrium characteristics, succession, evolution, and dynamic stability, which are all characteristic of real-time processes. In the attempt to achieve timeliness, the design of SFMs and digraphs "that will permit policy analysts to computerize the databases that describe processes, to model socioecological collectives, to determine the thresholds of deliveries, to monitor change, to allow for real-time order and response, and to conduct network evaluation" becomes an important tool of analysis (p. 185).

Finally, there are a number uses for the SFM in quantitative modeling; two of them – *Boolean algebra* matrix manipulations and *System Dynamics* – are discussed here. The customary use of zeroes and ones in the SFM's cells enables Boolean algebra matrix manipulations of the SFM (Hayden 1989, 2006a). The SFM itself is a form of adjacency matrix, which shows the one-step connections between parts of a network (Hage and Harary 1983). A short list of other Boolean-algebra-based matrix manipulations [as explained in Hage and Harary (1983)] includes the limited reachability matrix [which shows whether or not each component can be reached from each other component across a prespecified number of deliveries (or *n*-steps) through other components], the reachability matrix (which shows how many *n*-step connections there are for each pair of component in the matrix), the distance matrix (which indicates for each component of the matrix the smallest possible number of steps across other components taken to reach from one component to another), and measures of centrality [which estimate the control of flows by one or more components of a system (Freeman 1979; Bonacich 1987) and were applied using the SFM by Hayden and Stephenson (1995)].

The approach taken in *System Dynamics* simulations, like that taken in the SFM, is holistic, systems oriented in nature. Radzicki (1988) has suggested that incorporation of system dynamics computer simulation modeling into systems-based economic analysis can add mathematical rigor to the latter. Further, Radzicki (1990) illustrates how insights from chaos theory and the theory of self-organizing systems, both of which embed a systems perspective into analysis, can be joined with systems-based, holistic economic analysis through system dynamics simulations.

Of particular interest within the system dynamics literature is the modeling of the consequences of positive and negative *feedback loops* in a system, which are the sources of nonlinear and self-correcting behavior in real-world systems. In integrating system dynamics with socioeconomic analysis, Radzicki argues that the process of instrumental valuation can be modeled in system dynamics due to the fact that "it is a goal-seeking process that can be represented mathematically with negative feedback loops" (Radzicki 1990, p. 61). Significantly, feedback patterns in a system can be explicitly revealed through design of the SFM and subsequent digraph transformation of the SFM (Gill 1996). As Gill writes,

> The social fabric matrix is a powerful process through which an investigator might develop insights into the nature of system functionality. As a qualitative modeling procedure, the emphasis is on the development of insights shared with actual system actors. The social fabric matrix may be regarded as a systematic learning process. If some subsequent quantitative investigation is required, revealed system insights may be directly translated into a formal sytem dynamics model for further exploration. The two procedures are highly compatible, in both conceptual and applied terms. (1996, pp. 175–176)

Further, through construction of a SFM and through real-time descriptions and digraphs of the sequenced deliveries, minimum and maximum *thresholds* for system stability maintenance can be sought (Hayden 1987, 1989, 2006a). System dynamics simulations offer researchers the ability to simulate how different flows would affect the ability to maintain stability or how they might even affect the conditions required for stability. Dierdre McCloskey, in *The Rhetoric of Economics*, argues that it is more important for a researcher to know "how big is big" than to know if a given coefficient is "statistically different from zero." In the future, understanding how parts of a system and system evolution affect system stability thresholds ("bifurcations" or "phase transitions") and the ability of the system to remain within the threshold boundaries might constitute determining whether a given delivery was "big" or not; such analysis is a natural context for the integration of SFM and system dynamics methodologies.

In a recent exchange, Hayden (2006b) argues that System Dynamics is an inadequate tool for explaining the OIE principles of hierarchy, feedback, and openness. Radzicki and Tauheed (2009) argues that Hayden has misinterpreted and/or misunderstood System Dynamics, and suggests to the contrary and as above that the latter can be a powerful tool for blending OIE with quantitative modeling. The discussion over how the SFM and System Dynamics methodologies can potentially be blended is thereby clearly a continuing one, as chapters in this volume by Radzicki and Gill and Gray further suggest. Some studies utilizing the SFM-A and incorporating System Dynamics software have not necessarily employed the field's methodologies to digraph and quantitatively model real-world processes. For example, Hayden and Bolduc's (2000) analysis of a low-level radioactive waste compact integrated the SFM of the legal structure of the compact and a system dynamics simulation that predicted, according to the normative criteria set forth in legal documents, how the system would function. The study thus illustrated how cellular information from an SFM can be transformed into a System Dynamics *computer simulation* while not employing formal System Dynamics techniques or methods. The chapter by Hoffman in this volume similarly utilizes System Dynamics software, but not the methodology, to create a quantitative model of state school financing from SFM cellular information.

The SFM Approach to Policy Analysis

The complete SFM-A is shown in Fig. 3 (from Hayden 2006a, p. 17). Note that the process of policymaking follows a path of qualitative criteria from values, beliefs, and then goals to eventual quantification of system outcomes in social indicators. Via the SFM, the researcher has a method of organizing research that embeds a holistic, social systems perspective within it that is consistent with the relevant *beliefs, values, and norms* involved in the system. Once a system is detailed through the SFM, a researcher can determine which indicators ought to be gathered from the real world in order to assess the consequences of a particular policy according to instrumental criteria. Because "facts" are never value-free, one must choose the right values with which to generate facts. It is therefore necessary to design *social indicators* consistent with the goals of policy, the latter having been derived from social beliefs and cultural values (Hayden 2006a, Chap. 5).

Social indicators are at once both the culmination and the beginning of the policy research process. The outcomes of a particular process that are measured by social indicators are assessed for their consistency with values, beliefs, and policy goals. Overall, when measurements indicate that consequences do not conform to values, beliefs, and resulting goals, the process begins anew: policies may be altered, laws may be changed, and alterations to models are made as a result in order to generate indicators of the new policies. The success of markets, central banks, regulatory institutions, and so forth, must be judged in a social or cultural setting since "social efficiency requires a much broader base" than any one of these institutions (Hayden 1977, p. 133). For instance, evaluating the social efficiency of production of final

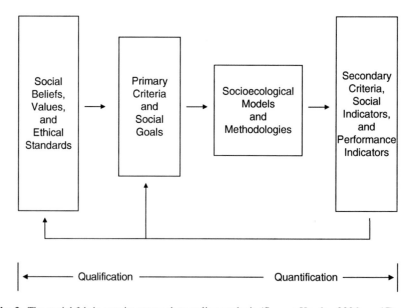

Fig. 3 The social fabric matrix approach to policy analysis (*Source*: Hayden 2006a, p. 17)

goods and services by whether or not GDP rises or falls is not consistent with the principles of instrumental valuation, since "in designing social evaluation indicators, it is tautological to use [only] an institution's own data as a criteria of its own efficacy" (Hayden 1977, p. 133).

Lastly, Hayden (2006a, Chap. 10) shows that the SFM approach has a central role within a comprehensive or "meta" framework for policy making and policy research. This framework, as should have been made clear in the foregoing, has rightly been referred to as "the most comprehensive effort yet made to define a specifically institutionalist approach to policymaking" (Lower 1993, p. 332).

Conclusion and Remarks on This Volume

The published research on the SFM-A spans more than 30 years. The methodology has been applied many times and thus honed further, often applied by Hayden himself in his capacity as a frequent policy advisor and consultant to local, state, and national level policymakers or as an appointed state commissioner, and it has been put into use by several of Hayden's students working in the public sector in various contexts and in various countries.

The SFM-A has proven to be tremendously adaptable as researchers have found it applicable to a wide variety of policy issues, including US farm policy (Meister 1990), French telecommunications (Groenewegen and Beije 1989), low-level radioactive waste disposal policy (Hayden and Bolduc 2000), the bee pollination industry in Australia (Gill 1996), overlapping corporate directorships (Hayden and Stephenson 1992, 1993, 1995), the operational tactics (Fullwiler 2001, 2003), and inflation targeting policies (Fullwiler and Allen 2007) of the Federal Reserve, cap-and-trade pollution reduction policies (Bolduc 2004), community development in rural India (Natarajan 2001), water resource management (Yang 1996), and state-level education funding (Hayden and Hoffman 2007).

Such adaptability is vividly on display yet again in this volume. The seven chapters contained in Part I highlight the SFM-A's methodological contributions and extensions of these contributions. In Chap. 2, Richard Adkisson defines the concepts of economic development and sustainability within the context of ecological, technological, and social criteria. James Sturgeon connects the SFM and institutional habit adjustment in Chap. 3. Sebastian Berger's chapter integrates the SFM-A and K. William Kapp's "normative economics," demonstrating how the former provides the "toolbox" for utilizing the latter in policymaking. In Chap. 5, Michael Radzicki provides a careful presentation of the system dynamics methodology and considers the possibilities and challenges of integrating it with the SFM. The chapter by Roderick Gill and Matthew Gray describes the use of the SFM in dealing with what they call "wicked problems," which by nature require holistic, transdisciplinary approaches to research and policy analysis. In Chap. 7, F. Gregory Hayden extends the SFM to normative systems analysis, which involves describing how normative criteria are articulated via rules, regulations, and requirements to guide institutional action.

Part II presents further applications of the SFM-A. In Chap. 8, Scott Fullwiler discusses the Federal Reserves operations, the SFM and normative systems analysis and applies general principles derived therein to the recent financial crisis. Saeed Parto and Akshay Regmi use the SFM to assess the introduction of microcredit in Afghanistan and provide recommendations for policy in Chap. 9. In Chap. 10, F. Gregory Hayden applies the SFM to government formulas for the distribution of funds to local public schools. Jerry Hoffman applies the SFM state finance systems for public elementary and secondary education and then from this develops a quantitative model using *ithink* computer software in Chap. 11. In Chap. 12, Steven Bolduc applies the cap-and-trade model of market-based pollution control to the SFM-A. Wayne Edwards' chapter identifies crucial factors in basic public service access rigidities in rural Alaska via the SFM methodology in Chap. 13. In Chap. 14, Tara Natarajan uses the SFM and its components to describe the process of trade liberalization, scientific research, and agricultural policy in India. Tristan Markwell presents analytical tools and techniques for the creation and editing of SFM displays and also for producing summary statistics from SFMs, in Chap. 15. Lastly, the concluding chapter by Richard Adkisson surveys research incorporating the SFM-A and considers how it has influenced actual real-world policies.

In closing this chapter as it began, flatly "value-free" analysis is not possible. Rather, scientists bring with them an approach to their research that influences the nature of the "facts" that are gathered. Values need to be handled in transparent, overt, and systematic ways. The SFM-A is a methodological tool to do so in complex, transdisciplinary contexts that are increasingly recognized as the norm. In conducting research useful for addressing socioeconomic issues, particularly when policy matters are the concern, the necessary preconditions are then the *relevance* of research and an understanding of *instrumentally effective* outcomes in making predictions. As Hayden puts it:

> In addition to Albert Einstein's tremendous substantive contribution to physics, he pointed out that the results found in scientific investigation depend, even in physics, on the frame of reference and view of the investigators. This knowledge has had a pronounced impact on scientific methodology. This is true in all sciences, but it is especially true in the policy and decision sciences. Therefore, in order for research to be relevant to the problem, it is necessary to structure the policy research consistent with the decision maker's frame of reference and primary criteria. A policy research and information model can be designed which encourages researchers to ask the right questions and compile the appropriate information in order to answer them. In this way, diverse technical expertise can be harnessed into a unified system to strengthen evaluation and decision making. Thus, the context of the SFM is consistent with its use as a tool for organizing policy analysis for complex systems. (Hayden 1989, p. 27)

It is in this way that scientific knowledge and research capability may be led to more relevant, applied, policy-oriented, and future-based problem-solving. We have to go into it, getting dirty hands, as economic researchers and theorists doing societally and humanly relevant work.

This book shall demonstrate that this is possible, in a serious scientific, methodologically disciplining, but nevertheless properly complex frame.

References

Arthur WB (1988) Self-reinforcing mechanisms in economics. In: Arthur WB et al (eds) The economy as an evolving complex system, Santa Fe Institute, studies in the sciences of complexity. Addison-Wesley, Redwood City, CA, pp 9–31

Bonacich P (1987) Power and centrality: a family of measures. Am J Sociol 92:1170–1182

Bolduc SR (2004) Ceremonial dimensions of market-based pollution control instruments: The Clean Air Act and the cap-and-trade model, Utilities Policies 12:181–191

Commons JR (1924/1955) Legal foundations of capitalism. Transaction Publishers, New Brunswick, NJ

Davidson P (1996) Reality and economic theory. J Post Keynesian Econ 18:479–506

De Greene KB (1973) Sociotechnical systems: factors in analysis, design, and management. Prentice-Hall, Englewood Cliffs, NJ

Elsner W (2005) Real-world economics today: the new complexity, co-ordination, and policy. Rev Social Econ LXIII.1:19–53

Elsner W (2007) Review of policymaking for a good society: the social fabric matrix approach to policy analysis and program evaluation. Interv J Econ 4.1:200–203

Freeman LC (1979) Centrality in social networks: conceptual clarification. Social Netw 1:215–239

Fullwiler ST (2001) A framework for analyzing the daily federal funds market (PhD Dissertation). University of Nebraska, Nebraska

Fullwiler ST (2003) Timeliness and the Fed's daily tactics. J Econ Issues 37(4):851–880

Fullwiler ST, Allen G (2007) Can the Fed target inflation? Toward an institutionalist approach. J Econ Issues 41(2):485–494

Gill R (1996) An integrated social fabric matrix/systems dynamics approach to policy analysis. Syst Dyn Rev 12:167–182

Greene RR (1991) General systems theory. In: Greene RR, Ephross PH (eds) Human behavior theory and social work practice. Walter De Gruyter, New York, pp 227–260

Groenewegen J, Beije PR (1989) The French communication industry defined and analyzed through the social fabric matrix, the *Filière* approach, and network analysis. J Econ Issues 4:1059–1074

Hage P, Harary F (1983) Structural models in anthropology. Cambridge University Press, Cambridge

Hayden FG (1977) Toward a social welfare construct for social indicators. Am J Econ Sociol 36:129–140

Hayden FG (1982) Social fabric matrix: from perspective to analytical tool. J Econ Issues 16:637–662

Hayden FG (1987) Evolution of time constructs and their impact on socioeconomic planning. J Econ Issues 21:1281–1312

Hayden FG (1989) Survey of methodologies for valuing externalities and public goods. Contract No. 68-01-7363. Washington, DC: US Environmental Protection Agency, Office of Environmental Planning

Hayden FG (1993) Institutionalist policymaking. In: Tool MR (ed) Institutional economics: theory, method, policy. Kluwer Academic, Boston, MA, pp 283–331

Hayden FG (1998) Normative analysis of instituted processes. In: Fayazmanesh S, Tool MR (eds) Institutionalist theory and applications: essays in honor of Paul Dale Bush, vol 2. Edward Elgar, Northampton, MA, pp 89–107

Hayden FG (2006a) *Policymaking for a good society: The social fabric matrix approach to policy analysis and program evaluation*. Springer, New York

Hayden FG (2006b) The inadequacy of Forrester system dynamics computer programs for institutional principles of hierarchy, feedback, and openness. J Econ Issues 40(2):527–535

Hayden FG, Bolduc SR (2000) Contracts and costs in a corporate/government system dynamics network: a United States case. In: Elsner W, Groenewegen J (eds) Industrial policies after 2000. Kluwer Academic, Boston, MA, pp 235–284

Hayden FG, Stephenson K (1992) Overlap of organizations: corporate transorganization and Veblen's thesis on higher education. J Econ Issues 26:53–85

Hayden FG, Stephenson K (1993) Corporate networks: a U. S. case study. In: Groenewegen J (ed) Dynamics of the firm: strategies of pricing and organization. Cambridge University Press, Cambridge, pp 53–95

Hayden FG, Stephenson K (1995) Comparison of the corporate decision networks of Nebraska and the United States. J Econ Issues 29:843–869

Henry JF, Wray LR (1998) Economic time. Jerome Levy Economics Institute Working Paper No. 255. http://www.levy.org

Hickerson SR (1988) Instrumental valuation. In: Tool MR (ed) Evolutionary economics. I. Foundations of institutional thought. M.E. Sharpe, Armonk, NY, pp 125–166

Hoffman JL, Hayden FG (2007) Using the social fabric matrix to analyze institutional rules relative to adequacy in education funding, J Econ Issues 41:359–367

Katz D, Kahn RL (1969) Common characteristics of open systems. In: Emery E (ed) Systems thinking. Penguin Books, Baltimore, MD, pp 87–104

Lower MD (1993) Commentary. In: Tool MR (ed) Institutional economics: theory, method, policy. Kluwer Academic, Boston, MA, pp 332–341

Mattessich R (1978) Instrumental reasoning and systems methodology: an epistemology of the applied and social sciences. D. Reidel, Dortrecht, Holland

Mayhew A (1981) Ayresian technology, technological reasoning, and doomsday. J Econ Issues 15:513–520

Meister B (1990) Analysis of federal farm policy using the social fabric matrix. J Econ Issues 24:189–224

Mercuro N, Medema SG (1997) Economics and the law: from Posner to post-modernism. Princeton University Press, Princeton, NJ

Natarajan T (2001) Confronting seasonality: socioeconomic analysis of rural poverty and livelihood strategies in a dry land village. A case study of Theethandapattu, Tamil Nadu, India. PhD Dissertation, University of Nebraska, Nebraska

Neale WC (1980) Market capitalism as dispute resolution: the loss of legitimacy and the problems of the welfare state. J Econ Issues 14:393

Neale WC (1988) Institutions. In: Tool MR (ed) Evolutionary economics. I. Foundations of institutional thought. M.E. Sharpe, Armonk, NY, pp 227–256

Pattee HH (1973) Hierarchy theory: the challenge of complex systems. George Brazillar, New York

Polanyi K (1957) The economy as instituted process. In: Polanyi K, Arensberg CM, Pearson HW (eds) Trade and market in the early empires. Free Press, Glencoe, IL, pp 243–270

Radzicki MJ (1988) Institutional dynamics: an extension of the institutionalist approach to socioeconomic analysis. J Econ Issues 22:633–666

Radzicki MJ (1990) Institutional dynamics, deterministic chaos, and self-organizing systems. J Econ Issues 24:57–102

Radzicki MJ, Linwood Tauheed (2009) In defense of system dynamics: a reply to Professor Hayden. J Econ Issues 43(4) (December-forthcoming).

Samuels WJ (1978) Normative premises in regulatory theory. J Post Keynesian Econ 1:100–114

Samuels WJ (1981) Maximization of wealth as justice: an essay on Posnerian law and economics as policy analysis. Texas Law Rev 60:147–172

Swaney JA (1987) Elements of neoinstitutional environmental economics. J Econ Issues 21:1739–1780

Tool MR (1979) The discretionary economy: a normative theory of political economy. Goodyear, Santa Monica, CA

Tool MR (1986) Essays in social value theory. M.E. Sharpe, Armonk, NY

von Bertalanffy L (1974) General systems theory and psychiatry. In: Arietl S (ed) American Handbook of Psychiatry, vol I, 2nd edn. Basic Books, New York, pp 1095–1117

Yang Y (1996) Crafting hierarchical institutions for surface water resource management of the Platte River: a case study for the assessment of institutional performance and transformation, PhD Dissertation, University of Nebraska, Nebraska

Part I
Institutionalist Theory, Philosophy and Methodology for Applied Research

The Economy as an Open System: An Institutionalist Framework for Economic Development

Richard V. Adkisson

Abstract The main purpose of this chapter is to set the stage for the rest of this volume by describing the economic system in a way consistent with original institutionalist principles, principles that prescribe an open system view of economies. The chapter emphasizes the ways in which technology, nature, and culture transact with the economic process. From this view the terms sustainability and development take on broader meanings. Strict sustainability requires adherence not only to environmental criteria but also to technological and social criteria. Development implies that the socioeconomic system changes in the direction of improved adherence to social criteria broadly defined.

Introduction

Original institutional economics takes a broad perspective on economic analysis and policy formation. Petr (1984: 4) argues that the institutionalist approach to economic policy is (1) values-driven, (2) process-oriented, (3) instrumental, (4) evolutionary, (5) activist, (6) fact-based, (7) technologically focused, (8) holistic, (9) nondogmatic, and (10) democratic. Many of the chapters in this volume provide examples of institutionalist policy analysis built on this ten-point foundation. One purpose of this chapter is to set the stage by briefly describing the economic system in a way consistent with these policy principles – as an open system.[1] Hayden (2006: 13) insists that "policy paradigms should be consistent with the complexity of reality." This chapter aims to help the reader appreciate the complexity of reality.

R.V. Adkisson (✉)
Department of Economics and International Business, New Mexico State University,
Las Cruces, NM, USA

---

[1] The details and philosophical underpinnings of open systems analysis are discussed in Kapp (1976), Berger and Elsner (2007), Mearman (2006), Hayden (2006), Hodgson (2004), and elsewhere.

T. Natarajan et al. (eds.), *Institutional Analysis and Praxis*,
DOI 10.1007/978-0-387-88741-8_2, © Springer Science+Business Media, LLC 2009

The same complexity that colors the institutionalist perspective also shapes the institutionalist approach to economic development and sustainability. For one thing, the evolutionary approach of institutionalists means that economies are always developing. For another, sustainability takes on a richer meaning, for sustainability now means much more than the maintenance of natural systems. Sustainability in this context requires that the full set of environmental, technological, and cultural criteria be met to assure the sustainability of an economic system.

The Economic System

An economy is an important social system. An economy organizes a variety of people, objects, processes, and activities in such a way as to accomplish the purpose of the system. The economic system's purpose is to solve a society's economic problem(s). Economic problems can take many forms but, in the broadest sense, the problem is that of provisioning society. Scott Nearing referred to provisioning as "getting a living." Nearing wrote that the purpose of economics (the economy) is to:

provide and ensure an adequate and regular supply of the goods and services needed by a community in order to maintain its physical well-being. (Nearing 1952: 23)

Nearing's definition is equivalent to Tool's notion of the economic problem being one of providing "real income" (Tool 1985: 72). Alfred Marshall referred to economic activity as "social action which is most closely connected with the attainment and with the use of the material requisites of wellbeing" or "the ordinary business of life" (Marshall 1890: 1).

Society, as a broadly defined system, incorporates a number of interrelated subsystems. For example, a society will have subsystems for provisioning (the economy), for rearing its young, for making community decisions, and for defending itself from internal and external threats. Social subsystems do not stand alone; rather, they are intertwined with other social systems and all interact with nonsocial systems, in particular, the natural environment and technology that, while not a social system, is a social product. Each system or subsystem involves the coordination of various processes working together to cause the system to accomplish its goal. Kapp briefly describes the open systems approach to economics in this way: "[E]conomic systems are parts of a much broader political and institutional system from which they receive important impulses and which they, in turn, are capable of influencing and even changing in a variety of ways" (Kapp 1976: 91).

Georgescu-Roegen uses thermodynamics to emphasize the open nature of economic/productive processes: "From the viewpoint of thermodynamics, matter-energy enters the economic process in a state of *low entropy* [high grade energy] and comes out of it in a state of *high entropy* [low grade energy]" (Georgescu-Roegen 1993: 76–77). The implication is that without solar energy inputs (openness) to restore low entropy, the economic system would slowly lose its ability to convert energy and material into the objects of human need and desire as energy and materials devolved into less and less usable forms (see also Daly 1993).

As a social system, the economic system is where the economic process plays out. The economic process is the set of activities leading to the provisioning (production and distribution of real income – goods and services) of society (Tool 1985). For simplicity the economic process is broken down into several subprocesses to demonstrate the transactional character of economic activities (Hayden 2006). Nothing in the system stands alone.

The Economic Process(es)

The economic process transforms that which is available (resources) into that which serves society by providing goods and services. Transformation is required because the raw resources themselves do little to satisfy human needs. Perhaps more to the point purely natural production processes (unassisted by technology) will not sustain the human population at its current size or in the manner to which humans have become accustomed.

Neither the economic system nor the economic process is self-contained or otherwise independent of other systems or processes. Rather the economic system is intertwined with other social and natural systems. It is a complex system. Likewise the economic process incorporates several subprocesses and interacts with and/or relies on other processes both social and natural. To begin to understand how the economic system interacts with other systems and processes, it will be useful to define three other categories of processes: technological processes, natural processes, and social processes.

Technological Processes

Technology has been described as the accumulated tools, skills, and knowledge of humankind, used together (Ayres 1962). Eric Beinhocker discusses two technological categories: "Physical technologies are methods and designs for transforming matter, energy, and information from one state into another in pursuit of a goal or goals" (Beinhocker 2006: 244). Social technologies "are methods and designs for organizing people in pursuit of a goal or goals (Beinhocker 2006: 262). Ayres warns of the folly of considering tools (physical technologies) alone, or skills (a social technology) alone to be technology":

> [T]echnological processes can be understood only by recognizing that human skills and the tools by which and on which they are exercised are logically inseparable. Skills *always* employ tools, and tools are such *always* by virtue of being employed in acts of skill by human beings. (Ayres 1962: vii, emphasis in original)

The essence of Ayres' statement is that physical technologies must interact with social technologies to be made useful (and vice versa). It is possible to think of technology in the abstract, as a set of *possible* combinations of tools, skills, and knowledge that *could* accomplish a goal or goals. However, technological goals are only met when the physical and social interact.

Technological processes are those that employ accumulated tools, skills, knowledge, and energy. They would not continue without human intervention to coordinate them. For example, newspapers, automobiles, and skyscrapers do not appear in nature. Newspapers, skyscrapers, and automobiles can only be produced because, over time, humans have accumulated the tools, skills, and knowledge required to produce them, harnessed the energy required for production, and developed the social processes to make things work together. Technology enhances humans in their ability to transform that which is available into that which they want.

Natural Processes/Systems

Natural processes are those that would continue to function without the application of technology. Assuming the continued existence of earth in a form similar to its current form, it is safe to say that natural processes were at work before humans showed up and that they would continue should humans leave the scene. Like other processes, natural processes involve transformation and energy use. The primary energy source for natural processes is the sun. Using the energy of the sun, and working within the limits of the fundamental forces of nature, natural processes use a wide variety of inputs to produce a wide variety of outputs that will be referred to here as natural products. Some well-known natural processes are the carbon cycle, the hydrological cycle, the nitrogen cycle, and the sulfur cycle. Jointly these are referred to as biogeochemical cycles because they involve life, geological minerals, and chemicals. Some familiar natural products are crude oil, coal, timber, quarry, and oxygen.

Obviously, natural processes and cycles are many, and a thorough understanding of them is beyond the scope of these few paragraphs. The important points to remember are that natural processes use energy (solar) to transform inputs into outputs, that individual natural processes fit together to form a system we are inclined to call nature, and that the natural processes do not rely on technology or human intervention to continue. Although as discussed later, natural processes can be captured, displaced, or modified by human effort and the application of technology.

Social Processes/Systems

Social processes, combined in systematic ways, are the means a society uses to organize and reproduce itself. Social processes involve the use of social technologies, "methods and designs for organizing people in pursuit of a goal or goals" (Beinhocker 2006: 262). Because social processes are so intertwined with one another it is difficult to provide clear and simple examples, so a few general examples will have to suffice. Societies will have processes to bring potential mates together.

They will have processes for assigning status. They will have processes for educating and socializing children. They will have processes for organizing production. They will have processes for assigning responsibility. Social scientists spend their lives studying social processes and social systems.

System Diversity and Change

Even casual observation and a cursory understanding of history reveal that, like natural systems, technological and social systems and processes exhibit great diversity, interdependence, resilience, and variation. There is no one-best system. The environments in which systems operate change, sometimes suddenly and sometimes slowly, while at all times subject to physical constraints such as gravity, laws of thermodynamics, and the like. Observing the dynamic nature of the economic system, economists have found it useful to interpret and analyze the economy as an evolving system and apply evolutionary theories in the study of the economy.

The impetus for change can come from outside the system, for example, a destructive storm or an unanticipated terrorist attack (exogenous change). Change can also come from within the system through the ongoing interaction of natural, technological, and social phenomena (endogenous change). As in natural systems, environmental change (broadly defined) calls for the selection and replication of the individual and system characteristics that are fitted to the new changed environment. In this context, one might think of development as any change that brings the system closer to meeting system criteria – natural, technical, or social. The primary difference between natural and sociotechnical change is that the latter involves humans and introduces reason and/or discretion (Tool 1985) into the selection process, a process Beinhocker (2006: 264) referred to as deductive tinkering.

Sociotechnical (Economic) Subprocesses

Again, by Tool's (1985) definition, the economic process is that set of activities leading to the provisioning of society. In a sense, the economic process is a squirming nest of other processes, natural, technological, and social. Societies organize themselves, develop technologies, and coordinate their use to capture and/or modify natural processes in ways that (hopefully) serve social ends. For the sake of simplicity, consider that the economic process involves several categories of subprocesses, all of which both rely on and are constrained by natural processes and physical laws, involve the application of energy, and involve both production and consumption. When humans become involved in the processes, it is tantamount to saying that technology is being applied. The consequence of the imposition of these processes on the natural environment will be discussed later:

- *Extractive processes* capture natural materials and processes to feed other (natural/technological/economic) processes. Examples of extractive processes are human inhalation of air, pumping of water, mining, and logging. Extractive processes consume energy, natural materials, tools, and human resources. They produce raw materials and wastes. They also alter natural processes, social processes, and technology.
- *Productive processes* use technology, energy, and natural materials to convert raw (and intermediate) materials into goods and services. Examples are the conversion of coal to electricity, ore to metal, and metal to locomotives. Productive processes produce goods, services, and wastes and alter natural processes, social processes, and technology.
- *Consumptive processes* convert the products of the productive processes (as well as natural and recycled/reused products) into human satisfaction. Consumptive processes consume goods, services, energy, natural materials, human resources, etc. They produce both satisfaction and wastes and alter natural processes, social processes, and technology.
- *Disposal processes* involve the processing of wastes. They take three forms. Wastes are expelled back into natural systems in raw or processed form. Wastes are sometimes recycled. Sometimes they are reused. Disposal processes consume wastes. Depending on the degree of waste processing, natural materials, goods and services, human resources, and energy are also consumed. As wastes are reprocessed by nature they produce food for natural processes. In some cases wastes can produce death and illness (in nature and humans). When wastes are recycled or reused they are made useful again. Disposal processes also alter natural processes, social processes, and technology.
- *Distributive processes* are the flows between and within other processes. They consume goods and services, natural materials, human resources, and energy. They produce distributive services and wastes. They also alter natural processes, social processes, and technology.
- *Coordinating processes* work to organize the functioning of the other subprocesses. Traditionally, economists spend most of their time and energy discussing coordinating processes (market interactions or government policy, for example). Coordinating processes consume goods, services, natural products, energy, human resources, etc. and, hopefully, steer the economic process toward the end of provisioning society in socially satisfactory ways.

Notice that these processes are not uniquely human processes. All or most of these economic processes are evident in nature.

Nature, Humans, and Technology

Consider the relationship between nature, humans, and technology. Humans are ill-equipped to survive and thrive in nature without the aid of technology. If non-technological humans were to exist in this state their numbers and impact on the rest of nature would almost certainly be minimal. Without technology humans would find themselves several links down on the food chain. With technology, especially as it has advanced over the last few hundred years, humans enter the natural world with tremendous capacity to capture, alter, and displace natural processes. Extraction, production, consumption, disposal, and distribution processes are all evident in nature. However, with the human application of technologies the potential impacts of these processes can be substantial.

Figure 1[2] emphasizes the relationships between economic and natural processes. Society's ability to continue its economic process depends on nature's ability to maintain and reproduce itself through natural processes. At the same time, society relies on nature to accept and process its discards. Osvaldo Sunkel (1980) likens the situation depicted in Fig. 1 to the simultaneous existence of two environments. One, the natural environment, supports a second, human-created, artificial environment, which, once created, requires continued inputs of material and energy from the natural environment for its maintenance and growth.

The ability of natural processes to support society's demands on them depends on the rates and types of extraction and disposal commanded by the economic process. Without accumulated technology, natural checks and balances moderate the human impact on the balance of nature. With accumulated technology, humans gain the ability to expand their range, extract otherwise inaccessible natural products, and extract from and dispose into nature at nonsustainable rates without necessarily feeling any immediate consequences. The technological ability of humans gives humans the ability to dominate nature and exploit it to the fullest extent, if they have the will to do so. According to Edward Hall:

> The risk, of course, is that by enormously multiplying his power, man is in the position of being able to destroy his own biotope—that part of the environment that contains within it the basic elements for satisfying human needs. (Hall 1989: 38)

Coordinating the Technical and Natural Processes Through Institutions

The various processes previously discussed are largely physical processes involving physical movement, manipulation, and interactions. It is through these physical processes that the economy and the natural environment interact. Less evident in Fig. 1 are the coordinating processes that govern technological/natural interactions. Technologies must be applied in appropriate ways, in appropriate places, and at appropriate times if society hopes to exploit the technical/natural interaction to its advantage. Farm equipment and hybrid cotton seeds will not serve human wants if they are sent to Antarctica. Likewise, electric motors are of little use if electricity

---

[2] Inspiration for this figure comes from Bryant (1980).

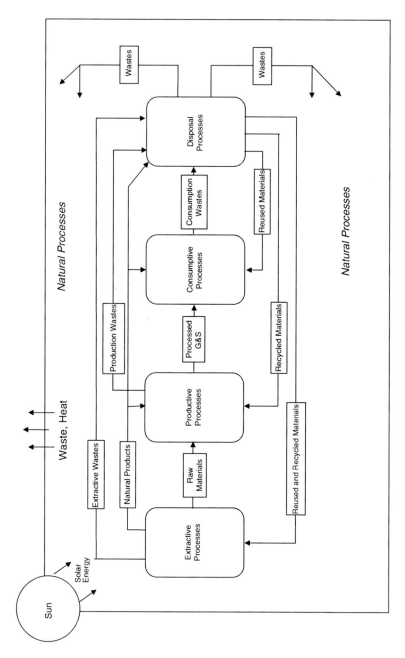

Fig. 1 Physical environment (nature) with economic (technological) processes imposed

is not available or if electrical power is available but provided at a voltage and/or frequency inappropriate for the motors. If workers are necessary for a process to function, the workers must show up at appropriate times. Additionally, the process of specialization and exchange that marks modern economies means that production and consumption decisions are not made by the same people. For the economic process to play out, the technological/natural processes must be coordinated. Coordination implies the need for evolving institutions that govern human behavior and, thus, govern technical/natural interactions.

Tool emphasizes the importance of institutions in the economic process:

> The economic process is given effect in experience only through institutions. The term institution means any prescribed or proscribed pattern of correlated behavior or attitude widely agreed upon among a group of persons organized to carry on some particular purpose. Institutions are the working rules, the codes, the laws, the customary ways which shape and pattern behavior and attitudes in a manner to accomplish some end-in-view or purpose. (Tool 1985: 73–74)

Similarly, Neale (1988) says that institutions can be identified by three characteristics. There are "people doing," that is, there are patterns of human activity. There are "rules" that give order to these activities, and there are "folkviews" that justify both the activities and the rules.

Institutions govern all sorts of human activity. They tell us when to applaud, when to dress up, what time to arrive at work, and what color socks to wear. Some institutions (rules) are explicit – traffic and bankruptcy laws, for example. Others are implicit – social norms that govern our day-to-day interactions, manners, and the like. Deviations from the institutional norms have consequences. Speeding can result in fines. Belching loudly or dressing inappropriately can result in social ostracism, job loss, or perhaps failure to find a mate. The present focus is on the role of institutions in coordinating technological/natural interactions. The fact that institutions permeate all social interactions should not be understated.

Figure 2 captures the essence of the relationships between nature, technology, culture (folkways), and institutions. The rectangle labeled, "Physical Environment (Nature)," represents the natural system from Fig. 1. The economic processes discussed are embedded in the circle labeled social institutions. The characteristics of these physical processes, the composition, rates, directions of flows, etc. are governed by the social institutions. In turn, the character of the institutions is shaped by the institutional criteria transmitted by the environment, the society's cultural values and beliefs, and technology. In other words, each component of the diagram is influenced by the others through feedback loops moderated by the social institutions.

The physical environment provides the original parameters for economic/institutional activity. Natural processes do not deliver the same materials at all times or places. Coal cannot be mined nor can bananas be grown everywhere. Water does not flow uphill. Barges do not float in a desert. These natural limits influence the evolution of social institutions by defining feasible patterns of activity. The arrow from the environment to social institutions represents this flow of environmental criteria.

The arrow in the opposite direction represents the influence of social institutions on natural processes. As societal activities modify natural processes, environmental

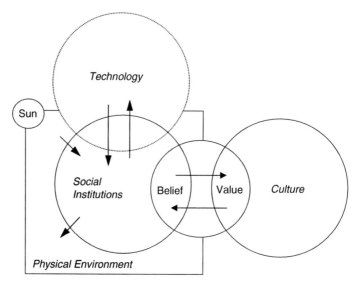

Fig. 2 Institutions as coordinating mechanisms

criteria may change, thus calling for institutional modification. For example, the presence of a river may invite the development of irrigated agriculture. Society organizes itself in ways that allow it to accomplish this end-in-view (irrigated agriculture). The diversion of water from its original path slows the river flow, alters the flora and fauna of the river channel, and perhaps causes silting of the river. Meanwhile, water is redistributed to previously dry land, changing the flora and fauna and perhaps causing salt to accumulate in croplands. If these things happen, new environmental criteria arise. For example, it may become necessary to change cropping patterns, to begin dredging channels to maintain the flow of the river, or to genetically modify crops to increase their salt tolerance. In other words, environmental criteria shape institutions but the criteria are not constants. They change as society changes the environment.

The circle labeled technology represents the stock of possible technologies. The stock of technology grows as technologies are used, combined, and recombined when applied by society. The adoption of any particular technology will impose institutional criteria on society. For example, the use of continuous flow steel production requires that machines be tended around the clock. If society wants to use this technology it will need to institute work patterns that bring workers to the machines at regular intervals over the 24 h of the day. The arrows from technology to social institutions represent flows of technological criteria. The arrow from social institutions to technology represents the contributions to evolving technology that result from the application of technology in the economy. For example, perhaps computer technology is combined with steel production technology, and the computerization of the controls in the steel mill allows the mill to run without direct, 24 h, human intervention. The technological criteria imposed on institutions then change. Instead of a regular flow of workers to the site, now remote workers with a different set of skills might be required.

In addition to the constraints of environmental and technological criteria, institutions are also faced with cultural criteria. Culture can be seen as the foundation of the "folkviews" mentioned earlier. Culture refers to "the collective programming of the mind which distinguishes the members of one category of people from another" (Hofstede 1994: 12). Hall says:

> Culture is man's medium; there is not one aspect of human life that is not touched and altered by culture. This means personality, how people express themselves (including shows of emotion), the way they think, how they move, how problems are solved, how their cities are planned and laid out, how transportation systems function and are organized, as well as how economic and government systems are put together and function. (Hall 1989: 16–17)

Culture, per se, is transcendent. All mature humans have a culture but exactly what it is and where it came from is not always obvious:

> Everything man is and does is modified by learning and is therefore malleable. But once learned, these behavior patterns, these habitual responses, these ways of interacting gradually sink below the surface of the mind and, like the admiral of a submerged submarine fleet, control from the depths. *The hidden controls are usually experienced as though they were innate* simply because they are not only ubiquitous but habitual as well. (Hall 1989: 42; emphasis added)

Museums are full of physical expressions of culture but, at the social interaction level, culture manifests itself through the values, beliefs, and attitudes held by a society (Hayden 1988). As suggested by the aforementioned Hall quote, once a culture is internalized it may become quite inflexible[3]; for the acculturated individual, right and wrong have been identified and internalized. Cultural values, individualism, or rule-based orientation, for example, are the most basic expressions of culture and tend to change little after their adoption. "Values are cultural criteria or evaluative standards for judgment with regard to what is ideal" (Hayden 1988: 416). Social beliefs [and attitudes], on the other hand, "are activity- and institution-specific" (Hayden 1988: 418). For a society's institutions to be socially satisfying and therefore sustainable, its members must be able to rationalize the patterns of activity with its cultural values. Beliefs and attitudes become the shock absorber between institutions and cultural values. Being more malleable than values, beliefs and attitudes can be adjusted until institutional changes demanded by environmental or technological criteria can be justified by the values. Consider the following example from McFerrin and Adkisson (2005):

> Think of a society that is guided by values of strong individualism and universal human dignity. The human dignity value might dictate that some minimum living standard be available to all members of the society. The individualist value might dictate that those who do not achieve the minimum standard of living must accept individual responsibility for their failure. In this circumstance, the society might institute a system of transfer payments (welfare) but also insist that welfare system promotes individual responsibility. To allow both criteria to be satisfied, beliefs (institutional rules) must be developed that can satisfy

---

[3]Culture is more malleable when viewed over generations of individuals.

both cultural values. For example, welfare recipients might be required to search for work, pursue training or education, accept low benefits, or accept a short duration of benefits. Any of these could be seen as a way to provide a minimum standard of living while also encouraging welfare recipients to accept individual responsibility for their well-being. (McFerrin and Adkisson 2005: 8)

Given the importance of institutions, one might ask, which institutions are the "right" institutions? Very simply, the right institutions are the institutions that match the ends (provisioning of society) to the means (technological and natural elements required to accomplish the provisioning of society), hopefully in a sustainable way. Such institutions are "right" because they are patterns of behavior driven by instrumental values – values that "correlate behavior by providing the standards of judgment by which tools and skills are employed in the application of evidentially warranted knowledge to the problem-solving processes of the community" (Bush 1987: 1,080). "Wrong" institutions are generally those driven by ceremonial values that reinforce "invidious distinctions, which prescribe status, differential privileges, and master-servant relationships and warrant the exercise of power by one social class over another" (Bush 1987: 1,079) and thereby constrain economic choice.[4]

Institutions, Development, and Sustainability

The perspective on the economy presented earlier leads to at least three fundamental conclusions about the economy and economic analysis. First, the economic process is coordinated by institutions. These institutions can take many forms from the simplest social norm governing supervisor–supervisee conversations to complex rules regulating the purchase and sale of corporate shares. Institutions are both shaped by social, technological, and natural environments and, in turn, shape the environments around them. Second, the interactions of nature, technology, and society are dynamic and nondeterministic. Humans can act purposely to shape these interactions. Finally, sustainability cannot be viewed narrowly.

Sustainability, in its strictest definition, implies that a pattern of activity can continue indefinitely. This would mean that extraction rates could not exceed nature's ability to replace the materials and energy being extracted. Neither could disposal rates exceed nature's ability to reprocess the waste products. At the same time, the level of goods and services delivery would have to satisfy society's demand that the economic process provides for its living. The demands of technology would need to be heeded as would the values and beliefs that dictate a society's sense of right and wrong. To be strictly sustainable, all system criteria would need to be completely and simultaneously satisfied.

Since it is unlikely that any pattern of economic development will fulfill the requirements for strict sustainability, it may be more useful to view sustainability

---

[4]Details on this dichotomy of values are discussed in the following chapter by James Sturgeon.

by degrees. Different patterns of economic development will have different degrees of compliance with the full set of systemic criteria. From a policy perspective, if sustainability is desired, the goal would be to think in terms of activities as being more or less sustainable rather than sustainable or not sustainable and would consider social sustainability as well as environmental sustainability. This approach to development is similar to what Colby (1989) has called the "eco-development" paradigm of environmental management.

Conclusion

The earlier discussion briefly outlines a view of the economy that is consistent with the original institutionalist paradigm. Moreover, the aforementioned model conforms to the general systems principles outlined by Hayden (2006), in particular, that the economy be viewed as an open system. Not all institutionalists will agree on every point and some might view it as overly simplistic. It could be expanded. In particular, the discussion assumes only one natural environment, only one set of available technology, only one culture, and a single set of institutions coordinating it all. Obviously the real world is much more complicated. Still, the chapter should set the stage for the work presented in the other chapters of this volume.

References

Ayres CE (1962) The theory of economic progress: a study of the fundamentals of economic development and cultural change, 2nd edn. Shocken Books, New York
Ayres CE (1978) The theory of economic process. New Issues Press, Kalamazoo
Beinhocker ED (2006) The origin of wealth: evolution, complexity, and the radical remaking of economics. Harvard Business School Press, Boston, MA
Berger S, Elsner W (2007) European contributions to evolutionary institutional economics: the cases of 'cumulative circular causation' (CCC) and 'open systems approach' (OSA): some methodological and policy implications. J Econ Issues 41:529–537
Botkin DB, Keller EA (2003) Environmental science: earth as a living planet, 4th edn. Wiley, Hoboken, NJ
Bryant JW (1980) Flow models for assessing human activities. Eur J Oper Res 4:73–83
Bush PD (1987) The theory of institutional change. J Econ Issues 21:1075–1116
Clark JOE (ed) (2004) The essential dictionary of science. Barnes & Noble Books, New York
Colby ME (1989) The evolution of paradigms of environmental management in development. The World Bank Strategic Planning and Review Department, Strategic Planning and Review, Discussion Paper No. 1
Daly HE (1993) Introduction to essays toward a steady-state economy. In: Daly HE, Townsend KN (eds) Valuing the Earth: economics, ecology, ethics. MIT Press, Cambridge 11–50
Georgescu-Roegen N (1993) The entropy law and the economic problem. In: Daly HE, Townsend KN (eds) Valuing the Earth: economics, ecology, ethics. The MIT Press, Cambridge 75–88
Hall ET (1989) Beyond culture. Anchor Books, New York
Hayden FG (1988) Values, beliefs, and attitudes in a sociotechnical setting. J Econ Issues 22:415–426

Hayden FG (2006) Policymaking for a good society: the social fabric matrix approach to policy analysis and program evaluation. Springer, New York

Hodgson GM (2004) The evolution of institutional economics. Routledge, London

Hofstede G (1994) Business cultures: every organization has its symbols, rituals, and heroes. UNESCO Courier 12–16

Kapp KW (1976) The open-system character of the economy and its implications. In: Dopfer K (ed) Economics in the future. Westview, Boulder, CO 10–105

Marshall A (1890) Principles of Economics, 4th edn. McMillan, London

McFerrin R, Adkisson RV (2005) Quantifying culture? Unpublished manuscript presented at the annual meeting of the Association for Institutional Thought. Albuquerque, NM

McShaffrey D (2005) Environmental biology – ecosystems. http://www.marietta.edu/~biol/102/ecosystem.html. Accessed 18 May 2005

Mearman A (2006) Critical realism in economics and open-systems ontology: a critique. Rev Social Econ 64:47–75

Moran EF (2000) Human adaptability: an introduction to ecological anthropology, 2nd edn. Westview, Boulder, CO

Neale WC (1988) Institutions. In: Tool MR (ed) Evolutionary Economics, vol I. M.E. Sharpe, New York 227–256

Nearing S (1952) Economics for the power age. John Day Company, New York

Petr JL (1984) Fundamentals of an institutionalist perspective on economic policy. J Econ Issues 18:1–17

Sunkel O (1980) The interaction between styles of development and the environment of Latin America. CEPAL Rev 12:15–49

Tool MR (1985) The discretionary economy: a normative theory of political economy. Westview, Boulder, CO

Zimmerman EW (1964) Introduction to world resources (edited by Henry L. Hunker). Harper and Row, New York

The Social Fabric Matrix, the Principles of Institutional Adjustment, and Individual Action

James I. Sturgeon

Abstract The social fabric matrix (SFM) together with the principles of institutional adjustment (PIA) may be used within the theoretical framework of the Veblenian dichotomy. This combination advances the conceptual and empirical reach of both. The Veblenian dichotomy is used to analyze the relationship of instrumental and ceremonial behaviors to institutions. It ties together the PIA and the SFM. The SFM identifies and incorporates several components for examining a problem and attempting to develop policies. The analysis of change is an important aspect of Institutional economics. Change involves adjustment of ceremonial behaviors to instrumental ones. Change in both group and individual behavior is controlled by the PIA. Habit adjustment is the individual counterpart to institutional adjustment. Perception of circumstances and consequences control behavior, and perceptions are controlled by habits. The potential directions and ability of an institution/habit to change can be informed by use of the SFM. The subject matter of this chapter is the connection of these and their application to institutional and individual adjustment.

Introduction

F. Gregory Hayden's work, grounded in his invention and application of the social fabric matrix (SFM), has importantly advanced policy analysis and formulation. The SFM is an analytical construct based on a dichotomy of social forces at work in human affairs. J. Fagg Foster developed three principles of institutional adjustment (PIA). These form the bases for understanding, at a conceptual level, the process of change in institutions and how institutions adapt to bring their elements into closer correlation. The same principles that govern institutional adjustment are applicable to the process of individual behavioral change. One thesis of this chapter is that these principles may be joined, if only in a rudimentary way, with the SFM. The combination advances both the conceptual and empirical reach of both. I shall argue that the SFM implicitly employs the PIA.

J.I. Sturgeon (☐)
Department of Economics, University of Missouri-Kansas City, KS, USA

T. Natarajan et al. (eds.), *Institutional Analysis and Praxis*,
DOI 10.1007/978-0-387-88741-8_3, © Springer Science+Business Media, LLC 2009

The Veblenian dichotomy is a theoretical construct that ties together the PIA and the SFM. After each of these is explained the interrelationship of the SFM and PIA is examined. Finally, it is argued that individual behavior is connected to the PIA and may be revealed by the SFM, thus connecting individual behavior to the behavior emerging through value change and adjustment.

Theoretical Framework: The Veblenian Dichotomy

A principle of institutional economics is that human activity is organized by institutions. Using Veblen's distinctions as a starting point the Veblenian dichotomy has been developed into an analytical tool.[1] This tool is a main part of the theoretical framework of institutional economics in the Veblenian school. Analytically, institutions are separated into two primary aspects: instrumental behavior and ceremonial customs. Each is a way of knowing, doing, and valuing. This means that there are two ways of knowing (method), two ways of doing (action), and two ways of valuing (valuation). Both are aspects of human behavior and both help explain human activities, including economic activities. We make a living, at bottom, as an interactive process of these two learned behaviors. They are the "stuff" of which the economy is made. Thus, both of these aspects of human behavior are used to analyze the functioning of the economy. Figure 1 illustrates the major components of the Veblenian dichotomy.

Instrumental behavior covers a broad range of learned activities. It forms correlated patterns based upon and deriving from a functional process. Instrumental behavior derives from sequences of cause and effect, understanding of consequences, warranted experimental/scientific knowledge, trial and error, and instrumental logic. It is technological and pragmatic.[2] The instrumental process is a tool-using process (both physical and symbolic). And, while the instrumental aspect of behavior involves tool-using activities, it is not merely tools. It involves patterns of behavior that are instrumentally verifiable and justifiable. It is best understood as internal, a part of human behavior; just as the head and hands are internal and transactional so too are tools and tool-using behaviors. Instrumental behavior is cumulative and developmental. It involves the accumulation and elaboration tools and tool using through processes of combination of existing tools and skills.

Ceremonial behavior is also defined to cover a broad range of learned behaviors and it too forms correlated patterns. Its patterns come from and are validated by processes comprising myths, legends, and traditions. This behavior is past-binding

---

[1] See Waller (1982). I came of age on C.E. Ayres' version of the Veblenian dichotomy, but gradually came to Foster's view. The main force in changing my thinking was the *Principles of Institutional Adjustment*. Bill Williams had much to do with it. Those who knew Bill or his work will recognize his influence on this present chapter.

[2] Pragmatic is used in the classical sense as found in the work of C.S. Peirce and John Dewey. See Webb (2007).

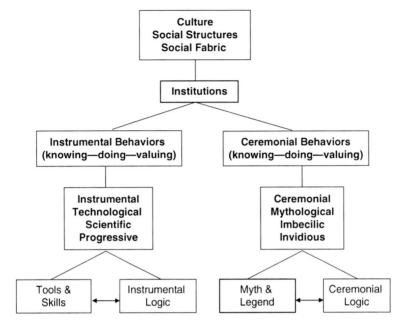

Fig. 1 A dichotomy of culture (social fabric) and institutions

and involves combined continuities and discontinuities with antecedent ceremonies. Past-binding resistance persists in part because we are taught to believe in the truthfulness and worthiness of traditional reactive habits of behavior that derive from activities that cannot be experimentally verified. For example, prosperity myths prescribe the traditional behavior necessary for continued well-being and the traditional way of life or calamity and decline befall the society; for example, balanced yearly budgets and self-adjusting markets qualify as part of the contemporary prosperity code. In addition, vested interests have a supreme incentive to perpetuate arrangements of which they are the chief beneficiaries. They usually exercise a major influence over many institutional arrangements.

Included in both instrumental and ceremonial behavior is the arts of associated living, the rules, customs, laws, ideologies, accumulated folklore, myths, licenses, policies, and traditions that form the constraints and freedoms of human interaction. These arts, not unlike the industrial arts, are cumulative and developmental, learned, and evolving. If not adjusted to correlate with institutional changes they grow stale and outdated and restrain unnecessarily the ability to compromise and resolve conflict, social tensions, and disagreements. Among the assertions here is that the PIA may be more accurately and pragmatically achieved as these arts progress and that the SFM may be used to discover and reveal these patterns of association and consequently advance the ability to develop arts of associated living. Notice too that the social fabric may be included in this dichotomy with no necessity to adjust the conceptual apparatus. And, of course, the SFM is analytically grounded in the dichotomy.

Social Fabric Matrix

Societies have traditions, beliefs, and habits that are believed necessary, revered, and taught to succeeding generations. Behavioral attributes display many patterns, but they are not an undifferentiable conglomeration of activities. The SFM may be used to differentiate these patterns by applying it to the structure and functioning of a situation, problem, or circumstance. It represents a snapshot of the constitute elements of the network of social behaviors. The first degree of differentiation in the analysis, based on the Veblenian dichotomy, is to separate behaviors into instrumental and ceremonial aspects. From there further analytical elements form the constitute elements of the SFM.

Hayden developed the SFM "to allow the convergence and integration of conceptual works in instrumental philosophy, general systems analysis, Boolean algebra, social system analysis, ecology, policy analysis, and geobased data systems" (Hayden 2006). It allows multiple forms of data to be incorporated into one analytical tool. While not comprehensive, it identifies and incorporates six main components in examining a problem and in attempting to develop a policy to solve the problem. These elements are (1) cultural values, (2) societal beliefs, (3) personal attitudes, (4) social institutions, (5) technology (here termed instrumental behavior), and (6) the natural environment (Hayden 2006). Each component is analyzed with an eye toward determining the flow and delivery of one component to another. By conducting the analysis in this manner the SFM can "express the attributes of the parts as well as the integrated process of the whole" (Hayden 2006).

There are seven major characteristics of the SFM itself: (1) it is based on the concept of delivery, (2) rows deliver to the columns, (3) it is a noncommon-denominator matrix (meaning that all kinds of data can be incorporated), (4) cell observations are the flows of the system (that is a 1 in a cell represents a direct delivery; therefore, indirect deliveries are not counted), (5) the number of cells is dependent on the study at hand, (6) the matrix defines the system as it exists, and (7) the matrix allows for model building and data collecting consistent with theory (Hayden 2006).

In addition to the SFM Hayden uses digraphs that allow a pictorial display of the delivery and flows of the elements connected in the SFM. Digraphs "illustrate the sequential structure of the system and provide a picture that is easier to comprehend than the matrix" (Hayden 2006). Later a model of behavior (knowing, doing, and valuing) that helps visualize the principal elements of behavior as they relate to both the PIA and the SFM is presented. This model is not a SFM or a digraph, but rather is a simplified combination of the PIA, the SFM, and a digraph.

After a discussion of the PIA there follows a discussion of how the SFM helps identify and disclose the fabric or network of connections among institutions and individuals that are not easily discerned. In the process it discloses junctures of activity that may be particular points of focus for institutional adjustment.

Principles of Institutional Adjustment

Change and its analysis are important aspects of institutional economics, possibly the most important. The idea advanced here is that the ability of an institution/habit to change can be analyzed by use of the SFM. It can reveal quantitative and qualitative aspects of an institution that indicate how and in what direction adjustment is possible or more probable. Change requires adjustment (closer correlation) of ceremonial behaviors to instrumental ones. In this section the PIA are enumerated and explained.

1. Instrumental primacy is the principle that indicates that change is predicated on the actual ability to do something. This involves technological progress – additions to the warranted stock of knowledge.[3] Instrumental primacy, as the impetus to adjustment, may be read to mean that one requirement for change is a reasonably accurate perception of what can be done in relationship to what is now being done. This is a critical part of instrumental correlation.
2. Recognized interdependence is a principle that specifies that the pattern of adjustment is bounded by the pattern of interconnectedness and interdependency of the members affected by the change (Foster 1981). It is almost axiomatic that recognized interdependence is more likely to be achieved in institutions that are structured around participation – cooperative interaction, since the participants will be better able to understand their interaction and the consequences of changing them. The pattern of dependency is, in part, indicated by the SFM. It helps show the levels of dependency and indicates the areas where receipts and deliveries will be affected. To recognize and to experiment with different ways of bringing about change requires consideration of the means–ends–consequences continuum. These can be simulated with the SFM so that actual consequences may be better anticipated, accepted, or avoided. Just how close that perception is to the instrumental reality is a critical feature in the adjustment process. This relates to the other two principles.
3. Minimal dislocation deals with the circumstance that adjustments must actually be capable of integration into the remainder of the existing social fabric. The principle discloses the limits, in term of rate and degree, of any adjustment (Foster 1981). This does not mean that adjustments are necessarily small, only that there is a limitation based on the integration of associated institutions. The social fabric of any institution is finitely elastic at any point of change implementation. The adjustment is more likely to be achieved if the adjustments follow a

---

[3] Foster's term was technological determinism (Foster, 1981). In this chapter it has been renamed as instrumental primacy. The latter is more in line with terminology used to define the Veblenian dichotomy and in light of contemporary usage of technological determinism, it is less likely to be misunderstood.

path with relatively small increments of continuous change. If adjustments are deferred and build to a situation where change involves significant dislocation there will be more resistance as vested interests accumulate around the prevailing institutional structure. This situation is more likely to create the condition of ceremonial encapsulation (Bush 1987), making adjustments less likely and less susceptible to deliberative processes.

Notice that none of the principles is ceremonially derived. This is because adjustment is a change in the relationship or synchronization of the ceremonial behaviors to instrumental. In other words, while adjustment is an interaction of ceremonial and instrumental behavior, the causative agent is instrumental behavior while ceremonial behavior is the passive and resistive force.

Means–End Continuum

In addition to the aforementioned three principles there are two processes involved in institutional adjustment. Each of these is implicit in the SFM and the PIA. The first is the relationship of means–ends–consequences. This process relates to the problem of selecting actions that will bring about the desired change including the axiom that choosing means *is* choosing ends. It is a hypothesis about what to do, but without the knowledge to do it. This continuum is an endless succession of means, which become ends. The means–ends continuum is deceptively simple, but it may sometimes have complex implications. How are means chosen, especially when there are multiple ways to solve a problem? Are they workable? If they are not workable what adjustments are in order? These questions involve not only how we know, but what is known, what is valued, and what action (doing) is undertaken. The answer lies in the process of instrumental knowing, based on experiment and learned by trial and error.

Selection processes are based not only on the "immediate" consequences of a choice but future consequences as well. Means cannot be separated from ends since the very arrival at an end has consequences for where we will be able to go once we have "arrived." It is a truism that means are ends and their continuum is based on seeking to understand the consequences stemming from choosing alternative means. Institutional theory sees these selections as derived from two different ways of knowing, valuing, and doing. One relies on trial and error, experiment, science, empirical evidence, and openness to using these. It is instrumental. The other is based on superstition, myth, ideology, the forces of vested interest and the like. It is ceremonial. Both posit a fact-based cause-and-effect relationship, but the former is while the latter is not. For example, the most reliable way to stop an automobile is to apply the brakes. Nobody would seriously entertain praying as a means of stopping– at least they would not actually use it very long.

Deliberation

Deliberation is a process that precedes instrumental choice and action. It is an intellectual process of examining the consequences of actions prior to acting – a dress rehearsal as it were. It is an intellectual experiment in which the consequences of alternative means are extended into the calculable future. The goal is to sort out alternative paths and their possible consequences and to evaluate the means with an eye toward directing choices in a way that is consistent with the goal and the instrumentalities of a situation. In the process of institutional adjustment deliberation improves the likelihood of reasonable choices. The analytical process is concerned with discovering whether the possible choices or action plans prove reliable. Deliberation involves (a) a felt difficulty, conflict, or discrepancy; something is clearly wrong; (b) clarification of the specific problem to be solved, (c) development of hypotheses concerning the nature of the problem and possible solutions; this means that traditional theories are not to be accepted a priori as correct; they may well be a mixture of folk beliefs and facts; (d) examination of the logical consequences of proposed hypotheses, a rehearsal in imagination of the possible hypotheses and lines of action. No action has been taken beyond recall. And finally, (e) choosing – hitting in imagination upon a line of action that permits overt action.[4]

Deliberation and choice are in conjunction with a relevant problem, a reaction, or adjustment to a situation. It arises to help solve a recognized difficulty. Ideas serve as plans of action because they suggest themselves as problem solvers. We may seek to choose an action that is perceived as "better," "more satisfactory," or "more successful" for the problem in hand. In this context, it is analogous to saying that this diagnosis is "better" or "more successful" than that one. The "success" or "satisfactoriness" of a plan of action is to be understood in terms of predicted and actual consequences. In science a general pattern of inquiry has been developed which is competent to integrate and test our ideas about the nature of the world. The hypothesis here is that the rationale of scientific methods is applicable to human behavior (knowing, doing, and valuing) and that in any particular situation, by the use of intelligent methods of analysis, one course of conduct can be established as "better" than another. These elements of inquiry for the process include (a) sensitivity to the uniqueness of different situations, (b) patience and persistence to carefully formulate the problem, (c) creative imagination to envision new possibilities, (d) a bias for objectivity and an ability to discount one's own prejudices, and (e) the courage to revise one's beliefs in the light of new experience.

In a reasonable or deliberative choice multiple hypotheses may be considered in dealing with a problematic situation. No choice is to be given precedence over others, meaning that one is just as diligent in looking for knowledge that may question a plan of action as knowledge that questions other plans. We criticize our hypotheses or ends by inquiring into what results come from the use of the means designed to realize

---

[4] For a more complete explication of deliberation as used in pragmatic philosophy see Dewey (1922).

them. When action is intelligent and responsible, the *means* are part of the *end*. We carefully consider the probable consequences of acting upon one or another hypothesis. Unreasonable choice leads to a path of action in which some preconception, some desire, overrides all alternatives and secures the sole right of way, usually without benefit of intelligent habits and deliberative processes.

Social Fabric Matrix and Principles of Institutional Adjustment

The SFM forms a useful and potentially powerful source of social analysis. As an empirically based analytical tool it assists in laying bare the relationships that, if known, provide an improved probability of understanding and anticipating the consequences of means selection. It helps illuminate transactions types and points to nodes of activity where these occur. Functioning as an integral part of inquiry, the SFM adds to the stock of knowledge about the structure, function, and interconnectedness of socioeconomic activities. In this it adds to the scope of instrumental primacy by enhancing our understanding of the arts of associated living. This is related as well to insights about interdependencies of activities and as such exposes (helps recognize) for better understanding these interdependencies. Further, by revealing interdependencies the SFM helps lay bare the interconnection of institutions that will have to be accommodated (minimally dislocated) as part of the adjustment process.

In this section the analysis achievable with the SFM is related to the explicit knowledge and value premises of the PIA via a schematic model of the behavioral interaction. The SFM requires information and data, and the PIA provide guides to the types of information that may be useful. Further the SFM provides a guideline for connecting the PIA with the social circumstances in question (institutions up for adjustment).

Figure 2 is a model of the interactive processes of instrumental knowing, doing, and valuing (K–D–V model) and the relationships of each to institutional adjustment. The model is also a simplified combination of the logic that underpins the SFM and the PIA and points to the behaviors that emerge from a deliberation process of individual and collective choice that result in institutional adjustment. In the pragmatic/instrumental view of the life process there is no separation of knowing, doing, and valuing. Life involves a process of constant adjustment to problematic situations and control of perceptions. The adjustment process also embodies the idea of progress as the enhancement of alternatives in any problematic situation. The model illustrates, in simplified form, the relationships among these. The basic structure of the model employs the PIA as well as the processes of deliberation as related to choosing means and evaluating consequences. The process of understanding and explicating the underlying social fabric that defines, determines, and reveals the context of the problem (area of adjustment of an institution) under consideration is included in the model in the form of both the processes of inquiry and of judgment as they interact to shape behavior. The contingent rather than determinate qualities of this dynamic

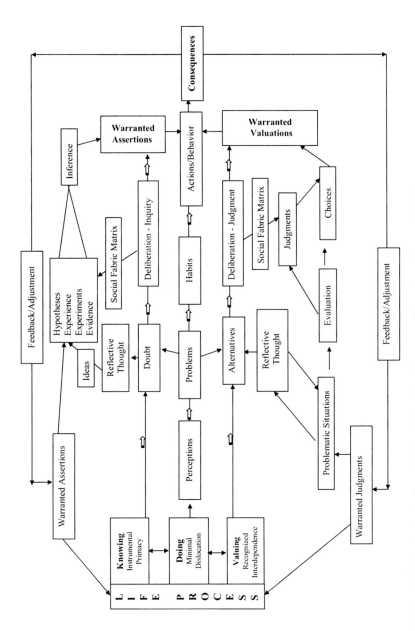

Fig. 2 Simplified model of institutional adjustment in relationship to instrumental knowing, doing, and valuing

process are embodied in the PIA. These are considered in light of their relation to the adjustment process as indicated in the K–D–V model. The strike point is the choosing of a means to adjust and the consequences that result from that choice. Actual behavior results in consequences not all of which can be known in advance. But the SFM and the PIA used in concert increase the likelihood of an improved understanding of the potential consequences and perhaps more importantly of more timely future adjustments as the consequences, desirable or undesirable, emerge.

The PIA work together and depend upon a perception of the objective circumstances of possible achievement. The SFM aids in achieving this perception. Meeting the contours and requirements of instrumental function depends upon the relative strength and depth of the layers of ceremonial imagination and practice. If enough of these can be peeled back an adjustment toward more instrumental correlation is more probable. Recognized interdependence and minimal dislocation depend critically on the participant's perception. Instrumental reality may be seen as unacceptable because it will cause too significant a change in the status relations of the community. Whatever may be the outcome, a prerequisite to institutional adjustment is the perception of a gap between what is instrumentally possible and what is being done. The SFM is used to disclose these interrelationships and to those activities to be targeted for the application of the PIA.

Adjustment occurs as a change in perception leading to a change in behavior – an adjustment of habit. The ease of adjustment depends on habit structure and tenacity. In part, a change in habit is a process of discovering and adjusting to error in knowledge and judgment. Institutional adjustment depends in part upon an individual psychology of perception of the objective circumstances of possible achievement. But, only individuals can perceive. The psychology of perception means that behavior is the control of perception. The ability to control perception and adjust it to meet the contours and requirements of instrumental function depends upon the relative strength and depth of ceremonial practice interacting with instrumental capability.

Ceremonial means are without genuine causal or experimental linkages. Thus, selection of such a means has little hope of solving a problem in a way that permits continuity or even of solving a problem. But within the bounds they set, however elastic, there is a required accommodation for a successful adjustment. Progressive change requires adjustment of behaviors to instrumental requirements. Change is not found in reenactment or routine – but by experiment and trial and error. Error is born in unfulfilled expectation. Instrumental behavior involves the correlation of expectation and action, error detection, and adjustment. It strives to bring action into correlation with expectation – without prejudice. Ceremonial behavior is imaginary, misspecified, misplaced, or mistaken if–then relations/correlations.

Instrumental patterns impose structure and behavior on other patterns, but these impositions are not necessarily known in advance or addressed in advance of technological change. Instrumental primacy can be discerned by the SFM. Since the actual ability to do something is a prerequisite to any adjustment it is necessary to know what is now possible or may soon be possible. The SFM is suitable to this task and can also disclose patterns of power and control in a situation.

Synchronization of tools and tool-using behaviors, what Veblen called the machine process, is a process of deliberate or rational behavior. The SFM is capable of disclosing the required connections to assist in this synchronization. An absence of this creates a stretch of tension in the social fabric or institutional collage. The SFM, while it does not necessarily reveal what is needed to make an adjustment, helps disclose where institutional adjustment is likely or required. Rational behavior is exhibited with the deliberate synchronization of the instrumental possible with the institutionally actual.

Consider a simple example of institutional adjustment, based primarily on tool synchronization that may be illustrated by railroad track gauge. In the USA the period from 1830 to 1840 was one of experimentation with locomotive power, tracks, rolling stock and the like. After two decades railroad gauge in the USA was without a national standard, that is, accepted institutional pattern. Western railroad construction in the 1850s created a "web of transport" binding together the east and west. But the web of rails was not tightly tied together. The lack of a standard gauge, a lack of correlation of the instrumental tool processes with the individual business practices of the separate railroad companies, frequently made it nearly impossible for a car of one company to roll on the track of another. In 1861, eight changes of cars were required on a trip between Charleston and Philadelphia (Stover 1987). Teamsters, porters, tavern keepers, and yet to be born Keynesians were happy that not a single rail line entering either Philadelphia or Richmond made a direct connection, that is, on the same gauge track, with any other railroad entering the city. Consequently cross-country shipments often had to be moved to other cars. It was a tool using system that was out of synchronization. After a not inconsiderable period of discussion the lines began to shift to a "standard gauge" often by relaying one rail and changing axel lengths of rolling stock. Sometimes during a single night or on Sunday hundreds of miles of track were adjusted to the standard. For example, the Louisville & Nashville railroad changed more than 2,000 miles of track from 5′4″ to 4′8.5″ on Sunday May 30, 1886. The Erie laid a third rail between the two existing ones shifting gradually from one to the other. Clearly this is recognized interdependence. And the fact that they standardized on the "narrow" gauge is evidence of minimal dislocation, that is, there is less disruption and cost in moving from broad gauge to narrow gauge, than conversely. Note that the adjustment does not mean that the "best" solution was chosen only an instrumentally/ceremonially workable one. This, as it turned out to be a mistake that locked the USA into a narrow gauge system. But it demonstrates that institutional adjustment is an evolutionary process not an "optimal" one. Of course, the series of inventions leading to railroads was the impetus that "created" the problem in the first place and was instrumental primacy. It had to be technologically possible to standardize and it was the machine process, or instrumental logic of tools, that required a standard if there was to be rational behavior, that is, a behavior leading to an adjustment of the actual to the possible.

A more socially complex example may be drawn for the experience of instituting the social security system in the USA. This was an adjustment, in part, from the institutions of an agricultural/rural economy to an industrial/urban one. In order to accommodate these changes specific institutions had to adjust. First, the technology of production had to be sufficient to maintain a dependency ratio allowing specific persons (retirees/disabled) to be exempt from employment. Second, there had to be recognition of a need to adjust the existing system of elder care – the institution of the family – to another system. As technology permitted greater mobility the family structure changed from an extended structure to a nuclear one – instrumental primacy. In this regard more families faced similar situations making it more and more difficult to care for elderly dependents – recognized interdependence. Third, the new system had to be capable of being integrated into the existing pattern of institutions. Consider, for example, in the USA it was part of the process to explicitly exempt social security benefits from a means test. This accommodated the strong ceremonial resistance to "welfare" programs – minimal dislocation. Fourth, the various constitute elements and interests had to be identified and understood. The first three involve the PIA and the last one the SFM. The Social Security Act was passed in the USA in the midst of the depression in 1930s. This somewhat extreme condition eased the enactment because there was pressure on existing ceremonial patterns of resistance to change. These patterns were weakened and feathered out, making it easier to adjust. Even so it was necessary, even in the depression to exempt part of the population from paid productive activity. Since many were unemployed this was easier to permit.

Of course, at the time of both of the earlier examples the SFM and PIA were not yet available to the participants. The former would have made the adjustment process better understood and possibly yielded improved results. The latter are actually revealed by the examples. Once articulated, the PIA may be more or less easily seen in the adjustment of institutions.

Individual Action

If we follow John R. Commons in defining an institution as "collective action in control and liberation of individual action" we are led to place individual action in the context of institutional adjustment, in other words to analyze individual action as it relates to institutional adjustment. Actions in the context of institutional adjustment flow from valuations of alternatives in a problematic situation. Adjustments arise as part of the patterns of social arrangements and derive from the transactional activities of individuals with each other as well as with the environment. The significant fact of human behavior is not found in instinct or reason, but in habit.[5] Individual habit may be thought of as equivalent to institutions, and the processes of institutional adjustment and individual adjustment are amenable to the same principles, that is, habit adjustment is the individual counterpart to institutional adjustment. Perceptions are controlled by habits, and habits are formed by the inchoate interaction of the mass of instincts present in human abilities with the total environment and experience[6] of the individual.

---

[5] Here, the argument is not significantly different from that made by Dewey (1922). It is only in its application to the theory of human behavior as the control of perception that the argument is expanded.
[6] Here, the term experience is meant as Dewey expresses it, perhaps best in *Art as Experience*, Chap. 3: "Having an Experience."

Individuals acquire their values from both the instrumental and the ceremonial forces of a social process. Instrumental values are experiential in character since they are formed by experiment, trial and error. John Dewey made instrumental values directly related to science. ". . . without physics, chemistry, and biology a grounded empirical theory of valuation, capable of serving as a method of regulating the production of new valuation was out of the question. With no adequate knowledge of physical conditions and propositions regarding the relationships to one another, the forecast of consequences of alternatives by was impossible" (John 1929).

This lodges intellectual habit and instrumental values in experiential processes capable of being verified by the consequences emerging from their application to action.

Ceremonial values are dictum in character and formed by the transmission of traditions, beliefs, and habits that are deemed necessary, revered, and faithfully taught to oncoming generations. These ceremonial norms that justify and sanctify power, authority, class inequality, rank, status, and superior/ subordinate are based on the ceremonial aspect. The norms and mores teach belief in the correctness of the inequalities of authority. The ceremonies form a network of means which they support and reinforce the validity of each other. The method of knowing and arriving at the validity of ceremonial values involves tradition, appeal to authority – "self-evident" truths.

Instrumental values, being based in instrumental logic, exhibit the ability to adjust and adapt as knowledge and experience change. However, as they change they put pressure on ceremonial values that are based on myth and tradition. Problems create stresses in the value structure. The stress may be thought of as a two-way stretch in the value structure – a tension between the two ways of valuing: instrumental and ceremonial. This stretch in the value structure cannot be indefinitely sustained. When the tension reaches a breaking point either the instrumental process of value formulation is stalled or the ceremonial values will crumble.

This is illustrated later in Fig. 3. The illustration points to the process of increasing tension between the two ways of valuing. The tension is applicable to the process of individual habit adjustment and formulation. As intellectual habit and instrumental processes expand they put pressure on the ceremonial values, which are inherently unchanging since they are dictum in nature. For behavior to change a break or adjustment in ceremonial values is required. This often leads to an expansion of the application of intelligence to the process of habit formation. If the dictum values do not change the process of habit formation continues to be lodged in ceremonial practice and it arrests the ability of an individual to adjust to changing circumstances. This may push the value structure to the breaking point.

Consider the so-called Giffen paradox as an example drawn from the theory of consumption. Many think it is inconsistent with the standard theory of demand since it gives rise to the paradox of an increase in consumption of a good when its price increases. Yet in institutional theory it is no paradox at all, being explained with a theoretical argument based on habit adjustment and perception.

Suppose one's diet consists of meat and potatoes in amounts just enough to maintain basic nutritional requirements. If the price of potatoes increases it is impossible

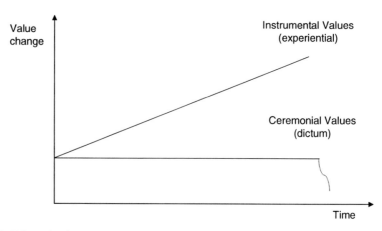

Fig. 3 Schematic of two-way stretch in the value structure

to consume the same amounts in the new situation. The situation is problematic for the retention of the old pattern of consumption and requires an adjustment to the new circumstances. Yet, before the required adjustment is possible several things are required. First, there must be the actual perception that a change in diet is required. Reduced to its simplest form the individual is faced with four interrelated conditions.

1. An instrumental function – in this case a minimum number of nutrients for a subsistence diet [some combination of meat and potatoes such that the price to nutrient ratio (p/n)] is lower for potatoes than for meat.
2. A preference (ceremonial) function – in this case a preference for meat over potatoes of a least the combination of the previous situation.
3. A budget limitation such that no more can be spent on the two than previously.
4. A perception of the need to adjust based on the aforementioned conditions.

The latter does not require a particular adjustment; only a perception of that one is needed. The individual may prefer to remain with the habits and patterns of behavior of the previous situation, but the environmental conditions have changed such that it cannot. The situation can be analyzed as follows. From the K–D–V model, if meeting the instrumental function is the action chosen at the conclusion of the process, the adjustment of habits will begin with an increase in potato consumption and a decrease in meat consumption. This is because it is the only way to get enough nutrients to forestall malnutrition. It means that the individual has perceived the instrumental requirement of maintaining a sufficient number of nutrients for basic requirements – the presence of felt difficulty and an adjustment to it. If the difficulty is passed through the comb of deliberative inquiry and if the warranted stock of knowledge allows for proper judgment of the diet, one may act to adjust to meet the instrumental function. This results in an increase in consumption of potatoes and a reduction in meat. In the alternative, one may decide to meet the preference (ceremonial) function first. This does not mean immediate starvation, but it does involve malnutrition. Note that there is no necessity of an immediate perception of the instrumental consequences. In fact, it may take a while to notice that one cannot eat as much meat as before. Nonetheless, this choice would lead to an increase in meat consumption and a decrease in potato consumption. The simplicity and home-liness of the example should not reduce its importance in understanding human behavior. It may be applied to any level of finite budget constraint, type of instrumental function and preference function. Further, it illustrates that habit adjustment involves a tension, a stretch in the value structure. In the aforementioned example the tension is between the two sources of habit formation. It involves the instrumental value function (nutrition) and the ceremonial function – preference for meat over potatoes. This two-way stretch creates a situation where either the preference function cannot be sustained over time and will eventually either adjust or the individual will starve. This is the equivalent of an institution being unable to adjust.

Conclusion

The relationship between the SFM and PIA exists and is compatible and synergis-tic. This essay has sought to demonstrate aspects of that compatibility and to illustrate the synergisms. For example, it was shown that recognized interdependence has patterns and that these can, in part at least, be revealed by the SFM. It helps show the levels of dependency and indicates the areas where receipts and deliveries will be affected. It is almost axiomatic that recognized interdependence is more likely to be achieved in organizations that are structured around participation – teams, since the participants will be better able to understand their interaction and the consequences of changing them. Further, the social fabric of any society/economy is finitely elastic at any point of change implementation. The adjustment is more likely to be achieved if policy development and implementation follows a path with increments of continuous change. This involves the principle of minimal dislocation. To recognize and to experiment with different ways of bringing about change requires the principle of the means–ends–consequences continuum as well as an understanding of how these changes may affect the existing matrix of social relations. Thus, the combination of the SFM and the PIA may yield an advance in institutional theory that ties together more strongly institutional theory and policy analysis derived from an institutionalist perspective. Hayden's work thus will be seen as a significant step in this direction.

In the evolution of a species an adaptation requires the replacement of some trait with another. There is a loss of something that was once adequately adapted and useful. This is likely the case in social evolution as well. The PIA take this into account and therefore may be relied upon to assess the process of social change, and the SFM is a way to disclose and analyze the transactional relationships involved in the process of adjustment and how institutional adjustment may be achieved. Any adjustment means the loss of something that was once useful or thought to be useful to the life process. This helps explain why there is resistance to change; it is sometimes seen as the loss of something of value. If the improvement from the adjustment is not recognized as worthwhile the resistance continues and the social shackles retard institutional change. An extension in the use of the SFM in conjunction with the PIA represents one way to improve the rate and progress of institutional evolution.

References

Bush PD (1987) The theory of institutional change. Journal of Economic Issues 21(3):1075–1116
Dewey J (1922) Human nature and conduct: an introduction to social psychology. Modern Library, New York
Dewey J (1929) Experience and nature. Dover, New York
Foster JF (1981) Syllabus for problems of modern society: the theory of institutional adjustment. Journal of Economic Issues 15(4):929–935
Hayden FG (2006) Policy making for a good society: the social fabric matrix approach to policy analysis and program evaluation. Springer, New York
Stover JF (1987) History of the Baltimore & Ohio railroad. Purdue University Press, West Lafayette
Waller WT (1982) The evolution of the Veblenian dichotomy: Veblen, Hamilton, Ayres, and Foster. Journal of Economic Issues 16(3):757–771
Webb JL (2007) Pragmatisms (plural), part 1: classical pragmatism and some implications for empirical inquiry. Journal of Economic Issues XLI(4):1063–1086

The Normative Matrix of Social Costs: Linking Hayden's Social Fabric Matrix and Kapp's Theory of Social Costs

Sebastian Berger

Abstract One of the most promising applications of Gregory F. Hayden's Social Fabric Matrix is within the context of policymaking to counter environmental degradation and social costs. Developing his institutional theory of social costs since the 1930s, K. William Kapp proposed policymaking that is very similar to Hayden's approach. Both aim at minimizing social costs by working with primary and secondary criteria based on systems principles, such as openness, negative and positive feedbacks. By presenting Kapp's "normative economics" this paper shows how primary and secondary criteria serve policymaking as a basis to evaluate social costs in a nonutilitarian way and to avoid the theoretical and practical limitations of the purely formal Coasian and Pigouvian frameworks. The paper concludes that Hayden's SFM provides the tool box for putting Kapp's normative economics to work in policymaking.

Introduction

This article is inspired by Gregory F. Hayden's *Policymaking for A Good Society: The Social Fabric Matrix Approach to Policy Analysis and Program Evaluation* (Hayden 2006), a foundational work for policymaking that combines insights of American Institutionalism and Pragmatism into a unique methodology. Hayden calls it a "how to" book for policy analysts and policymakers in order to design policies and programs that more efficiently and effectively solve problems.

Environmental degradation is one of the most pressing problems that modern policymakers have to grapple with particularly in the form of social costs. Rational evaluations of a situation as a means for deliberation require knowledge about social as well as private costs and benefits. An elaboration of different paths and scenarios depends on the adequate representation of alternative total costs and benefits. The three major theoretical contributions dealing with the problem of social

S. Berger (✉)
Roanoke College, Salem, VA, USA
e-mail: sberger@roanoke.edu

T. Natarajan et al. (eds.), *Institutional Analysis and Praxis*,
DOI 10.1007/978-0-387-88741-8_4, © Springer Science+Business Media, LLC 2009

costs are by the neoclassical economists Pigou and Coase, and the institutional economist Kapp. Since the 1950s Kapp proposed a kind of policymaking to minimize social costs that is similar to Hayden's approach in that it emphasizes working with primary and secondary criteria and the application of systems principles, such as openness, negative and positive feedbacks.

First, this chapter explores how Hayden's main concern is closely linked to problems of social costs and why he insists on the importance of primary criteria. The paper then presents Kapp's "rational humanism" or "normative economics" because it shows how primary and secondary criteria can be applied to evaluate social costs in a nonutilitarian way to avoid the theoretical and practical limitations of the Coasian and Pigouvian frameworks. The paper concludes that Kapp is an important precursor of Hayden's approach whose work provides important insights for policymaking to minimize social costs.

Framing Social Costs: The Need for General Systems Analysis and the Limitations of Utility Theory

Hayden refers to the problem of social costs explicitly in relation to the importance of General Systems Analysis (GSA): "The function of GSA in evaluating government programs, social costs, public goods, and environmental policy is a tool kit of principles for understanding systems. The principles are to be used to describe and explain the working of the socioecological systems in order to allow for the evaluation of the system and its parts [...] They are theories for organizing analysis, explaining systems, and judging policies." (Hayden 2006:51) It can thus be inferred that Hayden considers GSA useful for evaluating social costs because their systemic nature requires a systems approach.

Hayden's belief is that policymaking paradigms should be consistent with the complexity of reality. One important principle of Hayden's GSA is the open system approach: "All real-world systems are open systems, and all open systems are non-equilibrium systems. 'Open systems are those with a continuous flow of energy, information or materials from environment to system and return'" (ibid:52). This is in the tradition of ecological institutional economists Kapp and Nicholas Georgescu-Roegen who applied institutional economics to conceptualize problems of environmental degradation (Berger and Elsner 2007). The principle of positive and negative feedbacks is another important and logically connected GSA principle. "For policy purposes, especially with regard to the natural environment, the system concept of negative and positive feedback is very important. [...] What makes the open systems approach so vibrant from a policy standpoint is the fact that it views the environment as being an integral part of the functioning of a [...] system. Thus, external forces that affect the system need to be accounted for in the analysis of the system. [...] Positive feedback systems [...] tend to be unstable since a change in the original level of the system provides an input for further change in the same direction" (ibid:58). This GSA principle was applied by Gunnar Myrdal and Kapp under the name of "circular cumulative causation" to address social costs (Berger 2008) and will be dealt with in the second part of the paper.

Consequently, approaches that simplify or even distort the problem at hand are rejected: "Ideas like utility maximization ignore culture, social beliefs, institutions, power relations, traditions, procedures, and so forth, and, therefore, are not useful with regard to real-world policy analysis and decision making" (ibid:14). Hence, Hayden concludes that "utilitarian ideas for capturing and analyzing the real world are irrelevant to those who want reliable policy analysis" (ibid:15). By arguing that utility maximization and utilitarian ideas are not fit to deal with the complexity of the real word, Hayden actually reiterates Kapp's argument regarding the limitations of neoclassical "solutions" to problems of social costs, which Kapp had based in an understanding of openness and circular cumulative causation. This point will be further elaborated in the second part of the paper.

Another limitation of utilitarianism that concerns the framing of social costs is the assumption that the pecuniary prices charged by the corporation can be utilized as "the measure of benefits and costs for the analysis of public programs and that monetary prices are to be the common denominator" (ibid:15). Hayden argues that by adopting price as the measure of value, neoclassical policymaking concepts, such as cost–benefit analysis and the Coase theorem, endow the corporations with exaggerated legitimacy and power because its analytical apparatus becomes the dominant model of analysis. "In terms of policy power, the selection of the corporation's criterion of success – that is in dollar flows – as the social criterion of success provides [corporations with] a definite advantage in terms of political legitimacy, standing and power" (ibid:16). Hayden calls it a category mistake to take price as a measure of social value for the purpose of a policymaking paradigm. "The willingness to pay for a good is a subjective want. That is inconsistent with the purpose of public policy. The purpose of public policy is to provide for social beliefs through political association and public processes [...] [and not] to submit to the criterion of market price" (ibid:16). Hayden argues, that neoclassical economists have selected money making as the dominant policy criterion, as narrowly focused and misguided criteria that lack a concern for multisocietalism and multiculturalism (ibid:39). This usually leads to following market rules of pecuniary enhancement so as not to have to judge consequences by society's criteria (ibid:46). "Our system will not be allowed to prosper if the neoclassical standard of the market is to be the scientific criterion for making judgments about ecological systems policy" (ibid:48–49).

A Normative Matrix for Social Costs: Primary Criteria and Socioecological Indicators

Against the aforementioned background of GSA and the limitations of utilitarian criteria for analyzing and evaluating social costs, Hayden raises the important question regarding the role of primary and secondary criteria that stand between the social system and policy evaluation (ibid:37). Hayden stresses the importance of deriving alternative norms and values, that is, primary and secondary criteria. Criteria are to be consistent with belief clusters in the relevant context which does not preclude that beliefs are sometimes the object of policymaking themselves (ibid:40–41). Importantly, criteria also become the object of inquiry in evaluating their effects on socioecological processes: "[…] a major part of policy analysis will be to study the community structural changes that take place as a result of the application of a set of criteria and their resulting policies, and to change the criteria if they lead to undesirable consequences" (ibid:41–42). Criteria can be modified and refined: "The refinement of the interpretation and application of criteria is achieved through discretionary processes made up of legislative bodies, judicial proceedings, research inquiries, advocacy efforts, and so forth" (ibid:42). What is more, Hayden denies that there is one single set of criteria and argues that a different set of criteria are needed for every context particularly if contexts overlap (ibid:43). This matches his rejection of seeking and enforcing one unified common ground with regard to normative criteria (ibid:43). Yet, Hayden argues that it is possible that the problem itself generates the criteria of its resolution (ibid:36) so that, for example, the primary normative criteria for the ecological system have to be consistent with the mainte-nance of a particular kind of ecological systems (ibid:19).

This is why Hayden deals with the difficult task of generating a database of information for the guidance of the policymaking process and presents a methodol-ogy for developing socioecological indicators. "As was emphasized in the social indicator movement that began in the 1960s [cf. Kapp], all useful measures are ultimately social. They are recognized as social indicators to indicate that they are relevant to some social context, rather than as ultimate 'measures' having universal applicability" (ibid:61–62). Hayden applies John Dewey's measurement standards for the design of indicators "from quality to quantity," mentioning especially site-specific ecology and consistency with the problem. In addition, Hayden underlines that the indicators must be consistent with the primary goal because operationally the indicator becomes the public policy decision criterion. Indicators as secondary criteria become *the* action criteria (ibid:62–63). In reality, policy indicators determine the final policy result because the evaluation of alternatives depends on indicators used for their valuation. Hence, it becomes important that the indicators used to measure and value alternatives are consistent with the primary goals.

In conclusion, Hayden's approach points to the difficult task of subjecting values and criteria to the policymaking process as they are not outside the scope of science but can be evaluated in terms of their consequences. This hints at the primary task of an institutional approach to social costs, that is, to develop alternative criteria for the evaluation social costs when utilitarian criteria are not considered. Since social costs and benefits cannot meaningfully be measured in terms of market prices, there is a need to outline alternative criteria for measurement and evaluation. The question arises as to what forms of criteria exist that are suited to measure social costs. If problems provide the criteria for their solution, as Hayden argues, then it should be possible to find a normative common ground for the problem of social costs. It is here that Kapp's approach to policymaking for the environment (social and physical) can be fruitfully incorporated into Hayden's approach. Kapp proposed the universal value of basic human needs from which context-dependent criteria (social minima) can be developed as primary criteria. The degree to which social minima are not fulfilled would then be an objective nonutilitarian measure of social costs.

Kapp's Humanist Approach to Policymaking and Social Costs

Kapp is perhaps best known as the economist who developed a theory of social costs in the tradition of American institutionalism (Veblen 1904) (Kapp 1950, [1963] 1977) and a policy approach that links Dewey's pragmatic instrumentalism (Dewey 1922) with Max Weber's substantive rationality (Weber [1925] 2005).

The Complexity Theory of Social Costs and the Limitations of Utilitarian Policies

According to Kapp's theory, the extent to which social costs are accounted for depends on the political structure of society requiring environmental policy and institutional reforms to minimize them. "[Social costs] are damages […] which under different institutional conditions could be avoided. For, obviously, if these costs were inevitable under any kind of institutional arrangement they would not really present a special theoretical problem. […] to reveal their origin the study of social costs must always be an institutional analysis. Such an analysis raises inevitably the question of institutional reform and economic policy which may eliminate or minimize the social diseconomies under discussion." (Kapp 1963:186) "No democratic society can and will tolerate this subordination of the social system to the dictates of formal rationality. The universal reaction of society to the neglect of social costs […] has taken a variety of forms […] compelling private producers to internalize […] social costs" (Kapp 1963:202)

Realizing the normative-political character of the problem of social costs and its problematic dependency on asymmetric power relations, Kapp sought a way of dealing with problems of social costs scientifically without resorting to formal approaches of the utilitarian kind. In fact, his divergence from Pigouvian (1924) and Coasian (1960) policy approaches does not only result from the realization of the problem's normative-political character but also from their faulty logic and practical limitations. For instance, Kapp considered it as logically faulty to define the concept more precisely than is justified: "An element of inescapable indeterminacy may remain either due to the lack of homogeneity of the facts or of people's valuations or due to a lack of knowledge about causal interrelationships." (Kapp [1971b] 1977:309) Kapp pointed to circular cumulative causation in the ecological system and fundamental uncertainty: "Pollution and the disruption of the environment are the results of a complex interaction of the economic system with physical and biological systems which have their own specific regularities. Moreover, pollutants from different sources act upon one another and what counts are not only the effects of particular effluents and toxic materials but the total toxological situation. [...] Those who have studied these complex relationships know that environmental disruption can easily become cumulative with pervasive and disproportionate effects per unit of additional pollutants" (ibid:314–315). Kapp's theory of social costs stresses "the cumulative character and complexity of the causal sequence which gives rise to environmental disruption and social costs" (ibid:315) and "the delicate system of interrelationships" (Kapp [1963] 1977:94). His theory can in this sense be coined a "complexity theory" of social costs that does not exclude less tangible effects. Kapp emphasized that social costs cannot be considered as being minor side effects in relatively isolated locations, but have to be seen as all pervasive. He even combined this with a historical hypothesis: "as the economy becomes more complex, nonmarket interdependencies are likely to assume greater significance. For this reason social costs are bound to become increasingly important." (Kapp [1965a] 1983:5) Under conditions of complexity and uncertainty the price mechanism that relies on individual subjective evaluations alone cannot identify a viable output position. It is largely impossible for "the individual to ascertain the full range of short and long run benefits of environmental improvements, or for that matter, of the full impact of environmental disruption upon his health and well-being." (Kapp [1971b] 1977:314) Likewise, it can sometimes be difficult to causally determine who is responsible for effects either because of incomplete knowledge or because effects are out of proportion to each individual cause. Referring to Myrdal, Kapp reminded us "that statistical convenience and measurement must *not* be permitted to set limits to concept formations and thus to exclude relevant elements" (ibid:309–310).

Kapp rejected the application of the utilitarian principle, that is, the willingness to pay or accept compensation that assigns monetary exchange values to ecological effects. This method is, according to Kapp, as arbitrary as the distributional inequality which it expresses because the "willingness to pay" depends on the "ability to pay" and has nothing to do with the objective and real exigencies of states of socioecological balance. "The use of the willingness to pay as criterion of quantifying and evaluating the quality of the environment has the insidious effect of reinterpreting original human needs and requirements into a desire for money and of evaluating the relative importance of such needs in terms of criteria which reflect the existing inequalities and distortions in the price, wage and income structure" (ibid:313). Kapp made the case that monetary criteria such as the willingness to pay are not appropriate because they do not evaluate the characteristics that define the quality of the environment and its potentially negative impact on human health, human well-being, and human survival (ibid:316). In addition to these theoretical inconsistencies, Kapp argued on practical grounds that formal approaches have the effect of neither guaranteeing the fulfillment of the requirements of socioecological balance nor the satisfaction of basic human needs because they focus on rule-following, that is, their solutions are predetermined and limited by a prescriptive formal apparatus. In addition, they remedy social costs only ex-post, which can be too late if damaging effects are irreversible, and they can be too little if the formal calculus prevents taking into account the whole range and full extent of repercussions: "making the content and extent of the control of environmental quality dependent upon individual willingness to pay could at best lead to piecemeal measures and an ineffective formal suboptimization if it does not become the pretext for endless delays or a policy of doing too little too late" (ibid:315).

Rational Humanism and Primary Criteria

Kapp proposed a new rational humanism that would humanize economics by starting from a clear notion of universal human needs (Kapp [1967] 1985:99–120). According to Kapp basic human needs are universal values and should become the basis of substantive rationality in the tradition of Max Weber (Weber [1925] 2005). "Any substantive treatment of human needs and the resulting notion of substantive rationality is based in part on the normative axiom that human life and human development and survival are values which need no further proof or demonstration" (Kapp, unpublished manuscript, Chap. 4:11). In his unpublished manuscript "The Foundations of Institutional Economics" Kapp argued that Marxists and Institutionalists start from the value premise of human needs (ibid:11).[1] Kapp also referred to the concept of "social reproduction," which was first developed by the Physiocrats and later adopted by Marx and Engels. Social reproduction is considered as a goal in itself and as a useful tool for elaborating hypotheses regarding defects and inefficiencies of the social system (Kapp 1974:132, 134–135).

Regarding values Kapp explicitly refers to, on the one hand, the Myrdalian position that value judgments always influence economic science and that they have to be made explicit in order to escape the danger of claiming value-free results (Myrdal [1929] 1954; Kapp 1968:6). On the other hand, however, Kapp seems to have gone further than Myrdal when he proposed that a substantive (value-laden) formulation of concepts with "objective" categories that does not depend on an infinite variety of subjective values is in fact possible. For him "objectively" ascertainable values exist and therefore a "science of the essential being" (Wissenschaft des wahren Seins) (Blum 1982:49, 1977:51). For Kapp facts and values are not only interlinked but values, especially the universal value of human existential needs is the object of science. Regarding the interrelationship of facts and values, Kapp also adopted Marx's point of view that the analysis of facts is capable of yielding normative conclusions (Sollenspostulate), while rejecting naive empiricism (Kapp 1974:39).

To understand Kapp's rational humanism as a version of Weber's substantive rationality it is helpful to take a look at what is considered the central humanistic reference point (Blum 1977:49; Steppacher 1994:435). Kapp started from the "uniqueness of the biological structure of the human organism" (Kapp 1961:139). His biocultural concept argues that beyond certain basic physiological needs no

---

[1] In this context it is interesting that the importance of K. Polanyi's "substantive" meaning of "economic" has been emphasized more recently because of its usefulness for the integration of modern heterodox economics, such as neo-marxist and neo-institutionalist approaches (O'Hara 2000:128–134).

innate needs exist. Yet the human being has to satisfy certain universal or essential needs if he is to develop as a human being. These needs result from the fact that humans are born in a quasiembryonic state without the safety of a fixed instinct hierarchy and experience helplessness, anxiety and dependency: (1) the need for cooperation and communication, (2) the need for self-esteem, self-affirmation, and individuation, (3) the need for safety, order, and security. These needs are social in character because they can only be satisfied in society, so that humans and society are interrelated aspects of life that cannot be meaningfully separated. This consti- tutes the unique biological structure of humans that is "open" and that necessitates a "process of growth" as a condition of the actualization of latent potentialities (Kapp 1961:156). The failure to satisfy these needs may lead to various forms of stress, tension, and anxiety (ibid:174). From this Kapp concluded that human beings share universals by virtue of being human in close accordance with findings of theorists, such as Abraham Maslow and Erich Fromm. According to Blum, even depth psychology shows that there is an objectively observable and scientifically determinable "common denominator" in humans that expresses a quality that is both uniquely and universally human (Blum 1977:50). Kapp formulated the usefulness of such an understanding of human nature: "An empirically validated concept of man and human nature and an understanding of the impact of the enculturation process on the human personality and self-actualization may ultimately enable the social scientist to appraise [...] [the] impact [of the social and physical environ- ment] on the individual" (Kapp 1961:178).

This background allowed Kapp to derive criteria for a rational humanism that are substantive, meaning that they are sought and found in the degree of satisfaction of human needs. This process embodies a differentiation of human needs according to their urgency into basic and higher needs. According to Kapp, it is possible to determine minimum standards in the fields of public health, medical care, education, housing, transportation, and recreation based on empirical data with greater agreement than usually assumed. Hence, human needs become operable as social minima. While remaining subject to revision in the light of new scientific research they have to become ends in themselves because they reflect basic human and social needs (Kapp [1971a] 1983:117). In this context, Kapp praised Carl Menger for having faced the difficult task in the 2nd revised edition of *Grundsätze der Volkswirtschaftslehre* of differentiating between needs of first order and those of higher order (Menger 1923:32–56; Kapp 1972:217). As criteria human needs are clearly very different from the formal subjective maximizing, undetermined utility functions, or abstract money units of formal rationality that conceal great disparities (Blum 1982:67, 69). Referring to Immanuel Kant, Kapp argued that that which cannot be exchanged has no exchange value but intrinsic absolute value. Thus, for him human life and survival are not exchangeable commodities and their evaluation in terms of market prices is in conflict with reason and human conscience (Kapp 1974:132).[2]

---

[2] This is analogous to Polanyi's concept of "commodity fiction" (Polanyi 1947).

Kapp emphasized that the door remains open for empirical validation and refutation and the possibility of disproving evaluations (Kapp 1963:188–189). Kapp applies the term "objectivity" of norms in a pragmatic sense of a susceptibility to revision in the light of experience and the empirical test. Human needs as norms become a reference point that makes it possible to say which means and ends are "healthy" or "good." Norms and values are open to scientific evaluation and guide economic policy. In this, rational humanism links Weber's concept of substantive rationality to Dewey's pragmatic instrumentalism that considered value judgments to guide theoretical and empirical analysis (Bush and Tool 2001:198–200). In elaborating rational humanism Kapp drew farther away from Weber and closer to Dewey who stated that all crucial decision making must invariably include an exploration of the objectives pursued both as far as their content and their implications are concerned (Kapp 1965b:59). Kapp also referred to Dewey's distinction between the "manipulative" use of reason (formal rationality) and the "constructive" use of intelligence. He favored the latter because it is concerned with the realization of genuine opportunities, the exploration of new possibilities, and it requires the projection of the full repercussions of action under different circumstances (Kapp 1963:194–195).

Rational humanism moves beyond the limit of Weber's notion of objectivity that was tied to his version of "scientific" instrumental reasoning that is not concerned with criteria. Building on the contribution of Dewey, Kapp found a way to treat value-related decisions as also "objective" in a pragmatic sense. It seems that Kapp associated freely with Weber's notion of substantive rationality and it can be considered his innovation to build this orientation toward higher norms, in particular human needs, into economic reasoning and to render them operational as primary criteria. The very concepts of substantive rationality and value-related reasoning are evidence of Weber's intuition that even his scientific instrumentalism has certain limits. This is what inspired Kapp's theoretical innovation and brings into the open what Weber had only hinted at. Kapp's concept of universal human needs demonstrates that there is not an infinite amount of possible standards of value and that values are not beyond the scope of science. Yet, it is important that rational humanism does not enter into what Weber called "ethics of conviction" with its uncritical and unconditional devotion to an absolute idea and fixed aim which leads to a neglect as to its consequences. Instead it remains within the confines of what Weber called "ethics of responsibility" (Kapp 1963:188–189). Kapp fully agreed with Weber by emphasizing that science must never be used to impose dogmatic value judgments (Blum 1977:51).

Kapp's rational humanism in policymaking means that fundamental requirements of human life and survival are integral parts of the constellation of goals of economic policy and social controls. For example, particular aspects of the quality of the environment such as clean air and water must be an end in itself via scientifically derived environmental norms that reflect basic human needs. Kapp's policymaking places the human being and basic needs in the center by proposing social minima, ecological maximum tolerance levels, socioecological indicators, and social controls (Kapp [1971a] 1983, [1973] 1974, [1974] 1983). Kapp was convinced that the solution to the problem of social costs required a new *Political* Economy (Kapp 1950, [1963] 1977) or normative economics: "the new task of [normative] economics would be to elucidate the manner in which collectively determined social goals and objectives could be attained in the most effective and socially least costly manner" (Kapp 1976:102). In elaborating his humanist approach to policy-making Kapp relied on Dewey's instrumentalism: "the instrumental elaboration of the paths to be followed, the choice of means in its broadest sense, both belong to the rational setting of objectives and their rational achievement, i.e., rational in the light of empirically testable criteria [i.e. social minima]. [...] The logic of the deter-mination of objectives is added to the logic of the achievement of objectives by the introduction of means suited to the objectives. When political economics is oriented towards the preservation of life and providing the means of existence [...] it includes the exploration of what is necessary and possible and, in the form of political action, deals at the same time with the question of how appropriate reforms may be used to realize sets of objectives that have been recognized as necessary and found social acceptance." (Kapp [1967] 1985:112–113)

Social Minima and Socioecological Indicators for Measuring Social Costs

Rational humanism applied to policymaking aims at objectifying scientifically and making operational the value of human needs via social minima. Social minima are objective criteria – a kind of measuring rod – for the appraisal of the "health" of the social and physical environment which enables economists to establish norms and values scientifically. Social minima can further be transformed into maximum tolerance levels. These are ecological norms, which allow evaluating and exploring different means and ends in the light of their differing costs and benefits, their effects on the physical and social environment, hence their effect on the satisfaction of human needs. Maximum tolerance levels can be used to measure social costs in terms of existing deficiencies by comparing, for example, the actual state of pollution with the maximum permissible concentration of pollutants. "What we suggest as undeniable is the fact that as we extend the applicability of [social minima] we 'rationalize' and 'objectify' the determination of social costs and social benefits and remove their evaluation increasingly from the realm of subjective or ideological self deceptions and distortions" (Kapp 1963:202).

At this point it becomes clear that Kapp's realization about the social nature of the problem of social costs and the importance of finding workable and scientifi-cally sound solutions forced him to break with Weber's position on value-free instrumentalism: "In contrast to M. Weber we suggest that the substantive definition of social costs and social benefits is possible in terms of objective requirements [...] [because they] can be determined with a considerable degree of scientific method and objectivity. That is to say, the identification of social costs and social ben-efits calls for scientifically determined social minima" (Kapp 1963:193–194).

Yet, at the same time Weber's notion of substantive rationality remained the main inspiration for his rational humanism: "The identification of social costs and social benefits derives its objectivity from an orientation toward a substantive rationality which reflects the extent to which a given group of persons is or could be adequately provided with goods and services, or protected against unnecessary losses" (Kapp 1963:190, 193). Kapp acknowledged that social minima do not make the decision process free of conflict. "We do not deny that the social evaluation of the relative importance of social benefits and social costs will always carry elements of political decision as to social purposes and goals. [...] Admittedly this relationship [social minima] does not give rise to an unequivocal and self-evident determination of social goals and social values; but it [...] facilitates the formulation of aims and priorities which are accessible to scientific interpretation and the pragmatic test" (Kapp 1963:203).

Kapp's policy approach also offers derived (secondary) criteria for environmental policy. Kapp argued that environmental policies, the evaluation of environmental goals and the establishment of priorities require a substantive economic calculus in terms of social use values (politically evaluated) for which the formal calculus in monetary exchange values fails to provide a real measure. Hence, an integral part of Kapp's policymaking is a comprehensive system of social accounting with a diversity of heterogeneous socioecological indicators that reflect the present state and exigencies of the socioecological system and its effect on the condition of human life in the light of explicitly stipulated environmental objectives (minimum environmental standards). Socioecological indicators include an inventory of the total situation, a kind of stock taking as a departure point. This inventory of the present state of the environment has to contain the actual and potential dangers for human health and well-being, to social productivity and indeed to human life and survival. Yet, Kapp cautions, that it is important not to conceal that vested interests are affected by implementing a more comprehensive accounting system (Kapp [1973] 1974).

Conclusion

In conclusion, Kapp's approach fits into the framework of Hayden's Social Fabric Matrix (SFM) because both are based on the same philosophical foundation, that is, Dewey's pragmatic instrumentalism and a nonutilitarian approach to value. SFM's key system principles and components are also found in Kapp's open system approach to social costs. Thus, SFM is *the* technique that makes it possible to apply Kapp's theory of social costs in concrete problem settings to effectively resolve problems of social costs. The real advantage is SFM's graphical-formal tool box that allows the framing of the problem situation by better understanding circular cumulative causation between the open economic system and its physical and social environment. In addition, SFM's method to policymaking as a social process under the influence of different values allows for approaching social costs as Kapp did, i.e. by means of primary criteria (social minima and maximum tolerance levels) and secondary criteria (socioecological indicators).

References

Berger S (2008) Circular cumulative causation (CCC) à la Myrdal and Kapp – political institutionalism for minimizing social costs. J Econ Issues 42:357–365

Berger S, Elsner W (2007) European contributions to evolutionary institutional economics: the cases of cumulative circular causation (CCC) and open system approach (OSA) – some methodological and policy implications. J Econ Issues 41:529–537

Blum FJ (1977) Professor Kapp's approach to a science of man in society in the light of the emerging new consciousness and social order. In: Rolf S et al (eds) Economics in institutional perspective – memorial essays in honor of K. William Kapp. Lexington Books, Lexington, pp 47–60

Blum FJ (1982) Die Bedeutung des Universalen für alternative Theorien der Gesellschaft: Max Weber und William Kapp. In: Leipert C (ed) Konzepte einer humanen Wirtschaftslehre. Offene Welt, Frankfurt am Main, pp 41–72

Bush PD, Tool MR (2001) The evolutionary principles of American neoinstitutional economics. In: Dopfer K (ed) Evolutionary economics: program and scope. Elsevier, Boston, pp 195–230

Coase RH (1960) The problem of social costs. Law Econ 3:1–44

Dewey J (1922) Human nature and conduct – an introduction to social psychology. The Modern Library, New York

Hayden GF (2006) Policymaking for a good society: the social fabric matrix approach to policy analysis and program evaluation. Springer, Berlin

Kapp KW (1950) The social costs of private enterprise. Harvard University Press, Cambridge, MA

Kapp KW (1961) Toward a science of man in society – a positive approach to the integration of social knowledge. Martinus Nijhoff, The Hague

Kapp KW [1963] 1977 The social costs of business enterprise (second enlarged edition of The social costs of private enterprise (1950)). Spokesman, Nottingham

Kapp KW (1963) Social costs and social benefits – a contribution to normative economics. In: Beckerath EV, Giersch H (eds) Probleme der normativen Ökonomik und der wirtschaftspolitischen Beratung, Verein für Sozialpolitik. Duncker & Humblot, Berlin, pp 183–210

Kapp KW (1965a) Social costs in economic development. In: Ullmann JE (ed) Social costs, economic development and environmental disruption. University Press of America, Lanham/London, pp 1–38

Kapp KW (1965b) Economic development in a new perspective: existential minima and substantive rationality. Kyklos 18:49–79

Kapp KW [1967] 1985 Economics and rational humanism. In: Ullmann JE, Preiswerk R (eds) The humanization of the social sciences. University Press of America, Lanham/London, pp 99–120

Kapp KW (1968) In defence of institutional economics. Swed J Econ 70:1–18

Kapp KW [1971a] 1983 Implementation of environmental policies. In: Ullmann JE (ed) Social costs, economic development and environmental disruption. University Press of America, Lanham/London, pp 111–142

Kapp KW [1971b] 1977 Social costs, neo-classical economics, and environmental planning. In: Kapp, K. William [1963a] 1977. The social costs of business enterprise, Appendix. Spokesman, Nottingham

Kapp KW (1972) Umweltgefährdung als ökonomisches und wirtschaftspolitisches Problem. Schweizerische Zeitschrift für Forstwesen 123:211–222

Kapp KW [1973] 1974 Environmental indicators as indicators of social use value. In: Kapp KW (ed) Environmental policies and development planning in Contemporary China and other essays. Mouton, Paris/The Hague

Kapp KW (1974) Environmental policies and development planning in contemporary china and other essays. Mouton, Paris/The Hague

Kapp KW [1974] 1983 Governmental furtherance of environmentally sound technology. In: Ullmann JE (ed) Social costs, economic development and environmental disruption. University Press of America, Lanham/London, pp 143–207

Kapp KW (1976) The open-system character of the economy and its implications. In: Kurt D (ed) Economics in the future. The Macmillan Press, London, pp 90–105

Kapp KW (undated) The foundations of institutional economics (unpublished manuscript). Kapp Archive, Basel

Menger C (1923) Grundsätze der Volkswirtschaftslehre, 2nd, revised edn. Hölder-Pichler-Tempsky A.G./G. Freytag G.m.b.H, Wien and Leipzig

Myrdal G [1929] 1954 The political element in the development of economic theory. Harvard University Press, Cambridge, MA

O'Hara PA (2000) Marx, Veblen, and contemporary institutional political economy. Edward Elgar, Cheltenham/Northampton

Pigou AC (1924) The economics of welfare, 2nd edn. MacMillan & Co., London

Polanyi K [1947] 1968 Obsolete market mentality. In: Dalton G (ed) Primitive, archaic, and modern economies – essays by Karl Polanyi. Beacon Press, Boston

Steppacher R (1994) Kapp, K. William. In: Hodgson GM, Samuels WJ, Tool MR (eds) The Elgar companion to institutional and evolutionary economics, vol 2. Edward Elgar, Aldershot, Hants and Brookfield, pp 435–441

Veblen TB (1904) The theory of business enterprise. Charles Scribner's Sons, New York

Weber M [1925] 2005 Wirtschaft und Gesellschaft. Zweitausendeinsverlag, Frankfurt am Main

Convergence of the Social Fabric Matrix and Complex Modeling

Michael J. Radzicki

Abstract System dynamics is a computer modeling technique that is used to solve problems in complex socioeconomic systems through the design or redesign of system structure. Its application often involves the elicitation and mapping of knowledge from experts and stakeholders who possess detailed information about the relevant structure and behavior of the system under study. A digital computer is then used to accurately trace through the dynamics inherent in the mapping – a task that humans cannot do reliably via thought and debate due to their inherent cognitive limitations.

The purpose of this chapter is to illustrate how Hayden's Social Fabric Matrix can add value to system dynamics modeling by introducing discipline and an organizational framework based on institutional economic theory to the knowledge elicitation process. Potential pitfalls are discussed and examples are provided. An important conclusion is that the combination of the two tools can be profitably used for consensus building among experts – a result that is vital for effective policy formulation.

Introduction

In the early 1980s, F. Gregory Hayden (1982a, b) revealed his now famous social fabric matrix (SFM) method to his fellow economists. Since that time he has used it to help policy makers from a variety of public sector institutions systemically think through the implications of changes to complex socioeconomic systems. The applications to which Hayden has applied the SFM method are numerous and diverse (Hayden 2006), and the impact on actual policy making, particularly at the state and local levels, has been significant (Tool 2003). Hayden's successes in the policy arena, however, raise an important question: Can the SFM method, which is now quite mature, be improved and extended? The purpose of this chapter is to

M.J. Radzicki(✉)
Worcester Polytechnic Institute, Worcester, MA, USA

T. Natarajan et al. (eds.), *Institutional Analysis and Praxis*,
DOI 10.1007/978-0-387-88741-8_5, © Springer Science+Business Media, LLC 2009

provide at least one answer to this question. More specifically, the case will be made that the SFM is a tool that can profitably be combined with system dynamics computer simulation modeling to form a more powerful approach to socioeconomic policy analysis.

The System Dynamics Modeling Process

System dynamics is a computer simulation modeling process that is used to solve problems in complex socioeconomic systems through the design or redesign of system structure. Its intellectual origins lie at the interface of feedback control theory, cognitive psychology, and digital computer simulation. Although a comprehensive presentation of the details of system dynamics modeling are beyond the scope of this chapter a brief overview of the method will be presented.[1]

The most fundamental idea in system dynamics modeling is that a system's structure causes its dynamic behavior. Broadly, a system's structure consists of its:

- Physical structure

  - Resources
  - Constraints and limiting factors
  - Delays

- Organizational structure

  - Organization of the system's decision making units
  - Lines of authority
  - Information availability and quality

- Psychological decision making structure

  - Heuristics
  - Culture and tradition
  - Habits and routines
  - Standard operating procedures
  - Incentives and rewards
  - Values and goals
  - Forecasts and expectations

The goal of a system dynamics modeler is to identify and map-out the particular elements of a system's structure (i.e., its socio-techno-environmental-economic "fabric") that interact to create its problematic behavior. Once this has been accomplished the resulting model can be used to run "what-if" experiments aimed at determining which changes to the system's structure can alter its behavior in a desirable manner.

---

[1] For detailed information on the system dynamics method the reader should consult Sterman (2000).

System dynamics modeling is a pattern modeling process (Wilber and Harrison 1978) that essentially yields a dynamic case study of a system experiencing a problem. In mapping out a system's crucial structure, the modeler acts like a detective who is trying to piece together an explanation for a crime or a physician who is trying to diagnose a disease afflicting a patient. As shown in Fig. 1, the modeler is guided in this problem-solving process by knowledge of "generic structures," which are models and/or pieces of system structure that have been found to be common to many system dynamics studies, and "principles of systems," which are the fundamental rules of system dynamics to which all generic structures and system dynamics models must adhere.[2] In this sense, a system dynamics modeler acts very much like a lawyer who is assembling a legal argument related to a particular case, using insights from other, similar, cases and fundamental legal principles. Note too that this pattern modeling process is endogenous in that new models can lead to new generic structures and principles of systems.

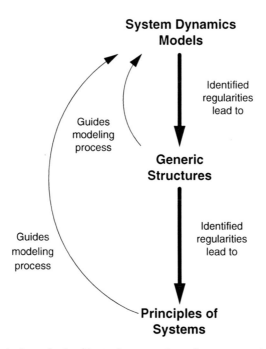

Fig. 1 Endogenously determined guides to the system dynamics pattern modeling process

---

[2] See Forrester (1968).

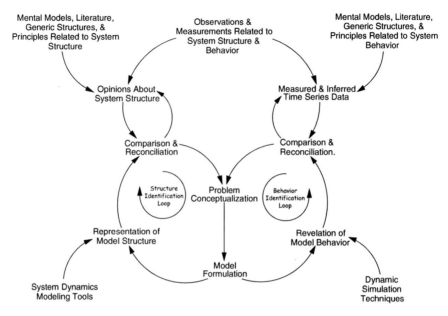

Fig. 2 Iterative nature of the system dynamics modeling process: identifying structure and behavior (Adapted from Saeed (1992))

System dynamics modeling is also an evolutionary learning process. Figure 2, adapted from Saeed (1992), shows that the creation of a system dynamics model is an iterative process involving the modeler's interpretation of measurements and observations about system structure and behavior in the light of information from the mental models of system experts and stakeholders, the relevant scientific literature, generic structures, and principles of systems. These interpretations help the modeler form opinions about important system structure and relevant system behavior that serve as targets for model structure and behavior. Based on these targets, the modeler creates a mapping of the system's crucial structure (i.e., the system dynamics model) and simulates it to reveal its inherent behavior. Comparisons are then made to target the structure and behavior. Discrepancies are resolved by either modifying the model and its associated behavior and/or by the modeler changing his/her mind about the relevant target structure and behavior, in the light of the results from the simulation. Seen from this vantage point, the structure of a system dynamics model evolves over a period of time and the evolutionary learning *process*, not the "finished" model, is the thing that generates value (Forrester 1985).

The Components of a System Dynamics Model

To map out the structure of a system that is generating problematic behavior, a system dynamics modeler utilizes four main building blocks: stocks, flows, feedback loops, and limiting factors. Stocks can be thought of as bathtubs that accumulate physical or informational flows over a period of time. Flows can be thought of as pipe and faucet assemblies that fill-up or drain the tubs. The process of flows accumulating in stocks is called integration in the calculus and is the fundamental source of the dynamics of any system.

Stocks and flows are components of feedback loops. Feedback is the transmission and return of information about the amount of "stuff" that has accumulated in a system's stocks over time. This information feeds back, directly or indirectly, to the system's flows and, based on a specified set of rules (often representing the system's psychological decision making structure), governs the behavior of the flows.

Two types of feedback loops exist in system dynamics modeling: positive loops and negative loops. Positive loops represent self-reinforcing processes such as speculative bubbles, wage-price spirals, and capital accumulation. They tend to destabilize systems and are responsible for the growth or decline of socioeconomic systems. Negative loops, on the other hand, represent goal-seeking processes such as inventory control mechanisms, basic supply and demand relationships, and open market transactions by a central bank aimed at keeping an overnight interest rate at its target value. They tend to stabilize systems, although when their corrective action is significantly delayed they have a tendency to make systems oscillate around their targets. As such, negative loops are responsible for both equilibrium and cycles in socioeconomic systems.[3]

Negative loops are also responsible for a phenomenon that is quite common in socioeconomic systems called "policy resistance." This behavior occurs when the goals of policy makers are in conflict with the goals of other agents in the system. Any intervention by policy makers that pushes a system in a particular direction is often counter-acted by the actions of the other agents in the system, as their negative loops try to pull the system back toward their (conflicting) goals (Sterman 2000, pp. 5–12). Policy resistance can be overcome if policy makers align their goals with those of the other agents in the system.

To sum up, from a system dynamics perspective the behavior of a system is significantly influenced by the types and numbers of its feedback loops and their associated strengths. The positive and negative loops can be thought of as fighting for control of the system with the dominant loops determining the system's time path.

A fourth building block used to map-out a system's structure is limiting factors. More specifically, since almost any conceivable stock cannot contain an infinite amount of material or information, the factors that limit the capacity of a system's important stocks must be identified and modeled. This forces a system dynamics modeler to look for the physical, financial, and psychological limitations that constrain a system's components.

In order to describe how a system behaves as it approaches any of its limiting factors, a system dynamicist must often specify nonlinear relationships. This has

---

[3] Of course, most evolutionary economists such as Gregory Hayden feel that actual socioeconomic systems never reach a state of equilibrium.

two important implications. The first is that simulation must be used to solve system dynamics models because in almost all cases nonlinear dynamic models do not have closed-form analytical solutions. The second is that the existence of nonlinearities means that the strength of the system's feedback loops (i.e., its "active structure") can change endogenously over a period of time. This imparts an evolutionary flavor to system dynamics models and makes it nearly impossible to predict their future time paths with the unaided human mind. Figure 3 offers an example of a simple generic system dynamics model that contains each of the four building blocks described above.[4]

Group Model Building

One of the most important uses of system dynamics modeling (and of the SFM method) is to help a group of experts and stakeholders reach a consensus about policy prescriptions. Indeed, it is quite common for experts and stakeholders to disagree on policy choices, as they bring different mental models to the policy

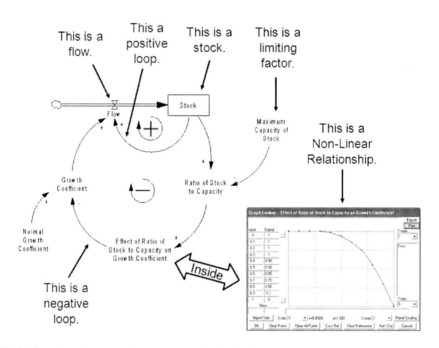

Fig. 3 Generic components of a system dynamics model

[4] Figure 3 was created with a system dynamics software package called Vensim. The figure is essentially a user-friendly picture of the equations that underlie the system dynamics model. If a user wishes to see the equations, they are a simple mouse click away.

formulation process. From a system dynamics point of view, the key is to use the modeling process to surface individual assumptions, test proposed strategies that are "obvious" and "known to be effective," and structure debate so that a shared mental model can be developed and a "learning organization" can be created (Vennix et al. 1997, p. 103).

Over the years, a lot of research has been conducted into what works and what doesn't when using system dynamics to do group model building.[5] The fundamental research questions involve uncovering, codifying, and standardizing best practices for systematically eliciting knowledge from a group of experts and stakeholders and for dealing effectively with group interactions. To a larger degree, answering these questions involves introducing insights from behavioral decision theory, small group dynamics, and group facilitation into the system dynamics modeling process (Vennix 1996; Vennix et al. 1997, p. 103).

A key aspect of group model building is the knowledge elicitation process. The goal of this endeavor is to accurately map-out the knowledge of the system and its problems that is held by the various experts and stakeholders who are participating in the modeling exercise. Moreover, to be useful this process must proceed in a manner that is amenable to the creation of a system dynamics model. This usually involves introducing the experts and stakeholders to "systems thinking" concepts so that they can organize and present their knowledge from both a holistic and dynamic point of view. A useful tool for accomplishing the former goal is causal loop diagramming and it will be argued that the SFM can become an important tool as well.

Causal Loop Diagramming

Causal loop diagramming is often used in the conceptualization or brainstorming stage of a group model building project (Randers 1980; Gill 1996; Lane 2008).[6] The goal is to have experts and stakeholders identify important variables in the system experiencing the problem and connect them in chains of cause and effect until feedback loops are formed. This forces the participants to think holistically and endogenously, and turn their thoughts about the causes of system problems inward toward the design of the structure of the system (Lane 2008). The interconnected set of feedback loops that emerges from this process is considered to be a "first cut" of a possible explanation for a system's problematic behavior.

---

[5] Excellent summaries of most of the research that was conducted in group system dynamics model building up through the mid-1990s can be found in Vennix (1996) and Vennix et al. (1997).

[6] Causal loop diagrams are also often used to present key feedback relationships from a *completed* system dynamics modeling project to an audience or reader.

As an example, Fig. 4 presents a "raw" or unrefined causal loop diagram that was created during an actual brainstorming session, held in July of 2007 that was aimed at uncovering the main cause of exchange rate problems in the nation of Columbia.[7] Each arrow represents an important cause and effect relationship perceived to exist by at least one economist participating in the exercise. The variable at the tail of each arrow (the independent variable) is assumed to cause a change, *ceteris paribus*, in the variable at the head of each arrow (the dependent variable). A plus sign next to the head of an arrow indicates that an increase in the independent variable will cause an increase in the dependent variable above what it would otherwise have been, and a decrease will cause a decrease below what it would otherwise have been. A minus sign next to the head of an arrow indicates that an increase in the independent variable will cause a decrease in the dependent variable below what it would otherwise have been, and a decrease will cause an increase above what it would otherwise have been.[8] Whenever possible, the arrows or "causal links" in Fig. 4 were joined to form closed feedback loops.[9]

Although causal loop diagramming can be a very useful part of the system dynamics modeling process, it must be used with caution because it possesses several inherent limitations (Richardson 1986, 1997; Sterman 2000, Chapter 5; Lane 2008). According to Lane (2008) these include:

- *A lack of precision.* Due to their inherent simplicity, the thought processes underlying some of the links in a causal loop diagram may be unclear to someone who has not participated in the brainstorming session.
- *A lack of variable and link distinctions.* Causal loop diagrams do not distinguish between stocks and flows or between conserved flows (flows of "stuff" between two stocks) and information links (flows of information about stocks). As such, the logic behind some causal links can be misleading. For example, in a causal loop diagram of a simple demographic model in which a birth rate influences a population and the population feeds back to influences the birth rate (i.e., a higher population leads to more births per year and more births per year causes a higher population), each causal link would have a plus sign at the head of its arrow. Yet, if a population decrease is considered, the causal chain would seem to indicate that a smaller population causes fewer births per year and fewer births per year causes a smaller population. Of course, this is silly because a smaller birth rate will still, *ceteris paribus*, *increase* the population, albeit at a slower rate.

---

[7] Actually, the causal loop diagram was first drawn iteratively on a white board during the brainstorming session, then copied onto notebook paper, and finally reproduced in a software program for presentation in this chapter.

[8] In the case in which the dependent variable is not a stock, a causal link is actually a picture of a partial derivative. See Sterman 2000 (p. 139).

[9] Most of the variables in Fig. 4 that are not part of a feedback loop(s) were not conceptualized to be exogenous, but rather as important components of feedback loops that exist in other sectors of the model economy. In other words, they represent points of linkage to other sectors of the model.

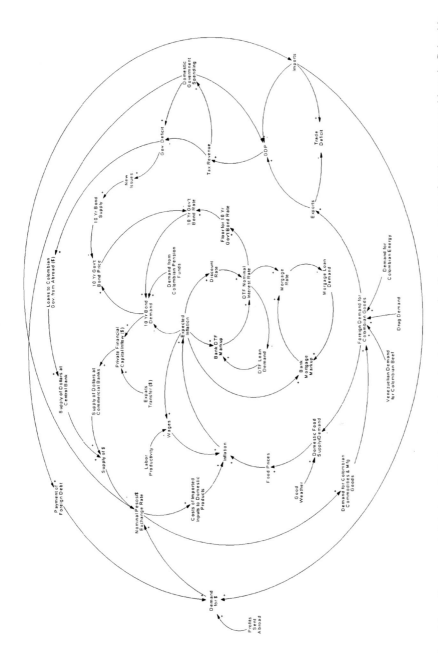

Fig. 4 Causal loop diagram created during a brainstorming session aimed at uncovering the primary causes of exchange rate problems in Columbia

- *Loop polarity errors.* The lack of variable and link distinctions can also cause the polarity of some feedback loops to be misidentified. A classic example from Richardson (1986) involves a simple causal loop diagram of the feud between the Hatfields and the McCoys. What appears to be a positive loop that wipes out one family and makes the other grow exponentially is actually a negative loop that gradually reduces the size of both families, when the appropriate stock and flow structure is considered.
- *Inability to reveal the dynamics of a system.* By far, the biggest problem with any causal loop diagram is that the dynamics of the socioeconomic structure it represents cannot be determined through simple inspection. Instead, the conversion of the causal loop diagram into a full-blown system dynamics model, and its subsequent simulation, is required to accurately reveal the dynamics inherent in its structure.

The last limitation of causal loop diagrams has been the source of some controversy over the years in the field of system dynamics. Practitioners of what is called "soft systems" or "soft OR" argue that significant insight into socioeconomic problems can be gained from causal loop diagramming and other knowledge elicitation and systems thinking techniques and as such, it is often unnecessary to go beyond this level to formal modeling and simulation. Of course, traditional system dynamicists have disagreed with this view for the reasons outlined above.[10]

Turning a causal loop diagram derived during a brainstorming session into a full-blown system dynamics model is not a trivial task. Indeed, anyone new to system dynamics modeling would find it incredibly difficult in all but the most trivial of cases, because, in and by themselves, causal loop diagrams do not contain enough information to facilitate simulation. Instead, a modeler must use his/her experience and knowledge to convert the ideas embodied in a causal loop diagram into dynamic equations and their equivalent stock-flow-feedback loop-limiting factor representation. Several authors, however, including Burns (1977), Burns and Ulgen (2002), and Binder et al. (2008), have proposed formal methods for fixing the problems associated with causal loop diagrams and allowing computer algorithms to automatically turn them into system dynamics models. Although automating the causal loop diagram conversion process takes away most of the learning that occurs during a system dynamics policy intervention, it represents an interesting (and perhaps inevitable) area of research that is currently being pursued by some within the field of system dynamics.

Social Fabric Matrix and System Dynamics

Gregory Hayden's SFM approach can be used to add significant value to the system dynamics modeling process by providing a powerful way of organizing knowledge elicitation sessions with system experts and stakeholders. In fact, getting experts

---

[10] For a collection of papers devoted to this controversy see Richardson et al. (1994).

and stakeholders to take what they know and offer it in a manner that easily facilitates the creation of an insightful (consensus) model may be the most important advancement that can be made in the field of system dynamics.

The SFM approach is essentially a way to map out the feedback structure of a complex socioeconomic system in a disciplined and organized fashion, with the organizational framework coming from institutional economic theory. In other words, it is a way of helping experts and stakeholders produce a causal loop diagram by helping them structure their thinking from a particular point of view. It is also potentially valuable to system dynamicists because it requires experts and stakeholders to include information that goes beyond what is minimally required in traditional system dynamics knowledge elicitation sessions.

Figure 5 presents a simple example of a generic SFM. It contains five primary categories of influence that have their origins in institutional economic theory: Societal Institutions, Technology, Environment, Norms (Beliefs), and Values. Although the details of the individual components grouped within each category (e.g., A1, A2, etc.) are not specified in this example, in practice they would be identified by the experts and stakeholders participating in the modeling exercise and included in the matrix.[11]

Receiving Components → / Delivering Components ↓	A. Societal Institutions	A.1.	A.2. Etc.	B. Technology	B.1.	B.2. Etc.	C. Environment	C.1.	C.2. Etc.	D. Norms	D.1.	D.2. Etc.	E. Values	E.1.	E.2. Etc.
A. Societal Institutions															
A.1.				1 +											
A.2. Etc.															
B. Technology															
B.1.	1 −						1 +								
B.2. Etc.															
C. Environment															
C.1.										1 −			1 +		
C.2. Etc.															
D. Norms															
D.1.	1 −						1 +						1 −		
D.2. Etc.															
E. Values															
E.1.				1 −			1 −								
E.2. Etc.															

Fig. 5 Simple generic social fabric matrix

---

[11] See Hayden (1982a, b, 2000) and Gill (1996) for more details and examples.

In Fig. 5, row components are assumed to deliver a flow of something to column components. The deliveries must be specified as occurring via processes of reciprocity (e.g., deliveries from one industry to another via cartel arrangements) and redistribution (e.g., deliveries from one industry to another via government agreement) and exchange (e.g., deliveries from one industry to another via market transactions).[12] Further, the process of creating a SFM requires experts and stakeholders to specify, for each cell, the sufficiency level (i.e., the required/desired/contractual amount to be delivered), locational aspects (i.e., the beginning and end points of deliveries), and appropriative aspects (i.e., the details of the transactions) of each delivery.

As in Hayden's original approach, the SFM can be converted to Boolean matrix that can in turn be used to make a causal loop diagram.[13] In Fig. 5, a one in a cell indicates that a flow of deliveries are made from the row component to the column component. Information about the link's polarity can be added by including a plus or minus sign in the cell. Figure 6 shows the causal loop diagram that corresponds directly to the SFM in Fig. 5.

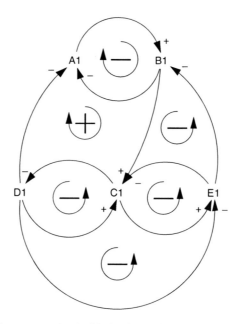

Fig. 6 Causal loop diagram associated with simple generic social fabric matrix

---

[12] Hayden (1982a).

[13] Hayden calls causal loop diagrams "sequence digraphs."

Discussion

As the SFM forces experts and stakeholders to structure their knowledge about the fabric of a socioeconomic system holistically and endogenously, *and* according to the characteristics of delivery flows organized into five categories based on institutional economic theory, it represents a potentially superior way of organizing knowledge elicitation sessions during a system dynamics group modeling intervention. In fact, during the mid-1990s Roderick Gill (1996) explored this very idea by using a SFM to produce a system dynamics model of the slow developing Australian bee pollinating industry. Unfortunately, after several years of research, Gill and his colleagues concluded that an "IdeaMaP" approach is preferable to the SFM method because experts and stakeholders found it difficult to make the conceptual jump from the SFM to the actual system dynamics model. Gill and Wolfenden (1998) write:

> In an earlier work, Gill (1996) proposed the prefacing of formal system dynamics modelling with the community participative development of a social fabric matrix (after Hayden 1982a). Though it was invariably successful in generating a high level of shared insight and learning, a major problem remained in effecting an intuitively seamless transition from the matrix to the model. The matrix approach is laterally different at least in appearance to the graphical interface underlying subsequent system dynamics modeling efforts though it is directly analogous to 'mud mapping'. It was always difficult (though never impossible) for participants to consider both aspects as two components of a unified overall process. Following an extensive review of cognitive mapping procedures, the current format for IDeaMaP was developed as a successful process for bridging the gap between the articulation of intuitive system understandings and computerized scenario testing and analysis.

With the IdeaMaP approach, experts and stakeholders brainstorm by producing a "mud map," which is essentially a hand-drawn causal loop diagram. The mud map is then translated into a quasi-system dynamics model on the computer (no equations, parameters, initial values, etc.). A sub-group of the experts and stakeholders then meets to add hard/soft data to the quasi-system dynamics model (equations, parameters, initial values, etc.), which turns it into a traditional system dynamics model. Finally, the traditional system dynamics model is turned into a "flight simulator" or "learning laboratory," which enables participants to interact with the model (e.g., run scenarios, test ideas) in a user-friendly manner (e.g., via buttons, switches, slider bars, gauges, etc.).

Hence to sum up, Gill's initial research showed that Hayden's SFM method can be profitably used to do group system dynamics model building, but his subsequent research led him and his colleagues to conclude that an alternative method, which eliminates the use of the matrix, is superior. The outstanding research question thus appears to be whether or not it is possible to eliminate participant confusion generated during the transition from matrix to simulation model while preserving the utility generated by the intellectual discipline and organizational framework inherent in the SFM method. Clearly, research conducted in the controlled setting of a laboratory instead of the uncontrolled environment of the field is required to answer this question. Moreover, the ultimate solution might involve a modification of the SFM method to include the specification of the polarities of the causal links, the stocks that accumulate the delivery flows, and a reference mode.[14]

Some Comments on the Notion of "Open" and "Closed" Systems

One of the issues that have historically generated confusion in both institutional economics and system dynamics involves the distinction between open and closed systems. More specifically, institutional economists such as Gregory Hayden have argued (correctly) that socioeconomic systems are "open," which means that they draw in inputs from, and expel outputs to, their environments. As a consequence institutional economists believe that, to be deemed appropriate for institutional analysis, a modeling technique must be able to create "open" models of socioeconomic systems. Some institutional economists, however, also argue that system dynamics models represent "closed" systems, which do not import inputs from, nor export outputs to, their environments because their structures consist of closed feedback loops that generate endogenous behavior.[15] Unfortunately, this belief is totally incorrect. Although it is certainly technically possible to create system dynamics models that are "closed," it is fairly uncommon to do so. The overwhelming majority of system dynamics models of socioeconomic systems are in fact "open."

The decision about whether or not to model a system as open or closed is really a decision about where it is best to draw a model's boundaries. Since models are by definition simplifications of reality, system dynamicists do not try to include all aspects of the systems they study in their models.[16] Indeed, experienced system dynamicists are experts at leaving things out of, as opposed to putting things into, their models!

Figure 7a presents a simple demographic model in which people migrate to and from the state of Massachusetts. In this example the particular place from which immigrants arrive, and the particular place to which emigrants depart, are unimportant for the purpose of the model and thus omitted. Instead, the flow of immigrants originates from a "cloud," which is an infinite source from the model's environment, and the flow of emigrants terminates in a cloud, which is an infinite sink into the model's environment. In this example, the clouds define the boundaries of the model and the model can be defined as "open."

---

[14] See Randers (1980) for more information on specifying a reference mode during the system dynamics modeling process. Specifying a reference mode would help experts and stakeholders tie the fabric of a socioeconomic system to its dynamic behavior.

[15] Mathematically, open systems are "dissipative" and closed systems are "Hamiltonian." For more on this distinction see Radzicki (1988).

[16] In the extreme, the models would end up being exact replicas of the actual systems.

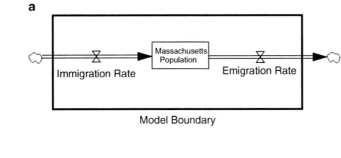

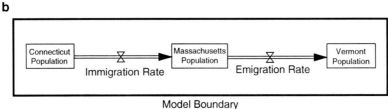

Fig. 7 (**a**) Simple demographic model of an open system. (**b**) Simple demographic model of a closed system

On the other hand, Fig. 7b presents an alternative version of the state demographic model. In this case the particular place from which immigrants arrive (Connecticut), and the particular place to which emigrants depart (Vermont), are deemed important for the purpose of the model and thus included within its boundaries. Therefore in order to facilitate this modification of the model, the clouds in Fig. 7a have been replaced by population stocks. The immigrants and emigrants never leave the system and the model does not interact with its environment. As a result, *if this is the complete model*, it can be defined as "closed."[17]

From Fig. 7a, b it is clear that the distinction between open and closed systems has nothing to do with feedback loops. The confusion surrounding this issue seems to have arisen from two sources. The first is Ludwig von Bertalanffy, the father of general systems theory. Richardson (1991, p. 122) writes that von Bertalanffy:

> might have confused the concept of a closed loop of circular causality with his own notion of a 'closed system.' The latter is a system that exchanges no material or energy with its environment, an entirely distinct and independent idea from the notion of a closed sequence of causes and effects. Alternatively, [he] may have equated information with 'material' and 'energy,' and thus found information loops equivalent to materially closed systems.

---

[17] Since the clouds in Fig. 7a represent an infinite source and an infinite sink, there are no limits to the number of immigrants and no constraints on the number of people who wish to leave Massachusetts (except a Massachusetts Population stock of zero) in the model. On the other hand, since the stocks in Fig. 7b cannot hold an infinite number of people, they implicitly have limits. Feedback from these stocks to the rates of immigration and emigration could be added that would reduce these flows as the system's limits are approached.

The second source is, ironically, Jay Forrester, the father of system dynamics. Forrester (1968, pp. 1-5–1-7) chose to classify systems as either "open" or "feedback" (i.e., "closed"). According to Richardson (1991, pp. 297–298):

> The concept of the closed boundary signals the system dynamicist's endogenous point of view...It also serves indirectly to show Forrester's independence of von Bertalanffy and the general systems theorists...A 'closed system' in general systems theory is a system that experiences no interchange of material, energy, or information with its environment – a corked bottle at constant external conditions, for example. In contrast, Forrester's concept [of a "feedback or "closed" system] represents a system that is not 'materially closed,' but rather 'causally closed' – the closed boundary separates the dynamically significant inner workings of the system from the dynamically insignificant external environment...The two views of closed systems – materially closed and causally closed – are related but are significantly different. No serious system dynamics model is closed in the general system theory sense. Every one exchanges material with its environment – the little clouds representing sources and sinks in Forrester-like flow diagrams representing stocks of material outside the system boundary. Because of such exchanges, Forrester's 'closed boundary' systems are, in von Bertalanffy's terms, 'open systems.'

Conclusions

Gregory Hayden's SFM method is an efficacious and mature approach to holistic socioeconomic analysis and he should be applauded for both its creation and its many successful applications. From a system dynamics point of view, however, it is essentially a tool for eliciting knowledge from a group of experts and stakeholders in a rich, disciplined, and theory-based fashion, to produce a causal loop diagram of a socioeconomic system's feedback structure or "fabric." As a consequence, the SFM method suffers from the same strengths and weaknesses as traditional causal loop diagramming. In order to take the SFM to the next level, research into how it can best be used as a part of the system dynamics modeling process is required. Field studies by Gill have suggested that experts and stakeholders find it difficult to make the conceptual leap from the SFM to the system dynamics stock-flow-feedback loop nomenclature. As such, research in the more controlled setting of the laboratory is required to determine how participants in system dynamics modeling interventions can be taught to easily make the transition from matrix to model. In the mean time, institutional economists need not worry that combining system dynamics with the SFM method will result in "closed" models of socioeconomic systems, as any concern along these lines stems primarily from definitional differences and historical confusions.

References

Binder T, Vox A, Belyazid S et al (2008) Developing system dynamics models from causal loop diagrams. http://www.inb.uni-luebeck.de/publikationen/pdfs/BiVoBeHaSv04.pdf. Accessed 17 Feb 2009

Burns JR (1977) Converting signed digraphs to Forrester schematics and converting Forrester schematics to differential equations. IEEE Trans Syst Man Cybernet 7:695

Burns JR, Ulgen O (2002) A matrix architecture for development of system dynamics models. Proceedings of the twentieth annual conference of the System Dynamics Society. Palermo, Italy. http://systemdynamics.org/conferences/2002/proceed/PROCEED.pdf. Accessed 17 Feb 2009

Forrester JW (1968) Principles of systems, 3rd edn. MIT Press, Cambridge, MA

Forrester JW (1985) 'The model' versus a modeling 'process'. Syst Dyn Rev 1:133–134

Gill R (1996) An integrated social fabric matrix/system dynamics approach to policy analysis. Syst Dyn Rev 12:167–181

Gill R, Wolfenden JAJ (1998) A system dynamics based planning solution for integrated environmental management and policy: the IDeaMaP toolbox. Proceedings of the sixteenth annual conference of the System Dynamics Society. Quebec City, Canada. http://systemdynamics.org/conferences/1998/PROCEED/00088.PDF. Accessed 17 Feb 2009

Hayden FG (1982a) Social fabric matrix: from perspective to analytical tool. J Econ Issues 16:637–662

Hayden FG (1982b) Organizing policy research through the social fabric matrix: a Boolean digraph approach. J Econ Issues 16:1013–1026

Hayden FG (2006) Policymaking for a good society: the social fabric matrix approach to policy analysis and program evaluation. Springer, New York

Lane D (2008) The emergence and use of diagramming in system dynamics: a critical account. Syst Res Behav Sci 25:3–23

Radzicki M (1988) A note on Kelsey's 'The Economics of Chaos or the Chaos of Economics'. Oxford Econ Papers 40:692–693

Randers J (1980) Guidelines for model conceptualization. In: Randers J (ed) Elements of the system dynamics method. MIT Press, Cambridge, MA

Richardson GP (1986) Problems with causal loop diagrams. Syst Dyn Rev 2:158–170

Richardson GP (1991) Feedback thought in social science and systems theory. University of Pennsylvania Press, Philadelphia, PA

Richardson GP (1997) Problems in causal loop diagrams revisited. Syst Dyn Rev 13:247–252

Richardson GP, Wolstenholme EF, Morecroft JDW (1994) Special issue: systems thinkers, systems thinking. Syst Dyn Rev 10:95–336

Saeed K (1992) Slicing a complex problem. Syst Dyn Rev 8:251–261

Sterman J (2000) Business dynamics: systems thinking and modeling for a complex world. Irwin McGraw-Hill, New York

Tool MR (2003) The 2003 Veblen-Commons Award Recipient: F Gregory Hayden. J Econ Issues 37:239–241

Vennix JAM (1996) Group model building: facilitating team learning using system dynamics. Wiley, New York

Vennix JAM, Andersen DF, Richardson GP (1997) Special Issue: Group Model Building. Syst Dyn Rev 13:103–204

Wilber CK, Harrison RS (1978) The methodological basis of institutional economics: pattern model, storytelling, and holism. J Econ Issues 12:61–89

Tackling "Wicked" Problems Holistically with Institutionalist Policymaking

Matthew Gray and Roderic A. Gill

Abstract One of our most pressing needs in creating a more sustainable world is the explicit development of holistic policy. This is becoming increasingly apparent as we are faced with more and more "wicked problems," the most difficult class of problems that we can conceptualize. Such problems consist of "clusters" of problems and include socio-political and moral-spiritual issues.

This paper articulates a methodology that can be applied to the analysis and design of underlying organizational structures and processes that will consistently and effectively address wicked problems while being consistent with the advocated "learning by doing" approach to change management and policy making.

This transdisciplinary methodology – known as the institutionalist policymaking framework – has been developed from the perspective of institutional economics synthesized with perspectives from ecological economics and system dynamics. In particular it draws on the work first presented in Hayden's 1993 paper "Institutionalist Policymaking" – and further developed in his 2006 book, at the heart of which lies the SFM – and the applicability of this approach in tackling complex and wicked problems.

Introduction

One of our most pressing needs in creating a more sustainable world is the explicit development of holistic policy. Such problems consist of "clusters" of problems; problems within these clusters cannot be solved in isolation from one another, and include socio-political and moral-spiritual issues (see Rittel and Webber 1973). Wicked problems are problems defined within the realistic setting of complexity; a setting wherein the behaviors of those systems are described by interacting "loops" of positive and negative feedback relationships. These real-world systems are too "uncontrollable" for preconfigured policy responses. At least some of the relationships that

M. Gray (✉)
Queensland University of Technology, Brisbane, QLD, Australia

T. Natarajan et al. (eds.), *Institutional Analysis and Praxis*,
DOI 10.1007/978-0-387-88741-8_6, © Springer Science+Business Media, LLC 2009

describe the behavior of any system will always remain beneath the resolution of any model. This is equally so for quantitative and mental models alike. We simply cannot know all the "facts" that describe contemporary problems, including environmental problems that are the focus of this paper. Those facts change continuously.

Following on from the earlier work of co-author Roderic Gill on planning for sustainability as a learning concept (Meppem and Gill 1998), this complex systems setting for dealing with the complex real world of environmental policy making, and with its inherently wicked problems, requires a shift in paradigm and an intentional reflexivity in relation to how each and every one of us (and in particular those of us engaged directly in the policy making process) sees the world and understands it. There can be no single overriding world view to underpin our progress, rather, the need is to accept a multiplicity of world views and understandings and to proceed by working with those sometimes divergent understandings towards more "robust pathways" through which to direct change. Finally, the "transdisciplinary learning perspective" we advocate also implies much about how the change management process should work as well. Again, the simultaneous existence of sometimes divergent world views and understandings of any problem set will suggest a change management process characterized by great caution, with an emphasis on experiential learning and continuous reflexivity in relation to how our collective understandings of these problem settings emerge over time. The need is, in other words, for a process that is supportive of continuous learning and that learning should work with the realities of "hermeneutical diversity" or a multiplicity of world views.

This multiplicity of world views is very evident in the case study context chosen as the focus in the paper. Forestry issues around the world have for many years been highly contentious and divisive problems and have been called – and can quite easily be argued as being – a wicked problem. Forestry on the island State of Tasmania has been an even more highly charged issue than that seen on the Australian mainland. It is argued here that it is in large part the divergent world views held by those involved in this issue in Tasmania that perpetuate the ongoing conflict revolving around conservation, land use, and resource management. The current institutions and processes being employed in Tasmania are insufficient to adequately address the complexity of interacting "loops" of positive and negative feedback relationships that are at play.

This paper articulates a methodology that can be applied to the analysis and design of underlying organizational structures and processes that will consistently and effectively address wicked problems while being consistent with the advocated "learning by doing" approach to change management and policy making. This transdisciplinary methodology – known as the institutionalist policymaking framework – has been developed from the perspective of institutional economics synthesized with perspectives from ecological economics and system dynamics. In particular it draws on the work of Hayden's 1993 paper and 2006 book – at the heart of which lies the SFM – and the applicability of this approach in tackling complex and wicked problems.

Substantive and lasting solutions to wicked problems need to be formed endogenously, that is, from within the system. These solutions are the product of interactive learning. They are not end point solutions given the likelihood of never ending learning pathways; rather, the solutions we seek are to be regarded as "steps along the way," or in more enlightened language, the solutions we seek should be regarded as points of intervention within a system that might exert leverage on the behavior of the system in directions considered to be desirable by those participating in the discourse we recommend. The institutionalist policymaking framework is a trans-disciplinary, discursive, and reflexive vehicle through which this endogenous creation of solutions to wicked problems may be realized.

Wicked Problems

> Continuing to seek solutions to 'tame problems' when we face 'messes', let alone 'wicked problems', is potentially catastrophic hence fundamentally irresponsible. (King 1993:n.p.)

Rittel and Webber (1973) were the first authors to use and define the term "wicked problem." Since then it has been applied to describe a range of issues (natural resources in particular), with Wolfenden (1999) stating that typical examples of wicked problems include urban design, social policy, and environmental problems, and King (1993) applying the term to the American nuclear industry.

Rittel and Webber in their original work (1973) describe two types of problems, "tame" problems and "wicked" problems. Ackoff (1974) expanded upon this to describe "messes," an intermediate type of problem. Kesik (1996, cited by Wolfenden 1999:37) developed a similar typology for classes of problems, named "Well Defined," "Ill-Defined," and "Wicked" problems.

Tame problems are solvable through analytical methods, and as such are amenable to reductionist problem solving approaches; King (1993) states that this type of problem has been the "forte of science for several hundred years." They may also be called convergent problems; the more the problem is studied, the more different answers tend to converge towards a single correct solution. Some examples are alphabetical sorting, analytical geometry (Kesik 1996, cited in Wolfenden 1999), development of a vaccine for smallpox, or analyzing the chemical components of air pollution (King 1993). Typically, a mono-disciplinary approach is most appropriate for tame problems (Wolfenden 1999).

"Messes" consist of "clusters" of problems and problems within these clusters cannot be solved in isolation from one another. A range of systems methods have been used to solve "messy problems"; the understanding of the interactions between the parts is as important as the parts themselves. Such methodologies are appropriate because they are non-linear and explorative in nature and develop solutions in an iterative and evolutionary way (Wolfenden 1999). Some examples of messy problems include automobile congestion, water pollution (King 1993), architectural design, and management systems (Wolfenden 1999).

Policy makers by-and-large have difficulties coming to terms with messy problems. Sterman (2002) addresses this problem when he says, "Thoughtful leaders increasingly recognize that we are not only failing to solve the persistent problems we face, but are in fact causing them." There seems to be an underlying inability of traditionally trained leaders, managers and policy makers to understand and come to terms with problems other than tame problems. King (1993) offers some insight into this situation when he suggests that "messes offend our sense of linear logic, the linear syntax of our language, and our continuing belief in prediction." Typical mental models that our political leaders use are, largely, unsuitable for the resolution of messy problems. Political leaders seem to be called upon by their constituents to "make tough decisions," to "take the reins," and to "solve the problems." Such approaches are perfectly applicable for tame problems, but inapplicable for messy or wicked problems. Indeed, King (1993:n.p.) suggests:

> Politically, messes require top and middle managers to relinquish traditional authority and forms of control, something most are loath to do. More disturbing, in turbulent times people often feel insecure and threatened, turning to those who offer reassuring but simplistic answers.

Rittel and Webber (1973) coined the term "wicked problems" to refer to the most difficult class of problems that we can conceptualize. Applying the typology of problems explained here, they may be thought of as messy problems that have had their boundaries expanded to include socio-political and moral-spiritual issues (King 1993).

Such problems call for a new approach, and more particularly for an approach which goes beyond the typical mono-disciplinary, multi-disciplinary, or even inter-disciplinary approaches. To deal with wicked problems a transdisciplinary approach is most appropriate, and institutional economics and ecological economics are two communities of practice that have claimed significant contributions to such approaches.

Integration of Institutional Economics and Ecological Economics

Institutionalist policymaking is a vehicle through which the reflexive and iterative integration of institutional economics (IE) and ecological economics (EE) can be accomplished. This integration of IE and EE has been argued for by Radzicki (2003b) and this framework facilitates this integration.

Ecological economics has been described as a methodologically pluralistic approach because it "tries to integrate and synthesize many different disciplinary perspectives" (Costanza et al. 1991:3). Institutionalist policymaking (Hayden 1993, 1995, 2006a) as a methodology can be pragmatically selected from an EE perspective as an appropriate methodological approach for policymaking and as a framework within which policy can be made in an institutionalist (i.e. a holistic) way. This framework articulates many steps (detailed in Hayden 1993, 2006a) in a complicated process that for most policymakers is implicit. As it is an implicit process, many policymakers are unaware of the underlying assumptions and perspectives they bring to the process. The explicit graphical form of the institutionalist policymaking framework is shown in Fig. 1. In developing and implementing policy using this framework, one moves roughly from the top left box to the bottom right box. Boxes either vertically or horizontally adjacent inform each other. Rather than being a linear, prescriptive approach, the process is intended to be iterative and reflexive, with progress in each part of the process reflected upon in light of progress in other parts of the process. Boxes from left to right indicate the progression of the policymaking process. Moving from top to bottom indicates the level at which the phase is being tackled, from theory, to strategy, and then tactics. All three levels are necessary to make the complete process work, but no one level can be used in isolation to formulate holistic policy.

In applying the methodology of the institutionalist policymaking framework, the policymaker is given an opportunity to articulate explicitly her epistemological position (Fig. 1, box 1). The importance of this phase cannot be reiterated strongly enough. A policymaker's epistemological position underpins all subsequent thinking and theories with regard to policymaking and decision-making, and all analyses begin with epistemology, either implicitly or explicitly. The importance of a constructionist approach from the point of view of developing the best approach to policymaking is also important (see Crotty 1998; Honderich 1995). Totally objectivist or subjectivist epistemologies may result either in the illusion that reality can be directly accessed by humans as totally objective observers (when in fact we are simply objectifying subjective truths), or in radical subjectivism and solipsism (Hayles 1991, 1995, 1996, cited in Binkley 1998).

An instrumental or pragmatic approach to policymaking in (Fig. 1, phase II) is the approach that both IE and EE recommend as most appropriate, as they are problem-focused approaches (remembering not to confuse "instrumental" and "pragmatic" terms with "instrumental rationalist" and "pragmatist," which are starkly different in their meaning; see Honderich 1995).

Phase III of the institutionalist policymaking framework (Fig. 1, phase III) involves reflection on and articulation of the ideology of the policymaker. All policymakers have underlying ideologies in forming their decisions, because they are humans with underlying cultural values and societal beliefs (see Hayden 1995, 2006a).

The underlying ideology seen as essential by Hayden (1993, 2006a) is one that treats the world as a complex place displaying emergent properties. In relation to human affairs, Hayden uses the word communitarian, meaning that human society is not a collection of unrelated parts, but it displays complex, emergent behavior. This perspective is consistent with the perspective of EE, in which complexity is seen as a vital contributor to both natural and social systems (see van der Lee 2002; Grant et al. 1997; Stacey et al. 2000; Brooks 2005; Gleick 1987; Bar-Yam 2000:1; Gell-Man 1994).

Having explicitly defined the position of the policymaker and having reflected upon the underlying assumptions and biases of that position, the stage is set for the appropriate articulation of the policy problem at hand; the phase of problem definition is defined from the perspective of wicked problems (Fig. 1, phase I). The explicit definition of the problem as a wicked problem brings with it the powerful realization that attempts to simplify the complex problem to common flows such as money in

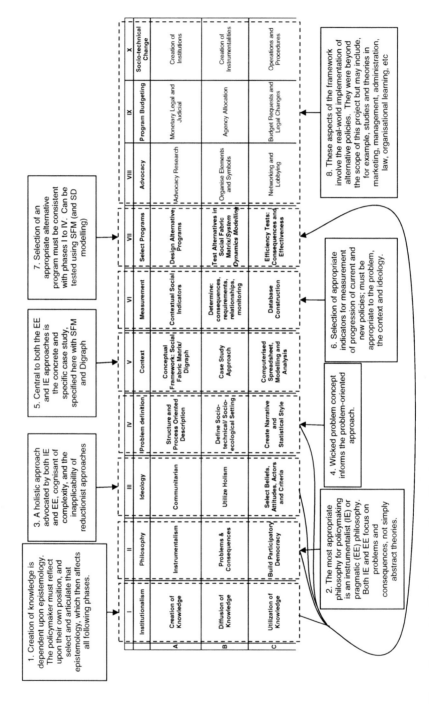

Fig. 1 Phases of the institutionalist policymaking framework

order to resolve it are totally inappropriate and to deal with the situation approaches that deal with multiple system components simultaneously are required.

It is not possible to reduce systems to simple money flows but flows of environmental and social capital must be included as well, and the economic system is only part of much larger socio-ecological system (see Costanza et al. 1997). It is arguable that wicked problems often arise when this fact is not foremost in the minds of policymakers. When economists insist on the use of money flows as the dominant concern, it assists in the conversion of our system from one in which government is the dominant governing institution to one in which corporations become dominant (Hayden 2003). Citizens within a democracy (largely) expect (rightly) that their elected government should be the dominant governing institution. When the situation that Hayden alludes to above occurs, it disenfranchises those citizens, and may lead to the development or exacerbation of wicked problems, as communitarian ideas are abandoned, to be replaced by attempts to maximize "net present value." Important in the definition of wicked problems is the EE concept of optimal scale (see Holling 2004; Kremen et al. 2000; Wolfenden 1999). Wicked problems often consist of nested problems, or problems within problems, and to effectively deal with such problems they must be addressed at the highest level possible, which institutionally often means State or Federal governments. Beyond these national institutions lie international institutions, and it may be that these higher levels may need to be addressed, including their beliefs, values, and epistemologies. At whichever higher level it is most appropriate, addressing an institution without addressing the underlying beliefs, and the cultural values and epistemologies that form those beliefs may be a fruitless exercise.

Once again, the approaches of IE and EE converge within the institutionalist policymaking framework in the contextualization of problems (Fig. 1, phase V). Both argue the need to make policy within the context of concrete and specific cases (Shi 2004). A variety of techniques may be used at this phase (again a convergence of IE and EE in their methodologically pluralistic approaches); the method recommended by Hayden (1993, 2006a) is the SFM (first introduced by Hayden 1982). Measurement of the system under investigation (Fig. 1, phase VI) may incorporate a number of methods from a number of fields, such as economics, ecology, botany, zoology, geology, anthropology, sociology, criminology, ethnography, statistics and so on. The integration of these techniques within the institutionalist policymaking framework makes it a transdisciplinary approach, one which unifies these diverse fields that are able to deliver valuable insights into the important variables of the policy problem. Ecological economics stresses the importance of social and biological indicators for the assessment of system performance rather than just the use of monetary indicators (Low 2003; Simon 2003). Concurrent with this concern for social and biological indicators is the need for analyses to evaluate multiple variables (Hamilton 1994:63; Munda 2003). The development of a complete set of indicators is a time consuming task and must be undertaken for each policy problem. The design of alternative programs is an important phase of the institutionalist policymaking framework (Fig. 1, box 7). Both the institutionalist policymaking framework and EE agree that the creation of models that allow these alternative programs to be tested is an important component of the processes of the framework. The SFM is an approach that allows such an analysis. Another applicable methodology is the use of System Dynamics (SD) to model the behavior of these policy alternatives (Forrester 1961; Sterman 2000). While SD modeling is a methodology that is relevant and useful for implementing the institutionalist policymaking framework, it is not the only methodology that may be suitable for such a task. Further, the development of an SD model needs to be undertaken by the researchers and stakeholders who are actually involved in the implementation of the framework in the actual development of alternative policy and management approaches. This is in contrast to more common "imposed solutions" where the development of models is undertaken far removed from the stakeholders of the system. Any SD model that might be presented here would simply be illustrative of the possible usefulness of such an approach in the context of the institutionalist policymaking framework. It has been argued that SD should be integrated with IE (Gill 1993, 1996; Radzicki 2003a) and with EE (Wolfenden 1999). The use of SD within the institutionalist policymaking framework allows the integration of all three, EE, IE, and SD. It should however be noted that Hayden (2006b) takes issue with the use of conventional Forrester-type computer programs which he considers to be "inconsistent with institutional economics" (p. 535).

The implementation stages of the institutionalist policymaking framework are shown in Fig. 1, box 8. As suggested by this diagram the implementation of policies can involve a broad range of approaches and methodologies, as long as these are consistent with the foundational phases of the institutionalist policymaking framework, which are utilizing holism, instrumentally focused and reflecting a constructionist epistemology, and built upon a participatory, democratic system. Such systems have been discussed by other researchers in this area (for example, Wolfenden 1999; Meppem 1999, 2000; Smith 2003). There is a potential cornucopia of research focused around these latter phases of the institutionalist policymaking framework, but they have not been the focus of this research.

The full development of the institutionalist policymaking framework for any given example is beyond the scope of any single researcher. Hayden (1993, 2006a), in developing the institutionalist policymaking framework stated, "institutionalists need to fill the 30 boxes in [the framework] with tools and integrate them in a complete policymaking process. No one scholar, or policymaker, can be an expert in all the areas; each box is an area of study and expertise." It is therefore appropriate that it should act as a vehicle for the integration of perspectives from IE and EE; the framework is itself a transdisciplinary approach to policymaking.

Epistemological and Philosophical Underpinnings

The strength of the institutionalist policymaking framework in the resolution of wicked problems is its usefulness as a transdisciplinary framework through which epistemologies, theoretical perspectives, methodologies, and methods suitable for addressing the elements of wicked problems may be integrated into a novel and system specific approach that will allow the resolution of wicked problems. The application of the institutionalist policymaking framework is predicated, of course, upon there being a policymaker at the appropriate level who has a desire to tackle a wicked problem in a novel way. This may come, for example, from someone with a strong latent commitment to holistic, reflexive policymaking, who has come into a position where that commitment may be realized; alternatively, a long-term policymaker may simply see the institutionalist policymaking framework as an opportunity to "try something different." It is in a situation such as this that the institutionalist policymaking framework may be an appropriate tool for allowing policymakers at, say, the State and Federal government level to, develop policy in a holistic and reflexive way, and in the process resolve the wicked problem they have been trying to address.

Features that may be thought of as contributing to wicked problems include conflicting paradigms, regulation and regulatory capture, environmental discourses, and complexity and chaos. The institutionalist policymaking framework can be used as an approach that specifically and systematically addresses these issues, and in doing so allows for the resolution of specific wicked problems.

One of the most important insights that the institutionalist policymaking framework brings into conflict between paradigms is a reflexive, constructionist epistemology. Such an approach recognizes that there are different ways of knowing, and that these different ways of knowing are held by people who may be said to operate within different paradigms. Two such conflicting paradigms relevant to wicked problems associated with "natural resource management" (the term itself reflects a particular underlying perspective of the natural world) are shown in Table 1, the "dominant" and "new" natural resource paradigms.

Table 1 Contrasting natural resource management paradigms (Shindler and Cramer 1999)

Dominant resource management paradigm	New resource management paradigm
Nature to produce goods and services (anthropocentric perspective)	Nature for its own sake (biocentric perspective)
Amenities are coincidental to commodity production	Amenity outputs have primary importance
Commodity outputs over environmental protection	Environmental protection over commodity outputs
Primary concern for current generation (short-term)	Primary concern for current and future generations (long-term)
Intensive forest management such as clear-cutting, herbicides, slash burning	Less intensive forest management such as "new forestry" and selective harvesting
No resource shortages – emphasis on short-term production and consumption	Limits to resource growth, emphasis on conservation for long-term
Decision-making by experts	Consultative/participative decision-making
Centralized/hierarchical decision authority	Decentralized decision authority

Through the institutionalist policymaking framework, and in particular through the contextualization of the wicked problem itself, the impact of conflicting paradigms may be deconstructed. Such deconstruction is seen by Dryzek (1997) as vital to the breaking down of the barriers between people holding divergent paradigms or discourses. The systematic uncovering of these divergent views is possible through the SFM, which is a central plank of the institutionalist policymaking framework. Having systematically deconstructed these relationships, it is possible then to develop systems which work to break down the barriers between these discourses and paradigms, to expand the "hermeneutic circles" (see Stones 1996) of those involved in the wicked problems and to allow for the fusions of horizons necessary for participants to come to terms with and resolve their issues.

What is required for either the transition from this old paradigm to the new paradigm, or a reconciliation of the two, is a change from a positivist, reductionist mindset, which objectifies and treats all problems as tame problems (Rittel and Webber 1973) to a holistic approach which recognizes not only that all the various elements of the problem must be addressed simultaneously, because they are all interconnected and interdependent, but also that an epistemologically constructionist and reflexive approach is needed. In addition, to be effectively addressed, these problems must be addressed at the highest level possible, which in the Australian case is the State and Federal Governments, although it may be argued that many wicked problems in Australia are a subset of global phenomena (see, for example, Buckman 2004; Clark 2001; Commission on Global Governance 1995; Daly 1993, 1998). While problems need to be addressed at these institutionally higher levels, governments should not intervene directly to implement their own "solutions" to problems, even though it may appear that their electorates are calling for such simple solutions. People often turn to those who offer reassuring but simplistic answers when they feel threatened or insecure (King 1993). However, substantive and lasting solutions to wicked problems need to be formed endogenously, that is, from within the system. The formulation of such solutions often requires the relinquishing of traditional authority and forms of control (ibid). In many examples top and middle managers have in the past implemented "technocratic" and "objectivist" solutions, but these "solutions" have themselves become contributors to wicked problems. Rather, the fundamental problem of these governments themselves must first be addressed, namely a lack of holistic, sustainability-focused systems thinking, essential in the application of an integrated and holistic approach to policymaking. If this underlying issue can be addressed, and a culture of holistic, system based, sustainability-focused decision-making can be inculcated in State and Federal Governments in particular, many current wicked problems may come closer to being resolved; the problem situations would be quite different if these institutions reconstructed their thinking from new fundamentals. The institutionalist policymaking framework presented in this thesis can be seen as a vehicle for the facilitated expansion of objectivist mindsets in the creation of policy and management alternatives, and in the synthesis of novel solutions from within the system. The superiority of solutions generated from within the system over those that are imposed from outside the system can be exemplified by regulation, a contributing component of a number of wicked problems.

Two types of regulation in particular may be identified as contributing to wicked problems, namely command-and-control regulation and self-regulation. Underlying those approaches is a common epistemology that may be called objectivism; that is, there is a truth and systems can be directed towards it. This truth is objectified in the selection of targets and the processes used to achieve them, with the main difference between command-and-control and self-regulation being whether those objectified truths are assessed by an external or internal agent. Such a perspective creates linear thinking, rather than complex or systems thinking, and is a perspective that assumes away feedback. In contrast, there are alternative regulatory instruments that are underpinned by a different epistemology, one that might be called constructionism. Such instruments may be seen as acting endogenously, and as such may be more effective in addressing ongoing regulatory problems and issues contributing to wicked problems. Within the regulatory approaches that fall within that epistemology, there may be said to be two groups. There are those that are *reflective*; that is, they reflect upon their position relative to *others*. Such instruments may be said to include some economic instruments, such as price-based instruments. The other group consists of instruments that may be thought of as *reflexive* (see Honderich 1995), requiring a degree of evaluation of epistemological position, and typically such instruments are those that involve the addressing of *one's own* position and ways of knowing, in the context of other stakeholders and their priorities (Shindler and Cramer 1999). The next section briefly explores the analysis of these stakeholders via the SFM for the case study examined for this project.

A Case Study: Forestry in Tasmania

Forestry is one of the areas which has been described as prone to produce wicked problems (King 1993), and the forestry situation in Tasmania is arguably one such problem. In attempting to grapple with this situation, tools such as the SFM and the institutionalist policymaking framework can assist in understanding, unraveling, and making explicit the complex interactions that can contribute to this situation and be so apparently intractable. Needless to say, there is insufficient space here to fully articulate a complete analysis of such a complex system. Table 2 does however show a condensed version of a SFM of the Tasmanian situation. This SFM has been further expanded elsewhere (Gray 2006); the resulting matrix contains over 3,000 potential relationships, far more than can be explained here.

From this simplified SFM, a digraph can be constructed that graphically represents the relationships between these system components; such an example is shown in Fig. 2. Note that most arrows (indicating "deliveries" between components) are bi-directional. Arrows that are single-headed have been drawn to be obviously so.

From this digraph more complex interactions can be extracted and explained, and obviously the creation of a single diagram that included all the relationships of the expanded SFM would truly earn the label "horrendogram"; this digraph shows only 84 such relationships.

Table 2 Simplified SFM of the Tasmanian forestry case study

Delivering components			Receiving components											
			Social institutions						Values	Beliefs	Technology		Environment	
			Federal gover- nment	Tasmanian govern- ment	Conser- vationists	Beek- eepers	Loggers	Comm- unity	Values re nature	Societal beliefs	Forestry	Bee keeping	Abiotic	Biotic
			1	2	3	4	5	6	7	8	9	10	11	12
Social institutions	Federal govern- ment	1	1	1	1	1	1	1		1	1	1		
	Tasmanian gover- nment	2	1	1	1	1	1	1		1	1		1	
	Conser- vationists	3	1	1	1	1	1	1		1	1		1	1
	Beekeepers	4	1	1	1	1	1	1		1	1	1	1	1
	Loggers	5	1	1	1	1	1	1		1	1		1	1
	Community	6	1	1	1	1	1	1		1	1		1	1
Values	re nature	7							1	1				
Beliefs	Societal beliefs	8	1				1	1	1	1				
Technology	Forestry	9	1	1	1	1	1	1			1	1	1	1
	Beekeeping	10	1	1	1	1	1				1	1		
Environment	Abiotic	11	1	1	1	1	1	1					1	1
	Biotic	12	1	1	1	1	1	1					1	1

The key strengths of such tools however lie not in the ability of a researcher such as the author to create them with ever increasing complexity, but in the use of such visual tools to be the catalyst of dialog, learning, and the evolution of shared under-standing by conflicting stakeholders of the complex relationships they find them-selves within. This is especially the case if these diagrams are constructed within an interactive environment where stakeholders are providing the guidance regard-ing these relationships. The SFM in particular acts as a systematic tool for the extraction of information regarding the relationships that are contributing to the wicked problem and the value and beliefs that influence those relationships, as the "empty boxes" cry out for data (are they *really* empty?) and the simple indication that a relationship exists demands further elaboration. Conflicts between stakehold-ers with different underlying value and belief sets, such as for example between anthropocentrism and ecocentrism (see Dryzek 1997), may be thought of as occur-ring because both "camps" objectify the "truths" they hold regarding the environ-ment. An approach to the development of policymaking and management that brings these people into a situation where dialog is possible allows the expansion of "hermeneutic circles." Within this now reflexive and constructionist space, the resolution of wicked problems can begin. Expansion of their understanding through active dialog within a discursive cooperative management environment (see Meppem and Gill 1998; Meppem and Bourke 1999; Meppem 1999, 2000) provides an opportunity for a "fusion of horizons."

Meppem and Gill (1998) in particular sought to redefine "sustainability" (today with over 250 published definitions) as a concept which inherently involves the

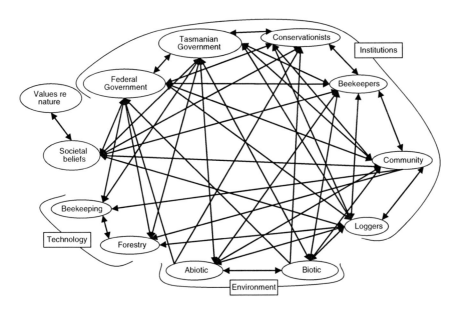

Fig. 2 Digraph of simplified SFM for Tasmanian forestry case study

breaking down of barriers between perspectives to produce a continual state of transition where the following can be noted:

- The objective of sustainability is not to win or lose and the intention is not to arrive at a particular point
- Planning for sustainability requires explicit accounting of perspective (world-view or, mindset) and must be involving of broadly representative stakeholder participation (through dialog)
- Success is determined retrospectively, so that the emphasis in planning should be on process and collectively considered, context related progress rather than on achieving remote targets. A key measure of progress is the maintenance of a creative learning framework for planning
- Institutional arrangements should be free to evolve in line with community learning
- The new role for policy makers is to facilitate learning and seek leverage points with which to direct progress towards integrated economic, ecological, and sociocultural approaches for all human activity

The expansion of understanding suggested here can arguably be brought about in a twofold way. First, the implementation of the institutionalist policymaking framework as a catalyst for reflexive processes of systems thinking can create alternative policies that are holistic and reflexive. Second, the implementation of these new approaches to management can itself continue to facilitate the ongoing expansion of stakeholder understandings.

Conclusion

When confronted by wicked problems, most policymakers and managers are unable to conceptualize appropriate responses and may even fail to recognize that they are dealing with a wicked problem at all. The use of the institutionalist policy-making framework provides an approach that makes the phases of the policymak-ing process explicit and through methods such as the SFM allows for the systematic unraveling of the complexity that lies at the heart of all wicked problems. This is accomplished in part through the inclusion of wicked problem stakeholders in the iterative policymaking process. The integration within this framework of perspec-tives from institutional economics and ecological economics is a vehicle for the further integration of the communities of practice of both ecological economics and institutional economics; the integration of these two areas that lay claim to being transdisciplinary makes significant progress in developing approaches that will adequately address a range of wicked problems. The institutionalist policymaking framework is one of the first methodologies to explicitly integrate institutional economics and ecological economics, but it is doubtful that it will be the last.

References

Ackoff R (1974) Redesigning the future: a systems approach to societal problems. Wiley, New York

Bar-Yam Y (2000) Dynamics of complex systems. http://www.necsi.org/publications/dcs/. Accessed 14 Feb 2009

Binkley CS (1998) Forestry in a postmodern world or just what was John Muir doing running a sawmill in Yosemite Valley. Policy Sci 31:133–144

Brooks M (2005) Spies, lies and butterflies. New Sci 19 Nov:32–35

Buckman G (2004) Globalization: tame it or scrap it. Zed Books, London

Clark J (2001) The global wood market, prices and plantation investment: an examination drawing on the Australian experience. Environ Conserv 28(1):53–64

Commission on Global Governance (1995) Our global neighbourhood. Oxford University Press, Oxford

Costanza R, Daly HE, Bartholemew JA (1991) Goals, agenda, and policy recommendations for ecological economics. In: Costanza R (ed) Ecological economics: the sciences and management of sustainability. Columbia University Press, New York

Costanza R, Cumberland JC, Daly HE, Goodland R, Norgaard RB (1997) An introduction to ecological economics. St. Lucie Press, Boca Raton

Crotty M (1998) The foundations of social research: meaning and perspective in the research process. Allen and Unwin, Sydney

Daly HE (1993) The perils of free trade. Sci Am 269:24–29

Daly HE (1998) Sustainable growth: an impossibility theorem. In: Dryzek JS, Scholsberg D (eds) Debating the earth: the environmental politics reader. Oxford University Press, Oxford

Dryzek JS (1997) The politics of the earth: environmental discourses. Oxford University Press, Oxford

Forrester JW (1961) Industrial dynamics. Productivity Press, Cambridge

Gell-Man M (1994) The Quark and the Jaguar. Little, Brown and Company, London

Gill RA (1993) The honeybee pollination market as a self-organising emergent system. PhD Thesis, University of New England, Australia

Gill RA (1996) An integrated social fabric matrix/system dynamics approach to policy analysis. Syst Dyn Rev 12:167–181

Gleick J (1987) Chaos: making a new science. Cardinal, London

Grant WE, Pedersen EK, Marin SL (1997) Ecology and natural resource management: systems analysis and simulation. Wiley, New York

Gray M (2006) Sustaining the Ecological, Social and Economic Values of the Forests of Southern Tasmania. Phd thesis, University of New England, Australia

Hamilton C (1994) The mystic economist. Willow Park Press, Fyshwick, ACT

Hayden FG (1982) Social fabric matrix: from perspective to analytical tool. J Econ Issues 16:637–662

Hayden FG (1993) Institutionalist policymaking. In: Tool MR (ed) Institutional economics: theory, method, policy. Kluwer, Boston/Dordrecht/London

Hayden FG (1995) Instrumentalist policymaking: policy criteria in a transactional context. J Econ Issues 29:360–384

Hayden FG (2003) Endangered democratic institutions and instrumental inquiry: remarks upon receiving the Veblen-Commons award. J Econ Issues 37:243–258

Hayden FG (2006a) Policymaking for a good society: the social fabric matrix approach to policy analysis and program evaluation. Springer, New York

Hayden FG (2006b) The inadequacy of Forrester system dynamics computer programs for institutional principles of hierarchy, feedback and openness. J Econ Issues 40:527–535

Holling CS (2004) From complex regions to complex worlds. Ecol Soc 9:11. http://www.ecologyandsociety.org/vol9/iss1/art11. Accessed 14 Feb 2009

Honderich T (ed) (1995) The Oxford companion to philosophy. Oxford University Press, Oxford

King JB (1993) Learning to solve the right problems: the case of nuclear power in America. J Bus Ethics 12:105

Kremen C, Niles JO, Dalton MG, Daily GC, Ehrlich PR, Fay JP, Grewal D, Guillery RP (2000) Economic incentives for rainforest conservation across scales. Science 288:1828–1832

Low N (2003) Is urban transport sustainable? In: Low N, Gleeson B (eds) Making urban transport sustainable. Palgrave Macmillan, New York

Meppem A (1999) Strategic policy development for public sector organisations: a communicative framework for sustainable regional development planning. PhD Thesis, University of New England, Australia

Meppem A (2000) The discursive community: evolving institutional structures for planning sustainability. Ecol Econ 34:47–61

Meppem A, Bourke S (1999) Different ways of knowing: a communicative turn toward sustainability. Ecol Econ 30:389–404

Meppem A, Gill RA (1998) Planning for sustainability as a learning concept. Ecol Econ 26:121–137

Munda G (2003) Internet encyclopaedia of ecological economics: multicriteria assessment. http://www.ecoeco.org/pdf/mlticritassess.pdf. Accessed 14 Feb 2009

Radzicki MJ (2003a) Institutional economics, post Keynesian economics, and system dynamics: three legs of a heterodox economics stool. Future of heterodox economics conference. University of Missouri, Kansas City 5–7 June 2003

Radzicki MJ (2003b) Mr. Hamilton, Mr. Forrester, and a foundation for evolutionary economics. J Econ Issues 37:133–173

Rittel HWJ, Webber MM (1973) Dilemmas in a general theory of planning. Policy Sci 4:155–169

Shi T (2004) Ecological economics as a policy science: rhetoric or commitment towards an improved decision-making process on sustainability. Ecol Econ 48:23–36

Shindler B, Cramer LA (1999) Shifting public values for forest management: making sense of wicked problems. http://www.fs.fed.us/eco/eco-watch/wickedpr.html. Accessed 14 Feb 2009

Simon S (2003) Internet encyclopedia of ecological economics: sustainability indicators. http://www.ecoeco.org/pdf/sustindicator.pdf. Accessed 14 Feb 2009

Smith J-AM (2003) Redesign of government sustainability education programs for business personnel – from awareness raising to changing behaviour. PhD Thesis, University of New England, Australia

Stacey RD, Griffin D, Shaw P (2000) Complexity and management: fad or radical challenge to systems thinking?. Routledge, London

Sterman JD (2000) Business dynamics: systems thinking and modelling for a complex world. McGraw-Hill Higher Education, Sydney

Sterman JD (2002) All models are wrong: reflections on becoming a systems scientist. Syst Dyn Rev 18:501–531

Stones R (1996) Sociological reasoning: towards a past modern sociology. MacMillan, Houndmills, Basingstoke

van der Lee JJ (2002) A decision-support framework for participative and integrated river basin management: an application of the triple bottom line. PhD Thesis, University of New England, Australia

Wolfenden JAJ (1999) A transdisciplinary approach to integrated resource management: a pragmatic application of ecological economics. PhD Thesis, University of New England, Australia

Normative Analysis of Instituted Processes

F. Gregory Hayden[1]

Abstract This chapter refines and formalizes the normative concepts of duty and obligation consistent with the ideas of institutional economics. To do so, deontic logic and normative system philosophy is utilized in order to formalize a methodology that enhances normative description, empirical investigation, and decision making. This formalization assumes the normative sets of social, technological, and ecological criteria as expressed in the social fabric matrix, and is grounded in the concepts of prohibition, obligation, and permission as emphasized by Karl Polanyi and John R. Commons. The deontic system necessary for a society to integrate authority and processing institutions to create and fulfill normative criteria through rules, regulations, and requirements is developed in a temporal setting. This explanation does not suggest that real-world normative systems are harmonious or continuous, or that they maintain commonality of normative criteria, avoid excess or inadequate redundancy, and are without gaps and conflict. In fact, it is quite to the contrary. The explanation is structured so studies can be completed to find the gaps, discontinuity, disharmony, and conflicts. Given the fragility of the modern world, analytical tools that assist in this task are of paramount concern.

Introduction

The conventional view with regard to scientific methodology and philosophy has been to emphasize a distinction between the analytical approach, which is based on linguistic or conceptual analysis, and the empirical approach, which lets empirical

F.G. Hayden (✉)
Department of Economics, University of Nebraska, Lincoln, NE, USA

[1]F. Gregory Hayden is Professor of Economics, Department of Economics, University of Nebraska-Lincoln, USA. The author is grateful to the editors and publisher for their permission to reproduce here the original publication of this chapter. The original was published in Sasan Fayazmanesh and Marc R. Tool (eds), *Institutionalist Theory and Applications*: *Essays in Honour of Paul Dale Bush*, *vol* 2. North Hampton, MA: Edward Elgar, 89–107.

findings guide science and philosophy as much as possible. The original institutional economics' view is that methodology and philosophy should be guided as much as possible by empirical investigations; a view that does not conform to the linguistic or conceptual tradition. Institutionalists usually designate the linguistic or conceptual approach as a formal approach in which formalized abstractions are laid down as immutable rules of the game (usually axiomatically) without respect to whether or not there is an empirical base for the rules of the game. They usually refer to the empirical approach as a substantive approach by which the results of real-world investigations are used to identify the substance of systems and to change the substance as social and technological changes, or the new investigations create problems for the systems methodology. Institutionalists agree with Richard Schlagel that: "Philosophical problems do not arise *primarily* from conceptual or linguistic confusions, but because of the dislocating effects of *our* established beliefs or conceptual linguistic frameworks owing to empirical discoveries or theoretical developments in the sciences and other intellectual or cultural disciplines" (Schlagel 1995, 1, original emphasis).

Empirical studies, as they reveal social, economic, and technological changes, continuously upset philosophical systems. When the properties of philosophical and methodological approaches are found to be inconsistent with the real world, the approach can be changed to conform to the new findings or it can be treated as a game and continue to perform analytical techniques allowed by the game. For example, when it was discovered that all real-world systems are open systems, it was clear that real-world systems cannot be equilibrium systems. This meant that formalized models based on equilibrium were not relevant analytical devices for analyzing real-world socioecological systems. Therefore, institutionalists abandoned equilibrium models while others continued to develop equilibrium models into more complex intellectual games.

Although institutionalists have traditionally termed the linguistic and conceptual approach to methodology and philosophy as formal, such terminology is misleading because empirical studies of substantive socioecological systems are completed according to a formal methodology. The emphasis of institutionalism should be that the methodological form should change as evidence indicates that it is inconsistent with empirical findings or that it is inconsistent with relevant linguistic and conceptual analysis. Paul Dale Bush recognized the need for developing formal methods for institutionalism and contributed significantly toward providing a formal base for institutional theory and methodology (Bush 1983, 1987, 1991). This is important for assisting empirical studies, for theoretical development and for policy applications. Bush (1983), 61–62 has suggested that the future work on his analytical model would require extension and refinement.

The purpose here is to refine part of Bush's formalization with the assistance of the ideas, tools, and nomenclature of normative philosophy and deontic logic. Bush has given an explication of the concept of a normative system as defined by institutionalists. The explication of the normative world is the method by which abstract concepts are transformed into more exact concepts so they become consistent tools of empirical analysis, thus providing for greater efficiency of research. Some have wondered whether such a method of reconstruction is by its nature incapable of assisting us in grasping reality, because they claim it proceeds by abstraction and leads to an impoverishment of our understanding. Objections of this kind are based on a misrepresentation of abstraction and appear to be unaware of the philosophy of the normative system. All scientific thought is based on abstraction. What is important is that such thought be relevant to understanding real-world systems which are guided by social norms. Institutionalists have traditionally emphasized the importance of duty and obligation embedded in socioeconomic institutions. Thus, to complete a normative system, it is necessary to turn to deontic logic, the logic of duty and obligation. Decisions within a normative system provide for a range of possible actions, called the normative range. Deontic logic provides the tools to define the extent of duty and obligation. Bush's work has provided a general framework for the concerns of institutionalists. With the assistance of normative system philosophy and deontic logic, analysis can be refined to allow for enhanced empirical analysis, decisions, and action.

The intent here is to take us a step closer to fulfilling a statement of purpose made by John Groenewegen of Erasmus University at a professional meeting. During a panel discussion he said that since there is no evidence of universal models, our goal should be to have well-developed models on the shelf for different types of institutional structure. Then, as investigations are undertaken to study different kinds of problems, institutionalists can retrieve the most appropriate model from the shelf. The intent here is to begin with the foundations laid by Bush, in order to discuss a methodology for building toward Groenewegen's *shelf* models.

It was stated above, that this work would depend on the ideas, nomenclature, and tools of the normative systems. Let me emphasize, however, that normative philosophers will not agree with some of the applications that will be made of their tools; although dependent upon, the applications will not always be consistent with. In an Ayresian sense, the work here is a new combination of normative technology for an alternative use. The purpose is to articulate a methodology to guide normative description and empirical investigation. The normative system of the real world does not always fit the normative requirements of normative philosophy. This is not meant as an adverse criticism; rather, it is to clarify the different purpose. Normative philosophers have been interested in logical systems based on axioms from philosophy, while institutionalists are interested in tools for articulation and evaluation of real-world socioecological systems.

Some normative philosophers emphasize that for a system to be valid, it must not contain contradictions or tautologies. Yet social systems contain numerous contradictions and tautologies. For example, the powerful ideology of supply-side economics is based on neoclassical methodology, which is constructed with the assistance of numerous tautologies. Supply-side economics cannot be ignored as an important normative force just because it is based on tautologies; its impact on social, economic, and ecological components has been too significant for social scientists to ignore. As another example, tautologies are the base of computers because computers are based on boolean mathematics which is, in turn, based on a series of tautologies. We cannot exclude the computer world and its social, economic, and ecological impacts because it contains tautologies. The tools of normative and deontic philosophers are important; the purpose here is to bend them toward the needs of institutionalism.

With regard to contradiction, Bush clarified with the axiom of transience the difference between the axioms of logical systems and the axioms of the real world. Neoclassical methodology assumes transitive relations. Yet Bush pointed out that empirical investigations have found dominance relations that are not transitive. He demonstrated a nontransitive dominance system based on graph theory from mathematics (Bush 1983, 44–45).

Foundation of Normative Systems and Deontic Categories

Karl Polanyi explained that the norms of a social situation include (1) prohibitions, (2) obligations, and (3) permissions. This was consistent with his advice that socio-ecological analysis should be centered on and guided by process, norms, and policy (Polanyi 1957, 248–250). To focus on process, norms, and policy, it is necessary to define the normative prohibitions (Ph), obligations (O), and permissions (P) that provide the rules for socioecological transactions. (A symbolic reference is provided at the end of the text/chapter for the readers' convenience.) These are the norms that guide the actions taken in an ongoing social process. They determine the patterns of institutional activity that give institutions correlative capability and statistical regularity. Polanyi emphasized the constant motion of social processes; thus, normative components are action oriented. John R. Commons had completed a particular application consistent with Polanyi's general theory prior to Polanyi's writing the general theory. In Commons's *Legal Foundations of Capitalism*, he described the normative criteria in a capitalist social system as the working rules of going concerns that specified what individuals (1) must do, (2) must not do, (3) may do, (4) can do with the aid of collective power, and (5) cannot expect from the collective power (1924, 6). The first three are consistent with Polanyi's obligation, prohibition, and permission. The last two can be deleted because all social norms are collective.

Although it will not be discussed here, Polanyi and Commons needed to add optional to their deontic categories of prohibition, obligation, and permission in order to include their respective concerns for privilege in socioeconomic situations. Both scholars explained that some actors may have the status and power to be indifferent toward a normative rule. That deontic modality allows that the norm-subject may either perform or not perform the act.

Walter C. Neale and Georg H. Von Wright are two scholars who have emphasized the question "why?" and provided answers to it in explaining the relationship between norms and human action. The most important aspect of their emphasis on that question is paradigmatic. Their paradigms explain that institutional action is completed for a reason or reasons. The answer to the question "why?" is the reason. In explaining institutional activity, Neale wrote that belief norms are a set of ideas or representations explaining or justifying the activities and governing rules and are answers to questions starting with "why" (Neale and Pearson 1962, 1). The reason includes the norm that orders, permits, or prohibits the doing of an action and the necessary connections that make (or do not make) the doing or forbearing of the action a practical necessity (Von Wright 1983, 74). Paradigmatically, institutional action has an end in view with normative statements to the effect that something ought to or may not be done. Neale and Von Wright have both clarified that persons involved in an institution can neither be depended upon to know the social belief criteria nor be depended upon to be truthful about them. Beliefs are social and are not necessarily known by all the different agents involved in a process. "Conscious awareness of the function of an institution is not necessary and will often be absent" (Neale 1987, 1,196).

The Social Fabric Matrix of Social, Technological, and Ecological Criteria

The literature of normative philosophy, although emphasizing social systems, has not developed a whole-system approach. The emphasis has been on particular logic rather than the transactional whole. The task here is to explain the analysis of normative systems within the context of the overall social fabric matrix (SFM). Figure 1 is a simple overall view of the social and cultural components and the reticulate fabric of a social system. The components are cultural values, social beliefs, social institutions, attitudes, technology, and ecological systems. With respect to Fig. 1, the analysis and discussion below will concentrate on the criteria that are concomitant with social institutions; the three normative sets are social belief criteria (N_B), technological criteria (N_T), and ecological system criteria (N_E). These norms are the standards for judging whether institutional patterns are appropriate. Since normative philosophy does not take a whole-system approach to normative decision making, N_T and N_E are seldom of concern in that literature, while the institutionalist tradition makes them apparent. N_T and N_E are not defined in any anthropocentric sense. Technology, which is the combination of tools, skills, and knowledge, does not think about and decide upon normative criteria. Technological norms are the criteria conveyed to society as a result of the combination selected by societal units such as corporations. Likewise, no assumption is being made that an ecological system is reflective about values and beliefs. N_E, instead, represents the normative criteria consistent with the maintenance of a particular kind of ecological system as institutions apply technology to that system.

The three sets of criteria (N_B, N_T, and N_E) are the first components entered in the SFM in Fig. 2. The SFM is an integrated process matrix designed to express the attributes of the parts as well as the integrated process of the whole (Hayden 1982, 1985). The rows represent the components which are delivering, and the columns represent the components which are receiving. The participle form serves to denote that the SFM is designed to model an action process. The SFM is "a systematic attempt to identify the relevant set of influences that shape the behavior of a system" (Gill 1996, 169). If the SFM in Fig. 2 were complete, it would include all the

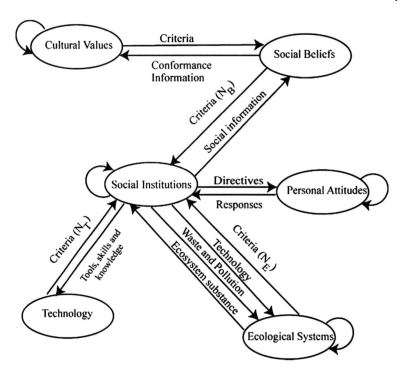

Fig. 1 Relationships among values, beliefs, attitudes, institutions, technology, and the ecological system

Delivering Components \ Receiving Components		Social norm (N_B)	Technological norm (N_T)	Ecological norm (N_E)	Authority institution (I_{A1})	Authority institution (I_{A2})	Processing institutions (I_p)	Action Sets of I_p
		1	2	3	4	5	6	7
Social norm (N_B)	1				1			
Technological norm (N_T)	2				1			
Ecological norm (N_E)	3				1			
Authority institution (I_{A1})	4					1		
Authority institution (I_{A2})	5						1	
Processing institutions (I_p)	6							1
Action Sets of I_p	7							

Fig. 2 Social fabric matrix of norms and institutions

components in Fig. 1. The SFM in Fig. 2 does not contain all components of a full SFM, nor does it indicate all deliveries among the components. It is limited to normative concerns. Deliveries made among matrix components (from rows on the left to columns on the right) are indicated by a 1 being placed in the cell where the delivery is made. If one wanted to complete Boolean manipulations on the matrix, 0 could be placed in the cells where deliveries are not indicated. Below in this chapter, when particular deliveries in the matrix are discussed, the cells of interest will be laid out in digraph format, with the deliveries in the cells indicated on the edge (directed line) between cells. The designation of the cells will be included in the textual discussion, designated as the ith row that is delivering to the jth column. The numbers of the rows and columns are indicated in Fig. 2.

Normative Criteria and Institutions

Each major norm that applies to numerous institutional settings has a number of subcriteria (n_B, n_T, and n_E) that apply to particular institutional situations or cases. Thus, N_B obligates the application of n_{B1}, n_{B2}, and n_{B3} under the conditions of the institutional authority of I_{A1}; N_T obligates the application of n_{T1} and n_{T2} under the conditions of I_{A1}; and N_E obligates the application of n_{E1} and n_{E2} when applied to institution I_{A1}. The first row of Fig. 3 informs us that N_B directs ($\supset$) an obligation (O) of n_{B1} & n_{B2} & n_{B3} given institution I_{A1}. The conjunction (&) means that the subcriteria are to be applied *together*. This is the delivery in cell (1,4) of the SFM. The second statement in Fig. 3 is similar in which the technological norm N_T directs an obligation for n_{T1} and n_{T2} to be applied together to institution I_{A1} and the third row contains a statement about a similar delivery for the subcriteria of N_E. The delivery in a SFM digraph format between norms N_B, N_T, and N_E and institution I_{A1} is found in Fig. 4 with the deliveries indicated on the edges (directed lines) from the norms to the institution I_{A1}. Normative criteria deliver instructions for subcriteria to be applied with other subcriteria in order to complete the respective super criterion. In turn, the designated subcriteria outlined above become the criterial standards to be applied by institutional authority I_{A1}, as indicated in Fig. 4.

As John R. Commons emphasized, institutional authorities come in many forms. They may be explicitly designated as government agencies or judicial branches. However, institutional authorities are also designated by those agencies within other kinds of institutions. For example, a used car salesperson may be given the

	SFM cells
$N_B \supset O\ (n_{B1}\ \&\ n_{B2}\ \&\ n_{B3})/\ I_{A1}$	(1,4)
$N_T \supset O\ (n_{T1}\ \&\ n_{T2})/\ I_{A1}$	(2,4)
$N_E \supset O\ (n_{E1}\ \&\ n_{E2})/\ I_{A1}$	(3,4)

Fig. 3 Norms and obligations for institutions

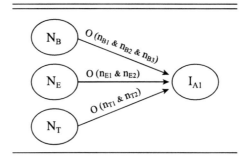

Fig. 4 SFM digraph: norm delivery of conjunctive subnorms to institutions

authority (obligated) to make sure that safety requirements are met on automobiles before they are sold. Thus, we do not attempt to find an authority institution within a particular kind of agency. As Bush has explained, institutions are patterns of correlated behavior (Bush 1987, 1,076), so the authority patterns of an institutional authority can be correlated across different kinds of agencies.

From the array of criteria delivered to the authority institution, rules (r), regulations (re), and requirements (rq) need to be articulated in order for the norms to influence and guide action. In the normative philosophy literature, r, re, and rq are often used interchangeably, and sometimes inconsistently. Here, we will designate rules as the broader and more authoritative code that guides regulation to achieve a particular conduct or establish a pattern with regard to particular institutions. Regulations are completed to control or govern the action of an institution through action requirements. Requirements are required responses to symbols. They usually take the form of orders, requests, and questions. Requirements are given externally. If requirements are consistent with the regulations and rules, they are instituted to carry out action to achieve the purpose of regulations. As instituted and presented to the agents, requirements exist, so to speak. Although agents undertaking the action often do not know the reasons for the required action, actions can still be consistent with a normative end (Von Wright 1983, 54). The human agent may have an end quite different than the normative reason for the requirement. A worker may be following order requirements for a paycheck without reflection on the normative end for which the requirement exists.

An example of a rule statement could be as follows: To permit maximum utilization of sources of radiation consistent with the health and safety of the public. A regulation consistent with that rule could be as follows: The calibration should be performed under the direct supervision of a radiological physicist who is physically present at the facility during the calibration. Requirements regarding calibration would be numerous, with precise instructions about when and how to calibrate and exactly what instruments to use.

Regulations are usually justified and explained, especially when codified in an operations manual. There are *reasons* given for carrying out the regulations. The reasons for carrying out regulations appeal to normative rules in the discourse because it emphasizes the actions the regulations are aiming to accomplish. In a corporate setting, managers, attorneys, directors and executives are expected to know and be accountable to the reasons given for the regulations. Without the reasons, administrative personnel will not know how to adjust requirements as situations change in order to achieve the intent of the rules.

Rules are made in order to fulfill norms and are usually explained in a discourse similar to norms discourse. Great effort usually goes into explaining the norms and the reason the rules are necessary in order to fulfill normative beliefs. Such rules are found in court decisions and legislation. An example is when the courts give trees standing in the courts to bring lawsuits in order that the courts can make rules to protect trees in a manner consistent with the norms of the ecological system. .

For the purpose of explaining normative systems, two types of authority systems are described with regard to carrying norms to the action field. The higher (meaning most authoritative) authority was designated as I_{A1} above. These are institutions that interpret norms for a particular situation and the particular properties of a situation and then frame, structure and explain the rules for the situations in which the rules are to be applied, and the acceptable reasons for applying the rules. I_{A1} authorities are institutions like courts and legislative bodies, and they "lay down the law" to other authoritative institutions, such as corporate authorities, designated as I_{A2}. I_{A2} represents authority as rule maker, while I_{A1} represents authority as regulator and enforcer.

Corporations are divided between authority institutions and processing or production institutions. The latter will be designated as I_p. The authority I_{A2}, often referred to as *headquarters* for a corporation, promulgates the numerous regulations that are utilized to determine the requirements of the corporate production process, I_p.

Rules of Institutional Authority

I_{A1} authorities deliver, as indicated in cell (4,5) of the SFM, a number of rules, r_1 . . . r_n, to I_{A2} authorities. Rules come in the form of rulings with regard to properties of a situation (S). Therefore, where r represents rules of obligation, prohibition, or permission with regard to situations, in general $I_{A1} \supset O(r_1 \ldots r_n)/S_1 \ldots S_n)$. I_{A1} obligates the application of an appropriate rule or rules given a particular situation or situations. We can think of numerous different possibilities. For example, $I_{A1} \supset O(r_2$ & $r_3)/S_1$ states that I_{A1} obligates rules r_2 and r_3 to be applied together to situation S_1.

Alternatively, cell (4,5) of the SFM can be expressed in digraph format as in Fig. 5, where I_{A1} delivers an obligation to I_{A2} to apply rules, $r_1 \ldots r_n$ to situations S . . . S_n as those situations are formulated in rulings by I_{A1}. In a more complete SFM, each of the relevant situations in the series, $S_1 \ldots S_n$, would be included in the SFM with its own row and column under I_{A2}.

Regulations of Institutional Authority

A major task for those studying a problem area is to identify the convergence of various rules, socioecological properties, and situations. Social life is never so simple as

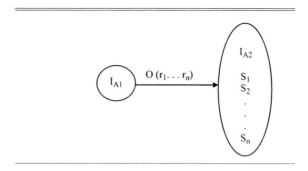

Fig. 5 SFM digraph: institutional delivery of rules to another institution

to have set rules and regulations that obligate or prohibit the same action in all situations within the same institution. We do not observe rules being applied to an institution as a whole. Rather, what can be observed are such activities in situations (see Neale 1987, 1,184). The situations are made up of properties. As the deontic content of social properties changes, the deontic status of particular action changes.

This can be demonstrated with a simple example of a real-world problem. It is the issue of whether waste from a production process, I_p can be spread on farmland in the region near the production centre in order to minimize production costs. This action issue can be called U. Under what conditions should I_p workers be obligated to spread the waste and under what conditions should this action be prohibited? To simplify, assume that there are three properties that make up situations that are relevant to the corporate leadership's decision making. The properties are: the river has a high volume of water, so the waste would be diluted and dissipated quickly if rainfall washed the waste from the land before being absorbed by the soil (F); the soil temperature is high enough to allow high rates of waste absorption (G); and the waste is spread (H). The compound of the properties (F, G, H) defines the socio-ecological situations. A simple technique from deontic logic for discovering the potential number of situations is 2^n where n is the number of properties. Given the three properties, there are eight possible situations, as demonstrated in Fig. 6.

We see in Fig. 6 that property F is negated (~) in situation S_2 which means the volume of water in the river is low. Which situations provide for what deontic requirement? That depends on the normative rules which, as explained above, depend on normative criteria. If the normative rule is that pollution of the river should be a concern, a regulation, re, could be promulgated that would obligate the spreading of waste whenever either F or G exists. This means situations S_1, S_2, and S_3 are situations obligating action U, or OU. The action solution is indicated in the right-hand column, given the regulation re. The solution content of situation S_4 is Ph U $\leftrightarrow$ ~F & ~G, or action U being prohibited is equivalent ($\leftrightarrow$) to a situation where the properties, F and G, are negated.

Although the paradigm here differs from that in the book, *Normative Systems* (Alchourron and Bulygin 1971), the book is very helpful, in general, and especially

Situation	Properties			Action Solution/re
S_1	F	G	H	OU/F V G
S_2	~ F	G	H	OU/F V G
S_3	F	~ G	H	OU/F V G
S_4	~ F	~ G	H	
S_5	F	G	~ H	
S_6	~ F	G	~ H	
S_7	F	~ G	~ H	
S_8	~ F	~ G	~ H	

Fig. 6 Properties of situations and consequential action, given a regulation

with regard to formulae (beyond the simple 2^n used above) for various combinations of properties and situations. There are more than three properties in most institutional situations, and there may be more properties in some situations than others in a specific institution, or, the number of properties may change on different occasions. For example, the religion of human entities may become a property in situations when persons of that religion become involved in those situations. Let us assume that Irish Catholics, for example, are not allowed to have jobs in a region and the rented trucks (from another region) that arrive to haul waste (property H) are driven by Irish Catholics, then that special property comes into play when such truck drivers enter the situation. The above advice to consult property and situation techniques in *Normative Systems* is not to suggest that such techniques be used to determine what is happening in a society. Rather, it is that such techniques can serve as tools to help identify potential possibilities that researchers should look for in institutions being investigated.

In the SFM digraph format, regulations are delivered to the processing institution, for example, a corporate production center, as in Fig. 7. Figure 7 is the delivery in cell (5,6) of the SFM in Fig. 2. I_{A2} delivers the regulation that I_p is obligated to undertake action U if confronted with situation S_1 or S_2 or S_3 and I_p is prohibited from undertaking action given situation S_4 or S_5 or S_6 or S_7 or S_8.

Requirements of Processing Institutions: Action Entities and Temporal Events

S_1, S_2 and S_3 are known by the condition of their respective properties. How are they known? By monitoring, indicating, measuring, auditing, observing, gauging, accounting, producing, storing, loading, hauling, spreading, supervising, and so forth. These are actions accomplished by requirements being delivered to agents and other entities that are in action settings. The relevant situations to which the

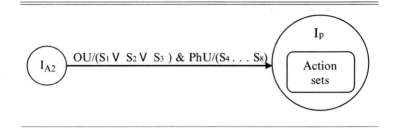

Fig. 7 SFM digraph: institutional delivery of action solution to another institution

process, I_p, are to direct entities have been defined by more authoritative institutional settings. As situations develop, and are recognized, entities are sent into action settings through requirements to accomplish their required action, that is, to fulfill their roles. Whenever ends and necessary connections justify a normative statement to the effect that a certain thing ought to (may, must not) be done, then a command (permission, prohibition) to somebody to do this thing, given by somebody in pursuit of these ends, has a teleological foundation in the ends of the norm-authority (Von Wright 1983, 74). The agents and other entities necessary to fulfill the requirements of any process are varied and numerous. They can be categorized as human entities (h), technological entities (t) and ecological entities (e), which are sometimes difficult to separate neatly. (Humans are biological as well as thinking and working beings.) To accomplish the action solution, say of spreading waste, the action solution U is divided into several subactions (W, X, Y, Z) that must be coordinated around an event or events (E). Thus the subactions are equivalent to U or U $\leftrightarrow$ [W & X & Y & Z]. The requirements $(rq_1 \ldots rq_n)$ prohibit, obligate, or permit the subactions by directing the human, technological and ecological entities to perform some act or acts depending on the action the normative system has formulated as appropriate.

Events, happenings, and occasions make the state of affairs temporal. Agents ought to act in conjunction with the appropriate events, happenings, and occasions. "For it is in the act and the state of affairs which together with their consequences, do or do not make the world preferable, and not the mere presence of an obligation. Thus we should restate all 'ought statements' so that whatever falls within the scope of an 'ought' operator receives an explicit temporal index" (Forrester 1996, 214). Requirements are given to entities to act on certain events, happenings, or occasions. Therefore, the delivery in SFM cell (6,6) would be as indicated in Fig. 8.

In Fig. 8, the production institution I_p directs, with requirements rq_1 to rq_n, to produce actions W, X, Y and Z with entities h, t and e on the occasion of event E to sustain the situation S_1 or S_2 or S_3. The coordinated action [W & X & Y & Z]$_{h\&t\&e}$ can be performed only on the condition that the combination of properties of a situation is present. S_1 as a whole, for example, ceases to exist unless some institution such as I_p maintains it because property H of S_1 is an institutional action.

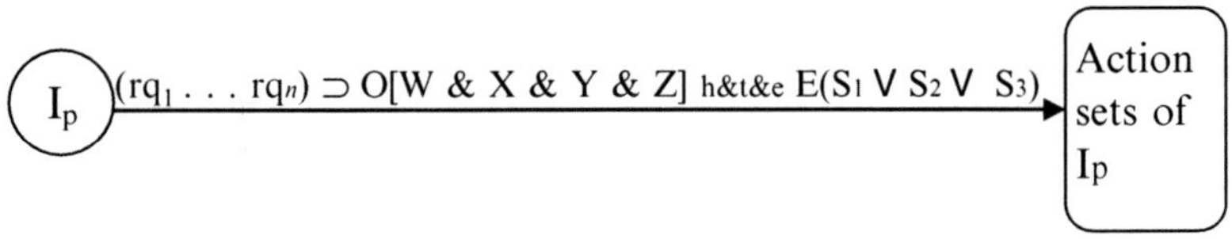

$$\left(I_p\right) \xrightarrow{(rq_1 \ldots rq_n) \supset O[W \ \& \ X \ \& \ Y \ \& \ Z] \ _{h\&t\&e} \ E(S_1 \ V \ S_2 \ V \ S_3)} \left[\begin{array}{l} \text{Action} \\ \text{sets of} \\ I_p \end{array}\right.$$

Fig. 8 SFM digraph: internal delivery of requirements by an institution

Conflict in the Modern World

This explanation of how to organize the analysis of a normative system is not presented in order to suggest that all real-world normative systems are harmonious or continuous, or that they maintain commonality of normative criteria, avoid excess or inadequate redundancy, and are without gaps and conflict. It is quite the contrary. This holistic approach to normative discourse is intended to encourage studies to be completed to find the gaps, discontinuity, disharmony, and conflicts. Given the fragility of the modern social world, the adequate redundancy of institutional patterns that assure conformance to ethical norms, and concomitant rules and regulations, is a paramount concern; likewise is the concern for providing for such redundancy through a policy when institutional patterns are changing. The current global economic system has very much gained the upper hand in defining institutional patterns, regulations, and requirements and, in turn, in creating global chaos. This is all the more reason why holistic studies of normative systems need to be completed in order to define the characteristics of the current system, so that we will have an opportunity to find the system particulars that lead to deleterious consequences and, in turn, recommend policy alternatives. However, system completeness, that is, creating redundancy, closing gaps, resolving conflicts and so forth, is not sufficient if the teleological beginning is flawed. That issue, which is a major issue in the modern world, is one that has been very much ignored by social scientists.

Conflict of Normative Ends

The teleological ends of the normative system were defined above as being made up of three sets or normative criteria. They were defined as social belief criteria (N_B), technological criteria (N_T), and ecological criteria (N_E). What has not been of much concern for either normative system philosophers or social scientists is whether these criteria are consistent. The concern for consistency of the normative criteria is not just a deontic concern for logical completeness and consistency. It is a real-world concern of major importance. Society has lost the institutional ability to make N_B, N_T, and N_E consistent with each other and consistent with an instrumental flow of events and actions in its processing institutions. The dominant norms are in conflict; therefore, the subnorms, as well as the consequent rules, regulations, and requirements for directing action, are conflicted.

Such conflicts lead to results that have left some agents destitute or destroyed, and others frustrated, when they learn of the resulting degradation and destruction. An example is the removal of peasant farmers from their land in South America so that European-based corporations can denude and intensely cultivate the land for soybean production, so the soybeans can be shipped to the United States to produce plastic used in weapons that are exported to Africa, so that different tribal groups, whose traditional societal patterns have been hopelessly disrupted, can slaughter each other. The peasant families move into a destitute status in slum areas, the numerous species that occupied the wetlands and woodlands of the peasant farms are destroyed as the wetlands and woodlands are destroyed, the soil becomes eroded by the agribusiness-selected technology utilized for cultivation, and water sources are polluted because of chemical runoff from the corporate farms and because of the waste byproducts of plastic production in the first world. The weapons lead to more dislocation and destruction in Africa. In addition, the whole process of production, involving overland hauling and oceanic and air shipping, is extremely energy intensive. Volumes could be filled with similar examples. We deplore this system. No one could call such a world efficient. Yet those kinds of examples continue to escalate at the community, regional, and global level. Why? Mainly because institutional structures have not developed to enforce the coordination of N_B, N_T, and N_E, nor has much effort gone into investigating how such coordinating institutions should be structured.

Conflict Between Bureaucracies and Institutions

What has happened is that more and more of our decisions are made by goal-oriented bureaucracies that have a narrow focus on what their goals ought to be. Lives in the modern world are dominated by bureaucracies rather than by broader-based institutions. An increasing proportion of the lives of decision makers is spent in bureaucracies, and they think increasingly in terms of bureaucratic goals. The automatic impulse to fulfill bureaucratic goals has replaced social reflection of social norms. Those in academic communities watch their colleagues race after research funds to fulfill bureaucratic goals of money acquisition rather than reflecting on what kind of research is consistent with social needs. How can professors very easily acquire money for research; by following the research goals of the multinational corporate bureaucracies? Those in homes watch marketing bureaucracies define consumption impulses via television. How do family members learn how they will be most admired by others; by following the marketing bureaucracies' goals? How can corporate executives stationed around the world by global corporations get promoted; by following corporate goals. Societal decision making becomes a series of impulses to bureaucratic goals rather than a reflection of consistent social, technological, and ecological norms. Bureaucracies are overpowering social institutions, especially democratic institutions. In addition, given the power of modern technology, impulses can cause immense damage, first, because the impulsive decisions direct powerful technology and, second, because modern communication technology quickly transmits bureaucratically designed goals into reality across the globe.

We can use Fig. 1 to help conceptualize the magnitude of the issue. As displayed, a set of institutions is at the center. The information processing and decision making of those institutions are, increasingly, determined by bureaucracies and, increasingly, those bureaucracies are not guided by transcendental norms or transactional analysis. Some of those institutions are important in defining the combinations of tools, skills, and knowledge that define technology. As demonstrated in Fig. 1, the kind of technology utilized defines criteria (N_T) for how institutions are to function. Thousands of years of human history have demonstrated that new technological combinations can improve and sustain social and ecological life and can be coordinated and adjusted to fit other socioecological components. Numerous examples exist to the contrary, especially recently. We know of new technological combinations that have depleted and contaminated water supplies, poisoned wildlife and people, and made the expression of important social norms impossible. We should not expect otherwise if those making decisions about technological combinations are not being guided to provide for criteria commensurate with appropriate social and eco-logical criteria.

Figure 1 indicates a relationship between institutions and ecological systems. This connection has become increasingly important in determining the functioning of ecological systems. Nature is not as natural as in the past. The application of technology establishes the relationship between the ecological systems and social institutions that establishes normative criteria (N_E) for society to follow. For example, the combination of technology for growing peanuts (to provide peanut oil to Europe) in Africa imposes a set of criteria upon society requiring it to convert land into deserts. A different technology would direct a different set of criteria.

Currently the matrix of social institutions, technology, and ecology creates criteria that, in turn, direct the formation of rules, regulations, and requirements to function which further erode commitment to social beliefs. Societies are falling apart because institutions that carried and enforced norms across different organizations have become less important to people. Those institutions are increasingly ignored in some cases, and despised in other cases. A society that has the basic criteria by which it lives dissolves and disintegrates which is neither pretty nor predictable, and it often loses its ability to recognize authority that is not authoritarian. Without strong commitment to consistent norms, the only real authority in a society is the one with a monopoly on weapons. We learn this in reports about cities in Russia where a mafia-type fascism is providing authority and also come across it in similar reports from all around the world. The new world disorder brought about by the attempt to rapidly replace legitimate social processes (often with bureaucratic market processes) is creating authoritarian systems which are not at all concerned about the coordination of the normative components of society, technology, and ecological systems. Those closest to the environment (for example, workers and managers in African peanut fields) may be able to see the damage caused by the criteria directing societal action. Yet there is seldom a social means for those observations to change the ecological criteria (N_E) or to direct a change in technological criteria (N_T) or social beliefs (N_B) in order to bring about a change in the normative system.

The social belief (N_B) connection in Fig. 1, beyond needing to be coordinated with N_T and N_E, needs to be protected and slowly adjusted when change is needed. Beliefs cannot be coordinated or their adjustment paced if analysis does not identify an institutional means for such control. The importance for coordination has been made above in the discussion about technological and ecological criteria. Pacing change is even more important with regard to social beliefs. Karl Polanyi explained in the *Great Transformation* the fragility of social institutions if change is too rapid and the suffering of humans if institutions break down. If an attempt is made to change social beliefs too quickly, human society loses its ability to know its own social norms and to recognize legitimate authority; therefore, institutions cease to function to provide for human needs. This is a current problem because rapid deviations from social norms, in order to fulfill bureaucratic goals, have become a dominant trend across the globe.

Concluding Remarks

The normative systems approach explained above clarified the importance of normative belief criteria, along with technological and ecological criteria, for the maintenance of authority and the working of socioecological processes. Professor Bush devoted most of his work to the understanding of evolutionary change and the process of instrumental decision making. As world affairs are revealed to us today, it would be difficult to find two more important concerns. Consistent with Professor Bush's leadership, the work here has attempted to utilize the assistance of normative philosophy and deontic logic to refine the description of normative processes. The approach is more holistic than that found in normative philosophy, yet the suggested way to describe normative relationships calls for more precise description than has been practiced in institutional economics. If this kind of description can be used to more precisely define normative systems, databases can be created consistent with the description; normative gaps and inconsistencies can be identified; and research agendas can be refined to determine the way that social, technological, and ecological system norms should be structured to provide for a more instrumental instituted process.

We need to become precise in the modeling of requirements in institutions in order to know whether the consequences of the requirements are consistent with the normative standards, because it is through requirements being placed on the human, technological, and ecological entities that beliefs and value criteria are manifested in reality. A small change in a requirement with regard to radiation exposure can lead to results quite different than were expected. A change of a few degrees in water temperature in a river due to industrial activities can render a species extinct. What are the requirements regarding radiation and temperature levels consistent with normative standards? We cannot know this without precise modeling that connects requirements to the normative system through the instituted process.

Appendix: Symbol Reference

SFM	social fabric matrix
Ph	prohibited or forbidden
O	obligation or obligatory
P	permission or permitted
N_B	social belief norms or criteria
N_T	technological norms or criteria
N_E	ecological norms or criteria
n_{B1}, n_{B2}, and n_{B3}	subnorms or subcriteria of N_B
n_{T1} and n_{T2}	subnorms or subcriteria of N_T
n_{E1} and n_{E2}	subnorms or subcriteria of N_E
I_{A1}	authority institution for making rules
I_{A2}	authority institution for making regulations
I_p	processing institution for delivering requirements
r	rules
re	regulations
rq	requirements
E	event happening or occasion
F	situational property of a high volume of water in the river
G	situational property of high soil temperature
H	situational property of spreading waste
S	situation
U	action to spread waste to solve a problem
W	subaction of U
X	subaction of U
Y	subaction of U
Z	subaction of U
h	human entities
t	technological entities
e	ecological entities
n	number
~	negation
&	conjunction
V	disjunction
⊃	directs or necessarily implies
↔	equivalence
/	given

References

Alchourron CE, Bulygin E (1971) Normative systems. Springer, New York

Bush PD (1983) An exploration of the structural characteristics of Veblen–Ayres–Foster defined institutional domain. J Econ Issues 17:35–65

Bush PD (1987) The theory of institutional change. J Econ Issues 21:1075–1116.

Bush PD (1991) Reflections on the twenty-fifth anniversary of AFEE: philosophical and methodological issues in institutional economics. J Econ Issues 25:321–346.

Commons JR (1924) The legal foundations of capitalism. University of Wisconsin, Madison

Forrester JW (1996) Being good and being logical: philosophical groundwork for a new deontic logic. M.E. Sharpe, New York

Gill R (1996) An integrated social fabric matrix/system dynamics approach to policy analysis. Syst Dyn Rev 12:167–249

Hayden FG (1982) Social fabric matrix: from perspective to analytical tool. J Econ Issues 16:637–661

Hayden FG (1985) A trans-disciplinary integration matrix for economics and policy analysis. Social Sci Inf 24:869–903

Neale WC (1987) Institutions. J Econ Issues 21:1177–1206

Neale WC and Pearson HW (1962) Institutions and economics. Unpublished paper 1–12

Polanyi K (1957) The economy as instituted process. In: Polanyi K et al (eds) Trade and market in early empire. Free Press, Glencoe, IL, pp 243–270

Schlagel RH (1995) Unpublished letter to F. Gregory Hayden 1–2

Von Wright GH (1983) Practical reason. Basil Blackwell, Oxford

Part II
Applications of the Social Fabric Matrix Approach

The Social Fabric Matrix Approach to Central Bank Operations: An Application to the Federal Reserve and the Recent Financial Crisis

Scott T. Fullwiler

Abstract This chapter utilizes the social fabric matrix approach (SFM-A) to provide a detailed description of the Federal Reserve's (Fed's) daily operations and the recent financial crisis. The SFM of the Fed's operations presents the primary components – major norms, institutions, technologies – relevant on a day-to-day basis. The SFM is then used for normative systems analysis (Hayden 1998) to show the articulation of major norms via sub-criteria, rules, regulations, and requirements into significant influences on the actions of authorizing and processing institutions in the Fed's operations. From the normative systems analysis, three types of time – intraday, maintenance period, and seasonal – in the Fed's daily operations can be explained. Overall, the Fed's operations are driven by the goals of stabilizing the payments system and the financial system. Other major norms, such as market efficiency, are important in terms of their influence, but they can become counterproductive to the Fed's ability to stabilize the payments system and the financial system at times, as they were during the mid-to-late 1990s. Given the SFM, normative systems analysis, and description of time and timeliness in the Fed's operations, seven general principles of the Fed's operations are presented, several of which are contrary to popular opinion (even among economists) regarding how central bank operations actually work. Of overarching importance is the realization that the Fed's operations are concerned with setting an interest rate, not controlling the money supply, which is in fact not possible. The events of August 2007 through December 2008 relevant to the Fed's daily operations are described and considered within the context of the previously laid out general principles, while as a result of information gathered during this period, three additional general principles of the Fed's operations are provided.

Introduction

While a detailed understanding of monetary operations has been central to research in the Post Keynesian endogenous money tradition for decades, it is not a stretch to suggest that it is now also a well-established area of research within neoclassical

S.T. Fullwiler
Wartburg College, Waverly, IA, USA

T. Natarajan et al. (eds.), *Institutional Analysis and Praxis*,
DOI 10.1007/978-0-387-88741-8_8, © Springer Science+Business Media, LLC 2009

monetary economics. Until recently, however, neoclassical research related to bank behavior in the US federal funds market had little relation to research on the Fed's behavior, and vice versa, beyond a few notable exceptions. This all change in the late 1990s, as neoclassical economists "found" several policy issues that required an understanding of Fed operations and bank behavior together – such as concerns about policy options at the zero bound for interest rates, retail sweep accounts, payments system crises, and increased use of non-central bank wholesale settlement options.

Particularly noteworthy is that a number of authors in the Post Keynesian tradition, and a few in the neoclassical tradition (e.g., Bindseil 2004), have argued that central bank operations bear little resemblance in reality to the traditional models such as the money multiplier that have nonetheless been overwhelmingly prevalent. Fullwiler (2001, 2003) applied the social fabric matrix approach (SFM-A, presented in Hayden 2006) in detailing the Federal Reserve's (the Fed's) operations and came to similar conclusions. The purpose of this chapter is to extend previous analyses applying the SFM-A to the Fed's operations and to consider this within the context of the functioning of US money markets during the recent mortgage or "subprime"-related financial crisis. The significance of the SFM-A for this particular area of research is that the institutional context under investigation is at the core of the United States' financial system; clear thinking about this core enables the subsequent development of a larger paradigm for future macroeconomic policy research that is more consistent with real-world financial interactions than has traditionally been the case.

Social Fabric Matrix of the Fed's Daily Operations

Figure 1 presents a basic social fabric matrix (SFM) of the Fed's daily operations. Each of the components listed vertically on the left as "delivering components" are also listed horizontally across the top as "receiving components." As is normal practice, a "1" within a cell of a matrix denotes that a delivery occurs from a particular delivering component to a particular receiving component. From the figure, nearly every component aside from the beliefs has several deliveries and receipts, and due to space constraints it is not possible to explain in a detailed manner every one of the deliveries; instead, the approach here is to begin by discussing the components and then to discuss deliveries in individual cells as they become important to the analysis.

Beliefs are indispensable to understanding the normative context of the Fed's operations. The beliefs listed in Fig. 1 are denoted as NBi (where i = 1, 2, 3, and so forth), which is the notation in Hayden (1998) used to model beliefs as "normative belief" criteria within a normative systems analysis; this is discussed in more detail and applied in the following section. The belief that the Fed controls the money supply (NB1) is at the core of the neoclassical paradigm and is readily seen in economics textbooks from the introductory to the doctoral level in the form of the money multiplier model, in which the central bank deliberately alters the quantity of reserves in order to achieve a desired rate of bank deposit expansion. Also central to the neoclassical paradigm is a belief that markets are efficient (NB2).

Delivering Components \ Receiving Components	NB1	NB2	NB3	NB4	NB5	IA1-1	IA2-1	IA2-2	IA2-3	IA2-4	IA2-5	IP-1	IP-2	IP-3	IP-4	T1	T2	T3
NB1. Central bank controls money supply						1	1											
NB2. Market efficiency						1	1						1	1	1			
NB3. Stabilization						1	1	1	1	1	1	1						
NB4. Neo-Jeffersonian view of banks						1												
NB5. Taxes/bonds finance govt spending						1												
IA1-1. Congress & President	1	1	1	1	1	1	1	1	1	1	1	1	1	1	1	1	1	1
IA2-1. FOMC/Board of G'vners/Fed Banks	1	1	1			1	1	1	1	1	1	1	1	1	1	1	1	1
IA2-2. FDIC			1			1	1		1	1	1		1	1		1	1	1
IA2-3. Comptroller of the Currency			1			1	1	1		1			1	1		1	1	1
IA2-4. State bank regulators			1			1	1	1	1				1			1	1	1
IA2-5. Treasury			1			1	1	1				1	1	1		1	1	1
IP-1. NY Fed Open Market Desk			1			1	1				1		1	1	1	1	1	1
IP-2. Banks				1		1	1	1	1	1	1	1		1	1	1	1	1
IP-3. Primary dealers				1		1	1				1	1	1		1	1	1	1
IP-4. Private payment clearinghouses				1		1	1				1	1	1	1		1	1	1
T1. Double-entry accounting						1	1	1	1	1	1	1	1	1	1			
T2. Payment clearing/settlement						1	1	1	1	1	1	1	1	1	1			
T3. Financial innovations						1	1	1	1	1	1	1	1	1	1			

Fig. 1 Social fabric matrix for the Federal Reserve's operations

In this case, the reference is primarily to finance literature suggesting that financial markets are efficient in pricing risk, providing liquidity, allocating scarce funds, settling payments, and so forth. The social belief criteria for NB3 refers to the policy goal of stabilization or the desirability of ensuring that economic and financial outcomes are well within certain thresholds. The neo-Jeffersonian view of banks (NB4) refers to a traditional American suspicion of enabling the amassing of economic power in the financial system, and banks in particular, in contradistinction with the Hamiltonian view of banking and finance; in modern times, this belief is often held by political liberals and some small government, more populist-oriented political conservatives (such as Pat Buchanon or Lou Dobbs). Both political liberals and conservatives – as well as economists of either persuasion – subscribe to the view that there are financial constraints upon the federal government (NB5) that must be taken into consideration when evaluating policy and policy proposals.

The institutions listed in the SFM range from key law making institutions such as Congress and the President (here listed together for simplicity instead of breaking down further, as the distinction is not overly crucial to the analysis in this case); regulatory institutions such as the Fed (in this case, again for simplicity, the Board of Governors, Federal Open Market Committee (FOMC), and regional Federal Reserve Banks are listed as a single institution), bank regulators (which also includes the Fed), and the Treasury; and, finally, the rest of the institutions listed are directly involved in some manner in the Fed's monetary operations. As with beliefs, a more detailed discussion of the institutional structure (and of the notation used in Fig. 1 for labeling the different types of institutions) is in the normative systems section below.

There are three important technologies (Ti) in the SFM for the Fed's operations. The most fundamental of these is double-entry accounting (T1). That double-entry accounting has impacted the system is beyond dispute, particularly where financial markets are concerned, as the creation of any financial asset by definition simultaneously creates an entry on the liability/equity side of a balance sheet. Views on how important double-entry accounting has been to the origins of the capitalist system and its continued evolution range from those suggesting it is a key technology in creating a conceptual framework for planning and control (e.g., Sombart 1924, Most 1972) to suggestions that accounting practices instead respond to changes in the business environment rather than vice versa (e.g., Yamey 1964, Edwards 1991). Consistent with Hayden's (1982, 1998, 2006) incorporation of technology and technological criteria into the SFM methodology, Previts and Merino's (1998) history of accountancy in the USA suggests a middle view in which double-entry accounting is "a 'condition' affecting and affected by market evolution" (5).

In the present context, the Fed's daily operations are financial transactions that occur on its own balance sheets and those of other banks, primary dealers, and other financial institutions. The development of electronic payment systems (another important technology in the Fed's monetary operations discussed below) that enable trillions of dollars to change hands daily is built upon the reality that loans, trades, and other sorts of electronic payment flows – including Fed operations – are simply credits and debits on the balance sheets of various institutions. In fact, financial assets (such as stocks, bonds, and deposits) largely do not exist in tangible form anymore, but instead exist solely as balance sheet entries. Similarly, the various trading and valuation techniques that were at the center of the rise and fall of mortgage-related securities, as well as the attempted policy responses to the latter, are necessarily embedded within the modern technology of accounting. In short, to understand the Fed's operations, one must understand the technology of double-entry accounting.

Payment clearing and settlement technologies (T2) – which, as noted above, are likewise necessarily embedded within modern accounting methods – have been referred to as the infrastructure of the modern business world (Shen 1997). Most of the Fed's operations are concerned with wholesale payment clearing and settlement, which is therefore the focus here. Large value transfer systems (LVTS), such as Fedwire, the Fed's LVTS, and CHIPS, a private clearinghouse whose member ship consists of primarily large New York banks and which handles most international transactions that involve the US dollar, are the largest wholesale settlement systems. In 2007, average daily value of funds transfers on Fedwire was $2.7 trillion, or around 20% of annual nominal GDP (Board of Governors 2008). Fedwire also operates a book-entry security settlement system which enables bonds issued by the Treasury, government sponsored enterprises, and other institutions to deliver ownership of securities against payment; in other words, these securities exist only as accounting entries, not in physical form. Securities transfers on Fedwire's book-entry system were about \$1.7 trillion per day in 2007 (Board of Governors 2008). Total dollar value of payments settled via CHIPS rival Fedwire funds transfers. A large percentage of securities transactions are cleared through subsidiaries of the Depository Trust and Clearing Corporation (DTCC) including the Depository Trust Corporation (DTC), National Securities Clearing Corporation (NSCC), and the Fixed Income Clearing Corporation (FICC), which together provide clearance services for "virtually all equity, corporate debt, municipal debt, government securities, mortgage-backed securities, and emerging market sovereign debt trades in the USA totaling more than \$1.7 trillion daily" (Bond Market Association and the Depository Trust and Clearing Corporation 2003, 9). Lastly, there are several small- and medium-size payment clearing systems in the US, such as automated clearinghouses (ACH) and check clearing, which actually account for the majority of payment transfer volume.

Wholesale payments systems settle payments either via netting (where only net changes to an institutions account must be settled at the end of the day or at specific times) or via real-time gross settlement (RTGS, where final settlement via debits and credits to accounts occurs immediately). Fedwire is the largest of the RTGS, while CHIPS moved in 2001 from netting to a sort of RTGS/netting hybrid that settles most payments immediately but nets others for final settlement later in the day. DTCC's subsidiaries settle netted transactions via Fedwire transfers of reserve balances, while most small banks use local clearinghouses to clear local transactions and then settle netted obligations using Fedwire.

Financial innovations (T3) in the private sector financial system related to the Fed's daily operations – particularly in the money markets and in the wholesale payments system – have been ongoing. Hyman Minsky recognized in 1957 that the continued evolution of the federal funds market as a central borrowing and lending market for banks was enabling fewer reserve balances to support the same level of economic activity (Minsky 1957). The proliferation of liability management techniques by banks and the continuing evolution of wholesale markets for short-term borrowing such as the federal funds, Eurodollar, repurchase agreement, and commercial paper markets influence the Fed's operations since they provide avenues for banks to quickly meet reserve requirements, payment needs, or the maturing of short-term commitments.

Innovations in the wholesale payments system have had similar effects on the Fed's operations. As noted, electronic payment clearing and settlement is simply a method of crediting and debiting account balances in a double-entry accounting system. For instance,

> A typical Fedwire transaction takes only a few seconds... Once Fedwire receives the payment instruction from [a] bank, the bank's account at the Federal Reserve will be debited ... while the account of [the receiving] bank at the Federal Reserve will be credited ... . Once this funds transfer is completed, the payment is said to be settled. Fedwire sends an electronic message to [the receiving] bank to confirm the settlement. (Shen 1997, 46)

However, since payments can be cleared electronically and the information can be stored in computers, the same quantity of reserves is able to facilitate far more payments due to the increased speed that results. Consequently,

> In recent decades, even while the banking industry was growing faster than real economic activity, the dollar value of funds transmitted via large-dollar electronic payments systems was growing relative to the size of banks... . Two decades ago, daily transfers were less than one-tenth as large as total bank liabilities. By the mid-1990s, the ratio had risen to seven times its value in the early 1990s... .
>
> [Over the same period] the sum of banks reserve and clearing balances ... at Federal Reserve Banks relative to their total liabilities fell markedly: After averaging close to 4% in the early 1970s, reserve balances as a proportion of liabilities averaged less than 1% by the mid-1990s. As a consequence, the value of banks' electronic payments relative to their reserve balances increased dramatically: By 1994, the ratio of the value of fedwire transfers to reserve balances was about forty times its 1973 value. (Hancock and Wilcox 1996, 871)

At present, it is not uncommon for individual banks to have daily payment flows that are 100 or 200 times the reserve balances that are kept in a bank's reserve account at the Fed (Furfine 2000).

A Normative Systems Analysis of the Fed's Daily Operations

Putting together a SFM is but a first step within the SFM-A approach, albeit an important and indispensable one. One must then decide how to use the completed SFM. Here, normative systems analysis based on Hayden (1998) is carried out in order to define and describe the normative criteria guiding relevant institutional interactions in the context of the Fed's daily operations. The normative systems analysis thus complements the SFM by providing a framework for more detailed investigation into the interaction of normative criteria and institutional action. Specifically, it requires the researcher to detail the criteria, rules, regulations, requirements, authoritative institutions, and processing institutions; together these determine the ends toward which the system is dynamically evolving. The process of normative systems analysis will generally lead the researcher to primary sources such as legal or regulatory documents, speeches or other accounts by regulators and policymakers, and well-documented accounts by other researchers of the normative characteristics of the system. In short, the normative systems analysis enables a researcher to answer the question "how do we know that we know how a system works?"

Subcriteria, Authorizing Institutions, and Processing Institutions in the Fed's Daily Operations

The beliefs or major norms described in the previous section are, to use Hayden's words, normative criteria that serve as standards for evaluation of institutional processes. The application of Hayden (1998) here is to recognize that these beliefs or major norms have direct or indirect influence at a number of different points in the process, and to provide a framework for explicating these influences.

To begin, Hayden (1998, 95) writes that "each major norm that applies to numerous institutional settings has a number of sub criteria … that apply to particular institutional situations or cases." Thus, sub-criteria or sub-beliefs are evaluative criteria in particular circumstances that are consistent with primary belief criteria or major norms; they can also reflect or further elaborate upon the ideological or otherwise theoretical basis for the belief itself. Table 1 lists the beliefs or major norms (NBi) from Fig. 1; the right-hand column of Table 1 lists corresponding sub-beliefs or sub-criteria (nb$i$-j, where i refers to the corresponding major norm, and j= 1, 2, 3, etc., to denote different sub-criteria for a given NBi).

Consider NB1 ("Central Bank Controls the Money Supply") from Table 1, which has three sub-criteria, nb1-1 ("Deposits and Reserve Balances Fund Bank Loans"), nb-2 ("Reserve Requirements Constrain Banks' Abilities to Lend"), and nb1-3 ("The Fed Exogenously Controls Reserve Balances"). As previously noted, NB1 is central to the neoclassical economics paradigm for monetary policy and originates in the money multiplier model. Specifically, these sub-criteria reflect the belief – which remains influential among policy makers – that the quantity of excess reserve balances is set directly and exogenously (in the policy sense) by Fed actions (the traditional "three tools" of monetary policy: discount lending, open market operations, and setting reserve requirements) and this quantity has a direct effect upon the growth or contraction of bank liabilities, if not immediately then at least over some time horizon. NB2 ("Market Efficiency") and NB3 ("Stabilization as a Primary Policy Goal") are shown in Table 1 to each have three sub-criteria, as with NB1. NB4 ("Neo-Jeffersonian View of Banks") and NB5 ("Taxes and Loans Finance Government Spending") are a bit different in the context of this paper than

Table 1 Major norms and beliefs in the Fed's operations

Major norms (NBi)	Subcriteria (nb$i$-j)
NB1. Central Bank controls the money supply	nb1-1. Deposits and reserve balances fund bank loans
	nb1-2. Reserve requirements provide control over loan creation
	nb1-3. The Fed can exogenously control reserve balances
NB2: Market efficiency	nb2-1. Markets efficiently price risk and allocate funds
	nb2-2. Markets can efficiently and safely settle payments
	nb2-3. Government intervention creates instability/moral hazard
NB3: Stabilization as a primary policy goal	nb3-1. Stabilization of the payments system
	nb3-2: Stabilization of the financial system
	nb3-3: Stabilization of the macroeconomy
NB4: Neo-Jeffersonian view of banks	nb4-1: Government should not subsidize banks
NB5: Taxes and Bonds Finance Government Spending	nb5-1: Avoid negative effects on the federal government's fiscal position

NB1, NB2, and NB3. This is due to the fact that while the former have only a single sub-criteria each in Table 1, both have several more sub-criteria that would become relevant were the context of the analysis expanded beyond monetary operations.

The notation for the institutions in Fig. 1 is to denote sub-categories presented in Hayden (1998). These are higher institutional authorities (denoted as IA1-*i*), other or lower institutional authorities (denoted as IA2-*i*), and processing institutions (denoted as IP-*i*). The US Congress and the President are listed together as the primary higher institutional authority (IA1-1). Together, they are responsible for important legislation (such as the Federal Reserve Act, and revisions to it) and operational directives (such as foreign exchange rate policy) that influence the normative context of the Fed's operations. The FOMC, Board of Governors, and Federal Reserve Banks together are the most important lower institutional authority (IA2-1), since they set monetary policy given the criteria and rules (defined below) set down by the higher authorities; this component will be referred to simply as "the Fed" below. Other institutional authorities are the other bank regulators besides the Fed (FDIC (IA2-2), Office of the Comptroller of the Currency (IA2-3), and state bank regulators (IA2-4)), which are discussed in more detail in the later section on recent events in the financial system, and the Treasury (IA2-5), whose authority in this context is primarily derived from its role in the collection of taxes.

The processing institutions are denoted as IP-*i*; these institutions receive regulations and requirements from institutional authorities which set the context for their behavior. The Open Market Desk at the New York Fed (IP-1) is responsible for carrying out open market operations in accordance with the policy and strategy set by the Fed. Banks (IP-2) are the key processing institutions for monetary policy, the payments system, and the financial regulatory structure; they trade reserve balances held in Fed accounts in the federal funds market, use reserve balances to settle payments, meet Fed regulations and requirements, and are subject to requirements of bank regulatory agencies. Primary dealers (IP-3) are dealers in US Treasury securities, some of which are also banks, which engage in the private sector side of the Open Market Desk's trades related to open market operations. Private wholesale or retail payment clearinghouses (IP-4) encompasses a number of institutions, some very large and some very small, that clear and settle private and public sector payments; many of these clearinghouses settle payments on a netted basis, leaving only a small percentage of gross payments to be settled by direct payments sent usually via balances in Federal Reserve accounts.

Rules, Regulations, and Requirements in the Articulation of Major Norms

Hayden (1998) writes that both John R. Commons (1995) and Karl Polanyi (1957) demonstrated that normative criteria were established and then implemented or otherwise "carried out" through prohibitions, obligations, and permissions, or what Commons referred to as "working rules." As Commons put it,

A working rule lays down four verbs for the guidance and restraint of individuals in their transactions. It tells what the individual *must* or *must not* do (compulsion or duty), what they *may* do without interference from other individuals (permission or liberty), what they *can* do with the aid of collective power (capacity or right), and what they *cannot* expect the collective power to do in their behalf (incapacity or exposure). (1995, 6; emphasis in original)

Hayden (1998) presents a taxonomy utilizing the terms rules, regulations, and requirements, which is inspired by Hayden's reading in the area of normative philosophy. Hayden's approach explicitly incorporates the normative process by which institutions articulate prohibitions, obligations and permissions such that major norms ultimately guide or at least significantly influence institutional action.

The normative systems analysis framework presented in Hayden (1998) might be summarized as follows: primary normative criteria – such as major norms NB1 through NB5 in Fig. 1, and their respective sub-criteria shown in Table 1 – give rise to policy goals, standards, and so forth. To carry out the process and achieve the desired normative ends, the appropriate rules, regulations, and requirements are articulated and implemented. Figure 2 illustrates the relationships between major norms, institutional authorities, and processing institutions as described by Hayden. From the figure, the sub-criteria are delivered to the higher institutional authorities as standards for rules, which frequently appear in legislation and are written to both embody and be consistent with the primary criteria. Hayden (1998, 97) writes that higher institutional authorities generally undertake great effort to explain the norms and the reason the rules are necessary; the higher institutional authorities additionally frame, structure and explain the rules, the situations in which the rules are to be applied, which rules are to be applied, and the acceptable reasons for applying the rules. Lower authorizing institutions design regulations that appeal to rules as reasons for their existence and which attempt to control, govern, or otherwise shape the behavior of processing institutions in a manner consistent with rules by setting

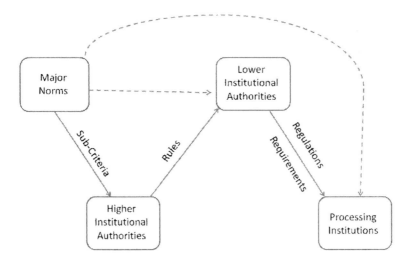

Fig. 2 Articulation of major norms into rules, regulations, and requirements

down various requirements. Requirements require responses by processing institutions to situations in order to fulfill the regulations, such as a bank adhering to an established required reserve ratio on deposits, capital requirements against assets, criteria and collateral requirements for receiving loans from the central bank or against government deposits held by the bank, or the specific procedures for managing a reserve account at the central bank.

Overall, institutional actions occur within the context of rules, regulations, and requirements and are thus normative in that "working rules" that dictate prohibitions, obligations, and permissions are in place and ultimately derive from the primary belief criteria. The dotted lines in Fig. 2 correspond to the indirect influence of major norms on the actions of lower institutional authorities and processing institutions via the design and implementation of rules, regulations, and requirements. This is consistent with the SFM in Fig. 1, which – as is common practice – presents beliefs or major normative criteria being delivered to a variety of institutions at various levels of authority; however, even as there is an implied influence of major norms upon processing institutions in Fig. 2, Hayden (1998, 96) notes that institutional actions may be consistent with the desired normative ends even as the individual processing institutions may not know or at least may not be in agreement with the required action. Thus, while deliveries in Fig. 1 present belief criteria specific to individual institutions (i.e., banks and other private financial institutions have a general belief that financial institutions can efficiently price financial assets, settle payments, and generally abhor government intervention in these areas; financial regulatory institutions are generally designed to be concerned with stability of particular parts of the financial system), the articulation of major norms into rules, regulations, and requirements may provide prohibitions and obligations that result in behaviors inconsistent with some other belief criteria. As Hayden (1998, 100–103) points out, when such conflicts are significant, the negative consequences for the entire system can be significant.

Major Norms, Subcriteria, and Rules in the Fed's Operations

Given space constraints, neither each entry in the SFM in Fig. 1, nor the role of each rule, regulation, and requirement related to the components of Fig. 1 can be described completely. But enough of the key characteristics of the system can be explicated within this framework to create an understanding of the Fed's daily operations. The approach here is to begin with two important rules: The Federal Reserve Act of 1913 (FRA), and the Depository Institutions Deregulation and Monetary Control Act of 1980 (DIDMCA), which amended the FRA. The analysis will then broaden and deepen in order to develop a working framework for understanding the normative context of the Fed's operations.

The FRA established the Federal Reserve System as the nation's central bank, and thus as a lower institutional authority according to the framework here. There are several primary belief criteria from Table 1 for the FRA with respect to the Fed's operations, namely control of the money supply (NB1), market efficiency (NB2), stabilization (NB3), and a neo-Jeffersonian view of banks (NB4). The FRA defines the existence and powers of the regional Federal Reserve Banks in Sects. 2, 4, 5, 13, and 14. The establishment of the Board of Governors is made in Sects. 10 and 11. The power of the Federal Reserve Banks to print Federal Reserve notes is given in Sect. 16. The establishment and powers of the FOMC are in Sect. 12A. The establishment of commercial banks as member banks of the Fed – that is, as processing institutions according to the normative systems analysis here – is explained in Sects. 6–9. The Board of Governors' power to set reserve requirements on member banks is provided in Sect. 19. Section 15 enables the Secretary of the Treasury to deposit Treasury funds in the Federal Reserve Banks and to use the Federal Reserve Banks as its fiscal agents.

Stabilization (NB3) was originally one of the most important, if not *the* most important, primary evaluative criteria – and remains so – particularly in regard to the payments system (nb3-1) and the financial system (nb3-2) as far as the Fed's operations are concerned, though there was also significant emphasis placed upon promoting operating procedures consistent with a "sound currency," a reference to macroeconomic stabilization (nb3-3) as understood at the time. The first paragraph of the FRA announces that the purpose is "to provide for the establishment of Federal reserve banks, to furnish an elastic currency, to afford means of rediscounting commercial paper, to establish a more effective supervision of banking in the United States, and for other purposes." The statement "to furnish an elastic currency" is generally interpreted as obligating the Federal Reserve to ensure liquidity and stability in the payment system – again, as in nb3-1 – particularly in regard to difficulties frequently encountered with both prior to 1913 that often led to broader financial panics (e.g., Spahr 1926; Myers 1970).

A neo-Jeffersonian view of banks (NB4) was and still is significant as there has been political opposition to a central bank throughout the nation's history; for instance, the separation of powers within the Fed and the twelve district banks presiding over regions drawn according to the distribution of the population in 1913 arise essentially from the influence of this primary belief. Political opposition to the Fed's existence has become less significant (though some opposition certainly still exists), however the Jeffersonian perspective remains important with respect to the role of regional Fed banks in the Fed's operations such as managing the payments system and extending credit to commercial banks.

Regarding the daily operations, Sects. 13 and 14 define the possible scope of discount loans and open market operations. Section 13 requires that discount loans be done only for depository institutions (including US branches of foreign banks). The assets eligible as collateral for discount loans are US Treasury securities, government agency securities, some mortgages, banker's acceptances, and "notes, drafts, and bills of exchange issued or drawn for agricultural, industrial, or commercial purposes." A number of financial assets normally considered "investments," including private equity issues, are not permitted as collateral. Section 14 sets the types of financial assets that can be purchased by the Federal Reserve in open market operations, which primarily encompasses obligations of the US federal government and its agencies.

Significantly, there is no express authority provided in the Federal Reserve Act for the Federal Reserve to purchase corporate bonds, commercial paper, mortgages, equity, or land (Johnson et al 1999; Small and Clouse 2000; Clouse et al. 2000). Rather,

> In contrast to bills of exchange ... debt instruments such as corporate bonds and mortgages are "promises to pay": they are two-party instruments [while a bill of exchange is a three-party instrument]. Thus, [the] first paragraph of section 14 of the Federal Reserve Act places a restriction on the Federal Reserve's open market operations because the only promises to pay that the paragraph authorizes for purchases or sale are bankers' acceptances. Because private-sector promises to pay other than bankers' acceptances are not made eligible for purchase under the first paragraph of section 14 or under any other part of the Federal Reserve Act, there is no express authority under which they may be purchased by the Federal Reserve. Thus there is no express authority for the Federal Reserve to purchase such promises to pay as corporate bonds, bank loans, mortgages and credit-card receivables, for example. Nor is there any express authority for the Federal Reserve to purchase equities. (Clouse et al. 2000, 54)

However, and importantly, Sect. 13 *does* provide for possible purchases of an expanded class of private sector debt instruments under special circumstances, which again recognizes the need for payments system stability (nb3-1) and financial stability (nb3-2) to override other concerns:

> The class of private-sector debt instruments eligible for purchase could be expanded to include corporate bonds, mortgages, and other instruments under section 13(3) of the Federal Reserve Act. Under 13(3), if the Board of Governors found there to be "unusual and exigent circumstances" and voted by a majority of at least five governors to authorize lending under 13(3), the Federal Reserve could discount [that is, make discount loans] to individuals, partnerships, and corporations "notes, drafts and bills of exchanges ... . indorsed or otherwise secured to the satisfaction of the Federal Reserve Banks ..." This broadening of the class of instruments eligible for discount would correspondingly broaden the class eligible for purchase. (Johnson et al 1999, 27n)

In other words, by expanding the class of institutions eligible for receiving discount loans from depository institutions to include firms and households, through the first paragraph in section 14 an expanded class of assets would be eligible for open market purchases whenever the Board of Governors decides conditions are "unusual and exigent." This obviously has been a significant provision in the FRA during the most recent difficulties in the financial system.

The limitations placed upon open market operations and discount lending in the FRA are frequently explained by reference to NB2 (market efficiency). That is, the Fed's daily operations are normally viewed as "interventions in the markets" and thus these "interventions" should be as limited as possible, except for instance in which failing to facilitate stabilization (NB3) is at risk. For instance, in a study drafted by the Fed in 2002 regarding potential "alternative" operations (that is, operations different from standard practice) permitted by the FRA for use in the event that more standard or typical uses of the discount window and open market operations became "ineffective," the authors set out market efficiency (NB2) as one of four primary evaluative criterion derived from the FRA. In their words,

In general, market price mechanisms allocate resources most effectively when undistorted by government actions. (Federal Reserve System Study Group on Alternative Instruments for System Operations 2002, I-3)

The monetary mission of the Federal Reserve is statutorily cast in terms of macroeconomic outcomes. In contrast, outcomes for specific sectors and for relative prices of credit or assets are within the purview of private markets and fiscal policy... . The broad mission of monetary policy and its transmission through the reserves market, together with the desirability of allowing private decisions to allocate credit, imply that, the Federal Reserve, *in choosing its portfolio composition*, should attempt to minimize effects on relative asset prices. (I-3; emphasis in original)

However, conducting monetary policy operations requires designating instruments and counterparties, thus potentially giving those instruments and counterparties at least some advantage over others. While fulfilling its needs to acquire assets, the Federal Reserve should avoid as best it can any such favoritism. Not only would the favoring of specific entities in the private sector distort resource allocation, but even appearing to influence relative asset prices in the financial sector through asset selection might invite pressure from special interest groups to achieve specific outcomes. (I-3, I-4)

From this, it is clear that sub-criteria nb2-1 (markets efficiently price risk and allocate funds) and nb2-3 (government intervention can create moral hazard) significantly influences the context within which the Fed views its mandate for carrying out its daily operations.

The belief that the central bank controls the money supply (NB1) had been a guiding tenet of the Fed's public statements regarding its tactics since the 1920s when the Fed "discovered" open market operations as a policy tool (e.g., Bindseil 2004; Meulendyke 1998). However, the DIDMCA even more explicitly embedded both the belief in central bank control over the money supply (NB1) and market efficiency (NB2) as major norms related to the Fed's daily operations. Regarding the former, the DIDMCA directed the Fed (and thereby gave it the authority) to set reserve requirements for all commercial banks, whether Fed members or not (i.e., the state banks), in order to enable better control over the money supply. The DIDMCA sets specific ranges for the Fed to set reserve requirements on transaction accounts (3%minimum on deposits below $25 million, 8–14% on deposits beyond that), savings accounts (same as for transaction accounts), and time deposits (0–9%). These were enacted for the sole purpose of increasing the amount of reserves "to a level consistent with the conduct of monetary policy" in accordance with nb1-1, nb1-2, and nb1-3 and as described in the money multiplier framework. Regarding market efficiency (NB2), the DIDMCA required the Fed to charge banks for its services related to processing and settling payments, which had heretofore been provided free of charge to banks, primarily in order to promote private sector payment clearing and settlement. In promoting private sector payment clearing and settlement, the DIDMCA required the Fed to price its services not just based upon its costs but also required the Fed to determine its imputed cost of capital (as in a shareholder's required return to capital) and add that to its operating costs in setting prices its services. Regarding sub-criteria, this is based upon nb2-1 and nb2-2.

Rules, Regulations, and Requirements in the Fed's Daily Operations

Table 2 presents a list of some of the more important rules (denoted as ri, for $i = 1, 2, 3$, and so forth), regulations (rg$i$), and requirements (rq$i$) in the Fed's daily operations, within the context of institutional authorities (Congress/President (IA1-1) and the Fed (IA2-1)) and processing institutions (the New York Fed's Open Market Desk (IP-1), Banks (IP-2), Primary Dealers (IP-3), and Private Payment Clearinghouses (IP-4)). The following discusses these in relation to the Fed's discount lending, management of the payments system, reserve requirements, and open market operations.

Discount Lending

As described above, the FRA (r1) sets out a number of guidelines for the Fed's discount lending to banks. The Fed's Regulation A (rg1) lays out its policy regarding these loans, including required collateral, interest rates, and maturities. Since 2003, the Fed has provided collateralized loans, mostly on an overnight basis, to banks at a rate set as a "penalty" above the federal funds target rate. This replaced a long-standing policy of lending at a rate slightly below the target rate, but with the added condition that a bank had already attempted to attain credit from other sources. The latter were frequently referred to as the Fed's "frown costs," as it made no secret of the fact that it "frowned" on banks taking out discount loans for anything other than seasonal liquidity needs. The changes to Regulation A since 2003 eliminated the "frown costs" and enable all banks in good standing to borrow at the "primary credit" rate set initially at one percent above the target (since fall 2008, this has been reduced to 0.25% above the target rate); other banks are generally offered "secondary credit" at an additional penalty that is currently 0.5%. The basic requirements and procedures banks must follow for establishing and maintaining an account at the Fed are provided in the Fed's Operating Circular No. 1, while the various collateral requirements and lending rates are spelled out in the Fed's Operating Circulars No. 10 and No. 8 (Operating Circulars are listed as rq1 in Table 2). Step by step guides regarding how banks go about receiving credit from their regional Fed Bank are also provided and updated in real time on a website maintained by the Fed (www.frbdiscountwindow.org, which is rq2 in Table 2).

Payments Clearing and Settlement

The FRA (r1) directs the Fed to make stability in the payments system (nb3-1) a priority for the Fed's operations. As the Board of Governors puts it, "a reliable payments system is crucial to the economic growth and stability of the nation. The smooth functioning of markets for virtually every good and service is dependent

Table 2 Institutions, rules, regulations, and requirements in the Fed's operations

Higher authorizing institutions (IA1)	Rules (r)	Lower authorizing institutions (IA2)	Regulations (rg)	Requirements (rq)	Processing institutions (IP)
	r1. Federal Reserve Act		rg1. Regulation A rg2. Regulation J	rq1. Operating circulars rq2.www.frbdiscountwindow.org	
			rg3. Pricing Principles	rq3. Account Management Guide rq4. www.frbservices.org	
IA1-1. Congress and the President	r2. Depository Institutions Deregulation and Monetary Control Act	IA2-1. FOMC, Board of Governors, and Fed Banks	rg4. Payments System Risk Policy	rq5. Payments System Risk Policy Reference Manual and Guide rq6. Reserve Maintenance Manual	IP2: Banks
			rg5. Regulation D	rq7.www.reportingandreserves.org	
	r3. Garn-St. Germain Act		rg6. Authorization for Domestic Open Market Operations	rq8. FOMC Directive	IP1. New York Fed's Open Market Desk

upon the smooth functioning of banking and financial markets, which in turn is dependent upon the integrity of the nation's payments system" (Board of Governors 1990, 2). To facilitate stability, the FRA authorizes all commercial banks, government agencies, government sponsored agencies, and several other institutions to have access to reserve accounts at the Fed. The DIDMCA (r2) in fact required the Fed to provide the same access to Fed reserve accounts and to all of the Fed's payment services that Fed member banks already have to all non-member banks.

It is useful here to define terms, as "clearing" and "settlement" have distinct meanings:

> Clearing comprises three main steps: processing payment instruments, delivering them to paying banks, and calculating interbank payment obligations. Settlement involves discharging the payment obligations. To illustrate the distinction between these two functions, consider the clearing and settlement of checks among banks that are members of a clearinghouse. Banks rely on the clearinghouse to perform the clearing function when they exchange checks drawn on each other. Then the clearinghouse calculates the multilaterally netted payment obligations due to and due from each clearinghouse participant. Banks participating in the clearinghouse have various options for settling these obligations. Members of the clearinghouse can agree to settle using cash or more likely the deposit liabilities of a private bank, which might also be a member of the clearinghouse, or through another institution. (Summers and Gilbert 1996, 6)

Because most Federal Reserve services in the payment system combine the clearing and settlement functions, the two terms are frequently used interchangeably when referring to Federal Reserve services (6).

Obviously, though, as the above statement points out, clearing and settlement are not the same. This is most clearly the case with the private sector clearing and settlement organizations that provide clearing but usually only netted settlement that is only finally settled via reserve account debits or credits. As the discussion of the SFM in Fig. 1 earlier in the chapter describes, there are a number of significant private payments systems that use Fedwire or at least bank Fed accounts for final settlement. Beyond settling payments, final netted settlement of trades involving US Treasury securities and obligations of US agencies and government sponsored enterprises also occurs exclusively via Fedwire's book-entry settlement system. Thus, as also noted, total dollar value of payments settled via reserve accounts approaches 20% of *annual* US GDP on an average business day.

Consistent with the goal of stability in the payments system, the Fed provides in Regulation J (rg2) that payments sent from one institution's reserve account to another's reserve account are final and irrevocable "at the time a Federal Reserve Bank notifies the receiving bank that a payment has been credited to its reserve account, regardless of whether the sending bank makes good on the payment request" (Hancock and Wilcox 1996, 871–872). In practice, this means that the Fed provides both intraday overdrafts to banks whenever their reserve accounts are drawn down, while collateralized loans at the regional Fed Banks' discount windows (discount lending) are available if an overdraft cannot be cleared by the end of the business day. For banks, the Operating Circulars (rq2) contain procedures for using reserve accounts to purchase currency from the Fed (Operating Circular 2), check clearing and float (Operating Circular 3), using reserve accounts to settle Automated Clearing House payments (Operating Circular 4), sending payments via Fedwire (Operating Circular 6), and final settlement of securities using Fedwire's book-entry system (Operating Circular 7). Additional information for banks is available in Fed's *Account Management Guide* (rq3) that also describes procedures for payment settlement and overdrafts, and on a website maintained by the Fed to provide guides and information for utilizing the Fed's payment services (www. frbservices.org (rq4 in Table 2)).

As mentioned, the DIDMCA requires the Fed to charge banks for its payments services, and required the Fed to set pricing principles by September 1, 1980. The Board of Governors thereby set out its *Principles for the Pricing of Federal Reserve Bank Services* (rg3), while the Fed then provides more detailed content for banks regarding up-to-date fee schedules and precise calculation of charges for services in its *Account Management Guide* (rq3) and its informational website on its payment services (www.frbservices.org (rq4)). Recall that an overarching goal of the DIDMCA in requiring the Fed to set fees for its payment settlement services is to encourage the development of private sector settlement systems, a result of the primary belief in market efficiency (NB2). By requiring the Fed to recoup its own costs of providing payment clearing and settlement services plus an imputed cost of capital, the opportunity obviously arises that private sector providers may be able to gain market share by providing banks and other financial institutions with the same clearing and settlement services at a lower price.

Returning to the Fed's overdrafts in promoting "elasticity" in the quantity of reserve balances to enable the settlement of payments, the Fed has since the 1980s been concerned about default risks related to the large quantities of credit it extends to banks while enabling payment settlement to continue as normal. Prior to 1986, the Fed essentially provided these overdrafts as unsecured loans at no cost, and the Fed apparently believed that banks were taking advantage of the underpriced credit (Richards 1995).

> By the early 1980s, banks' daylight overdrafts of their reserve accounts had become very large, and regulators recognized that at some point a very large bank might be unable to repay its unsecured, and possibly very large, overdraft.... During the period, the maximum value of daylight overdrafts grew as rapidly as the value of transfers, which in turn grew faster than the value of bank liabilities .... By the early 1990s, daily maximum aggregate overdrafts often exceeded $150 billion and averaged about $125 billion. (Hancock and Wilcox 1996, 871)

Starting in 1986 the Federal Reserve imposed limits on maximum daylight overdrafts, and in 1994 it began charging a modest fee, which amounts essentially to an interest charge, for daylight overdrafts beyond a percent of a bank's capital (see Richards (1995) and Panigay-Coleman (2002) for a discussion of the evolution of payments system risk policies at the Fed). It also imposed collateral requirements and caps on total overdraft privileges (beyond which significantly greater penalties are incurred). On an average business day in 2005 the Fed was providing around $36 billion in overdrafts to the banking system *every minute*, and over $116 billion during a typical day's peak settlement period near the end of the day (Bank for International

Settlements 2007); researchers found, however, that daylight overdrafts were significantly reduced as a result of the fees, collateral requirements, and caps at the time they were implemented, rising slowly over time to again nearly reach mid-1980s levels around 20 years later but this time in support of a vastly greater dollar volume of payment settlement (e.g., Richards 1995; Hancock and Wilcox 1996; Shen 1997; Panigay-Coleman 2002).

In order to further minimize its own credit risk, the Federal Reserve is very clear in discouraging banks from permitting a daylight overdraft to become an unsecured overnight overdraft by imposing a substantial penalty of 400 basis points above the day's federal funds rate with a minimum charge of $100 (Federal Reserve System 2007, VI-2). Higher overdraft charges are assessed if an institution exceeds three overdrafts in a moving twelve-month period. Chronic overdraft problems can result in administrative controls. As a result, banks attempt to avoid these unsecured overnight overdrafts at nearly any cost (Clouse and Elmendorf 1997; Furfine 2000).

Within the context of the normative systems analysis, fees, collateral requirements, and caps for overdrafts detailed in the Fed's *Payments System Risk Manual and Guide* (rq5), the *Account Management Guide* (rq3), and on the Fed's informational websites for banks (www.frbservices.org (rq4) and www.frbdiscountwindow. org (rq2)) are requirements that shape bank behavior in the payment system. As a result, banks manage daily reserves closely, and whereas they might have utilized more federal funds trades requiring gross settlement on Fedwire in previous decades to manage liquidity for payment settlement and to perform asset/liability management, they now accomplish a large percentage of both via netted settlement using competing settlement systems (IP-4). Finally, researchers have also found that banks routinely wait to send payments at high payment flow periods during the beginning and end of the business day since an overdraft cleared within a minute does not count as an actual overdraft according to the Fed's Payments System Risk Policy (McAndrews and Rajan 2000; Armantier et al. 2008).

Reserve Requirements

The DIDMCA (r2) requires the Fed to set reserve requirements. The Fed has laid out its policies on reserve requirements in Regulation D (rg5) of the Federal Reserve System. Regulation D prescribes a computation period during which banks' end-of-day deposits and holdings of vault cash are averaged over a two-week period; a bank's reserve requirement is then the relevant reserve requirement ratio multiplied by its average deposits held during the period less its average vault cash holdings. Regulation D then prescribes a two-week maintenance period beginning seventeen days after the end of the computation period during which time banks are obligated to hold end-of-day average balances in their reserve accounts equal to or greater than their reserve requirement. A bank deficient in meeting reserve requirements for a given maintenance period will be provided with a loan to cover the deficiency by the Fed and be charged the Fed's collateralized loan rate plus one percent. The Fed publishes a *Reserve Maintenance Manual* (rq6) for banks that explains in detail how reserve requirements are calculated and met, and also explains various technical details and adjustments that might be necessary in a number of specific instances (Federal Reserve System 2008). The Fed also publishes updates to its manual in real time and offers additional day-to-day reserve requirement management procedures on a special website for banks (http://www.reportingandreserves.org (rq7)).

Open Market Operations

The FOMC's annual Authorization for Domestic Open Market Operations (rg6) is the source of the New York Fed's Open Market Trading Desk's (IP-1; hereafter, Desk) authority for purchasing different types, quantities, and maturities of financial assets in its open market operations. The FOMC delivers instructions in its directive (rq8) after each FOMC meeting, which since 1988 has set the target for the federal funds rate that the Desk then attempts to achieve via its open market operations.

Timeliness in the Fed's Daily Operations

This section is based on Fullwiler (2003), albeit in revised and updated form here, which applied "time" and "timeliness" as defined in Hayden (2006, Chap. 8) to the Fed's operations. Hayden defines time within the context of a given system as a series of event sequences. Time or the particular sequencing of events within any socio-economic system is unavoidably framed by the normative characteristics of the system that define the rights, obligations, permissions, and prohibitions. The event sequences in the Fed's daily operations are similarly and unavoidably linked to the primary beliefs, sub-beliefs, rules, regulations, and requirements that provide the context for interactions among various institutions involved in these operations. The point of policy in any socio-economic system, though, is to effect instrumentally efficient outcomes for that system. The normative criteria established by policy makers to influence system behavior ought to therefore be enhancing or at the very least consistent with the manipulation of event sequences such that outcomes or consequences are consistent with normative policy goals. The successful design and implementation of normative criteria at various levels of the socio-economic system is referred to by Commons (1995) and by Hayden (2006) as "timeliness." The overarching goal of timeliness thereby suggests the system's dynamic stability during a given sequence of events, while recognizing, of course, that "stability" and other terms such as "optimal" or "efficient" often used to describe outcomes have meaning only within the normative context.

From a tactical standpoint, timeliness within the Fed's daily operations is currently defined by the Desk's (IP-1) ability to achieve the FOMC's target rate. Doing so is considered consistent with stability (NB3) in the payments system (nb3-1), the financial system (nb3-2), and the macroeconomy (nb3-3). The Desk (IP-1) regularly announces, for instance, that "the [FOMC's] objective for the [federal] funds rate will be achieved if the rate is sufficiently certain to trade close to the indicated target over the long run, so that temporary deviations from the target do not influence other asset prices" (Federal Reserve Bank of New York 1999, 2). Consistent with minimizing deviations in the federal funds rate, the Desk attempts to keep volatility in the rate at low levels, too. As former Fed Governor Laurence Meyer (2000, 4) suggests, "A significant increase in volatility in the federal funds rate ... would be of concern because it would affect other overnight rates, raising funding risks for most banks, securities dealers, and other money market participants." This view is also backed by a good deal of published empirical and theoretical research in monetary economics, which suggests that such volatility would become problematic "if [it were] transmitted to maturities which are deemed directly relevant for decisions of economic agents" (Bindseil 2004, 100–101).

Central to understanding how the Fed's daily operations function within the normative context described in this chapter to this point is an understanding of double-entry accounting (T1) for the balance sheets of the Fed and banks, and most importantly how it relates to reserve balances. Table 3 presents the components typically found on the Fed's balance sheet. Due to double-entry accounting, both sides of the balance sheet must equal; more importantly in this case, only changes to either assets or liabilities aside from reserve balances can affect the quantity of reserve balances. This means that, for the aggregate banking system, only changes to the Fed's balance sheet can affect the system-wide quantity of reserve balances. Individual banks may lend or borrow reserve balances in the federal funds market or other competing money markets, but these activities can only shift existing reserve balances between banks, not alter the aggregate quantity. In other words, the Fed is the *monopoly supplier* of aggregate reserve balances held in reserve accounts via changes to its balance sheet. Several economist have recently taken to labeling accounting identities such as this one (i.e., aggregate reserve balances held in reserve accounts   Fed assets – Fed liabilities other than reserve balances) as "operational" realities, as they are true by definition, and necessary for any relevant, real-world analysis.

The operational realities of double-entry accounting (T1) must similarly be applied to reserve accounting for individual banks in the loan-creation process. As is well known by economists familiar with the literature on endogenous money,

Table 3 Items commonly found on the Fed's balance sheet

Assets	Liabilities and equity
Treasury securities held outright	Currency in circulation (including vault cash)
Repurchase agreements	Reserve balances
Loans	Treasury account balance
Float	Foreign accounts
Gold and special drawing rights	Other liabilities
Other Assets	Equity

the creation of a loan by a bank at the initiation of a credit worthy borrower creates a liability on the bank's balance sheet (normally a deposit, but not necessarily) for the borrower on the bank's balance sheet. In other words, in contradiction to the sub-criteria "deposits and reserve balances fund bank loans" (nb1-1), neither deposits nor reserve balances actually fund bank loan creation. Many have difficulty understanding that loans are created "out of thin air," but of course this is what any number of non-bank businesses do daily when they provide trade credit to business customers or offer credit to retail customers. For banks, though, the bank liability created by the loan can and probably will be withdrawn by the borrower, perhaps immediately, and the latter is the key difference from credit creation by non-banks. The borrower generally instructs the bank to make a payment on his/her behalf, and at this point (and not before) the bank's reserve account at the Fed can come into play.

Note, however, that as the bank carries out the borrower's request to deliver funds, the bank may or may not need to debit reserve balances from its own account at the Fed. For instance, if the borrower's payment is going to a current customer of the same bank, then the bank simply debits the borrower's account and credits the receiver's account. Or, if the borrower's payment is to be sent via any number of private wholesale payments systems (IP-4), then recall that the bank is usually only responsible for delivering reserve balances if there is a net debit in its position with the clearing house at the end of the day (or at various points in the day), which again may or may not require the bank to debit its reserve account. And if a debit to the account is necessary as a result of the netted settlement, then recall that Regulation J (rg2) ensures that the payment will be sent and that the bank will receive an overdraft automatically in the case of its account balance turning negative. Finally, if the borrower's payment is to be delivered via Fedwire or any other debit to the reserve account as with ACH payments, then again Regulation J (rg2) ensures an overdraft is provided in the case of the account balance turning negative.

Thus, in every conceivable scenario, and (again) in contradiction to sub-belief nb1-1, neither prior reserve balances nor prior deposits funded the loan. Rather, if the bank needed reserve balances to settle a payment resulting from the loan, the regulations and requirements designed according to the FRA (r1), which itself is the result of belief criteria in support of stability in the payments system (nb3-1), ensured any needed reserve balances for settling the payment were provided via overdrafts (at penalty rates set in the Fed's payments system risk policy (rg4)). Consequently, there is no loan officer anywhere in the US that consults with his/her bank's liquidity manager to see how many reserve balances or deposits the bank has before approving a loan; it is simply not how the real-world loan creation process works. The role of deposits in the bank's decision to make the loan relates to the profitability of the loan; that is, if the bank can increase core deposits as it creates new loans, this is less costly than borrowing from the Fed or in the money markets, and the profit margin on the loan is that much greater. Finally, instead of the quantity of reserve balances, it is the bank regulators such as the Fed (IA2-1), the FDIC (IA2-2), the Comptroller of the Currency (IA2-3), and state bank regulators (IA2-4) that are empowered and charged by Congress and the President (IA1-1) with ensuring that banks hold capital (placing their own shareholders sufficiently at risk for management's activities) and are not expanding their balance sheets via loan creation in ways that unnecessarily risk insolvency or, even worse, more systemic risks related to instability in the financial system (nb3-2) or the macroeconomy (nb3-3).

In achieving timeliness in the Fed's daily operations, the Desk balances three different forms of time created by the combination of normative criteria and operational reserve accounting identities: *intraday time, maintenance-period time,* and *seasonal time.* First, there is intraday time, which refers to the needs of banks to settle payments throughout the day. Of course, intraday overdrafts are provided by the regional Fed Banks, not the Desk. Nonetheless, to avoid the risk of an overnight overdraft, or a collateralized discount loan at the Fed's penalty rate, banks in the aggregate have held a "buffer" of reserve balances that typically changes from day-to-day. Partly, this is also due to the lack of perfect coordination among the several thousand banks in the US system, as national banking systems with more precise coordination of lending between banks holding surpluses and those with overdrafts hold little to no aggregate buffer for this purpose. At the same time, US banks have historically preferred that this buffer be as small as possible, since Congress and the President (IA1-1) would not permit the Fed to pay interest on balances banks held in reserve accounts (the recent change in the law to permit remuneration on reserve account balances is discussed in more detail below).

The end result is a daily demand for reserve balances that is quite interest inelastic at the "buffer" banks desire to hold on a given day. If there are fewer balances in the aggregate, overdraft banks can have difficulty finding surplus banks willing to lend, and the federal funds rate can be bid up until a bank in overdraft turns to its regional Fed Bank for a collateralized overnight loan. At times, the federal funds rate may move well above both the FOMC's target rate and the Fed's collateralized lending rate, as prior to 2003 Regulation A (rg1) strongly discouraged banks from using this source of credit. On the other hand, if more balances are supplied than the desired aggregate "buffer," then banks are left holding more surplus reserve balances than are desired in the aggregate and would not be able to find enough banks with overdraft positions to lend the balances to. Prior to October 2008, the Fed paid no interest on reserve balances, and until November 2008, the rate the Fed paid (hereafter, the remuneration rate) was set below the FOMC's target rate. As a result, the larger than desired "buffer" of reserve balances would result in the federal funds rate being bid below the Fed's target rate.

Recall that the Desk's job is to prevent deviations from the federal funds rate from occurring, on average. The source of the change in the rate could be demand-driven, as in a change in the desired "buffer," or supply-driven, as in a change in some component on the Fed's balance sheet that by definition changes the aggregate quantity of reserve balances. For the demand-driven sources, the Desk attempts to predict these via various technical means, though some changes are as predictable as the days of the week. For instance, Mondays tend to be higher payment flow days than Fridays. Similarly, beginnings and ends of months and ends of quarters tend to be high payment flow days, as well as days on which Treasury auctions settle. On the supply side, the Desk prepares each day a forecast of changes to its balance sheet, most notably bank purchases of currency (which debits their reserve accounts) and changes in the Treasury's balance at the Fed, but there can also be other significant sources such as changes in float and repurchase operations on behalf of foreign accounts. Regarding the Treasury's balance, the Treasury is the largest transactor in the world (Garbade et al. 2004, 1), and thus flows to and from its account have potentially the largest effects on the quantity of reserve balances. The Treasury therefore maintains a rather complex system of hundreds of accounts in private commercial banks to and from which it transfers balances toward the overarching purpose of minimizing the net effect on reserve balances of the Treasury's total transactions (see Garbade et al. 2004 for a thorough description). The Desk's forecasts of the Treasury's balance are thus enhanced by a conference call with the Treasury regarding the latter's plans and expectations for the day's net flows (Thornton 2003).

The Desk's operations to manage intraday time are short-term repurchase agreements (to temporarily add balances) and reverse repurchase agreements (to temporarily reduce balances). The operations to add balances temporarily far outweigh operations to reduce them, as the Desk's management of maintenance period time and seasonal time (both discussed below) generally leave an anticipated shortfall in the projected difference between the supply of reserve balances and the average demand for them, which it then attempts to manage more precisely at the intraday frequency. Typically the Desk undertakes all of its operations (that is, operations for various maturities) on a given business day early in the morning as settlement from the previous day in the repurchase markets is occurring.

Maintenance period time is related to reserve requirements and Regulation D (rg5). As previously described, a bank is required to hold an average end-of-day balance over the two-week maintenance period at least equal to its requirement. Maintenance-period time has two significant effects on banks' behavior in the federal funds market. First, it raises the overall demand for reserve balances and thereby reduces the likelihood that banks will be in overdraft at the end of the business day. Second, because banks are permitted to meet reserve requirements *on average* during the maintenance period, deficiencies or surpluses on any given day can usually be offset later in the maintenance period. This has the effect of increasing the elasticity of banks' demand for reserve balances on most days compared to the effects of intraday time alone, and provides the Desk with a bit more "room for error" than otherwise would be the case in terms of correctly forecasting the demand and supply for reserve balances and gauging its operations to achieve the target rate. It also provides the Desk with a bit more certainty in forecasting the demand for reserve balances, as Regulation D (rg5) since 1998 has stipulated that reserve requirements are determined prior to the beginning of the maintenance period.

Of course, this added elasticity reduces as the maintenance period continues and the days left for averaging surpluses or deficiencies shrink in number; not surprisingly, researchers have found that volatility in the federal funds rate rises significantly in the latter days of the maintenance period. Thus, the Desk's operations related to maintenance-period time must recognize that (1) while there is more "room for error," significant over- or under-shooting by the Desk in providing daily reserve balances will still create deviations in the federal funds rate from the FOMC's target, and (2) by the end of the maintenance period, much like intraday time, the aggregate demand for meeting reserve requirements becomes very inelastic and significant system-wide surpluses or deficiencies will bring large deviations from the FOMC's target rate until banks eventually (in the case of deficiencies) borrow from the Fed at the collateralized loan rate (or end up deficient and receive a Fed loan at one percent above the collateralized loan rate) or (in the case of system-wide surpluses) bid the rate down to the remuneration rate. As with intraday time, the Desk's primary tools for managing maintenance period time are short-term repurchase agreements (reverse repurchase agreements are rare for maintenance-period time), though these are frequently of a bit longer maturity, varying between overnight and several days.

For seasonal time, the Desk's operations offset changes in the Fed's balance sheet that are larger and longer lasting in their effect on the quantity of reserve balances in circulation than simply a day or a maintenance period. The purpose in this case is to leave a much smaller volume of operations to undertake at the intraday and maintenance period frequencies. As with intraday time and maintenance period time, the primary sources of changes in the Fed's balance sheet are currency in circulation and the Treasury's balance. Regarding the former, more permanent increases in the public's desired holdings of currency lead the Desk to conduct outright purchases of Treasury securities. Less permanent variations, such as the typical rise during the shopping season at the end of the year and the significant dip after the beginning of the year, result in longer-term repurchase agreements, the maximum length of which are set in the FOMC's directive (rq8). The Treasury's account balance tends to rise as important tax dates arrive and for some time thereafter as payments to the Treasury net of outflows can grow larger for some time than the maximum capacity in its accounts in private commercial banks. Again, the Fed uses repurchase agreements at a variety of maturities to offset add reserve balances and thereby offset the reserve drain caused by net tax revenues. Lastly, because the Treasury issues securities when it runs deficits, this aids the Desk by eliminating the need for the Desk to do the same to support the FOMC's interest rate target (since a deficit would by definition add more reserve balances than it drained).

Overall, the Fed's operations have been able to weather several minor or even major crises that otherwise might have brought significant disruption to the payments system and the financial system. For instance, during the months and weeks leading up to Y2K in late 1999, the public increased their holdings of currency by more than $100 billion, while there was also significant uncertainty among financial institutions regarding the effects of Y2K on private settlement systems. The Fed was able to rather seamlessly provide for the additional desired currency, and the Desk was able to use repurchase agreements to maintain the quantity of reserve balances such that, aside from the last few weeks of the year, there was little deviation in the federal funds rate from the FOMC's target (and the deviations in this case were not much greater than is usually the case during late December, as a number of seasonal factors and intraday factors regarding the demand and supply of reserve balances come into play). The Desk also offered call options to protect financial institutions from the possibility of significant increases in the federal funds rate in the event if the millennium date change proved to be chaotic. The date change came and went without event, and the Desk then again rather seamlessly offset the $100 billion increase in reserve balances caused by the reduction in desired currency holdings mostly via reverse repurchase agreements that occurred in the first few weeks of the year.

The Fed was also able to avoid serious problems in the payments system in the days and weeks following the terrorist attacks in September 2001. As the attacks created significant uncertainty with regard to the private settlement of payments, the Fed was able to raise the quantity of reserve balances circulating via overdrafts, discount lending, and repurchase agreements (by the Desk) by more than $130 billion on demand (McAndrews and Potter 2002). And when this temporary increase in balances then also resulted in rising deposits and thus rising reserve requirements for the next several weeks, the Desk was able to quite easily accommodate this increase without significant effect on the federal funds rate.

The Fed was able to achieve timeliness in its operations in the face of these events because the institutional structure designed by the FRA (r1) and related regulations and requirements were consistent with the primary goal of promoting and sustaining stability (NB3) within the payments system (nb3-1) and the financial system (nb3-2). The overarching goal spelled out in the FRA (r1) of ensuring an "elastic" currency has been achieved in terms of both the Fed's and the Desk's abilities to expand the quantity of reserve balances and currency circulating to meet the private sector's requirements for settling payments and obtaining overnight finance.

On the other hand, the proliferation of retail sweep accounts during the mid-to-late 1990s provides an example where there is less consistency in the normative structure within which the Fed operates daily and thus timeliness was much more difficult to maintain. The financial innovation of retail sweep accounts were enabled by computer software that allow banks to track the account activity of individual customers and "sweep" unused balances into money market deposit accounts (MMDAs), which were "invented" by the Garn-St. Germain Act of 1982 (r3 in Table 2). The Garn-St. Germain Act stipulates that banks are not required to hold reserves against MMDAs, so retail sweep accounts had the effect of reducing bank deposits (as deposits were "relabeled" as MMDAs at the end of the business day) and reducing required reserves. By the end of the 1990s, deposits had fallen by nearly 50%, and so many banks were able to meet reserve requirements via normal vault cash holdings that reserve requirements fell in kind to the point that they were essentially voluntary (Anderson and Rasche 2001).

The difficulties arose because with the decline in reserve requirements and reserve balances came an increase in the likelihood that banks would end the day with difficulties clearing overdrafts. In other words, the role of intraday time was magnified in the Desk's operations, and its room for error in achieving the target rate normally provided by maintenance period time was greatly diminished. With a decreased overall demand for reserve balances, and a more inelastic demand as well, small deviations from banks' desired "buffer" for settling payments (which now could frequently outsize banks' aggregate required reserve balances) could lead to large swings in the federal funds rate away from the FOMC's target. Furthermore, through the summer of 1998, Regulation D (rg5) had set the maintenance period to overlap the computation period almost completely, except for the last two days for the former; this was primarily in accordance with the sub-belief that reserve requirements provide the Fed with control over loan creation and thus money supply growth (nb1-2), since in the money multiplier model greater monetary control can be had if banks' reserve requirements can be more directly tied to the quantity of reserve balances. In reality, though, the effect was to significantly reduce the Desk's ability to correctly forecast the demand for reserve balances related to reserve requirements. And while Regulation A (rg1) set the collateralized lending rate below the FOMC's target prior to 2003, because the Fed strongly discouraged banks from utilizing this source of overnight liquidity via its "frowning," the federal funds rate could move well above its target range before banks in overdraft would think to turn to the Fed for a collateralized loan. Finally, as mentioned previously, until late 2008 the Fed was prohibited by Congress from paying interest to banks on reserve balances (this is discussed in more detail in the following section but is related to both the neo-Jeffersonian view of banks (NB4) and the widely held view that there are financial constraints on the federal government (NB5)), which would have reduced banks' desire to economize on their holdings of reserve balances and thereby raised the aggregate "buffer" banks were willing to hold at the FOMC's target. The effect of a larger desired "buffer," given that it would necessarily be accommodated by the Desk, would have been to reduce the likelihood of large numbers of banks ending the day in overdraft; this would have reduced the likelihood of large increases in the federal funds rate beyond the FOMC's target, while at the same time it effectively would have put a floor on how far below the FOMC's target rate the federal funds rate could be bid down in the event that the Desk "overshot" in its estimate of how many reserve balances to supply through repurchase agreements.

As a result of these factors, the federal funds rate became exceptionally volatile and frequently deviated significantly from the FOMC's target rate. The Fed's response was to alter both Regulation D (to begin the maintenance period 17 days after the end of the computation period) and Regulation A (to raise the penalty rate to one percent above the FOMC's target while ending the practice of "frowning" on banks that desired to obtain overnight collateralized credit) in 2003, while the Desk also put more emphasis on intraday forecasts than previously. And while the Fed was at that time not yet permitted to pay interest on reserve balances, it was able to encourage banks to hold greater numbers of "required clearing balances," which were voluntary agreements banks made with the Fed to hold a pre-determined (by each bank individually) quantity of balances during the maintenance period; these balances would earn "credits" equivalent to the FOMC's target rate that could be used only for paying off fees incurred by using the Fed's payments services. Since they could only be used for paying these fees, there was a limit to the quantity of required clearing balances each bank would hold, but nonetheless these agreements with the Fed raised the quantity of reserve balances circulating and thereby somewhat reduced the likelihood of large numbers of banks ending the day in overdraft.

By 2004, the Fed reported that volatility in the federal funds rate had been reduced significantly, partly as a result of the steps taken above, and partly as a result of the fact that the FOMC's target rate had been reduced so much that banks' opportunity costs of holding reserve balances had declined and so their desired "buffer" had increased (e.g., Federal Reserve Bank of New York 2008). What is significant to note here, though, is how the goal of stability in the payments system (nb3-1) and financial system (nb3-2), which are partly reflected by the volatility in the federal funds rate, became inconsistent with regulations and requirements in place that had been intended to enhance the Fed's control over the money supply (NB1), encourage banks to use alternative sources of liquidity (NB2), discourage subsidization of banks (NB4) and government outlays (NB5) via interest payments on reserve balances (NB4). It is also not a coincidence that volatility in the federal funds rate eventually diminished as more and more changes were made to rules and regulations that were increasingly consistent with the goal of stabilization (NB3) in the payments system (nb3-1) and the financial system (nb3-2) and less concerned with the other major beliefs.

General Principles for the Fed's Operations

Given the foregoing description of the Fed's operations derived from the SFM-A, a number of "general principles" are clear, some of which are counter to traditional monetary theory (see Fullwiler 2010 for a more detailed discussion of these and other "general principles" of central banking within a comparative context) and even counter to some of the important beliefs in Fig. 1. This section briefly describes seven such principles.

The Fed's Daily Operations Are Mostly About the Payments System, Not Reserve Requirements

Consider a world with no reserve requirements and no maintenance-period time. In this case, banks hold reserve balances only for the purpose of settling payments. The demand for aggregate reserve balances is very interest inelastic; if the Fed, as the monopoly supplier of reserve balances, provides more or fewer balances than banks desire to settle their payments results in large swings in the federal funds rate. This is because beyond the desired "buffer" of aggregate balances, banks have no need for more (since loans create deposits by double-entry accounting (T1)) and will be forced into overdraft and to the Fed for a collateralized loan if too few are provided.

Adding reserve requirements and maintenance-period time means banks now hold reserve balances to settle payments and also to meet reserve requirements. The maintenance period gives the Desk more "room for error" in accommodating the demand for reserve balances. But by the end of the maintenance period, just as without maintenance-period time, the Desk must accommodate an inelastic demand for reserve balances. Although most learn of central bank operations first via consideration of reserve requirements, this is backward; the Fed's obligation to the stability of the payments system (nb3-1) is primary and represents the general case, while the addition of reserve requirements is actually the special case. As an earlier report on comparative central bank operations by the Government Accountability Office put it, "the primary objective of all central banks is to ensure the smooth functioning of their countries' payments systems" (Government Accountability Office 2002, 2).

The Fed's Operating Target Is Necessarily an Interest Rate Target. The Money Multiplier Framework Is Inapplicable and Untenable in Practice

Because the demand for reserve balances is very interest inelastic on a daily basis (when payment needs dominate the aggregate demand for reserve balances) or at least by the end of the maintenance period (when reserve requirements dominate), to repeat from the previous principle, supplying more or fewer reserve balances than banks in the aggregate desire to hold will result in the federal funds rate falling to the remuneration rate (if too many balances are supplied) or rising to the penalty rate assessed on collateralized lending from the Fed (if too few are otherwise supplied). As such, a reserve balance "target" would be actually a *de facto* interest rate target at either the remuneration rate or the collateralized lending rate. In practice, a reserve balance operating target would send the federal funds rate fluctuating between these two rates as the demand for reserve balances shifted, sometimes significantly, from day-to-day.

Overall, the operating target is necessarily an interest rate target given the Fed's obligation to the payments system (nb3-1) and the Fed's stated desire to minimize volatility in the federal funds rate. Reserve aggregates can be targeted only *indirectly* via manipulation of the interest rate target – though the link between these has shown itself empirically to be rather unreliable since loans and deposits are created at the initiative of creditworthy borrowers whose motivations are often not easily explained by the FOMC's interest rate target alone. In short, this means, again, that support of the payments system (nb3-1) and financial system stability (nb3-2) are primary, while beliefs related to use of Fed operations and reserve requirements to enable more direct control over the money supply (NB1 and nb1-2, nb1-2, nb1-3) are essentially inapplicable if not counterproductive to achieving stabilization. Of course, again, due to double-entry accounting (T1), loans create deposits, and thus neither reserve balances nor deposits can provide additional "funding" for bank lending.

The Fed's Operations Accommodate Banks' Demand for Reserve Balances While Offsetting Changes to Its Balance Sheet Inconsistent with Such Accommodation

As the Fed's target is necessarily an interest rate target, the Fed's operations necessarily accommodate banks' aggregate demand for reserve balances at that target rate. In doing so, its operations must also offset changes to the Fed's balance sheet such as increases in currency in circulation or a rise in tax revenues received by the Treasury, which would (in these cases) reduce the quantity of reserve balances and send the federal funds rate above the FOMC's target. This means that the Fed's operations are largely defensive in nature; the textbook view of a central bank "flooding the economy with money" is inapplicable, as the Fed's balance sheet essentially grows only as banks' demand for reserve balances grow or as the public's demand for currency grows (since this brings forth an open market purchase by the Desk to replenish drained reserve balances). The exception to this is only in the historically exceptionally rare case that the remuneration rate is set equal to the central bank's target rate, as this would enable the Fed to oversupply reserve balances – and thus grow its balance sheet according to its own preferences – without having the federal funds rate fall below the FOMC's target rate. Here again, though, the additional reserve balances would not "fund" bank loan creation, and thus would not be any more inflationary, just as in the previous principles.

Reserve Requirements Have to Do with Interest Rate Targeting, Not Money Supply Targeting

As described above, reserve requirements do not constrain lending, since banks do not use reserve balances to create loans. What reserve requirements *do*, though, is provide the Desk with additional "room for error" in achieving the FOMC's target. Again, beliefs and sub-beliefs related to the proposition that central banks' directly control the money supply (NB1, nb1-1, nb1-2, and nb1-3), as well as rules such as the DIDMCA, are inapplicable and can even interfere with the Fed's ability to promote stability in the payments system (nb3-1) and the financial system (nb3-2).

Potential Deviations in the Federal Funds Rate from the FOMC's Target Rate Are Set by the Fed's Collateralized Lending Rate and the Remuneration Rate

While the Fed encountered difficulty achieving its target rate during the late 1990s as retail sweep accounts proliferated, most of this difficulty was either self-imposed or imposed by Congress and the President (IA1-1). Uninhibited by such constraints, there is no question about the Fed's "operational" ability to achieve its target rate as precisely as desired. For instance, the Fed's exceptionally high penalty on unsecured overnight overdrafts meant the latter was not an option for banks. A rise in the federal funds rate might have been avoided still as banks could turn to the Fed for a collateralized loan, but the Fed's historical "frowning" on banks obtaining such liquidity from their regional Fed banks led them to continuously bid up the federal funds rate when they were endanger of an overdraft but reluctant to turn to the Fed for collateralized credit. Similarly, as mentioned, the prohibition against paying interest on reserve balances (effectively setting the remuneration rate at zero) both increased the likelihood of overdrafts (as banks economized on reserve balances held to minimize opportunity costs) and meant that the federal funds rate could fall dramatically if the Desk over-estimated the desired "buffer" for banks on a given day.

In contrast, if the Fed sets either the unsecured overdraft penalty or the collateralized lending rate closer to the FOMC's target, and if payment of interest is permitted on reserve balances at a rate close to the target, then the potential volatility in the federal funds rate is obviously significantly reduced. The New York Fed recognized as much when it noted that the elimination of "frowning" and its replacement instead with a one percent penalty on collateralized lending combined with a historically low overall target rate (which, though the remuneration rates was still zero, effectively set a lower bound on the federal funds rate close to the target rate) led to substantially reduced volatility. As it stated,

> Volatility in the federal funds rate was exceptionally low in 2003 and 2004, when target rates for federal funds were at historical lows [one percent]. At that time, the gap between the target rate and the lower bound for rates – zero percent [since the Fed does not pay interest on reserve balances] – narrowed substantially which, in conjunction with the primary credit facility adopted in 2003, effectively limited the potential trading range for rates. (Federal Reserve Bank of New York 2008, 21)

Note once again that the lack of timeliness in the Fed's operations during the late 1990s was primarily due to normative constraints in place that were unrelated to the goal of stabilization in the payments system (NB3). Instead, large penalties and "frowning" are more related to instilling "market discipline" on the liability side of bank balance sheets, since it is believed that markets are efficient (NB2) and will efficiently price risk (nb2-1). As previously noted, objections to paying interest on reserve balances arise from concerns that such payment will subsidize banks (nb4-1) or that this will negatively affect the federal government's fiscal position (nb5-1). Again, these normative criteria have led to difficulties for the Fed in achieving its target rate at times, as institutional rules and regulations consistent with norms related to market efficiency (NB2), neo-Jeffersonian views of banks (NB4), and concerns with the federal government's fiscal stance (NB5), can be completely inconsistent with regulations and requirements related to stability in the payments system (nb2-1) and financial system (nb2-2).

There Is No Liquidity Effect Related to the Fed's Operations to Change Its Target Rate

Perhaps no one topic has been more researched in the field of monetary economics than the liquidity effects of central bank operations. A liquidity effect here is defined as operations by the Fed intended to permanently change the target rate. It is clear from the foregoing, though, that a liquidity effect so defined is not at work in the Fed's operations. This is because any attempt by the Fed to unilaterally add or subtract reserve balances to alter the target rate, if not consistent with banks' aggregate demand for reserve balances to settle payments and meet reserve requirements, will simply send the federal funds rate up to the collateralized lending rate (in the case of a deficiency in reserve balances) or reduce it to the remuneration rate (in the case of undesired excess balances). As Sandra Krieger (head of domestic reserve management and discount operations, New York Fed) put it,

> The conventional textbook view is that the Trading Desk buys and sells securities in response to easings and tightenings [i.e., the liquidity effect]. From the [Trading] Desk's perspective, however, the supply-demand balance is primarily a function of the demand for required balances, which is almost completely insensitive to small changes in policy. Consequently, any change in the target has no effect on excess supply or demand in the funds market. (Krieger 2002, 74)

Since there is no change in the supply-demand balance for reserve balances with a target rate change, there is no need for open market operations related to a liquidity effect as defined here. The suggestion that a liquidity effect is at work is related to the belief that reserve balances fund loans (nb1-1). But this demonstrates a lack of understanding of double-entry accounting (T1) as it applies to bank loan creation, since it assumes banks can "do" something with additional balances; recall again that reserve balances serve no purpose but to meet reserve requirements and settle payments. Instead of a liquidity effect, then, the Fed simply announces rate changes. This is all the more obvious when one considers an alternative tactic to minimize potential deviations from the target rate in which the Fed leaves a narrow range between its collateralized lending rate and the remuneration rate; in this case, it could simply announce new levels for both rates while the target rate would necessarily remain within this new range.

The Fed's Operations, Overall, Are About "Price," Not "Quantity"

The most common misconception about monetary policy operations is that they are primarily concerned with the quantity of reserve balances in circulation. As explained, though, the Fed's only available operating target is an interest rate target, regardless of whether the spread between the collateralized lending rate and the remuneration rate is large or small. Even during 1979–1982, when the Fed claimed it was not setting an interest rate target, it is widely acknowledged now that in fact the Fed was simply allowing a wider range for the federal funds rate to fluctuate within than it has during other periods. As the monopoly supplier of reserve balances, this is necessarily the case, since even with such a wide spread the Fed can quite obviously enable, exacerbate, or relieve whatever "pressure" exists for the federal funds rate to rise or fall according to its own preferred outcomes (while any such "pressure" exists in the first place due to the quantity of balances provided by the Fed itself relative to the banks' system-wide demand for them).

Moreover, the quantity of reserve balances circulating has nothing to do with the Fed's target rate or its ability to achieve the target rate. Recall that, absent reserve requirements, the quantity of reserve balances simply falls to the "buffer" level that banks desire to hold overnight, with no effect on banks' abilities to create loans. However, in the presence of an opportunity cost to holding reserve balances (as when the target rate is set above the remuneration rate), the buffer itself is primarily determined by a combination of the penalties banks are faced with for borrowing secured or unsecured from the Fed (since a negligible penalty would lead to less need to hold a buffer against it), the ability of banks to coordinate borrowing/lending between surplus and deficient banks at the end of the business day, and the Fed's ability to forecast and offset changes to its balance sheet. So, a desired overnight "buffer" of zero would indicate that at least one or more of these factors had been eliminated, rather than being an indication that banks could not lend or that the Fed's reserve balances were having difficulty "competing" with other means of payment. In Canada, for instance, banks have no reserve requirements, face a penalty of 0.25% on collateralized borrowing from the Bank of Canada, have absolute certainty that they can clear overdrafts or eliminate surpluses by the end of the business day, and the Bank of Canada can with absolute certainty offset any changes to its balance sheet. Perhaps not surprisingly, the quantity of reserve balances banks hold overnight in Canada has been zero for several years, as reserve balances there exist only in intraday form. At the same time, the Bank of Canada has also been able to achieve its interest rate target with significantly greater precision than the Fed.

At the other extreme, if the Fed were to set the remuneration rate equal to its federal funds rate target, it could raise the quantity of excess balances (beyond that desired to settle payments and meet reserve requirements) to virtually any positive level it desired, while still achieving the target rate (Fullwiler 2005; Whitesell 2006; Lacker 2006; Keister et al. 2008). This would also greatly simplify the Fed's unnecessarily complex daily operations. As Richmond Fed President Jeffrey Lacker explained, "the market funds rate would not rise above the [rate paid on balances] except to reflect borrower-specific risk. The New York Fed staff would merely need to provide an amount of reserves that will be sufficient to oversupply the system with reserves and meet daylight settlement needs. But they would not need to estimate daily reserves" (2006, 3). Since 2006, the Reserve Bank of New Zealand has used a similar procedure (Martin and McAndrews 2008, 20–22). Note, though, that this increased quantity of reserve balances would have no bearing on banks' abilities to create loans, since – yet again – loans create deposits. As with no reserve balances in circulation, even with a very large surplus of balances, the Fed's operations are "about" interest rates, not the quantity of reserve balances.

The Fed's Operations and the Recent Financial Crisis

Beginning in August 2007, events related to the problems in "subprime" mortgages – which themselves became readily apparent in the summer of 2006 – started having a substantial impact in the money markets closely related to the Fed's operations. The failure of Lehman Brothers in September 2008 added yet another level to the effects on the Fed's operations. The purpose of this section is to interpret events related to the Fed's operations using the SFM and normative systems analysis developed above. This also provides an opportunity to propose alternative approaches to dealing with such events, and has implications for day-to-day operations under normal circumstances, as well.

Brief Chronology of Events, August 2007 to December 2008

The details and causes of recent events in the US financial system have been covered by many others already, and are beyond the scope of this chapter. This section therefore confines itself to a brief chronology of events from August 2007 to the end of 2008 that are most related to the Fed's operations.

Significant volatility developed in the federal funds rate in late summer through fall 2007 as losses well above those previously expected began to emerge for institutions funding mortgage-related securities in money markets. Historically large spreads developed between the Fed's interest rate target and rates in both Eurodollar and commercial paper markets in August 2007. This reflected the difficulty financial institutions were having obtaining short-term funds as lenders shifted from term to overnight lending due to concerns of counterparty risk. For instance, the one- and three-month LIBOR-OIS spreads, which had been typically around 0.1–0.2%, rose to around a full percent. Commercial paper spreads were even wider. These events created upward pressure on the federal funds rate, according to the New York Fed, which led to a change in the Desk's tactics.

> In the first maintenance period in which these pressures appeared, the period ending August 15, the Desk effectively suspended its normal approach to controlling the funds rate. In order to combat severe and persistent upward pressures … the Desk provided a level of excess reserves above any amount banks would have chosen to hold at rates anywhere around the target. This extraordinary measure was taken to restore a more normal balance between risks of upward and downward rate pressures. (Federal Reserve Bank of New York 2008, 4)

The Fed also responded in mid-August 2007 by cutting the collateralized lending rate to 0.5% above the target rate. Overall,

> the ultimate rate effects of the heavy reserve provisions that the Desk provided … [were] evident in the tendency for the [federal funds rate and other overnight rates] to fall off during the day … which sometimes contributed to very low rates even early in the morning on subsequent days. For a time, until about mid-September, the Desk's reserve provisions contributed to an overall soft bias in daily average rates, despite a tendency for upward rate pressures to emerge many mornings. (Federal Reserve Bank of New York 2008, 28)

The New York Fed thus reported that for the period from August 9 through September 18 intraday standard deviations, daily trading ranges, and absolute deviations from the target were up substantially from normal levels (Federal Reserve Bank of New York 2008, 28–30).

Thereafter, though, "period-average excess levels were returned to more normal levels in subsequent maintenance periods in the year, [since] financial market strains did not appear to have any material impact on the period-average level of excess reserves that banking institutions wished to hold... ." (Federal Reserve Bank of New York 2008, 8). The corollary was that "since [September 18 through the end of 2007], the Desk has succeeded in maintaining daily rates on average around the target," (28) while, nevertheless, "volatility around the target, though somewhat dampened, has remained elevated" (28).

During this period, the Fed also lowered its target rate from 5.25 to 4.75% in early September, and then again two more times to 4.25% by the end of 2007. Even with the lower target rate and some success minimizing volatility and deviations in the federal funds rate, after mid-September 2007 spreads in term money markets continued to fluctuate while remaining at levels well above normal. The Fed therefore introduced on December 12, 2007 the Term Auction Facility (TAF) to auction a fixed dollar-value of collateralized loans available to banks at one-month maturities, with the purpose of spreading funds more broadly than typically could be achieved via open market operations. In early March 2008, the Fed also began providing a large number of 1-month repurchase agreements with agency mortgage-backed securities (MBS) as collateral, in order to reduce spreads between Treasury and agency MBS repurchase agreements and provide liquidity to holders of now less-liquid agency MBS.

As Bear Stearns' failure or takeover became imminent, on March 17, 2008 the Fed lowered its collateralized lending rate to a 0.25% penalty above the target rate. The target rate, which had been lowered to 3% in January, was lowered again on March 18 to 2.25%. On March 17, the Fed created the Primary Dealer Credit Facility (PDCF), which provided overnight collateralized loans at the Fed's collateralized lending rate to primary dealers. The Fed the previous week had also established the Term Securities Lending Facility (TSLF), which loaned up to $200 billion in US Treasuries held by the Fed to primary dealers in exchange for a greater dollar-value in other highly-rated fixed-income securities. The purpose here was to enhance dealers' abilities to obtain credit in private markets (which they could do by lending the Treasuries in reverse repurchase transactions) and also to improve settlement in Treasury repurchase markets that are crucial to overall functioning in the money markets (discussed in more detail below).

In May 2008, the Fed asked Congress for authority to pay interest on reserve balances. Congress did give the Fed authority to do so in the Financial Services Regulatory Relief Act of 2006, but the authority was not to take effect until 2011. The Fed's rationale was that it needed to expand its balance sheet in order to continue providing overnight and term liquidity at the levels commensurate with difficulties in those markets. During the period of August 2007 through May 2008, the Fed's balance sheet had remained around $900 billion in total assets, but there was a significant "reshuffling" of assets, as the TAF, PDCF, and MBS repurchase agreements had required the Desk to actively reduce its holdings of Treasuries by around $200 billion in order to achieve the Fed's target rate. The TSLF also reduced holdings of Treasuries by another $100 billion or so, though these operations were simply security swaps and had no effect upon total reserve balances circulating. In other words, in addition to managing these new facilities, the Desk had to offset all of the reserve affects from these facilities since banks' overall demand for reserve balances had not increased (that is, since the balances could not earn interest, banks minimized their holdings just as in normal times). This was all added to its normal activities of estimating the demand for reserve balances and forecasting balance sheet effects of changes in currency, the Treasury's account, and so forth.

Congress's reasoning in 2006 for delaying interest payment on reserve balances until 2011 was that its budgeting cycle is always five years, so spending related to such interest payment more than five years into the future was not required to be incorporated into a new bill. As previously explained, for years prior to 2006, though Congress had rejected interest payment due to concerns regarding the effect upon the federal government's fiscal position (nb5-1), and also that such interest payment unnecessarily subsidizes banks (nb4-1). The financial press repeatedly replayed both of these reasons in the public discussion regarding reconsideration remuneration for reserve balances in May 2008. Consequently, no action was taken by Congress at that time.

After Lehman Brothers' bankruptcy in mid-September 2008, and subsequent bailouts or buyouts of several other large financial institutions, the worst part of the crisis set in (to date, at least). Strains on the money markets were enormous, as "both term unsecured and secured financing markets ground to a halt" (Federal Reserve Bank of New York 2009, 43). In response, the Fed this time increased its balance sheet size from around $900 billion at the beginning of September 2008 to $1.8 trillion on October 16 and then to around $2.3 trillion by early November, where it remained through December. In doing so, the Fed did not further actively reduce its outright holdings of Treasuries, while it also expanded the TAF and PDCF, and continued other operations at roughly the same levels, such as repurchase agreements with agency MBS and traditional collateralized lending to banks. It further added significantly to its assets via new activities such as currency swaps with more than 14 foreign central banks totaling over $500 billion (which enabled the latter to provide dollar loans to their banking systems and thereby stabilize offshore dollar money markets); loans to the American International Group (AIG) were valued at around $50 billion by the end of 2008, and lending facilities for issuers of commercial paper and money market mutual funds totaled over $300 billion by the end of 2008. Though it did not affect the size of the Fed's balance sheet, the Fed also significantly expanded the TSLF to over $200 billion (whereas prior to September 2008 it had been around $50 billion) as "demand for US Treasuries again skyrocketed" and accompanied substantial problems in the settlement of term and overnight repurchase agreements (Federal Reserve Bank of New York 2009, 43–45).

The FOMC further lowered its target rate in early October to 1.5%, and then in late October to 1%. The New York Fed reports that "prior to mid-September, fed funds traded with some volatility but daily effectives were relatively close to the target rate …[but] after September 15, volatility increased and funds often traded well below the target rate as the banking system had large levels of excess balances"

(Federal Reserve Bank of New York 2009, 4). In other words, the corollary to the large increase in the Fed's assets was a large increase in reserve balances and therefore a large decline in the federal funds rate relative to the target rate; this was unavoidable since the Fed did not hold enough Treasuries to sell to offset its expanded liquidity and lending operations. Overall, reserve balances rose quickly from around $20 billion to over $200 billion in mid-September, and then continuously increased to around $800 billion by the end of 2008.

The Fed was finally provided with the authority to pay interest on reserve balances in the Emergency Economic Stabilization Act of 2008 effective on October 9. The Fed set the rate on excess balances initially at 0.75% below the target rate, but as the federal funds rate traded well below this level, the remuneration rate was raised to 0.35% below the target on October 22. With the federal funds rate still trading near zero, the remuneration rate was set equal to the target rate, as suggested in research cited above. However, the rate continued to hover near zero, even as the target remained at 1% until December 16. The following from the New York Fed's report explains why:

> In practice, a combination of circumstances prevented interest on reserves from working as designed. Several major participants in the fed funds markets, specifically Government Sponsored Entities (GSEs) and some of the Federal Home Loan Banks, are not depository institutions and thus not eligible to earn interest on reserves. As a consequence, they retained incentives to sell fed funds in the market at very low rates to earn some return. Perhaps more importantly, banks were not willing to arbitrage in the funds market to the extent necessary to keep the funds rate close to the target. Absent any balance sheet constraints, banks should be willing to purchase funds at a rate below that paid on excess reserves and earn a risk-free return by holding those balances in their accounts at the Federal Reserve. However, banks only marginally took advantage of this arbitrage as most viewed balance sheet flexibility to be more crucial [than slight income earned on additional overnight liabilities]. As a consequence, the funds rate regularly traded below the interest rate paid on excess reserves. (Federal Reserve Bank of New York 2009, 4–5)

On December 16, the Fed set the interest rate target to a range between 0 and 0.25%. For the Fed's operations, this meant that interest payment on reserve balances was essentially no longer necessary to expand the Fed's balance sheet while achieving the target rate. With no more room to cut the target rate, and with money markets somewhat stabilized, albeit still at historically high spreads (but lower than September 2008 highs), the Fed announced in November its additional plans to aid credit creation in the financial system in which the Fed's newly created Term-Asset Backed Securities Loan Facility (TALF) would begin in March 2009 purchasing $1 trillion billion in securities backed by newly originated student, auto, credit card, or small business loans.

The Financial Crisis and General Principles for the Fed's Operations

This section relates the above events to the general principles for the Fed's operations that derive from the SFM and normative systems analysis for these operations. There are four issues in particular to discuss here: (1) the substantial variations in the federal funds rate relative to the Fed's target rate; (2) the defensive nature of the Desk's operations; (3) the importance of the federal funds rate and the unimportance of the quantity of reserve balances; and (4) the payment of interest on reserve balances. In each case, consistent with the general principles, major norms unrelated or inconsistent with stabilization of the payments system (nb3-1) and financial system (nb3-2) that were primary criteria for setting rules, regulations, and requirements are again at best flawed and at worst contributors to the difficulties experienced in stabilizing the payments system and the financial system.

The rise in volatility reported by the Desk, beginning in August 2007 continuing through September 2007, was a direct result of the wide spread historically permitted between the collateralized lending rate and the remuneration rate. The one percent penalty on collateralized lending, while lower than the non-monetary costs previously associated with the Fed's "frowning," was among the highest for central banks. It was not until March 2008 that the penalty was reduced to a level more in line with most other central banks at 0.25%. Partly due to this large penalty (and potentially the reluctance of banks to borrow from the Fed given past history), and probably also partly due to the very high penalties on uncollateralized overnight loans, the Desk felt compelled to substantially oversupply the banking system with reserve balances. This over supply of reserve balances then led the federal funds rate to fall substantially since the Fed was not allowed to pay interest on reserve balances until October 2008. Thus, as the general principles explained, it is the width of the spread between the Fed's overnight lending rate and the remuneration rate that sets the potential swings in the federal funds rate. Under the circumstances, the Desk had very little chance during the worst periods of the crisis to achieve the Fed's overnight target rate, and this was precisely when stabilization of the price of refinancing of short-term funding was one of the most important contributions the Fed could make to stabilization of the financial system.

The Desk's tactics during the August 2007 through early September 2008 period are a rather extreme example of its necessarily defensive operations when the interest rate target is set above the remuneration rate. Many in the financial press did not understand this basic fact, and saw only the increased lending via the multiple programs the Fed designed as evidence of the Fed was "pumping money" into the economy. But in fact, because the overall demand for reserve balances did not increase during this period, and because no interest payment was yet permitted on reserve balances, the quantity of reserve balances therefore also needed to remain the same. The Desk was thereby required to engage in what was essentially an act of juggling, managing various new programs, attempting to forecast demand for reserve balances in an historically volatile environment, and also removing several hundred billion dollars in Treasuries from its balance sheet so that there might be some chance of achieving a federal funds rate close to the target rate.

Since September 2008, as both the Fed's balance sheet and the quantity of reserve balances have risen to historic highs, the financial press has labeled this "quantitative easing" (QE), which the Bank of Japan used (incorrectly) to describe its own actions in the early 2000s. Often forgotten is the fact that the Desk had no choice but to allow reserve balances to rise, as there were no longer enough Treasuries on its balance sheet to sell as an offset to the Fed's increased lending. The Fed had warned Congress of this possibility in May 2008. More importantly, though, is the general principle that the Fed necessarily sets an interest rate – in this case, with such large excess balances circulating, the rate was effectively zero percent – while the quantity of reserve balances or the size of its balance sheet are irrelevant to banks' "abilities" to create loans. In other words, yet again, the money multiplier view of the Fed's operations (NB1) is inapplicable. Nevertheless, such concerns were widespread in the financial press. A speech by FOMC Chair Ben Bernanke in February 2009 acknowledged these concerns about the size of the Fed's balance sheet (Bernanke 2009), and also correctly noted that most of the loans on the Fed's balance sheet will be self-liquidating once private sources of the same sort of financing are available. But Bernanke, unfortunately, did not point out that these concerns were inapplicable at any rate. While reserve balances held overnight had risen from a fraction of a percent to around 5% of GDP in December 2008, whether this quantity is zero (as in Canada) or 15% of GDP (as in Japan in the early 2000s), reserve balances simply settle payments and meet reserve requirements, while loans create their own deposits. Congressional outrage that banks were not "lending" capital injections received from the federal government's Troubled Asset Relief Program (TARP) was similarly inapplicable and inconsistent with the logic of double-entry accounting (T1): banks do not require capital, deposits, or reserve balances to create loans. Instead, banks increase their lending when they see profitable lending opportunities (which, in the current environment, may be sparse) assuming that their regulators approve the assets and consider the banks to be well-capitalized. As in the general principles, the effect of such large quantities of excess reserve balances being held overnight is that the federal funds rate will fall to the remuneration rate. Since both the target rate and the remuneration rate were already effectively zero percent, the excess quantity had little if any economic significance.

Finally, as the Fed's inability to pay interest on reserve balances was one of the key factors in the volatility and deviations of the federal funds rate from the Fed's target rate, it is useful to consider the argument here that such interest payment harms the government's fiscal position (nb4-1). The traditional argument has been that because the Fed is required by law to remit its profits to the Treasury, and with interest payments these remitted profits would be reduced (e.g., Abernathy 2003). But, consider the case with the greatest potential interest outlays by the Fed in which the remuneration rate is set equal to the Fed's target and a large quantity of excess balances circulates. Under normal circumstances with no financial crisis, such as the scenario envisioned by Lacker above, the Fed would hold on average a greater quantity of Treasuries in order to add a large surplus of balances (or, alternatively worded, a larger proportion of the national debt would now circulate on the non-government sector's balance sheets as reserve balances than would be the case without interest payment). To the degree that the Treasuries now held by the Fed (or at least now not held by the non-government sector) would earn a higher interest rate than the remuneration rate earned on reserve balances now being held by the non-government sector (which would frequently be the case, since Treasuries have longer maturities than reserve balances and the yield curve usually slopes upward), then the net effect upon the federal government's fiscal position is undeniably positive. Further, under extreme conditions – such as now – in which the Fed raises reserve balances significantly by creating loans to stabilize the financial sector (and then does not drain them as it would have to without interest payment in order to hit a positive interest rate target), to the degree the interest rate charged by the Fed on these loans is greater than the remuneration rate on the increased quantity of reserve balances (which like now would almost always be the case), the total impact upon the federal government's fiscal stance is again positive. In other words, it is simply *not* the case that interest payment on reserve balances hurts the federal government's fiscal position; in fact, the opposite is actually the case. This also shows the folly of the Fed's prohibition against the GSEs and other non-depository receiving interest on reserve balances, since this either means the Desk must drain excess balances by selling Treasuries (which, against Congress's own preferences, *worsens* the government's fiscal position) or leave the excess balances circulating and let the federal funds rate fall well below the target rate (which the Desk did during mid-September to mid-December).

Additional General Principles for the Fed's Operations as a Result of the Financial Crisis

As a result of the financial crisis, there are additional general principles for the Fed's operations that can be articulated. These include (1) the unnecessary interbank market; (2) the Fed's ability to set the term structure of risk-free lending rates; and (3) the role of the Treasury in stabilizing repurchase agreement markets. One might add a fourth principle, which would be that the Fed can set terms of credit in virtually any market it desires, since it is the monopoly supplier of reserve balances.

There Is No Public Purpose Served by the Federal Funds Market that the Fed Could Not Provide in a More Direct and Precise Manner While Also Expending Fewer National Resources

As noted, much like the DIDMCA's (r2) goal of encouraging private settlement systems (nb2-2), the Fed's payments system risk policy (rg4) likewise encourages settlement off of the Fed's balance sheet via overdraft penalties, collateral requirements, and so forth. Consequently,

> in practice, the daily operation of the payments system typically involves *sequential* use of [three different money markets]. Repo markets are most active in the (New York) morning when dealers arrange financing for continuing balance sheet positions and settle security trades made the previous day (or two). The Eurodollar market is then most active during the day, and the Fed Funds market is most active at the end of the day. (Mehrling 2006, 25)

An important reason for this structure is the preference for "market discipline" and the presumed benefits of such discipline in terms of efficiency gains (nb2-1).

> During the day, elasticity is the objective, and daylight overdrafts at all levels of the system
> are permitted in order to facilitate payments. But overnight, discipline is the objective and
> that means that credit expansion is ideally kept off the books of the banking system, and
> certainly off the books of the central bank. The point is to provide an ongoing incentive for
> economic agents to settle their debts, and not simply roll them over to the next day.
> (Mehrling 2006, 25–26)

While these respective interbank markets under normal circumstances are likely as efficient as any in the world in terms of liquidity, depth, and breadth, consider how much government "intervention" is necessary even in this case. First and second, the Fed obviously provides daylight overdrafts at little cost to enable a large percentage of intraday settlement to occur on its own balance sheet and also achieves its own target for the overnight rate in the federal funds market to anchor the other money market rates. Third, the federal government insures bank liabilities, which is only a step or two from the Treasury offering its own accounts to the public; an intermediate step would be deposits in banks that could only invest in Treasuries, but instead banks are allowed to invest in a variety of loans and securities, while regulators regularly evaluate bank assets and the sufficiency of bank capital. And fourth, as recently occurred, the Fed by necessity brings a large amount of this money market activity onto its own balance sheet if the prior three "interventions" are still insufficient to provide stability (NB3).

An alternative approach could be for the Fed to substantially reduce the spread between its lending and remuneration rates, perhaps even reducing it to zero as Mosler (2007) and Goodhart (2008) suggested. Some worry that eliminating or grossly reducing the penalty for borrowing from the Fed would encourage speculative activity among banks, possibly leading to asset price bubbles; however, such concerns neglect that (1) banks must collateralize their loans from the Fed, and (2) banks must submit their asset portfolios to bank regulators for approval on a regular basis. A related concern might be that eliminating such a penalty subsidizes banks (nb4-1) because central bank liquidity is effectively free (banks borrow from the Fed at the same rate they can invest the funds with the Fed), but of course bank liabilities are already effectively subsidized in that they are guaranteed by the federal government (enabling banks to acquire them for little to no interest cost in most cases), while, again, banks can only earn profits from investing in regulator-approved financial assets.

Instead of subsidizing banks, substantially reducing or eliminating the spread would further enable the smooth functioning of payment settlement (nb3-1) while also having the potential to remove a large degree of perceived counterparty risk in the financial system during a crisis (nb3-2). Indeed, it was precisely the Eurodollar and repurchase agreement markets for which the Fed encourages netted payment settlement during the day (and also the commercial paper market) that "ground to a halt" due to increased concerns regarding counterparty risk.

Another concern for some is that eliminating the opportunity cost of holding reserve balances by setting the target rate equal to the remuneration rate subsidizes banks (nb4-1) and eliminates their incentive to lend to other banks. Regarding subsidization, it is true that this would eliminate the "tax" on banks of holding reserve balances and thereby reduce their need to economize on their holdings. But with a reduced spread, any bank needing to borrow funds obviously can obtain balances from the Fed at the same rate they would borrow from another bank, so there are no additional profit opportunities available to banks holding excess balances in this case. Further, while any bank that simply acquires deposits and invests in reserve balances would now earn more than previously for the same activities, it is difficult to see why this would be a problem since this would be an extremely safe strategy (the equivalent of 100% reserve banking) while at the same time the strategy would be far less profitable (particularly after non-interest costs and taxes were deducted) than the traditional practice of holding a portfolio of regulator-approved loans and securities.

How would a reduced spread work in practice? Consider, as an example, an overnight reserve "market" in which the spread is zero or close to zero, and in which the Fed perhaps oversupplies significantly the banking system with reserve balances as in Lacker's (2006) suggestion above. In this system, the target rate is achieved at all times, banks are able to settle payments with a minimum of intraday or overnight credit in the case of an oversupply of balances (as an alternative to the Fed's payments system risk policy (rg4)), and there is no counterparty risk among banks given that each can access funds from the Fed at no penalty above the target rate. If, as the Fed apparently believes would happen, there are too many banks that are "not settling their debts," then Goodhart's (2008) suggestion that the spread be widened for individual banks after outstanding overdrafts reach a certain amount could be considered. Alternatively, perhaps the Fed could instead operate a clearinghouse via reserve accounts throughout the day or at the end of the business day, as the Bank of Canada already does, such that banks with overdrafts could be matched with banks in surplus, leaving only whatever net balances have been supplied by the Fed's open market operations. Or, to again remain somewhat in the spirit of Canada's interbank market and settlement system, the Fed could do both, leaving a modest spread to encourage banks to settle their overdrafts beyond a certain level while also acting as counterparty. The Fed as interbank clearinghouse and counterparty for all banks has been suggested by others (such as Kregel 2008) as a relatively simple change that would have significantly softened money market disruptions driven by concerns over counterparty risk. This is a "relatively simple change" since, for the Fed, the role is a natural one, as it already is the banker to all commercial banks, provides their intraday overdrafts and their overnight collateralized loans, operates the Fedwire payments system most commonly used by all banks for final settlement of payments and securities transactions, and is a bank regulator. That the Fed has not yet officially taken on this role has to do with major norms that favor market efficiency (NB2) via private settlement (nb2-1), market discipline and credit allocation (nb2-2) and less government "intervention" (nb2-3), which have led to rules, regulations, and requirements that have promoted the settlement of payments off the Fed's balance sheet.

Finally, a common mistake related to the arguments in favor of market efficiency or market discipline in the federal funds market (nb2-1) is not recognizing that there is no useful role in this particular case for price discovery. As Martin and McAndrews (2008) explain,

> The costs of reserves, both intraday and overnight, are policy variables. Consequently a
> market for reserves does not play the traditional role of information aggregation and price
> discovery. In fact ... many demand-management features determined by central bank pol-
> icy are intended to dampen price variability in the market for reserves. (1)

One could go even further, since the Fed necessarily sets an interest rate as the
monopoly supplier of reserve balances, so any price variation not dampened and
providing the appearance to some of "price discovery" occurring in the federal
funds market is instead an indication of an error in the Desk's estimation of reserve
demand, or otherwise an indication of how much of a "trading range" for the
federal funds rate the Fed is willing to allow (as during 1979–1982). The corollary
here is that there is little rationale for economically significant penalties on borrowing
from the Fed or opportunity costs for holding balances in Fed accounts, as they
contribute virtually nothing to, and can even be counterproductive to, the goals of
stability in the payments system (nb3-1) and the financial system (nb3-2). Instead,
as Mosler (2007) argues, "when the [central banks] fully understand their own
monetary operations ..., they will offer unlimited funds at or just over their target
rates and ... bid for funds at or just under their target." As above, the Fed then
becomes effectively the counterparty to banks in the final settlement of payments
and trades. And because the Fed *already is nearly that* except for the influence of
norms that favor settlement of payments and trades off the Fed's balance sheet, as
Martin and McAndrews (2008, 24) put it, "under this view, activity in the [interbank
market] is a waste of resources." Even worse, in the recent crisis, not using the Fed
as a counterparty in settling banks' payments needlessly hampered attempts to
stabilize the financial system.

The Fed Can Set Money Market Rates for Banks at Any Point in the Term Structure

In the first few months of the crisis, the Fed did not recognize its own ability – as
monopoly supplier of reserve balances – to control interest rates along the term
structure by intervening in term lending markets that were experiencing substantial
difficulties. As money market spreads widened for a large percentage of banks in
good financial standing, the Fed only in December 2007 began offering term loans to
all member banks through the TAF, and even then had to continue raising the quantity
of lending made available throughout 2008 as the quantity of funding offered each
time was fixed. Similarly, the rates on the TAF loans were allowed to float via auction,
even as they were ultimately lower than those in private term money markets.

Note that the point of the Fed's operations to achieve a target rate is not to simply
achieve an overnight rate target, but rather to influence via this target other interest
rates set in other markets. This aids financial stability (nb3-2) by stabilizing the price
of refinancing of short-term funding under normal circumstances when it is generally
accepted that simply setting the federal funds rate can be consistent with stable,
modest spreads in other money markets. But this process has not worked as normal
since August 2007, as spreads in several money markets remain at historical highs.

To this day, it is unclear if the Fed realizes it could have stabilized costs of refinancing short-term funding significantly in the financial system by simply setting lending rates to banks at one-, two-, and three-month maturities, for instance, that were equivalent or slightly higher than the spreads the Fed desired to see in the respective term lending markets. While some have noted that the TAF appears to have reduced spreads in term markets, this is not the same as recognizing that the spread was a potential policy variable, while spreads have remained at historical highs at any rate.

The Treasury Can Supply Unlimited Amounts of Treasuries to Help Stabilize Settlement and Reduce Counterparty Risk in Repurchase Agreement Markets

As the Federal Reserve Bank of New York (2009, 41) reports, "amid ongoing concerns about counterparty credit risk and increased risk aversion, demand for Treasury collateral was extremely elevated during several episodes throughout the year.... . This occurred in spite of the sizable amount of Treasury collateral that was available in the market through primary issuance, the [Treasury's Supplementary Financing Program], and other programs geared towards improving functioning in Treasury markets." This was a repeat, albeit on a significantly larger scale, of Treasury shortages in March 2008 at the time of Bear Stearns's failure (and these shortages have appeared in most instances of financial system strain during the past decade, as well). The Fed's response in both cases was to accept more forms of non-Treasury collateral for its standing facilities (in order to reduce the amount of Treasuries held as collateral by the Fed, freeing them for use in repurchase markets) and to first establish and then increase the size of the TSLF.

An additional or alternative option would be for the Treasury – which is obviously the monopoly supplier of Treasuries – to offer to lend any of its previous issues at a fixed spread (such as 0.25%) below the federal funds rate target. And given the extreme circumstances, as the owner of the Fannie Mae and Freddie Mac GSEs since August 2008, the Treasury could, like the TSLF (or as a more effective replacement for it), have offered to lend Treasuries against GSE obligations. While repurchase markets stabilized by November, there were options available to stabilize payment settlement (nb3-1) and this part of the financial system (nb3-2) more quickly that were not implemented.

Additional "Unconventional" Operations by the Fed (or the Treasury) Are Necessarily About Interest Rates and Spreads, Not Quantities

The proposed TALF, announced by the Fed and the Treasury, is expected to purchase nearly $1 trillion in securities backed by recent auto, home, student, and credit card loans. The purpose is to reignite lending in these sectors of the economy, where spreads above Treasury bonds remain at historical highs. Indeed, the success or failure of the TALF will be judged on how well it is able to reduce these spreads, much as analysts have evaluated the TAF and related standing facilities. But since the creation of a loan in the first place requires a willing borrower at the current rate of interest, it is unclear if there will be too few or too many loans for the Fed to purchase relative to the arbitrary TALF limits; it is also unclear how much this will affect spreads that are indicators of whether or not markets are functioning "normally," and how quickly these effects will occur. Mostly unmentioned, though, is the fact that if it is a particular spread or interest rate that is considered consistent with more "normal" functioning of credit markets, this could simply be set directly and immediately, allowing the quantity of loans purchased by the Fed to float. The spread could be set a bit above the historical or otherwise desired level, enabling financial institutions to purchase the loans at desired spreads once the financial system is willing and able to do so, which would then provide a clear signal that this moment had arrived. As an example, if it is deemed desirable to have conforming mortgages at four percent, which would put them near historical spreads over Treasuries (as of this writing in February 2009), then the Fed or the Treasury (which owns Fannie Mae and Freddie Mac) could purchase conforming mortgages at four percent. Overall, the use of values such as $1 trillion in discussion of such "unconventional" operations assumes the Fed controls the money supply (NB1) and the quantity of private lending, when it does not. On the other hand, the Fed – as monopoly supplier of reserve balances – *can directly set a price* (i.e., an interest rate) at which it will purchase or sell an asset, and allow the quantity of loans purchased to float.

Concluding Remarks

This chapter has applied the SFM-A to the Fed's operations, for which the core analytical framework is based upon the SFM (Hayden 2006, Chap. 6) and evaluative criteria (Hayden 2006, Chap. 5) derived from normative systems analysis (Hayden 1998). Together, these enable further extension into analysis of time and timeliness (Hayden 2006, Chap. 8) in the Fed's operations. The analysis results in a number of general principles for understanding the Fed's operations. The overarching implication of this analysis is that the institutional design and context of the Fed's operations are strongly influenced by an *instrumental-ceremonial dichotomy* (Bush 1987), where there are *instrumental* norms related to stabilization in the payments system and the financial system, but also *ceremonial* norms founded more or less on ideology and generally accepted but inapplicable theoretical models related to central bank control over the money supply, market efficiency, and concerns over the fiscal position of the federal government and subsidization of banks. Applications of this framework to events in the 1990s, early 2000s, and then to the recent financial crisis repeatedly suggests that the goal of stabilization should be the primary evaluative criteria for the design and articulation of the rules, regulations, and requirements related to the Fed's operations, as the other criteria that have more ceremonial bases can be and have been inapplicable or – much worse – in conflict with achieving stability in the payments system and the financial system.

References

Abernathy WA (2003) Business checking freedom act of 2003, H. R. 758 and H. R. 859. Testimony delivered before the Subcommittee on Financial Institutions and Consumer Credit of the Committee on Financial Services, U. S. House of Representatives, March 5

Anderson RG, Rasche RH (2001) Retail sweep programs and bank reserves, 1994–1999. Fed Reserv Bank St. Louis Rev 83(1):1–24

Armantier O, J Arnold, J McAndrews (2008) Changes in the timing distribution of Fedwire funds transfers. Fed Reserv Bank New York Econ Policy Rev 14(1):83–112

Bank for International Settlements (2007) Statistics on payment and settlement systems in selected countries. Committee on Payment and Settlement Systems Report 78, March

Bernanke B (2009) Federal reserve programs to strengthen credit markets and the economy. Speech given on February 10

Bindseil U (2004) Monetary policy implementation: theory, past, and present. Oxford University Press, New York

Board of Governors (1990) The federal reserve in the payments system. http://www.federalreserve.gov/paymentsystems/pricing/frpaysys.htm

Board of Governors (2008) Data on funds service, securities service, and national securities service. http://www.federalreserve.gov/paymentsystems/fedwire/fedwirefundstrfann.pdf

Bond Market Association and the Depository Trust and Clearing Corporation (2003) Issues and recommendations regarding commercial paper settlement practices (discussion paper). Bond Market Association and the Depository Trust and Clearing Corporation, New York

Bush PD (1987) The theory of institutional change. J Econ Issues 21(3):1075–1115

Clouse JA, Elmendorf DW (1997) Declining required reserve balances and the volatility of the federal funds rate. Federal Reserve Board, Finance and Economics Discussion Series, June

Clouse JA, D Henderson, A Orphanides, D Small, P Tinsley (2000) Monetary policy when the nominal short-term interest rate is zero. Federal Reserve Board, Finance and Economics Discussion paper, November

Commons JR (1995/1924) The legal foundations of capitalism. Transaction Publishers, New Brunswick, NJ

Edwards JR (1991) The process of accounting innovation: the publication of consolidated accounts in Britain in 1910. Account Hist J 18(2):113–132

Federal Reserve Bank of New York (1999) Annual report on domestic open market operations in 1998

Federal Reserve Bank of New York (2008) Annual report on domestic open market operations in 2007

Federal Reserve Bank of New York (2009) Annual report on domestic open market operations in 2008

Federal Reserve System (2007) Account management guide. http://www.frbservices.org/files/regulations/pdf/amg.pdf

Federal Reserve System (2008) Reserve maintenance manual. http://www.frbservices.org/files/regulations/pdf/rmm.pdf

Federal Reserve System Study Group on Alternative Instruments for System Operations (2002) Alternative instruments for open market and discount window operations. Federal Reserve System, December

Fullwiler ST (2001) A framework for analyzing the daily federal funds market (Ph.D Dissertation). University of Nebraska, Nebraska

Fullwiler ST (2003) Timeliness and the Fed's daily tactics. J Econ Issues 37(4):851–880

Fullwiler ST (2005) Paying interest on reserve balances: it's more significant than you think. J Econ Issues 39(2):543–550

Fullwiler ST (2010) Modern Central Bank operations: the general principles. In: Moore B, Rochon L-P (eds) Post-Keynesian monetary theory and policy: horizontalism and structuralism revisited. Edward Elgar, Cheltenham

Furfine C (2000) Interbank payments and the daily federal funds rate. J Monetary Econ 46(1):535–553

Garbade KD, Partlan JC, Santoro PJ (2004) Recent innovations in treasury cash management. Fed Reserv Bank New York Curr Issues Econ Finance 10(11)

Goodhart CAE (2008) The preferential access scheme. Paper presented at global macro economy: imbalances or passive outcomes, Valance Co., Inc., United State Virgin Islands, January

Government Accountability Office (2002) Payment systems: Central Bank roles vary, but goals are the same. GAO-02-303, February

Hancock D, Wilcox JA (1996) Intraday management of bank reserves: the effects of caps and fees on daylight overdrafts. J Money Credit Banking 28(part 2):870–908

Hayden FG (1982) The social fabric matrix: from analytical perspective to policy tool. J Econ Issues 16:637–661

Hayden FG (1998) Normative analysis of instituted processes. In: Fayazmanesh S, Tool MR (eds) Institutional theory and applications: essays in honor of Paul Dale Bush, vol 2. Edward Elgar, Northampton, MA, pp 89–107 (reprinted in this volume)

Hayden FG (2006) Policymaking for a good society: the social fabric matrix approach to policy analysis and program evaluation. Springer, New York

Hayden FG, SR Bolduc (2000) Contracts and costs in a corporate/government system dynamics network: a United States case. In: Elsner W, Groenewegen J (eds) Industrial policies after 2000. Kluwer, Boston, MA

Johnson K, Small D, Tryon R (1999) Monetary policy and price stability. Federal Reserve Board, International Finance Discussion Papers, July

Keister T, Martin A, McAndrews J (2008) Divorcing money from monetary policy. Fed Reserv Bank New York Econ Policy Rev 14(1):41–56

Kregel J (2008) A simple proposal to resolve the disruption of counterparty risk in short-term credit markets. Jerome Levy Economics Institute Policy Note, October 4

Krieger SC (2002) Recent trends in monetary policy implementation: a view from the desk. Fed Reserv Bank New York Econ Policy Rev 8(1):73–76

Lacker JM (2006) Central Bank credit in the theory of money and payments. Speech at the Economics of Payments II Conference, Federal Reserve Bank of New York, March 29

Martin A, McAndrews J (2008) Should there be intraday money markets? Federal Reserve Bank of New York Staff Report No. 337, July

McAndrews JJ, Potter SM (2002) Liquidity effects of the events of September 11, 2001. Fed Reserv Bank New York Econ Policy Rev 8(2):59–79

McAndrews J, Rajan S (2000) The timing and funding of Fedwire funds transfers. Fed Reserv Bank New York Econ Policy Rev 6(2):17–32

Mehrling P (2006) Monetary policy implementation: a microstructure approach. http://cedar.barnard.columbia.edu/faculty/mehrling/Monetary_Policy_Implementation_Final_Revision.pdf

Meulendyke A-M (1998) U.S. monetary policy and financial markets. Federal Reserve Bank of New York, New York

Meyer LH (2000) Payment of interest on reserves and fed surplus. Testimony delivered before the Committee on Banking and Financial Services, U.S. House of Representatives, 3 May

Minsky HP (1957) Central banking and money market changes. Q J Econ 71(May)

Mosler WB (2007) The trillion dollar day. http://www.mosleconomics.com/2007/12/19/the-trillion-dollar-day

Most KS (1972) Sombart's proposition revisited. Account Rev 47(4):722–734

Myers MG (1970) A financial history of the United States. Columbia University Press, New York

Panigay-Coleman S (2002) The evolution of the Federal Reserve's intraday credit policies. Fed Reserv Bull (February):67–84

Polanyi K (1957) The economy as instituted process. In: Polanyi K et al (eds) Trade and market in early empire. Free Press, Glencoe, IL, pp 243–270

Previts GJ, Merino BD (1998) A history of accountancy in the United States. Ohio State University Press, Columbus, OH

Richards HW (1995) Daylight overdraft fees and the Federal Reserve's payment system risk policy. Fed Reserv Bull (December):1065–1077

Shen P (1997) Settlement risks in large-value payment systems. Fed Reserv Bank Kansas City Econ Rev 82(2nd Quarter):45–62

Small D, Clouse JA (2000) The limits of the Federal Reserve act places on the monetary policy actions of the Federal Reserve. Annu Rev Banking Law 19:553–779

Sombart W (1924) Der Moderne Kapitalismus, 6th edn. Duncker and Humblot, Munich

Spahr WE (1926) The clearing and collection of checks. Banker's Publishing, New York

Summers BJ, Gilbert RA (1996) Clearing and settlement of U.S. dollar payments: back to the future? Fed Reserv Bank St. Louis Rev 78:3–23

Thornton DL (2003) Forecasting the treasury's balance at the Fed. Federal Reserve Bank of St. Louis Working Paper No. 2001-004D, May

Whitesell W (2006) Monetary policy implementation without averaging or rate corridors. Federal Reserve Finance and Economics Discussion Series No. 2006-22, May

Yamey BS (1964) Accounting and the rise of capitalism: further notes on a theme by Sombart. J Account Res 2(2):117–136

Microcredit and Reconstruction in Afghanistan: An Institutionalist Critique of Imported Development[1]

Saeed Parto and Akshay Regmi

Abstract This chapter investigates the inconsistencies in perceptions by the international donors of the positive role of microcredit in improving rural livelihoods in Afghanistan. We examine the interface between the role of "microfinance institutions (MFIs)" and the pre-existing rural institutions that have traditionally governed credit transactions for generations of rural Afghans. In our analysis, we view MFIs as introduced organizations with anticipated institutional roles by the international donors and the Afghan government to facilitate desirable socio-economic change. An institutionalist framework is applied to primary and secondary data to assess the outcome to date of introducing microcredit in Afghanistan. This chapter concludes with a series of recommendations for integrated policy and operational interventions to improve rural livelihoods in post-2001 Afghanistan.

Introduction

Afghanistan has come out of a decades-long intermittent period of armed conflict, which has severely limited the capacity and the ability of the state to provide services to meet even the most basic needs of the population. With an average per capita GDP of less than US$200, Afghanistan was in 2001 one of the poorest countries in the world, with its formal institutions and infrastructure virtually destroyed. An estimated 80% of the population lives in rural areas, with agriculture and agriculture-based employment providing income for 67% of the labour force. The amount of useable farmland comprises as little as 12% of the total land area, and land ownership is highly skewed with great regional differences. A significant portion of rural households possesses little or no land for sustenance.

S. Parto (✉) and A. Regmi
Faculty of Arts and Social Sciences, Maastricht University, Maastricht, The Netherlands
e-mail: saeed.parto@maastrichtuniversity.nl

---

[1] We acknowledge Anna Paterson's earlier and much valued input into this chapter.

T. Natarajan et al. (eds.), *Institutional Analysis and Praxis*,
DOI 10.1007/978-0-387-88741-8_9, © Springer Science+Business Media, LLC 2009

Afghan households need access to credit as a coping strategy – for consumption smoothing, crises, and life cycle events such as marriages and funerals. Access to credit is also purported to be key in expanding income-generating activities, investment in productive assets, and improvement of livelihoods, thereby adding to local economic growth. Small, medium, and large-scale entrepreneurs need access to credit for capital accumulation in setting up or expanding businesses. This need has attracted new attention in a time of economic reconstruction, promotion of economic growth in the formal sector, and development of rural markets. Access to credit is considered by donors and Afghan policymakers as an important service for promoting socio-economic inclusion, countering poverty and promoting growth in rural Afghanistan. The continued commitment to microfinance at the highest levels is reflected in the Interim Afghanistan National Development Strategy (I-ANDS), which contains a rural development benchmark relating to rural credit and financial services:

> To promote livelihoods and economic growth, the Government will expand access to quality financial services – especially for women and the poor – by further developing informal financial markets through the Microfinance Investment Support Facility in Afghanistan (MISFA), creating a legally independent yet regulated sector, and mobilizing resources and private institutions that will provide financial products for investment in small and medium-sized enterprises. Comprehensive rural financial services will also provide special products such as insurance that will encourage private sector investments in rural farm and non-farm enterprises. (I-ANDS 2005:148)

MISFA was established in August 2003 as the apex organization for "microfinance institutions" (MFIs) in Afghanistan. The number of MFIs has since grown to 15 (see Appendix A for a list and descriptions). The MISFA website recorded a total of US$252.8million in loans disbursed to 314,208 active borrowers by May 2007. This commitment to microfinance is based on the assumption of a large unmet demand for credit in rural communities. At its inception, MISFA estimated that as many as 2 million households were in need of credit. In December 2007, the World Bank official website reported that,

> The World Bank, CGAP (the Consultative Group to Assist the Poor), and the donors that followed, seized the opportunity [in 2002] to establish a model microfinance industry in this *virgin* territory – doing things right, from day one. Four years later, microfinance in Afghanistan is thriving despite deteriorating security in the country, and a new impact survey has found that the benefits to clients are real. ...Interviews with more than 1,000 households across five regions of the country in the spring of 2007 revealed that 700,000 employment opportunities have been created for women...[2] (emphasis added)

However, research has shown that a variety of informal credit mechanisms are commonly used across Afghanistan, pointing to the presence of highly evolved, albeit not always fair and equitable, credit markets throughout rural Afghanistan. Village-level case studies of informal credit conducted in Herat, Kapisa, and Ghor provinces as well as a pilot study in Balkh in 2006–2007 (Klijn and Pain 2007) raised a number of challenges to such assumptions on the unavailability of

---

[2] From: http://web.worldbank.org/WBSITE/EXTERNAL/NEWS/0,,contentMDK:21590188~page PK:64257043~piPK:437376~theSitePK:4607,00.html. Accessed 31 Dec 2007.

credit, finding that an array of credit options were available to rural households. The authors also questioned the understanding of credit mechanisms based on a preoccupation with "formality" (Klijn and Pain 2007:2):

> If we look at informal credit through the lens of formal systems where money exchange is treated as simply as a commodity exchange, does this not rather ignore the context of social relations in which most Afghans lead their lives and the meaning and role that informal credit plays within these relations?

To further investigate the inconsistencies in perceptions by the international donors of the positive role of microcredit in improving rural livelihoods, this research examined the interrelations between microcredit and traditional credit. Village-level in-depth interviews were held with households, loan officers and key informants in villages where microfinance is being offered. Data collected from Kabul, Bamiyan, and Balkh provinces were supplemented with data from a series of shorter and less in-depth key informant interviews and focus group meetings conducted in Herat. The interviews and focus group meetings in the four provinces took place between February and August 2007.

This chapter examines the interface between MFIs as introduced organizations with anticipated institutional roles in facilitating desirable socio-economic change and the pre-existing rural institutions that have traditionally governed credit transactions for generations of rural Afghans. An institutionalist framework is applied to primary and secondary data to assess the outcome to date of introducing micro credit in Afghanistan. This chapter concludes with a series of recommendations for integrated policy and operational interventions to improve rural livelihoods in post-2001 Afghanistan. The remainder of this chapter is organized as follows.

The next section provides a brief history of formal microcredit in Afghanistan. The third section outlines the objectives of this research, while the fourth section describes the methodology used in the analysis of the data from primary and secondary sources. The fifth section provides a detailed description of the context including a review of some of the relevant literature. The sixth section analyzes the data from primary and secondary sources, followed by a conclusion on the main findings. The chapter concludes with the section that outlines a series of policy and operational recommendations.

Microcredit in Afghanistan

In this study, microcredit refers to small amounts of money borrowed by clients from MFIs as part of the set of services described as Microfinance.[3] Loans can be delivered to individuals and groups with or without collateral and may or may not

---

[3] CGAP defines Microfinance as "the supply of loans, savings, and other basic financial services to the poor ... to run their businesses, build assets, stabilize consumption, and shield themselves against risks. Financial services needed by the poor include working capital loans, consumer credit, savings, pensions, insurance, and money transfer services." For more information see: http://www.cgap.org/portal/site/CGAP/menuitem.b0c88fe7e81ddb5067808010591010a0/.

contain a savings requirement. In Afghanistan, there are variations in the microfinance system across different MFIs, although they operate under the general policy guidelines as prescribed by MISFA. These variations occur in terms of targeted groups, nature of financial services provided, and the presence of capacity building components built into the loans. For instance, PARWAZ only offers loans to urban women, while FINCA cooperates with donor organizations such as USAID to contribute to nationwide programmes such as ARIES (Agriculture, Rural Investment and Enterprise Strengthening) and has established FAMA (FINCA Afghanistan Microfinance Academy) to train its employees in training its clients.[4]

There is an array of different regulations that govern formal credit provision through the 15 MFIs operating under MISFA. For instance, loan repayment cycle can start from 2 weeks after borrowing, such as in the case of OXUS, or 10 months, as is the case with ARMP. Each MFI has different loan cycles, with different amounts that can be borrowed after the end of a repayment cycle. Most MFIs require that savings be made before loans can be accessed. Some MFIs only give group loans, whereas others provide loans to individuals and groups. The Murahaba credit system utilized by FINCA is the world's first Sharia law compliant micro credit system. Under Sharia law, interest on loans is considered as sinful. To avoid this label, the Murahaba system charges "administrative costs" for its loans, which include interest calculated annually and payable by the borrowers as the service cost of their loan.

In traditional lending the mechanisms are rooted within local family, community, as well as Islamic notions and norms of social assistance and responsibility, linked in many ways to the practice of giving alms to the poor or to benefit from donating to the needy based on the Islamic notion of sawab (Table 1). They can also be bound up with local hierarchies and patronage arrangements as well as other

Table 1 Inventory of traditional credit practices and terms (Source: Klijn and Pain (2007) and Maimbo (2003))

Murabaha	A contract of sale between a lender and a client for the sale of goods at an agreed price plus an agreed profit margin for the lender. The contract involves the purchase of goods by the lender, who then sells them to the client at an agreed mark-up. Repayment is usually in instalments. Murabaha has been adopted by many banks as a means of lending that is consistent with Islamic law. However, murabaha is considered illegitimate by some Islamic scholars
Muzarebat	A partnership between an investor and a businessman in which one provides the money and the other provides the work; profit is divided between the two, while the loss is carried only by the investor
Qarz-i-hasana	Credit on goodwill terms with no interest
Qarz-i-khudadad	A loan given on the understanding that the debtor will repay when God provides the opportunity
Salam	A well-known form of advanced payment where credit is provided for a future harvest at an already fixed (low) price

[4] See Appendix A for a list and descriptions of MFIs under the MISFA umbrella.

social networks and may have a role in sustaining exploitative power relationships (Klijn and Pain 2007). An inventory of the traditional forms through which credit is transacted is listed in Table 1. Excluded from this inventory are voluntary donations such a Khairat (voluntary alms), Zakat (obligatory alms) and Hawala services (to transfer funds).

Objectives

In this chapter we examine the interface between the newly introduced MFIs and pre-existing (traditional) sources of lending and borrowing in rural areas. We pay particular attention to MFIs as organizations with intended institutional roles in relation to pre-existing institutions with key governance roles in rural livelihoods. A key assumption in our analysis is that the introduced organizations (the MFIs) with intended institutional roles can improve rural livelihoods, given the "right" interface between the new organization (the MFIs) and the pre-existing and mostly traditional institutions such as those described in Table 1. In the analysis, we drew on information from secondary sources as well as primary data collected from research in 2007 in the four provinces of Balkh, Kabul, and Bamiyan and Herat. The research was guided by the following objectives:

- Identify and inventory the traditional institutions that govern lending and borrowing credit
- Investigate the role of microcredit in rural communities
- Assess the interface between MFIs and the traditional forms of lending and borrowing
- Take stock of the changes in rural socio-economic conditions due to introduction of microcredit

An institutionalist framework based on Hayden's (Hayden 1982a, b, c) "social fabric matrix" (SFM) and Parto's (2005a, b, 2008) "typology of institutions" is employed to analyse the data from primary and secondary sources. The next section provides a description of these two approaches to institutional analysis and the methods utilized in the collection and analysis of the data.

Methodology

Our analysis is informed by Hayden's SFM and the concept of delivery and process. Hayden (1982b) uses as examples the "components" of electric companies delivering electricity, novels delivering myths, and values delivering belief criteria. Components may deliver more than one "element". For example, some industries can deliver goods and services as well as carcinogenic substances. Designing an SFM requires first defining the matrix components and their elements. In Table 2 the range "1...n" denotes the elements for each component.

The flows of goods, services, information, funds, and people collectively structure and maintain community relationships. Depending on the subject of study, the SFM that emerges from linking these elements may attribute more or less weight to each element. The system continues to function as long as there is delivery among its elements consistent with natural principles and social rules. A "sustainable" system has continuous delivery and receipt among its many elements. Absence of delivery–receipt relationship among elements undermines the continuance of relationships and can lead to a reconfiguration of the matrix. One main purpose of the SFM is to organize what we know as the basis to identify the key nodes or points in a given system and investigate possibilities for intervention through policy or other means toward more desirable outcomes.

The completion of the SFM for a research problem should also result in discovering linkages among the components/elements and the identification of weak and strong linkages. Placing a notation of "1" or "0" in any cell in Table 2 denotes the existence or absence of a delivery–receipt relationship. If more than one relationship are of interest, each relationship can be accounted for in this binary fashion. The number of cells in the SFM depends on the research or policy problem being addressed, i.e., it is scope-dependent. The boundary for the system represented by a constructed network is thus subjective and delineated by the researcher. Links or relationships between deliveries and receipts are established on the basis of reciprocity, and/or redistribution, and/or exchange.

The central nodes are entities or phenomena that are involved in more overlaps, have more reachability to other entities, and generate greater levels of deliveries, in terms of flows, than other entities or phenomena. Using the SFM, it is possible to identify the relevant set of influences that shape the behaviour of a system (Hayden

Table 2 Social fabric matrix (Source: After Hayden (1993))

Delivering component	Receiving component						
	Cultural value, $1\ldots n$	Social belief, $1\ldots n$	Pers. attitude, $1\ldots n$	Pers. taste, $1\ldots n$	Environment, $1\ldots n$	Technology, $1\ldots n$	Institutions, $1\ldots n$
Cultural value, $1\ldots n$							
Social belief, $1\ldots n$							
Pers. attitude, $1\ldots n$							
Pers. taste, $1\ldots n$							
Environment, $1\ldots n$							
Technology, $1\ldots n$							
Institutions, $1\ldots n$							

1998:94). As a means to model action processes, the SFM can be used to select the most important components, or regulatory factors, through highlighting the delivery and receipt relationships. Depending on the number and importance of the most central node(s), one might speculate about the resilience of the network or the stability of a particular institutional arrangement as a whole, were one or more of the central nodes to be eliminated or diminish in importance.

Consistent with Uphoff and Buck (2006) and Parto (2005a, 2008), this research also employed a notion of institutions as formal and informal structures that collectively organize a community. As such, institutions have relative permanency and longevity (Hodgson 1988; Parto 2005a; Uphoff and Buck 2006) and are manifest as a continuous spectrum consisting of formal, tangible entities (e.g., banks, government agencies, courts) at one end and less formal, intangible phenomena (e.g., customs, norms, and beliefs) at the other. The full spectrum may be depicted as in Fig. 1.

In this conception, institutions are viewed as reflections of learning in the broadest societal sense (Parto 2005b,2008;Voeten and Parto 2006). However, once established, institutions structure (constrain and facilitate) further learning in a continuous and interactive auto-catalytic process (Parto et al. 2005). Institutions are thus structuring phenomena and manifest at different levels of interrelation, scales of governance, and in different spheres of the political economy.[5] Applying the levels–scales–spheres perspective to institutions yields a loose but necessary typology of institutions (Fig. 1).[6]

In our analysis we use the typology in Fig. 1 in conjunction with Hayden's SFM to identify and map the formal and informal institutions as the components (and their elements) that collectively structure credit transactions in the four provinces of Balkh, Bamiyan, Herat, and Kabul. A full inventory is presented of the constitutive,

Behavioural	Cognitive	Associative	Regulative	Constitutive
Institutions as standardized (recognizable) social habits – manifest in deeply ingrained behaviour of individuals and groups as reflections of social norms	Institutions as mental models and constructs or definitions, based on values and embedded in culture – aspired to by individuals and groups	Institutions as mechanisms facilitating prescribed or privileged interaction among different private and public interests – manifest in activities of groups of individuals	Institutions as prescriptions and proscriptions – manifest as the immediate boundaries of action by individuals and groups	Institutions setting the bounds of social relations – manifest as the ultimate boundaries of action by individuals and groups

Informal; Social   Formal; Societal

Fig. 1 Characteristics and manifestations of institutions (Adapted from Parto (2008))

[5]For an elaborate discussion of levels, scales, and systems see Parto (2005a). See, also, Philo and Parr (2000) for a discussion of scale and institutions.
[6]This typology and the subsequent discussion are based on Parto (2005b).

regulative, and associative institutions based on reviews of secondary data and interviews with key informants. The information on the cognitive and behavioural institutions comes from the interviews recognizing, however, that more accurate data on these two latter institution types can only come from household surveys of representative household samples, a task which was beyond the scope of this research.

It is important to distinguish between each institution type and its catalyst(s). For example, the introduction of a new regulation on borrowing is not an institution but a catalyst. The catalyst may, or may not, result in the emergence of an institution that plays a significant role in structuring transactions and has relative permanency. If the regulation on borrowing is not enforced or complied with widely, it is not, for all intents and purposes, "instituted". In a similar vein, an association that comprises a group of organizations or individuals determined to protect and promote common interests may or may not emerge as an associative institution. If the association persists, actively lobbies on behalf of its members, and succeeds in changing the operating environment for its members, it can be said to have become an associative institution. Sustained lobbying by the association can result in the elimination of old or the formation new regulations (in the broadest sense) to benefit the members and thus the formation and persistence of the regulative institution.

The use of this typology in analysis elsewhere has illustrated that intervention through policy succeeds only if it resonates with the pre-existing behavioural and cognitive institutions within the area of focus for the policy. An important implication of this proposition is that governing to effect systemic change, as intended through the introduction of microfinance in rural Afghanistan, requires a continuum of measures to be pursued jointly through local arrangements and supported by territorially defined levels of government. In the case of microfinance, local arrangements have included the introduction of MFIs in villages, while the government and the international donors have provided structural support including funds, expertise, and regulation. The focus of this research has been to assess the compatibility of introduced change with pre-existing conditions.

A total of 32 households were interviewed in the four provinces in addition to a number of "chit-chats" on the streets with random individuals. Thirty-three focus group meetings were organized and 19 key informant interviews conducted with shopkeepers, local government officials, farmers, teachers, mullahs, eldermen, widows, and MFI staff.[7] The MFIs active in the four provinces studied for this research are listed in Table 3.

This research did not focus on specific MFIs in the four provinces. Due to time and resource limitations as well as the dispersion of MFI-originated credit among the MFIs operating in each province, and to maintain confidentiality rules, we use "MFIs" as the focal organization with intended institutional functions. The interviews and focus group meetings in each province were organized with assistance from local officials, NGOs, and MFI personnel to examine credit transactions involving MFIs

---

[7]We acknowledge access to data collected by teams of researchers from Afghanistan Research and Evaluation Unit (AREU) for an ongoing project on microfinance. We are also grateful for valuable comments from Erna Andersen, Floortje Klijn, Asta Olesen, and Amit Brar. All errors and omissions remain our responsibility.

Table 3 Active MFIs in case study provinces(Source: MISFA)

Kabul	AFSG (Mercy Corps), AMFI (CHF), BRAC, FINCA, MoFAD (Care Afghanistan), OXUS (ACTED), PARWAZ, WWI
Balkh	ARMP, BRAC, FINCA, FMFB, OXUS (ACTED), SUNDUQ (MADERA), WWI, WOCCU
Bamiyan	AMFI (CHF), ARMP, BRAC
Herat	ARMP, BRAC, FINCA, MADRAC

and rural borrowers in more general terms while making every attempt to distinguish between MFI-originated loan types and procedures. Some of key differences in lending arrangements among the MFIs are reported later in this chapter.

Description of the Context: The Rural Financial Landscape

Using this data, as well as other literature, we look at the formal credit systems alongside existing local and traditional understandings of credit, assistance, repayment, and interest and notions of community/social responsibility. We examine formal and informal credit institutions that collectively structure microcredit transactions in rural Afghanistan. The spectrum of institutions examined include Government measures and organizations which organize or oversee microfinance, banks and other organizations that disburse microfinance, and the customs and norms that govern community behaviour in relation to credit from traditional sources as well as Islamic notions of money lending (Fig. 2).

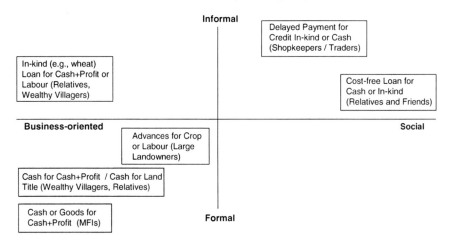

Fig. 2 Traditional rural financial landscape (Based on Klijn and Pain (2007))

To varying degrees, these traditional transactions can be formal and agreed upon in strict business terms or they could be highly informal and arranged based on kinship and/or social relations.

The introduction of MFIs fits into several of the Afghan Government's key priorities and commitments from the international donors. It is seen as a means for poverty reduction, fostering economic growth and productivity, and the formalization of legitimate economic activities and financial services. Microfinance programmes are bound up with the Government's commitment to gender mainstreaming through increasing the participation of women in economic life – many microfinance loans are targeted at women. According to I-ANDS (2005:44–45):

> The Afghan economy is dominated by the informal sector (as it is the case in many neighboring countries, such as India), running across all areas of production, but particularly the small holder economy.... Exchange of services and products between rural households is widespread, and women perform a major part of this work.

It remains open to debate whether attempts to formalize economic activity have been successful or indeed desirable, particularly given the fact that formalized borrowing through MFIs can lead to a strengthening of traditional forms of borrowing due to pressure on borrowers to make their repayment installments, forcing them to borrow from traditional sources.[8] Table 4 shows the World Bank's (2007) conceptualization of the range of traditional ("informal") economic transactions that make up the largest part the Afghan economy. The range of traditional transactions considered most nefarious isgrouped in the "illegal" category. The chart is highlighted here because it exemplifies the way legitimate or desirable economic activity and exchange can be perceived through the lenses of "formality" and "legality".

Table 4 is useful for categorizing the financial transactions that take place outside the formalized and registered sector. However, it does not fully capture the fact that these are social as well as financial transactions. Attempts through policy or other means to effect lasting change need to better resonate with these pre-existing conditions either by charting ways of working through social relations or by devising new institutional forms that compete with and, ultimately, replace certain traditional institutions deemed as detrimental to the emergence of a re-aligned, legitimate, accountable, transparent, and productive political economy as part of the larger agenda of post-conflict reconstruction.

Credit from traditional sources spans all of the categories in Table 4. Traditional loans may often take the form of in-kind transactions between households, placing them in the category of "in kind activities", but credit linked with the opium economy and the salaam system is also a well known form of traditional advance on a crop. Klijn and Pain (2007) point out that it is partly the informality of transactions in the opium economy that has led to a condemnatory attitude toward the traditional financial sector as a whole. This attitude is based on a lack of transparency in the hawala transaction system as well as the use of this system as a means for money laundering, largely from illicit activities centred around the opium economy. Nevertheless, a condemnatory attitude towards traditional means of transactions runs the risk of overlooking the need to work through and change the pre-existing institutional forms prevalent in rural economies and through which credit giving and borrowing have traditionally been conducted.

Understanding the interaction dynamics between introduced and traditional/preexisting institutions requires extensive and in-depth knowledge of these institu-

---

[8]See, in particular, Klijn and Pain (2007). This point was also brought up by interviewees in a number of cases during fieldwork in the Kabul, Balkh, Bamiyan, and Herat provinces.

Table 4 Range of Informal Activities as defined by the World Bank (Source: World Bank (2005a, b))

"In-kind" activities	More or less legal. Examples: Subsistence agricultural output; sharecropping; services such as blacksmith, carpenter, thresher; non-monetized exchange of goods and services between households
"Extra-legal" activities	Output and production with potential for formalization. Small scale transactions often involving casual labour. Examples: Money exchange dealers; small shops and traders; small manufacturing; agricultural production; construction; registered NGOs that are actually for-profit entities; economic activities of Kuchis
"Irregular" activities	Further away from legality. Production and transactions that break aspects of Afghan law. Examples: trade in illegally exploited resources, such as illegally harvested timber or illegally mined emeralds; illegal use of gravels and construction materials; smuggling; re-export of Pakistani imports back into Pakistan
"Illegal" activities	Output that is outright illegal. Examples: opium; bribe taking by officials; people trafficking; prostitution; forced labour; excavation and theft of archaeological artefacts; arms trafficking; land seizures. Activities encompass "war economy" (financing war and insurgency) and "black economy" (run for profit)

tions. In the case of credit, particular attention needs to be paid to social network arrangements and traditional values that govern borrowing. These aspects can be captured reasonably well through mapping the institutional landscape as illustrated later in this chapter.

Our focal organization in this study,i.e., MFIs, are the operational arms of the MISFA set up in 2003 to build a system to provide flexible, timely, and affordable finance to the poor as a means to alleviate poverty throughout Afghanistan. Table 5 is a list of MFIs active in Afghanistan as well as the number of clients per MFI and the value of loans. Information is not available for a provincial breakdown of MFI loan portfolios and the number of borrowers.

Table 5 Microfinance institutions in Afghanistan (Source: http://www.mixmarket.org/en/demand/demand.quick.search.asp. Accessed 30 Dec 2007)

Name	Gross loan portfolio (US$)	No. of active borrowers
AFS	925,905	6,217
AMFI	1,178,618	3,362
ARMP	16,889,524	30,346
BRAC – AFG	20,780,335	138,625
CFA	1,743,375	10,430
FINCA – AFG	6,192,768	27,570
FMFB – AFG	17,609,421	16,955
Hope for Life	Unknown	Unknown
MADRAC	1,195,027	8,249
MoFAD	966,520	4,499
OXUS – AFG	805,522	5,621
PARWAS	734,834	7,138
SUNDUQ	724,417	3,660
WOCCU – AFG	844,609	1,869
WWI – AFG	1,266,941	10,773

Analysis

Traditional lending is by far the most common way of acquiring credit for rural Afghan borrowers. Many of these forms of credit are given in kind. The national risk and vulnerability assessment (NRVA 2005), which surveyed over 30,000 households, found that traditional (informal) credit was an important source of income, allowing households to cope with unforeseen circumstances or opportunities. Thirty-eight percent of all households interviewed reported having taken a loan from traditional sources in the year prior to the survey. Moreover, the assessment found that informal loans were more commonly taken on by rural (42%) than by urban (25%) households, concluding that "these figures are indicators of a strong social network in rural areas in comparison to urban areas" (NRVA 2005:40).

The survey also asked households to report the use to which their largest informal loan had been put. The largest portion of loans was used for food purchases, indicating the role of credit in consumption smoothing and the possible impact of food insecurity on demand for credit. The impact of food security and agricultural productivity on demand for credit was further suggested by the fact that of rural areas, households in the Paktika province had the largest number of loans (96%) used for purchasing food, whereas the Kunduz province, which is an area of agricultural surpluses, showed the lowest occurrence of loans (27%) used for food purchases. In the urban areas, the use of loans to purchase food was less prevalent, and more households used their loans for business purposes.

MISFA was set up in 2003 at the invitation of the government of Afghanistan to pool diverse donor funding mechanisms and to convert funds into streamlined and flexible support to MFIs in Afghanistan.[9] MISFA serves as the means for the Ministry of Rural Rehabilitation and Development (MRRD) to build up the lower end of the financial sector through programmes to formalize at least a significant portion of microfinance, including microcredit, in rural Afghanistan. Specifically, MISFA was set up to

- Coordinate donor funding so that the conflicting donor priorities endemic in post-conflict situations do not end up duplicating effort and distorting markets
- Help young MFIs scale up rapidly, offering performance-based funding for operations and technical assistance
- Build systems for transparent reporting and instil a culture of accountability

In addition, MISFA's mandate is to provide technical support to MFIs and to monitor performance against the three main goals of scaling up as rapidly as possible to serve poor people throughout Afghanistan, especially women; to use public funding to invest in institutions (MFIs) that would become sustainable and able to grow further without requiring more subsidies; and to make a transition from international organizations with microfinance expertise to Afghan organizations with local expertise. MISFA receives its funds from the Canadian Government, the British

---

[9]This section is based on the official website for MISFA, available at: http://www.misfa.org.af.

Department for International Development (DFID), the Consultative Group to Assist the Poor (CGAP) of the World Bank, the Swedish International Development Cooperation Agency (SIDA), USAID, and the Dutch Oxfam N(o)vib.

As of September 2007, MFIs were active in 23 provinces (106 districts) and had active clients totalling 405,099. The number of women clients stood at 269,743 (70% of the total). A total of 882,103 loans had been disbursed for a cumulative value of $317,226,364. The outstanding loans total $94,572,179, distributed as follows:

- Trade and services ($56,876,378);household consumption – food, medical, house repair, education, etc. ($2,629,229);handicrafts and manufacturing ($12,848,158);agriculture ($7,846,699);livestock ($12,887,654);and other ($1,484,061).[10]

The performance of MFIs (and MISFA) has been evaluated as favourable by the World Bank, albeit inconclusively. It has to be noted that performance surveys to date have focused on the financial sustainability of MISFA and its MFIs and not the livelihood impacts of MFI-originated loans in rural Afghanistan.

The rationale for the Government of Afghanistan and its international donors to promote microcredit is based on an assessment of the post-2001 period as having "a huge unmet demand" for microfinance. In December 2001, according to MISFA,

> …the picture looked bleak with a non-functioning financial sector, a total absence of commercial players willing to serve the poor, and lack of delivery capacity among existing Microfinance Institutions (MFIs). [F]oreign donors were asked to step in. The issue facing everyone – foreign donors and Afghans alike – was how to meet that demand and energize the development of an entire microfinance sector that will serve the Afghan people beyond tomorrow.[11]

Previous research (Maimbo 2003, Hanifi 2004, Lyby 2006) suggests that the situation as described in the above quote from MISFA was not, and has not been, the case since 2001. Informal commercial financial services and credit have been operating in Afghanistan for hundreds of years. A study of cash, credit, debt and state–society relations in nineteenth century Afghanistan found that a number of social groups and financial institutions and instruments were associated with cash, credit and debt (Hanifi 2004). One of the informal financial services that has attracted most attention is the hawala system. The same historical study found that "In terms of credit, the key fiscal instruments were bills of exchange known in Afghanistan as hawalas…that circulated widely within and moved regularly through the country" (Hanifi 2004:200). A World Bank (Maimbo 2003:8–9) study of hawaladars in Kabul in 2003 notes that:

> Local money exchange dealers can be found in almost every community in Afghanistan. Traditionally, these dealers provide the community with numerous financial services in addition to funds transfers, for which they have attracted much attention. They also provide

---

[10]For more information see: http://www.misfa.org.af.

[11]From MISFA's website, available at: http://www.misfa.org.af/index.php?page_id=4. Accessed 6 Sep 2007.

deposit-taking facilities for those who want to save, microfinance for informal entrepreneurs, trade and finance for wholesalers and retailers; and currency exchange services for international business and personal transactions.

There has been an assumption that credit from traditional sources is more expensive than credit from MFIs. Derogatory phrases like "money lender" and "loan shark" have been used to describe some traditional lenders. But these terms do not explain the full range of credit services available to Afghans from traditional sources or the costs involved in borrowing on traditional terms. Reportedly, the interest rates charged for formalized microcredit loans are much lower compared to the rates offered by money-lenders. In Bangladesh, where Grameen Bank charges between 15 and 35% on the average loan, one author described these loans as "the only alternative for the poor to local moneylenders who regularly charge 10 times that amount" (Synovitz, RFERL, March 30 2007). However, there are no estimates provided by MISFA of the average cost of MISFA loans relative to the average cost of traditional credit in the regions where MISFA partners operate. This is a significant omission since some forms of traditional credit carry no interest or time limits on repayment (see Table 1).

It is often the case that hawaladars, and other sources of credit for business and trade purposes charge effectively more interest than MFIs. But, there are also indications that even in the case of hawaladars, this may not always be the case. Maimbo (2003) notes that the degree of competition in the market may have been bringing down charges for all hawala services, including loans. He also cites one hawaladar serving mostly large organisations claiming not to charge interest on loans at all, owing to "the Islamic prohibition against charging or receiving interest on loans and deposits" (Maimbo 2003:11). In any case, there is little evidence on the cost of lending in the informal commercial sector in Afghanistan. There is, however, evidence presented by Klijn and Pain (2007) on informal credit suggesting that rural households have access to loans from family, friends and community trust networks on better terms than microcredit loans or, in the case of qarz-e-hasana, with no charges at all.

Although microfinance continues to be discussed as a tool to fight poverty through acting as a mechanism to include the rural poor in mainstream economic activity, it is generally not targeted at the poorest groups. A World Bank study of microfinance and gender roles in Afghanistan in 2006 noted that loans were not reaching the "ultra poor". The report goes on to explain that fighting "abject poverty" is not the aim of microfinance worldwide, noting that the Consultative Group for Assistance to the Poor (CGAP) changed the last word in its name from "Poorest" to "Poor" in recognition of this fact (Lyby 2006:21). This is confirmed by Klijn and Pain (2007:51), who point out that whereas informal alms are accessible to the very poor, "both informal credit systems and formal micro credit will exclude the effectively destitute." Thus, while "the village moral economy clearly provides assistance to such people; micro credit does not address this group, nor does it aim to."

Primary data used in this research suggest that even the middle and higher income families targeted by microcredit are not necessarily drawing the intended benefits from these loans, with noted exceptions in Herat (see Klijn 2006).

Knowledge of MFIs' borrowing rules and eligibility criteria appears to be a factor in how effectively a borrower uses the money and assesses the ability to repay. A general lack of understanding of the rules by borrowers was noted during the interviews. The Bamiyan case indicates that a significant portion of the borrowers and potential borrowers are unclear about the rules on borrowing. In part, this is due to variation in the form of guarantee required to secure MFI loans as each MFI operating in Bamiyan has its own set of rules based on loan size.

MFIs in Afghanistan, as in other countries worldwide, often concentrate on loans to women as a means to increase women's participation in economic activity beyond the household level:

> In the implementation of micro-credit schemes, the Government will continue to pay particular attention to women, aiming to expand the number of female beneficiaries relative to men and encourage mechanisms for group savings. (I-ANDS 2005:94)

Some 70% of loans distributed in Afghanistan so far have been given to women. Women's loans are distributed in groups of women with the aim to enhance women's social mobility and participation in the economy. However, as we report later in this paper and as pointed out in other research, such aggregated statistics used outside their social and family contexts can exaggerate the positive impact of microcredit on women. Lyby (2006:1) states:

> ...Although most loans are given to women, the limitations faced by women with regard to gender roles in most regions ensures that the men continue to be actively involved when it comes to buying or selling goods in the market, even if the credit is received in the name of the woman. This has led to concerns as to whether the women merely serve as fronts or conduits of resources that effectively go to the men.

Lyby (2006) nuances this observation by suggesting that there may be, nevertheless, indirect benefits accruing to women from microfinance in terms of joining other women in borrowers' groups and training. Benefits to women may also be a by-product of a family's increased economic productive capacity facilitated through microcredit.

Lyby (2006:36) also reports that while men more commonly made the decision on how to spend the loans distributed to the women in their families, the number of women making this decision was significant. According to this report, a high number of women reported that the decision on how to spend the loan was discussed in the family. Women interviewed by Lyby (2006) reported improvements in their wellbeing and status in the family with one woman reporting that she felt more appreciated by the men in her home and was now consulted on financial matters, as a result of receiving microcredit.

Part of the rationale for introducing microcredit is that loan sizes can be larger and thus more likely to have an impact on economic productivity. A large number of borrowers in the Kabul, Herat, and Balkh provinces, however, complained that microcredit loans were too small to invest in significant productive assets, especially given the frequency of repayments. In Bamiyan it was reported that some MFIs offer larger loans with a longer grace period before repayment. Lyby (2006:35) also reports that: "[M]any men and women said the loans were too small to really make a difference, and additional money was frequently needed from other sources in order to start a project". Some interviewees reported that small-sized loans had a corrupting effect on powerful individuals who had become loan group leaders. Some of these leaders reportedly borrow from MFIs on behalf of the group but hoard the loan for their own personal use. These findings may indicate a failure of MFIs to effectively identify and respond to the needs of the different income groups they are intended to serve.

More generally, MFIs have not displayed significant changes to their programmes based on the feedback they have received from their clients or the limited research on microfinance in Afghanistan. There is incongruence between client needs and programme structures, evident in client behaviour of bypassing programme rules by borrowing through more than one borrowing book, as well as the seemingly high percentage of non-returnee clients, mostly due to the non-fulfilment of initial expectations from taking a loan or disqualification to borrow due to inability to repay previous MFI loans. Also, in the Bamiyan case it was reported that a number of borrowers get around borrowing rules by, for example, forming groups so that one individual secures access to a large loan. This illustrates the continued importance of social networking arrangements in credit transactions.

Research in the four provinces points to the need for a client-led approach to service delivery in credit provision. The only example that comes close to a client-led approach is the MFI in Bamiyan, which developed a lending system that follows the natural cash flow of the community, based on economically active summer and non-active winter months. Another example of systemic planning from the Bamiyan case is the MFI that offers larger loans and enjoys greater client satisfaction due to its transparent programme characteristics. It has to be noted, however, that the generally higher level of satisfaction with MFIs operating in Bamiyan is likely accentuated by a less severe environment of risk.

The key observation in the Bamiyan and other cases is that MFIs in general have not yet taken steps to monitor and evaluate the impact of their products, which must precede steps taken towards an adaptation of programmes to local context. Indeed, a focus note published by CGAP[12] emphasizes the importance of social performance indicators to measure microfinance success. The conceptualization of the idea is still in its infancy and actual changes in the day-to-day operation of MFIs may be a while in coming.

One of the main claims in promoting MFIs in rural economies is to lessen the negative livelihood impact of high interest (monetary or in kind) charged on credit from traditional sources. While this is certainly true in some cases, and compounded by ecological factors such as droughts, a challenge faced by MFIs is the public perception that the sudh (interest) payable on loans is viewed as haram (sinful) in the Koran, even if the sudh is lower compared to the interest paid on loans from

---

[12]The Focus Note is titled "Beyond Good Intentions: Measuring the Social Performance of Micro Finance Insitutions" and can be accessed in the World Wide Web at http://www.cgap.org/portal/binary/com.epicentric.contentmanagement.servlet.ContentDeliveryServlet/Documents/FocusNote_41.pdf.

traditional sources. A meeting with a Mullah in Bamiyan confirmed the sinful perception of MFI loans, with the Mullah declaring that any loan over a fixed period with an interest charge was sudh and therefore disallowed by the Koran. Similar instances were reported in Herat. During the field visit for this research in Herat, an MFI was said to have had to withdraw entirely from one village after the local Mullah posted the following message around the village condemning sudh charged on loans dispersed by MFIs as haram:

> We, the ulema and elders, declare that MFI loans are haram because of sudh. We request that people refrain from taking out MFI loans. Those who already have loans are asked not to take out further loans. (Sign posted in the Pashtun Zargun District, a similar sign was sighted in the Guzara District)

This announcement was said to have been made after borrowers had reported difficulty in making their MFI loan instalments, some having resorted to selling assets to make payments.

There are a variety of possible interpretations of what constitutes sudh according to Koranic law, and therefore what kind of credit is forbidden, and what kinds permitted. This often depends on the interpretation by individual Mullahs, rather than a locally specific feature: some Mullahs view interest on loans as haram, while others are more tolerant of it. There is, at the same time, evidence to suggest that some MFIs have made significant attempts to come to terms with the negative public perception of MFI-originated loans. In the face of opposition from Mullahs, for example, some MFIs operating in Bamiyan and Balkh have obtained fatwas from Islamic scholars declaring their operations as being consistent with Islamic law. Also, in recognition of religious prohibitions of charging interest, some MFIs provide murhaba style loans whereby the MFI buys products for its clients but adds a prearranged mark-up based on the accumulated interest that would have been accrued for the duration of the loan. In the case of other MFIs, however, many non-borrowing respondents identified the issue of sudh as the determinant for their decision not to take interest-bearing loans.

MFIs frequently rely on traditional mechanisms to launch a new operation in new villages. Many loan officers reported organizing introductory meetings in local mosques to spread awareness of the MFI being introduced in their communities. Local authority figures such as the maliks and village elders have also been noted to facilitate the establishment of MFIs. These processes can sometimes affect the flow of information to women, who are not involved in these initial meetings but who are deemed as a main group of target clients by the MFIs.

Institutional and Organizational Mapping

Definitions of formality and informality, such as those described in Table 4, do not fully capture the full range of institutions through which the giving and receiving of credit is governed, since these transactions are structured by individual as well as collective mental models and rules. Many of the institutions with which MFIs interact are not informal at all, such as the functions of Islamic leaders and maliks, or the hawaladars,

for example. However, MFIs still have to contend with deeply rooted understandings of
the way things are done through these traditional formal structures.

Informal / Social	Institution Type	Examples
	Behavioural: Standardized (recognizable) social habits – manifest in deeply ingrained behaviour of individuals and groups as reflections of social norms	Understandings and internalization of "how things are done" based on cultural (including religious) values such as the notions of halal (permissible) and haram (impermissible)
	Cognitive: Mental models / constructs or definitions, based on values and embedded in culture – (to be) aspired to by individuals and groups	Islamic notions of charity and community responsibility such as ashor (khoms in Shiaism) and zakat, both requiring that a portion of earned and accumulated wealth be given up to support the poor
	Associative: Mechanisms facilitating prescribed or privileged interaction among different private and public interests – manifest in activities of groups of individuals	Community and familial trust networks that facilitate interactions and transactions
	Regulative: Prescriptions and proscriptions setting the bounds of social relations – manifest as the immediate boundaries of action by individuals and groups	Formal regulative environment such as legislation and judicial capacity that facilitate interactions and transactions; rules and arbitration mechanisms laid out and conducted by elders, maliks or shuras to regulate transactions and interactions
Formal / Societal	Constitutive: Prescriptions and proscriptions setting the bounds of social relations – manifest as the ultimate boundaries of action by individuals and groups	Formal microfinance organisations and banks – formal and inflexible understandings of repayment schedules and interest; human / civil rights of individuals governed at the most fundamental level in the land

Fig. 3 Typology of credit institutions (Adapted from Parto (2008))

Figure 3 offers a more nuanced typology of the relevant institutions affecting
and being affected by credit transactions. This perspective on institutions is used to
identify (Fig. 4) and map (Fig. 5) a fuller range of institutions that collectively
govern credit transactions as follows.

Institutions of Microcredit

Two main sources of credit were identified: introduced microcredit system through
MFIs, and traditional forms of lending, grouped together under traditional microcredit system (Fig. 4). Secondary data and field research data gathered through
interviews and focus group meetings were used to identify the plethora of institutions that collectively govern microcredit transactions.

MFI-originated credit (on the left) and credit from traditional sources (on the
right) are characterized according to the typology presented in Figs. 1 and 3. Using

Hayden's SFM method the role(s) of each institution in relation to other institutions is mapped (Fig. 5) based on three simple criteria of Strong (3), Moderate (2), or Weak (1) relation (see Table B.1, Appendix B).

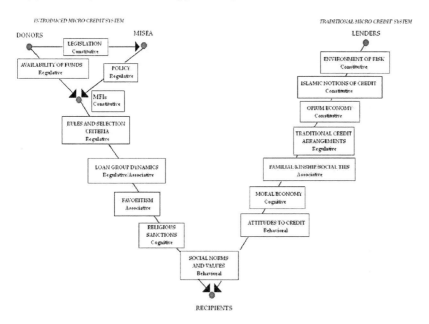

Fig. 4 Institutions governing microcredit transactions

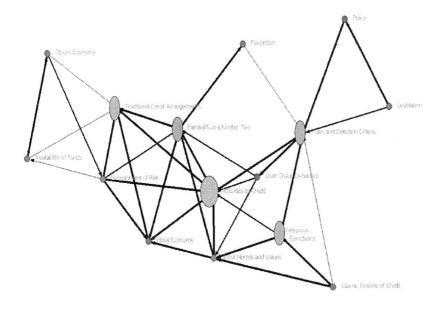

Fig. 5 Institutions of microcredit

The main purpose of the map in Fig.5 is to highlight the institutions most instrumental in credit transactions from introduced (MFIs) and traditional sources. Fifteen institutions were identified and used to generate this map (Appendix C). The blank cells in Table B.1 (Appendix B) indicate no relation between the listed institutions. The descriptions of the institutions used to generate Fig. 5 and the assumptions underlying the numerical values given to a given relationship with other institutions are explained in Appendix C.

Based on the mapping of institutions in Fig. 4, we can make the following observations:

- The behavioural institution "Attitudes to Credit" (Fig. 5) is manifest as a set of recognizable social habits based on deeply ingrained values. Attitudes to Credit occupies a central place in the institutional landscape of credit transactions. This suggests taking root in rural communities by MFIs depends very much on how they come to terms with, or overcome, the instrumental role played by Attitudes to Credit in structuring the relationship between lenders and borrowers. Deeply embedded social norms and values are at best very difficult to change. Change may be possible through introduction of systemic incentives over a long period of time, possible generations.
- The cognitive institutions "Religious Sanctions" and "Moral Economy" prescribe in ideal terms "doing the right thing" in lending and borrowing based on long-held traditions. Change in or replacement of these institutions is possible through the introduction (with incentives) of new ways of doing things. Educational and public awareness programmes and campaigns can be used to promote new mental models on how things ought to be and what new ways of doing things could be aspired for. Establishing new mental models takes a long time and can conceivably happen within one generation. It may take generations for a new mental model to become a shared mental model and ultimately a behavioural institution.
- The associative institutions "Favouritism", "Familial/Kinship/Social Ties", and "Loan Group Dynamics" are products of instrumentalism by the actors involved to facilitate prescribed or privileged interactions and pursue common interests. Because these associations are interest-based and instrumental, it is possible to introduce incentives and disincentives to constrain or enable the actors involved. Change can be effected relatively easily to discourage favouritism and redefine loan group dynamics. Changes in familial/kinship/social ties are more difficult to establish.
- The regulative institutions "Rules and Selection Criteria", "Policy", and "Availability of Funds" are prescriptions and proscriptions setting the immediate boundaries in societal relations and are enforced through public sanctions. In microcredit transactions, these institutions are all newly introduced. Changes in these institutions are relatively easy and can happen almost immediately. The regulative institutions, "Loan Group Dynamics" and "Traditional Credit Arrangements" are products of behavioural and cognitive institutions and, as such, are more difficult to change. Change would require the introduction of systemic incentives and disincentives.

- The constitutive institutions "MFIs" and "Legislation" are prescriptions and proscriptions setting the ultimate bounds of societal relations in microcredit. They are promoted and enforced through political structures and measures, ecology, geography, and place-specific mental models. Change in any of these institutions is relatively easy. In contrast, "Opium Economy", "Islamic Notions of Credit", and "Environment of Risk" are generations-old fundamental structuring phenomena, established by ecology, religion, and conflict. Change in these latter constitutive institutions is highly dependent on changed material and physical conditions and likely to take generations.

Changing the properties of the network mapped out in Fig.5 requires change in the main nodes such as "Attitudes to Credit", "Opium Economy", "Islamic Notions of Credit", and "Environment of Risk". But, these institutions are arguably the hardest to change, mainly because change would require a long time, a lot of resources, and long-term commitment by those wishing to effect change, i.e., the Government and its international donors. The introduction of a modern banking sector in opposition to the traditional arrangements can violate traditional norms and values, causing tensions with powerful traditional actors such as Mullahs or opium smugglers. To overcome these tensions, innovative ways of engaging powerful traditional actors need to be devised based on an appreciation of and respect for context-specific values, norms, and local conditions. This is particularly the case with illegal poppy growing as an established and ecologically sustainable economic institution. Despite the strong international stance against poppy growing in Afghanistan, the elimination of the opium economy may simply not be an option, at least in the short term.[13] Some have suggested at least part-legitimization of poppy growing as a means to control it and a source of income for reconstruction efforts (Senlis Council 2007).

Understanding institutions of microcredit as outlined in this section also suggests that access to finance by rural Afghans is not "the solution" to rural poverty. Microfinance needs to be viewed as one of many factors including access to basic services such as health and education or adequate infrastructure, which are necessary to create an enabling environment for the rural communities to help themselves. The main policy lesson here is to appreciate institutional complexity and have low expectations in setting policy objectives, while persisting over the long term and work with and through traditional institutions that govern credit lending and borrowing.

Organizations of Microcredit

There are some variations among the organizational entities (MFIs) involved in microfinance transactions in the four provinces. At a formal level, the legislation and the rules that MFIs operate under are standardized and prescribed by MISFA.

---

[13]It is worth noting that in Fig. 5, "Opium Economy" is off to one side as not being a key institution in microfinance. This is because the transaction sizes are far larger in opium dealings than transactions in microfinance. Figure 5 suggests that, at least initially, Opium Economy is a marginal though potentially important institution in lending and borrowing.

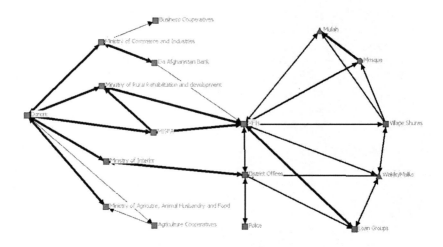

Fig. 6 Organizations of microcredit

In practice, however, how the rules are enforced by individual MFIs and how the borrowers respond to these rules vary and depend on the MFI, MFI personnel, and the operating environment.

The following map (Fig. 6) displays the relationship between the organizational entities dealing with microfinance in the four provinces. One key difference among the provinces is the make-up of the MFIs active in each province (see Table 3).

The map in Fig. 6 ilustrates the linkages between MFIs and other local and extra-local organizations and individual actors. The thickness of the linkages is based on four parameters: existence of relations (0 or 1), information exchange (0 or 1), influence (0 or 1), and resources (0 or 1) among the organizations that have a bearing on microcredit transactions (see Table B.2, Appendix B). What the map cannot show is the net impact of influence and information. To illustrate, MFIs routinely make contact with the local shuras, mullahs, district offices, and so forth before starting operation in a new location. There is a connection, a flow of information, and perhaps some influence from a given MFI toward other organizations and actors as far as making a convincing case to start operations. But, as was the case in Herat, if a mullah announces that taking MFI loans is against Islamic values, the mullah's influence on the affected MFI cannot be captured by this map. If there is a clash of influences from the mullah and the MFI, it is impossible to determine who benefits from the net impact.

That said, Fig. 6 adequately captures the lack of co-ordination, or indeed any connection between different organizational entities, e.g., different government ministries, that could potentially and positively affect service delivery in the microfinance sector. The Ministry of Agriculture, Animal Husbandry, and Food and the Ministry of Commerce and Industries are the two most prominent ministries that should be important government organizations in the operation of MFIs. Since agriculture is the mainstay of the majority of the population that access formal credit, some coordination between these ministries would be desirable. Similarly, the Ministry of Commerce and Industries, and organizations operating under it for the promotion of business activities, such as the Afghan International Chamber of Commerce (AICC), among others, do not have any form of organizational coordination with MISFA, or any of the individual MFIs operating in the same area. Despite having offices in all of the four provinces studied, the AICC did not appear to have any contact with the MFIs operating in the area.

At the time of writing, the governance of MFIs is solely under the Ministry of Rural Rehabilitation and Development (MRRD). The rules and regulations that govern MFIs are a nebulous mix of laws that apply to NGOs as well as commercial enterprises. Currently, the monitoring and evaluation of different MFIs is done via independent monitors and consultants. As commercial enterprises, the governance of MFIs should adequately fall under the Ministry of Commerce and Industries. Da Afghanistan Bank, the central bank of the state and a key implementing partner of the Ministry of Commerce and Industries, is said to be poised to take over the governance of MFIs. However, these steps had not materialized in 2007 when the research for this chapter was underway. MISFA remains the premier governing body under MRRD for the operation of microfinance in Afghanistan.

The lack of coordination among line ministries is not limited to microfinance. Numerous studies on post-2001 Afghanistan have underlined a general lack of coordination among line ministries as a major impediment to reconstruction efforts.[14] The existence of MISFA as an apex organization and as one that has continual interactions with the ministries and the international donors can and should be used as a platform to effect more cohesion among the ministries. This would require instituting formalized lines of reporting and accountability between MISFA and the ministries.

At a lower level of analysis, the activities of individual MFIs are also largely uncoordinated. The MFIs operating in the different provinces did not appear to be related to each other in any way. Numerous borrowers claimed that while being approved for a loan, they were asked if they had taken a loan from any other MFI, but were unaware of any follow-up or corroboration of their claims. Many households interviewed in field visits stated that they were able to access loans from more than one MFI operating in their area. This leads to the conclusion that MFIs not only enter a market populated by traditional credit products as just another provider, but are also in competition with one another. This lack of coordination among MFIs is by design, however, and a product of MISFA's desire to promote open competition among MFIs so as to maximize choice in the range of credit products available to potential clients. The resultant duplication of services, however, does not necessarily result in better service delivery or an adaptive business model that takes clients' needs into account. Loans from one or more MFIs may be the last resort for a con-

---

[14]See, for example, Lister (2005, 2006), The World Bank (2005a, b), and Asia Foundation (2007).

strained borrower unable to borrow from other sources. Arguments for increasing consumer choice as the way forward must take into account the factors that constrain choice making for the more desperate borrowers.

Discussion

In Afghanistan MFIs entered communities with the assumption that there is sizable unmet demand for microfinance. The analysis of the information from secondary sources and from the field visits undertaken for this research suggests that MFIs entered an already sizable credit market as just another product. The establishment and sustainability of MFIs depends squarely on how MFIs as new challengers manage to find their niche and fit in with the key institutions that govern transactions in a pre-existing market dominated by traditional credit providers. To illustrate, reducing the influence of traditional credit sources as a means to capture a part of the market for microfinance requires introducing incentives to make MFI loans and other financial schemes more competitive and attractive to the prospective borrowers. In the longer term, institutionalization of MFIs is contingent on how effectively long-established social norms and values are changed in favour of borrowing from microfinance organizations. This is not a task to be left only to MFIs, but a challenge for reconstruction programmes to provide other necessary elements, such as improved infrastructure and addressing the many-faceted water and land issues, conducive to increased economic activity.

Unchecked, microcredit from MFIs can become parasitic in combination with credit from traditional sources, with traditional credit being used to pay off MFI loans. There is also evidence to suggest that the reverse, with MFI loans being used to pay off loans from traditional sources, also takes place. Similar examples have been found in studies of microcredit loans provided in Bangladesh (Klijn and Pain 2007). Inter-reliance between microfinance from MFIs as a formal process and traditional systems also extends to the grass roots implementation of microfinance loans. Traditional community relations and trust networks are sometimes used to bend the rules in the implementation of microcredit, for example. Loan officers are sometimes from the same communities as borrowers, and are therefore part of the same community trust networks as the borrowers themselves. Working through these relations, some borrowers are able to take out more than one loan, or higher amounts and, through this process, reinforce the inequities evident in traditional power relations centred on gender, tribal connections, and wealth. Several loan officers interviewed in the four provinces reported that, based on trust and favouritism, they sometimes give borrowers more time to repay because of difficulties to meet repayment obligations.

Evaluations of the performance of microcredit loans appear to be preoccupied with the criteria of repayment. A recent publication (World Bank 2007) makes reference to a 95% loan repayment rate, the fact that the microfinance sector as a whole is already covering 89% of its costs from its own income earned from lending activities, and that some of the MFIs have already reached operational self-sufficiency, suggesting that it is expected that most of the other MFIs will achieve financial sustainability by the end of 2008. Clearly, the financial sustainability of MFIs operating under MISFA is prioritized over measuring the sustainability of loans in terms of income-generating gains to the borrowers. This preoccupation with repayment, coming from the highest donor and policymaking levels, is reflected in implementation by MFI staff in rural Afghanistan. All loan officers interviewed appeared to be under pressure to secure repayment, with reports in two locations that one MFI was docking loan officers' wages when clients failed to repay.

Unless microfinance leaves households with more productive assets than they had before the loan, it is difficult to conclude that there has been an overall positive impact on rural livelihoods, despite instances of microfinance being productively used in some cases such as Herat. Due to acute poverty in many rural areas, compounded by external factors such as droughts and persistent civil and military strife, households often spend microcredit loans on consumption-smoothing needs. In Herat, one borrower reported that she had taken out a microfinance loan to help pay for her son to get married, a story that was echoed in research from other provinces. Some borrowers spend all of their loans on consumption, while others divert portions of the loan for this purpose. If widespread, consumption smoothing based on credit from traditional sources and MFIs results in leaving the borrowers worse off than before. Desperate borrowers would borrow from anyone willing to lend, regardless of their future ability to repay. Those in debt and under pressure to repay may be forced to liquidate livestock and other assets or marry off, in some cases, their daughters to annul their debts, an outcome diametrically countered to the rationale of institutionalizing MFI credit as a means for increased income generating capacity and livelihood betterment. To be sure, MFI-originated loans alone cannot be expected to work around the pre-existing institutions that govern credit transactions in rural Afghanistan.

Microfinance is often presented as a way of fighting poverty, but it is not aimed at the very poorest groups, since ability to repay and to successfully invest in productive assets are often beyond the reach of the very poorest. An implicit argument for microfinance programmes including microcredit is that if they succeed in improving local economies as a whole, there are likely to be benefits for the poor through the trickle down effect. This research found, however, that it is possible that the strength of the local economy might have a decisive effect on the success of microfinance loans, rather than the other way around. Microfinance may be more successful in areas with a healthy existing market for a given crop or commodity, such as among potato farmers in Bamiyan, than in communities with a poorly functioning local economy. This suggests that, for microfinance schemes and programmes to take root locally with tangible net benefits for the borrowers and the local economy in the longer term, pre-existing economic conditions would need to be better than poor and destitute – a relatively productive local economy is less conducive to consumption-smoothing practices.

Credit and assistance from traditional sources, on the other hand, have been noted to have a positive impact on the livelihoods of the very poorest households in the community. The traditional sources of credit and assistance networks that support the poorest Afghan households are important features of the resilient livelihood strategies adopted by the Afghan poor under extreme conditions. Conclusive and comparable evidence does not yet exist to suggest an overall positive impact of microcredit on borrowers or the wider village economy. There is insufficient evidence to conclude that MFI-originated microfinance has resulted in making the rural poor, as a target group, more enterprising and economically more productive. This points to a need for more studies, spanning a longer period of time and covering larger samples of the population, to more accurately establish the benefits accrued to the rural poor through availability of loans from MFIs and in conjunction with credit from traditional sources. A longitudinal study is likely to capture the dynamics of loan cycles, drop out rates by borrowers and lenders from the system, and changes in the credit system as an outcome of learning, which is crucial in institutionalization processes, by both lenders and borrowers.

Where loans are tied to the building, expansion, or enhancement of an enterprise, it is vital that this should be linked to training and identification of business needs and viable markets for the end products of the enterprise. In the long run, external factors such as the strength of the local economy, irrigation issues in the case of agricultural enterprises, droughts, transport and energy infrastructure, and access to markets play quite instrumental roles in the success or failure of an MFI as far as making a lasting impact on livelihoods. Unless MFIs meet their declared aim of improving sustainable income generation in conjunction with improvements in all other facets of Afghan rural political economy, there is a risk that MFI-originated loans might feed cycles of debt, instead of improving livelihoods in a sustainable fashion.

Future research and efforts to reform how MFI funds are disbursed will need to pay particular attention to the non-financial and longer term impact of credit provision and borrowing through MFIs. The design of microfinance organizations to prioritize repayment as a measure of success filters down to the loan officers and may be clouding a comprehensive view of exactly how far loans are helping livelihoods. The design of loans with very frequent and inflexible repayment schedules may also combine with small loans in initial cycles, making it hard for households to make a sufficient investment with their loan and make enough profit to both repay and end up with more assets than they started with.

Despite the many shortcomings in the introduction of microfinance in rural Afghanistan, it is too early to conclude that microfinance has been a failure. There have been, in Bamiyan and in some instances in Balkh and Herat, cases of increased participation of women in productive economic activity. There are also cases of livelihood improvements, more so in Bamiyan than in the other provinces. The introduction of microfinance in rural Afghanistan remains a work in progress. The future success or failure of this experiment depends on how well MISFA and its MFIs adapt to their operating environment by learning and how the many institutional gaps and obstacles highlighted in Figs. 4–6 are understood and overcome.

Conclusions

Microfinance from traditional sources in Afghanistan is subject to a complex set of institutional arrangements. Numerous forms of credit transactions are governed by generations-old traditional institutions. Interventions through the introduction of MFIs to change the pre-existing lending and borrowing patterns and arrangements are thus difficult to institute in the short term and likely to be subjected to suspicion and mistrust, particularly if a given MFI fails to effectively "resonate" with the pre-existing institutions that govern credit transactions. There is clearly a perception among policymakers that microfinance is working in Afghanistan, although studies of microfinance have drawn mixed conclusions.

Evidence suggests that even the middle and higher income families targeted by microfinance do not always benefit fully, due to the small sizes of loans, short grace periods, and frequent repayment cycles of some loans in the first cycles. Longer grace periods and larger loans offered by microfinance organizations in the later cycles of lending are likely to increase the potential for long-term livelihoods benefits for borrowers. While some innovation has taken place, notably the implementation of the murhaba-based loans, there is clearly much more room for similar initiatives to make formal borrowing more acceptable to the potential borrowers. Future initiatives should focus on such issues as affordability to borrow (through flexible and/or reduced interest), longer grace periods, longer term loans, and larger loans.

There appears to be a desire by the government and international donors to regulate and supervise the variety of people involved in hawala style activities including the hawaladars grocers, merchants, and a host of other individuals. If identifying, licensing, and regulating the well-established system of hawala transactions is difficult because of the number of actors and the complexity of their relationships, the task will be many folds more difficult, and perhaps not very useful, for the less common but equally complex traditional forms of transaction such as alms. This calls for increased attention to and innovativeness in the development of new lending and borrowing arrangements with a capacity to replace the less transparent and difficult-to-document traditional institutions. Policy innovation in this regard is possible only through engagement of the target population to continually define and re-define community needs. As Reich (1988) has eloquently put it, policymakers' responsibility is not only to discover "objectively" what they think people want and then to devise solutions, but to provide the public with alternative visions through engaging with them so as to broaden the range of potential responses being wanted.

Given the need for re-visioning and re-examination, the replacement and transformation of traditional institutions of credit with MFIs is at best a medium-term objective. As such, it would require on the part of MFIs competitiveness of lending terms, receptiveness to client needs, and, most importantly, increased trust by the borrowers in MFIs. These requirements would only emerge over time through further adaptation by MFIs to better fit with local conditions (including what the public wants) and through positive livelihood impacts felt by the borrowers of MFI loans.

Recommendations

Policy Recommendations

- The emphasis on the financial sustainability of MFIs must be supplemented with equal emphasis on assessments of the social sustainability of MFIs if the introduction of microfinance is to lead to measurable, documented improvements in rural livelihoods.
- A change of thinking at policymaking levels is necessary regarding the moral framework in which traditional microfinance transactions are discussed. The discussion of "informal credit" or "moneylending" in a pejorative leads to an implicit assumption that all traditional sources of credit should wither away along with increased regulation of financial transfers and increased reach of formal financial services through, for example, MFIs.
- Policy options that recognize, respect, and work with and through the more equitable pre-existing lending and borrowing arrangements need to be more closely investigated to reduce the tension between the introduced and traditional forms of lending and borrowing. A starting point in this process is to engage the relevant community actors such as mullahs prior to introducing MFI-originated loans in rural communities.
- Introducing records or paper trails for traditional financial transactions is perhaps overambitious. However, MFIs could be regulated to perform an additional function in monitoring the debt to traditional sources.
- Ultimately, there needs to be recognition that, alongside a conceptual shift away from the negative perception of the traditional sector as something that should be replaced by formalized structures, microfinance alone will not achieve the poverty reduction and economic growth aims that it is intended to help deliver. Microfinance will need to be regarded as one component of the strategy to improve local services, employment creation, infrastructure, and market function.

Operational Recommendations

- The pervasiveness of microcredit (and finance) from traditional sources should be taken into account when assessing the demand for MFI-originated loans so as to avoid duplication of services that are already available locally, and sometimes equitably, and to ensure that microcredit targets the households where it can make a difference.
- The engagement of mullahs and other influential community actors needs to be sought and sustained to avoid resistance to and backlashes against MFIs and their services.
- To take root and become institutionalized, MFIs have to successfully compete with the traditional terms of lending and borrowing. Interest rates or service charges have to remain lower than those in the traditional sector.

- The size of MFI loans and repayment arrangements (commencement of repayment of instalments and the lifecycle of the loan) need to be re-thought so as to minimize undue pressure on the borrowers and discourage decapitalization through selling assets or additional borrowing to meet strict repayment deadlines.
- MFIs should fully assess and monitor levels of existing indebtedness in communities where they plan to operate so as to minimize contributing to cycles of indebtedness prevalent in many of the poorer rural areas.
- MFIs should standardize their methods of recording and responding to non-payment, involving the creation of mechanisms for assessing reasons for non-payment and for protecting households who may be going through decapitalization as a result of repayment pressures.
- MFIs should adopt a standardized system of evaluating the livelihood impact of their loans so that a general picture can be built of the types of loans and repayment schedules most appropriate in different Afghan contexts.

Appendix A: The Microfinance Institutions of Afghanistan

AFSG: The Ariana Financial Services Group (AFSG) was established by Mercycorps in April 2003. AFSG uses the group lending methodology to provide credit to predominantly female clients in Kabul City who are active in a wide range of small businesses. The organization has also started an individual loan product targeted at repeat cycle clients (both males and females).

AMFI: CHF International's Afghanistan Microfinance Initiative (AMFI) offers credit and working capital to low-income households in Bamiyan and Ghazni provinces. The programme uses solidarity group method to offer credit to business owners.

ARMP: The Afghanistan Rural Microcredit Programme (ARMP) was set up in 2003 by the Aga Khan Foundation (AKF). The organization offers a variety of loan services to individuals to improve their business activities or remedy cash flow problems.

BRAC: Set up by BRAC (Bangladesh) in 2003, it is the leading MFI in Afghanistan. BRAC offers individual loans to business owners in both urban and rural areas of the country.

CFA: Child Fund Afghanistan (CFA) was started by the international NGO, Christian Children's Fund (CCF), and currently (2007) operates in three provinces. CFA follows a solidarity group lending methodology and has already financial sustainability.

FINCA: FINCA Afghanistan was set up in 2004 by the NGO, FINCA International. The organization has pioneered the development of shari'a law-compliant lending (murabaha) in Afghanistan. FINCA operates in the city and surrounding areas of Kabul, Jalalabad, Herat, and Mazar-e-Sharif.

FMFB-A: The First MicroFinance Bank – Afghanistan was established in 2003 to lend in order to "reduce poverty, diminish the vulnerability of poor populations. and alleviate economic and social exclusion." It has operations in seven provinces.

Hope for Life: Affiliated with HOPE International, it is a global, faith-based, non-profit organization focused on poverty alleviation through microenterprise development.

MADRAC: Established in June 2005 by the Danish NGO, DACAAR, it has the main goal of providing microfinance services to low-income households in rural areas of Afghanistan. MADRAC uses a solidarity group lending method for its operation with group sizes of 10–20 members. MADRAC works in the Herat, Ghazni, and Laghman provinces.

MoFAD: The Micro Finance Agency for Development (MoFAD) is a savings-based microfinance program established in Kabul by CARE Afghanistan. MoFAD uses CARE's well-known savings and credit group (SCG) methodology to set up groups of women who rotate their savings and borrow from the MFI.

OXUS: Part of the OXUS Development Network (ODN), a global network of MFIs affiliated to ACTED, the French international development NGO. OXUS Afghanistan is currently providing loans to solidarity groups of women and men for income-generating activities. The organization works in Kabul, Parwan, Balkh, and Faryab provinces.

PARWAZ: The first woman-led MFI for Afghans by Afghans in Afghanistan established in 2002 to provide microcredit to male and female households in Kabul and Ghazni, and the surrounding areas.

SUNDUQ: Setup by MADERA, a French NGO, in 2005. The organization uses the village banking methodology to provide credit to rural households. MFI operations are spread across the Eastern part of the country.

WWI: Women for Women International (WWI) started a microfinance program in 2004 in Afghanistan to offer financial services to the poor and socially excluded women in rural and urban areas.

WOCCU: The apex organization of the international credit union system. Only owner-members have access to the savings and loan services provided by each credit union. WOCCU has established two credit unions in Balkh and Jowzjan.

Appendix B: Datasets for Institutional and Organizational Maps in Figs. 5 and 6 (appendix B begins on the following page)

Table B.1 Matrix for Fig.5 based on the strength of relations among institutions (3=strong, 2=moderate, and 1=weak)

	Legislation	Availability of funds	Policy	Rules and selection criteria	Loan group dynamics	Favouritism	Religious sanctions	Social norms and values	Environment of risk	Opium economy	Traditional credit arrangements	Familial/social/kinship ties	Moral economy	Attitudes to credit	Islamic notions of credit
Legislation		3	2								1				
Availability of funds				2						2					
Policy				3	3										
Rules and selection criteria														3	
Loan group dynamics								2				2		2	
Favouritism				1											
Religious sanctions				3				3						2	
Social norms and values												3	3	3	
Environment of risk		1									3	2	3	3	
Opium economy		3							2		1				
Traditional credit arrangements												3		2	
Familial/social/kinship ties						3					3		3		
Moral economy											3				
Attitudes to credit											3	3	3		
Islamic notions of credit				1			3	3							

Table B.2 Matrix of relationships among organizations of microcredit (mapped in Fig. 6) based on existence of relations (0 or 1), influence (0 or 1), information exchange (0 or 1), and resources (0 or 1)

	Donors	MRRD	MOI	MOAAHF	MOCI	MISFA	MFIs	District-offices	Agriculture co-ops	Businessco-ops	Village shuras	Wakils/maliks	Mosque	Mullah	Police	Loan groups	Da Afghanistan Bank
Donors		1,1,1,1	1,1,1,1	1,1,1,1	1,1,1,1	1,1,0,1	1,1,1,1		1,0,0,0	1,0,0,0							
MRRD	1,1,0,0																
MOI	1,1,0,0							1,1,1,1									
MOAAHF	1,1,0,0																
MOCI	1,1,0,0																1,1,1,1
MISFA	1,1,1,1	1,1,1,1					1,1,1,1										
MFIs	1,1,0,0					1,1,1,1		1,0,0,0			1,1,0,0	1,1,0,0	1,1,0,0	1,1,0,0		1,1,1,1	
Districtoffices		1,1,0,0	1,1,0,0												1,0,1,0	0,1,0,0	
Agriculture co-ops				1,0,0,0													
Businessco-ops					1,0,0,0												
Village shuras												1,1,0,0					
Wakils/maliks								1,1,0,0			1,1,0,0		1,1,0,0	1,1,0,0		1,0,1,0	
Mosque														1,1,1,1			
Mullah													1,1,1,1				
Police								1,1,0,0									
Loan groups							1,0,0,1					1,1,0,0					
Da Afghanistan Bank							1,0,0,0									1,1,1,0	

Appendix C: Descriptions of and Assumptions About Institutions of Credit Transaction

Legislation

Legislation refers to laws that govern the transfer of money from the donors to MISFA. Legislation has a direct, strong effect on the policy of the MFIs. The laws regarding the distribution, use, availability, and intended effect of funds form the basis for the policies enacted by MISFA for the operation of MFIs. Legislation also has a moderate effect on the rules and selection criteria of MFIs. The laws determine the policies of MISFA, which in turn forms the basis for the rules, selection criteria, punitive measures and other operational parameters of MFIs. As such, legislation is a constitutive institution (according to the typology in Fig. 3) in the introduced system because it sets the ultimate boundaries of action for MISFA and, consequently, for MFIs and their clients.

Availability of Funds

Availability of Funds to MISFA from the donors for the operation of microfinance programmes will havea moderate effect on the opium economy if MFI loans replace finance available to borrowers from participation in the opium economy. However, Klijn and Pain (2007) demonstrate that traditional credit arrangements are weakly affected by the availability of funds from the formal sector. Moreover, there is some evidence of borrowers borrowing from traditional sources to pay off their formal loans. From a livelihood perspective, this points to a conflictive, detrimental relationship between traditional forms of borrowing and finance arrangements with MFIs.

The availability of funds from MFIs is a regulative institution (Fig. 3) in the introduced sector since it determines the immediate boundaries of action by MFIs.

Policy

Actions by MFIs are structured through policy as determined by MISFA. The rules and client selection criteria (see below) for the MFIs are a direct result of the policy of MISFA for the operational parameters of MFIs. Policy, therefore, is a regulative institution (Fig. 3) within the introduced sector.

Rules and Selection Criteria

The borrowing rules and selection criteria used by MFIs regulate credit transactions in the introduced credit sector by setting the immediate boundaries on who receives the loans and what punitive measures may be taken against non-payment. As such, the rules and the selection criteria have a direct, facilitative impact on the dynamics of a loan group (see below).

Rules and selection criteria also affect attitudes to credit strongly. Traditional attitudes to credit are based on negotiable and flexible repayment arrangements,whereasfinance from MFIs tends to be stricter. The observed behaviour of borrowing from traditional sources to pay back MFI-originated loans is arguably an outcome of this relationship between rules and selection criteria and the attitude to credit. Also, the interplay between the flexible traditional attitude to credit and the restrictive mode of behaviour imposed on the borrowers by MFIs can result in a conflictive relationship.

Loan Group Dynamics

The loan group is one of the principal forms through which MFI-originated loans are dispersed to individual borrowers. The loan group dynamics represents regulative as well as associative institutions in transactions involving MFIs. An individual's relationship with the loan group and the ability to pay determine the individual's eligibility for future loans. Loan groups simultaneously serve as a means for individuals to secure MFI loans and a mechanism to exert peer pressure on borrowers (to repay) and thus in shaping repayment behavioural patterns.

Loan group dynamics hasa moderate effect on deeply ingrained social norms and values manifest as standardized habits of groups and individuals in social situations. The presence of a loan group can result in a realignment of social values associated with credit repayment and also have moderate effects on social and kinship ties. The presence of a loan group whose options to access credit are determined partly by individual action also affects the attitude that the individual has towards credit repayment. Group loan dynamics can come into conflict with traditional social norms and values and attitudes to credit repayment. However, their longer term impact can be facilitative if group and individual-in-group attitudes toward credit are changed without undermining the traditional norms embedded in social, kinship, and familial ties.

Favouritism

Loan group officers can exercise favouritism toward certain borrowers. Being (largely) based on familial, kinship, and social ties, favouritism is an associative institution (Fig. 3) in traditional and introduced forms of borrowing. Evidence from interviews with borrowers in the four provinces suggests that the rules and selection criteria used by MFIs can be undermined by favouritism. A weak relationship is assumed between favouritism and MFI rules and selection criteria since rules and selection criteria are not always clear to the borrowers.

Religious Sanctions (by Mullahs)

Traditionally, mullahs are interpreters of Islamic notions concerning behaviour in the community, including individual economic behaviour. The perception of sudh as being sinful is a cognitive institution (Fig. 3) or a mental model promoted by mullahs and expected to be complied with by believers. Wealthier mullahs can also act as money lenders based on terms that could be benevolent or draconic, depending on the mullah and his scruples.

Since mullahs usually act as watchdogs in enforcing social norms and values, their influence on perceptions within the community about introduced forms of credit is likely to be significant. Some MFIs have responded to the instrumental role of mullahs by modifying their interest system based on consultation with or buy-in from the mullahs in some cases. A moderate effect from religious sanctions on borrowing behaviour is assumed because the power of mullahs concerning sudh is not conclusive to attitude change, as has been reported in this research and other literature. Depending on the role assumed by the mullah in a given context, the relationship between religious sanctions and the rules and selection criteria of MFIs can be conflictive or facilitative.

Social Norms and Values

Social norms and values are behavioural institutions (Fig. 3) manifest as deeply ingrained, standardized patterns of behaviour. To a large extent, but not exclusively, attitudes to credit are manifest as social norms and values which in turn structure familial, kinship, and social relations as well as forming a key component part of the moral economy (see below).

Environment of Risk

According to Klijn and Pain (2007), "environment of risk" is the institutional expression of inequality, inequitable class relations, exploitation, social exclusion, and unaccountable power within rural Afghan society. These features cause the poor to seek protection through relations of patronage with the powerful actors and reinforce the dependency of the poor on the powerful. This relationship has a strong effect in defining traditional credit arrangements. The environment of risk is a constitutive institution (Fig. 3) since it sets the ultimate boundaries of action by individuals entering traditional credit relations.

The environment of risk has a weak effect on the availability of funds from donors to MISFA and a strong effect on attitudes to credit. An element in consideration to provide funds is the perceived scale of success in terms of improved socio-economic and political security. Higher risk areas are less likely to receive microfinance, making the relationship between environment of risk and availability of funds conflictive.

Opium Economy

The opium economy has proven to be a resilient agricultural activity and by all accounts has been a constitutive institution (Fig. 3) in the Afghan rural landscape for a number of generations. The salaam system of advance payment is a widespread credit arrangement in the opium economy. The practice is far less evident in rural economic activity. A weak effect is assumed of the opium economy on traditional credit arrangements.

Availability of Funds from donors is highly dependent on the state of the opium economy in an area. A high level of opium production generally implies low availability of funds for the area. The opium economy, due to the security risk element attached with opium cultivation, acts as a facilitator to the environment of risk in rural Afghanistan. This effect is assumed as moderate because the environment of risk is a pervasive aspect of rural Afghanistan, regardless of the role of the opium economy.

Traditional Credit Arrangements

Traditional credit arrangements, such as Qarz-e-hasana and Qarz-e-Khudad (Fig. 1), usually arranged as advance loan on crops, play a regulative role (Fig. 3) in the flow of credit from lender to borrower. These arrangements have a strong influence on familial/kinship/social ties (see below) because they facilitate the creation and reinforcement of existing ties within the community. The form of credit arrangement often corresponds to the structure of social power relations.

Traditional credit arrangements have a moderate influence on attitudes to credit. Klijn and Pain (2007) note a confidence among borrowers about their ability to access credit and repay loans, attributing this to the flexibility and negotiability of traditional credit arrangements. The structures of these arrangements themselves contribute to the shaping of attitudes to credit.

Familial/social/kinship Ties

This associative institution (Fig. 3) facilitates the major interaction among the lenders and borrowers within the traditional system of credit. Familial, social and kinship ties have a strong and direct effect on favouritism. The stronger the ties, the higher the possibility of rule-bending by the lenders and the expectation of preferential treatment by the borrowers. Moreover, traditional credit arrangements are negotiated on the basis of these ties. The moral economy (described below) also operates on the basis of familial, kinship, and social ties.

The Moral Economy

The set of expectations and choices concerning credit relations, with the aspect of morality that legitimizes the parameters of these relations, form the basis of the moral economy as a cognitive institution (Fig. 3) in informal credit practices. Traditional credit arrangements are affected strongly by the moral economy. Klijn and Pain (2007) refer to leniency in many cases in repayment arrangements as a product of the moral economy. The moral economy is affected by the attitudes to credit and reinforces traditional credit arrangements.

Attitudes to Credit

Attitudes to credit (Klijn and Pain 2007), refers to high confidence among the potential borrowers in finding loans and in repaying them. This behavioural institution (Fig. 3) is a key feature in traditional credit arrangements, the moral economy,and the familial/kinship/social ties. Since rural individuals have been reported to have a high confidence in accessing as well as repaying loans, they enter into traditional credit arrangements more readily. They also utilize their familial and kinship ties frequently to access credit, thus reinforcing these ties.

Islamic Notions of Credit

Islamic notions of credit are both cognitive and constitutive institutions (Fig. 3), which at once guide actions of individuals and set the ultimate boundaries for socio-economic activity. Islamic notions of credit have a weak impact on the rules and selection criteria formulated by MFIs concerning microfinance. MFIs have changed their rules to better accommodate Islamic notions, but this has been the direct result of the actions of mullahs, who are the purveyors of the Islamic notions of credit.

References

Asia Foundation (2007) An assessment of sub-national governance in Afghanistan. Asia Foundation, Kabul, Afghanistan

Hanifi SM (2004) Impoverishing a colonial frontier: cash, credit and debt in nineteenth century Afghanistan. Iran Stud 37(2):199–218

Hayden FG (1982a) Project evaluation in a futures real time system. J Econ Issues 16(2):401–411

Hayden FG (1982b) Social fabric matrix: from perspective to analytical tool. J Econ Issues 16(3):637–661

Hayden FG (1982c) Organizing policy research through the social fabric matrix: a Boolean digraph approach. J Econ Issues 16(4):1013–1026

Hayden FG (1993) Institutionalist policymaking. In: Tool MR (ed) Institutional economics: theory, method, policy. Kluwer, Norwell, MA, pp 283–331

Hayden FG (1998). "Normative Analysis of Instituted Processes", in Fayazmanesh, S. and M.R. Tool (eds.) Institutionalist Theory and Applications: Essays in Honour of Paul Dale Bush (Cheltenham, UK: Edward Elgar Publishing Limited), pp. 89–107

Hodgson GM (1988) Economics and institutions: a manifesto for a modern institutional economics. Polity Press, Cambridge

I-ANDS (2005) The Interim Afghanistan National Development Strategy (I-ANDS). Government of the Islamic Republic of Afghanistan, Kabul

Klijn F (2006) Informal credit practices in rural Afghanistan, case study 1: Herat. AREU, Kabul

Klijn F, Pain A (2007) Finding the money: informal credit practices in rural Afghanistan. (Kabul, Afghanistan: AREU)

Lister S (2005) Caught in confusion: local governance structures in Afghanistan. AREU, Kabul

Lister S (2006) Moving forward? Assessing public administration reform in Afghanistan. AREU, Kabul

Lyby E (2006) Microfinance and gender roles in Afghanistan: a study report. The World Bank, Washington, DC

Maimbo SM (2003) The money exchange dealers of Kabul: a study of the hawala system in Afghanistan– the World Bank Finance and Private Sector Unit–South Asia Region. The World Bank, Washington, DC

NRVA (2005) National risk and vulnerability assessment. Government of the Islamic Republic of Afghanistan, Kabul. http://www.cso-af.net/nrva2005/docs/Final%20NRVA%202005%20 Report.pdf. Accessed 11 Dec 2007

Parto S (2005a) Economic activity and institutions: taking stock. J Econ Issues 39(1):21–52

Parto S (2005b) "Good" governance and policy analysis: what of institutions? MERIT/Infonomics Research Memorandum 2005-001

Parto S (2008) Innovation and economic activity: an institutional analysis of the role of clusters in industrializing economies. J Econ Issues 42(4):1005–1030

Parto S, Ciarli T, Arora S (2005) Economic growth, innovation systems, and institutional change: a trilogy in five parts. MERIT/Infonomics Research Memorandum 2005-021. Maastricht University, Maastricht, The Netherlands

Philo, Chris and Hester Parr (2000) Institutional geographies: introductory remarks. Geoforum 31(4): 513–521

Reich R (1988) The power of public ideas. Harvard University Press, Boston

Senlis Council (2007) Poppy for medicine. http://www.senliscouncil.net/documents/poppy_medicine_technical_dossier. Accessed 5 Dec 2008

Synovitz R (2007) Could Islamic banks do more to help the poor? http://www.rferl.org/featuresarticle/2007/03/73f320d2-d89a-477c 8130-04a3e29c45bb.html. Accessed 30 Mar 2007

Uphoff N, Buck L (2006) Strengthening rural local institution capabilities for sustainable livelihoods and equitable development. Paper for Social Development Department, World Bank. The World Bank, Washington, DC

Voeten J, Parto S (2006)How do institutions matter in institutional capacity development? – Observations from Vietnam, Yemen, and Uganda, funded by Nuffic NPT (Nederlandse organisatie voor internationale samenwerking in het hoger onderwijs)

World Bank (2005a) World Bank country study: Afghanistan– state building, sustaining growth, and reducing poverty. The World Bank, Washington, DC

World Bank (2005b) Afghanistan: managing public finances for development (Report No. 34582-AF), volume I: main report. The World Bank, Washington, DC

World Bank (2007) World Bank Afghanistan update report, July 2007. The World Bank, Washington, DC

Utilization of the Social Fabric Matrix to Articulate a State System of Financial Aid for Public Schools and to Derive Conceptual Conclusions

F. Gregory Hayden

Abstract Central government education formulas for the distribution of funds to local public schools have a long history in numerous countries, with special importance at the state level in the United States. Such formulas have been formulated to express an array of concerns to include equity, ability to pay, adequacy, need, willingness to pay taxes, geographical sparcity, tax burdens, the political power to acquire more money for an area, and so forth. The differentiation and elaboration of school-aid formulas have led to the evolution of greater formula complexity and the emergence of very different kinds of school finance systems in different states. The social fabric matrix is utilized to articulate the Nebraska State system used for the distribution of financial aid to kindergarten- through- grade- 12 public schools. This demonstrates how states can model their systems in order to observe the interconnections through algebraic formula terms in order to determine the consequences of planned changes. The findings of the analysis are also drawn upon for conceptual conclusions about school-aid policy, rules, and systems.

Introduction

Central government education formulas for the distribution of funds to local public schools have a long history in numerous countries, with special importance at the state level in the United States. Such formulas have been formulated to address an array of concerns to include equity, ability to pay, adequacy, need, willingness to pay taxes, geographical sparcity, tax burdens, the political power to acquire more money for an area, and so forth (see Musgrave 1961; Morgan and Hayden 1970; King et al. 2003).

Consistent with the principles of open systems, the differentiation and elaboration of school-aid formula terms have led to the evolution of greater formula complexity and the emergence of very different kinds of school finance systems in

F.G. Hayden
Department of Economics, University of Nebraska-Lincoln, Lincoln, NE, USA

T. Natarajan et al. (eds.), *Institutional Analysis and Praxis*,
DOI 10.1007/978-0-387-88741-8_10, © Springer Science+Business Media, LLC 2009

different governmental units. This chapter utilizes a social fabric matrix (SFM) (see Hayden 2006, 73–108) to articulate the Nebraska state system used for the distribution of financial aid to kindergarten- through- grade- 12 (K-12) public schools. This demonstrates how states can model their systems with the SFM in order to observe the interconnections of various formula terms and to determine the consequences of planned changes. The findings of the analysis are drawn upon for conceptual conclusions.

The SFM context contains the matrix, digraph, and cell definitions. The cell definitions generate a continuous 600-page algebraic formula for each school district that is used to determine the amount of money that is distributed by the state to each school district. An integrated mathematical formula of the system's rules has not existed prior to this project. The formula is the articulation of the rules, regulations, and requirements as expressed in state law and by operational routines established in government departments. The matrix, digraph, and complete formula are available at the interactive SFM website http://cba.unl/academics/economics/sfm/. To demonstrate the utilization of the SFM, only part of the system will be explained here.

Social Fabric Matrix, Digraph, and Cells

Social Fabric Matrix

The 40×40 SFM is found in Fig. 1. The rows and columns are social belief criteria, authority institutions, and processing institutions (see Hayden 1998). The authority institutions deliver rules such as the legislative laws and court decisions to other authority institutions and to processing institutions; the rules are used to specify regulations and requirements for calculating associated formula terms; and processing institutions deliver calculations to other institutions for making other calculations that finally determine the amount of money to be sent to each local school district.

Social Fabric Matrix Digraph

A display of the information in the SFM is its digraph presented in Fig. 2. Each oval in Fig. 2 is a SFM component that is numbered with its respective row and column number in Fig. 1, and the directed edges between components in Fig. 2 represent the cells in Fig. 1 that indicate the delivery from the row components to the column components.

Components 1 through 6 appear from top to bottom on the left of Fig. 2. They are the normative social beliefs that have been explained, discussed, and debated on a regular basis in state legislative bodies and in state and federal courts. The deliberative process helps refine their meaning. The beliefs are delivered to components 7 and 8, which are the courts, legislature, and Office of the Governor. These authority institutions utilize the beliefs to make and deliver rules that are delivered to other authority institutions, represented as components 9 through 13.[1] Through that process, the meaning of the social beliefs becomes specified through the working of the institutional process that determines the allocation of school aid.

The Nebraska Department of Education (NDE) is the authority institution of greatest interest here because the legislative laws and court decisions give it the main authority for formulating the regulations from the rules. Additionally, NDE has the responsibility for specifying the requirements to be used by agents in various departmental groups for making the calculations of the state educational finance system, which is termed the Tax Equity and Educational Opportunities Support Act (TEEOSA) (Nebraska Department of Education 2007). TEEOSA calculations are guided by the deliveries of regulations and requirements, indicated by the edge coming from NDE to components 14 through 40 in Figs. 1 and 2. NDE directs its divisions and the niches within its divisions to fulfill regulations and requirements through coordination with other divisions and niches within its own department and with divisions and niches in other departments. The directed edges from NDE to components 14 through 40 inform those components about what data to use, from where to acquire the data, what calculations to make, and to which groups to deliver the calculations after they are completed. Components 14 through 40 are different working groups within departments and across departments that make different calculations for different parts of TEEOSA by coordinating workers, data, and computers across different institutional organizations. Formula terms require the institutional organizations to coordinate work and data from local, state, and federal government departments. Components 14 through 40 are given the names that correspond to the TEEOSA rules that designate the components' processes.

Social Fabric Cell Descriptions Through Algebraic Terms

An abridged 138-page version of the 600-page algebraic formula mentioned above is presented in the SFM website. It is an expression of the SFM cells which indicates the quantity, temporal dimensions, and spacial location of deliveries. For the purpose here, only the formula parts numbered (1) through (49), as found in Table 1, are

---

[1]Rules are delivered by institutional organizations, so, if possible, it is best to include the institutional organizations as the delivering and receiving components in the rows and columns of the SFM (as in Fig. 1) with the rules in the cells. This clarifies the row institutions that are responsible for the delivery of the rules and the column institutions with a 1 in the cells across the delivery row that help institute the rules. It is possible to list only the rules in the delivery rows of the SFM, but this does not explicitly indicate the source of rules, thus making it appear that rules stand alone. This is the way new institutional economists might use the SFM, or anyone who wants to emphasize the importance of a set of rules in a problem area without indicating the source of the rules.

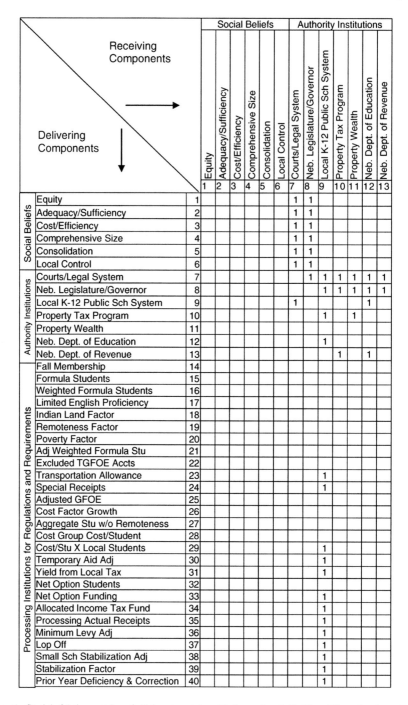

Delivering Components	#	Equity (1)	Adequacy/Sufficiency (2)	Cost/Efficiency (3)	Comprehensive Size (4)	Consolidation (5)	Local Control (6)	Courts/Legal System (7)	Neb. Legislature/Governor (8)	Local K-12 Public Sch System (9)	Property Tax Program (10)	Property Wealth (11)	Neb. Dept. of Education (12)	Neb. Dept. of Revenue (13)
Equity	1							1	1					
Adequacy/Sufficiency	2							1	1					
Cost/Efficiency	3							1	1					
Comprehensive Size	4							1	1					
Consolidation	5							1	1					
Local Control	6							1	1					
Courts/Legal System	7								1	1	1	1	1	1
Neb. Legislature/Governor	8								1	1	1	1	1	1
Local K-12 Public Sch System	9							1					1	
Property Tax Program	10									1		1		
Property Wealth	11													
Neb. Dept. of Education	12									1				
Neb. Dept. of Revenue	13									1		1		
Fall Membership	14													
Formula Students	15													
Weighted Formula Students	16													
Limited English Proficiency	17													
Indian Land Factor	18													
Remoteness Factor	19													
Poverty Factor	20													
Adj Weighted Formula Stu	21													
Excluded TGFOE Accts	22													
Transportation Allowance	23									1				
Special Receipts	24									1				
Adjusted GFOE	25													
Cost Factor Growth	26													
Aggregate Stu w/o Remoteness	27													
Cost Group Cost/Student	28													
Cost/Stu X Local Students	29									1				
Temporary Aid Adj	30									1				
Yield from Local Tax	31									1				
Net Option Students	32													
Net Option Funding	33									1				
Allocated Income Tax Fund	34									1				
Processing Actual Receipts	35									1				
Minimum Levy Adj	36									1				
Lop Off	37									1				
Small Sch Stabilization Adj	38									1				
Stabilization Factor	39									1				
Prior Year Deficiency & Correction	40									1				

Row groups (left side labels): rows 1–6 = Social Beliefs; rows 7–13 = Authority Institutions; rows 14–40 = Processing Institutions for Regulations and Requirements. Column groups: columns 1–6 = Social Beliefs; columns 7–13 = Authority Institutions.

Fig. 1 Social fabric matrix of Nebraska state aid for a local K-12 public school system, 2006–2007

	Processing Institutions for Regulations and Requirements																										
	Fall Membership	Formula Students	Weighted Formula Students	Limited English Proficiency	Indian Land Factor	Remoteness Factor	Poverty Factor	Adj Weighted Formula Stu	Excluded TGFOE Accts	Transportation Allowance	Special Receipts	Adjusted GFOE	Cost Factor Growth	Aggregate Stu w/o Remoteness	Cost Group Cost/Student	Cost/Stu X Local Students	Temporary Aid Adj	Yield from Local Tax	Net Option Students	Net Option funding	Allocated Income Tax Fund	Other Actual Receipts	Minimum Levy Adj	Lop Off	Small Sch Stabilization Adj	Stabilization Factor	Prior Year Deficiency & Correction
	14	15	16	17	18	19	20	21	22	23	24	25	26	27	28	29	30	31	32	33	34	35	36	37	38	39	40
1																											
2																											
3																											
4																											
5																											
6																											
7																											
8																											
9																											
10																			1								
11																											
12	1	1	1	1	1	1	1	1	1	1	1	1	1	1	1	1	1	1	1	1	1	1	1	1	1	1	1
13																											
14		1																									
15			1		1	1					1																
16								1						1				1									
17								1						1													
18								1						1													
19								1																			
20								1						1													
21																1											
22												1															
23												1							1						1	1	1
24												1							1			1			1	1	1
25															1												
26															1												
27															1												
28																	1				1						
29																			1						1	1	1
30																					1	1			1	1	1
31																									1	1	1
32																					1						
33																						1			1	1	1
34																									1	1	1
35																											
36																							1		1	1	1
37																										1	1
38																											1
39																											
40																								1			

Fig. 1 (continued)

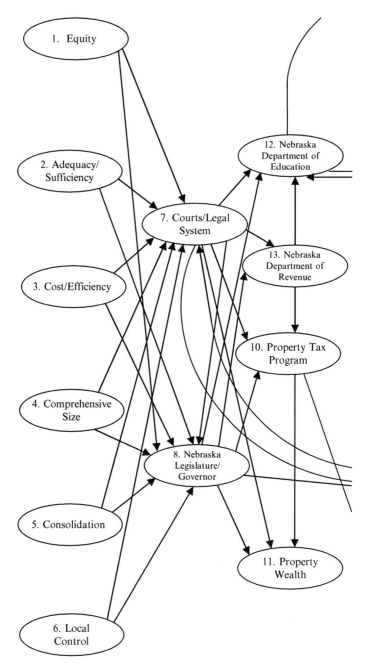

Fig. 2 Social fabric matrix digraph of Nebraska state aid for a local K-12 public school system, 2006–2007

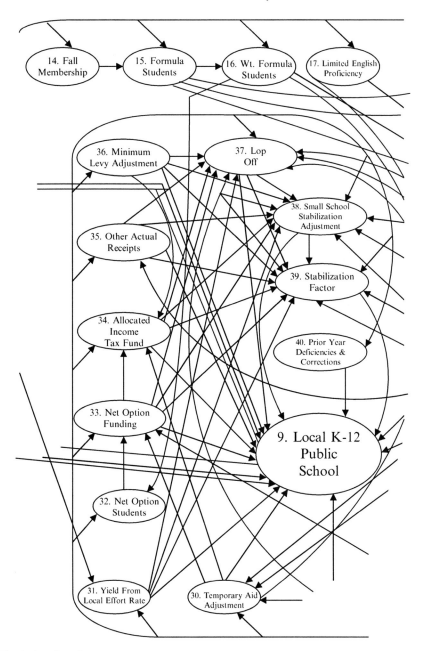

Fig. 2 (continued)

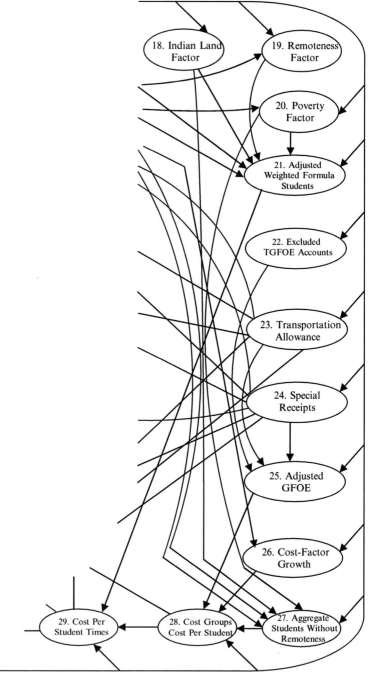

Fig. 2 (continued)

Table 1 Nebraska state school aid formula for each local K-12 school system, 2006–2007

$$\left\langle \left\{ \left[\left[.5 \left(\frac{\dfrac{ADM_{y-2}}{FM_{y-2}} + \dfrac{ADM_{y-3}}{FM_{y-3}} + \dfrac{ADM_{y-4}}{FM_{y-4}}}{3} \right) \left(K_{y-1} \right) + KC_{y-1} \right] \right. \right. \right. \tag{1}$$

$$+ \left[\left(\frac{\dfrac{ADM_{y-2}}{FM_{y-2}} + \dfrac{ADM_{y-3}}{FM_{y-3}} + \dfrac{ADM_{y-4}}{FM_{y-4}}}{3} \right) \left(FDKS_{y-1} \right) + FDKSC_{y-1} \right] \tag{2}$$

$$+ 1.2 \left[\left(\frac{\dfrac{ADM_{y-2}}{FM_{y-2}} + \dfrac{ADM_{y-3}}{FM_{y-3}} + \dfrac{ADM_{y-4}}{FM_{y-4}}}{3} \right) \left(SE_{y-1} \right) + SEC_{y-1} \right] \tag{3}$$

$$+ 1.4 \left[\left(\frac{\dfrac{ADM_{y-2}}{FM_{y-2}} + \dfrac{ADM_{y-3}}{FM_{y-3}} + \dfrac{ADM_{y-4}}{FM_{y-4}}}{3} \right) \left(NT_{y-1} \right) + NTC_{y-1} \right] \right\} \tag{4}$$

$$+ .25 \left(LEP_{y-2} \right) \tag{5}$$

$$+ .25 \left(IndLandADA \right)_{y-2} \tag{6}$$

$$+ .125 \left\{ \left[\left[\left(\frac{\dfrac{ADM_{y-2}}{FM_{y-2}} + \dfrac{ADM_{y-3}}{FM_{y-3}} + \dfrac{ADM_{y-4}}{FM_{y-4}}}{3} \right) \left(K_{y-1} \right) + KC_{y-1} \right] \right. \right. \tag{7}$$

$$+ \left[\left(\frac{\dfrac{ADM_{y-2}}{FM_{y-2}} + \dfrac{ADM_{y-3}}{FM_{y-3}} + \dfrac{ADM_{y-4}}{FM_{y-4}}}{3} \right) \left(FDKS_{y-1} \right) + FDKSC_{y-1} \right] \tag{8}$$

$$+ \left[\left(\frac{\dfrac{ADM_{y-2}}{FM_{y-2}} + \dfrac{ADM_{y-3}}{FM_{y-3}} + \dfrac{ADM_{y-4}}{FM_{y-4}}}{3} \right) \left(SE_{y-1} \right) + SEC_{y-1} \right] \tag{9}$$

$$+ \left[\left(\frac{\dfrac{ADM_{y-2}}{FM_{y-2}} + \dfrac{ADM_{y-3}}{FM_{y-3}} + \dfrac{ADM_{y-4}}{FM_{y-4}}}{3} \right) \left(NT_{y-1} \right) + NTC_{y-1} \right] \right\} \tag{10}$$

(continued)

Table 1 (continued)

if a local district has:

(1) Less than 200 formula students,

(2) More than 600 square miles in the local system,   (11)

(3) Less than .3 formula students per square mile in the local system, and

(4) More than 25 miles between high-school attendance centers.

$$+ \left\{ .05LI\left[\delta(.05) + \delta(.10) + \delta(.15) + \delta(.20) + \delta(.25) + \delta(.30) \right] \right. \tag{12}$$

$$-.05^2 \left\{ \left[\left(\frac{\frac{ADM_{y-2}}{FM_{y-2}} + \frac{ADM_{y-3}}{FM_{y-3}} + \frac{ADM_{y-4}}{FM_{y-4}}}{3} \right) \left(K_{y-1} \right) + KC_{y-1} \right] \tag{13}$$

$$+ \left[\left(\frac{\frac{ADM_{y-2}}{FM_{y-2}} + \frac{ADM_{y-3}}{FM_{y-3}} + \frac{ADM_{y-4}}{FM_{y-4}}}{3} \right) \left(FDKS_{y-1} \right) + FDKSC_{y-1} \right] \tag{14}$$

$$+ \left[\left(\frac{\frac{ADM_{y-2}}{FM_{y-2}} + \frac{ADM_{y-3}}{FM_{y-3}} + \frac{ADM_{y-4}}{FM_{y-4}}}{3} \right) \left(SE_{y-1} \right) + SEC_{y-1} \right] \tag{15}$$

$$+ \left[\left(\frac{\frac{ADM_{y-2}}{FM_{y-2}} + \frac{ADM_{y-3}}{FM_{y-3}} + \frac{ADM_{y-4}}{FM_{y-4}}}{3} \right) \left(NT_{y-1} \right) + NTC_{y-1} \right] \right\} \tag{16}$$

$$- \left[\delta(.05) + 2\delta(.10) + 3\delta(.15) + 4\delta(.20) + 5\delta(.25) + 6\delta(.30) \right] \right\};$$

$$where : \delta(c) = \left\{ 1, \frac{LI}{FS} \geq C \atop 0.else \right\} \tag{17}$$

$$\left(\sum_{i=1}^{n} \left\langle TGFOE_{y-2} \,; which\, includes: \left(TP + SS + AE + TfOF \right. \right. \tag{18}$$

$$+ CS + GFDSP + TransPd + StCat + RIP + SDA \right)_{y-2} \tag{19}$$

$$- \left(TP + SS + AE + TfOF + CS + GFDSP + TransPd + StCat + RIP + SDA \right)_{y-2} \right\rangle \tag{20}$$

$$- \left\{ \left(TRPT_{y-2} - TPd_{y-2} \right); if < PRM_{y-2} \left[(.405)(4.00) \right] + ILT_{y-2} \right\}; \tag{21}$$

OR

$$- \left\{ PRM_{y-2} \left[(.405)(4.00) \right] + ILT_{y-2} \,; if < \left(TRPT_{y-2} - TPd_{y-2} \right) \right\} \tag{22}$$

(continued)

Table 1   (continued)

$$-(TR2 + Trans2 + SpEdSchAge + WrdsSt \,\&\, Count + AorDCurr + MCCA)_{y-2} \Big\rangle \tag{23}$$

$$\left\{ 1 + 2 \left\langle \sum_{i=1}^{n} \left\{ \left[\left(\frac{\frac{ADM_{y-2}}{FM_{y-2}} + \frac{ADM_{y-3}}{FM_{y-3}} + \frac{ADM_{y-4}}{FM_{y-4}}}{3} \right) \left(K_{y-1} \right) + KC_{y-1} \right] \right. \right. \tag{24}$$

$$+ \left[\left(\frac{\frac{ADM_{y-2}}{FM_{y-2}} + \frac{ADM_{y-3}}{FM_{y-3}} + \frac{ADM_{y-4}}{FM_{y-4}}}{3} \right) \left(FDKS_{y-1} \right) + FDKSC_{y-1} \right] \tag{25}$$

$$+ \left[\left(\frac{\frac{ADM_{y-2}}{FM_{y-2}} + \frac{ADM_{y-3}}{FM_{y-3}} + \frac{ADM_{y-4}}{FM_{y-4}}}{3} \right) \left(SE_{y-1} \right) + SEC_{y-1} \right] \tag{26}$$

$$+ \left[\left(\frac{\frac{ADM_{y-2}}{FM_{y-2}} + \frac{ADM_{y-3}}{FM_{y-3}} + \frac{ADM_{y-4}}{FM_{y-4}}}{3} \right) \left(NT_{y-1} \right) + NTC_{y-1} \right] \tag{27}$$

$$- \left[ADM_{y-2} + TS_{y-2} \right] \right\} \Big/ \left\{ \sum_{i=1}^{n} \left[ADM_{y-2} + TS_{y-2} \right] \right\} ; only\ if > 0 \tag{28}$$

$$+ \left[BARG_{yo} + BARG_{y-1} + .50(SBG)_{yo} + .50(SBG)_{y-1} \right] \right\rangle \right\} \Big/ \tag{29}$$

$$\sum_{i=1}^{n} \left\langle \left\{ .5 \left[\left(\frac{\frac{ADM_{y-2}}{FM_{y-2}} + \frac{ADM_{y-3}}{FM_{y-3}} + \frac{ADM_{y-4}}{FM_{y-4}}}{3} \right) \left(K_{y-1} \right) + KC_{y-1} \right] \right. \right. \tag{30}$$

$$+ \left[\left(\frac{\frac{ADM_{y-2}}{FM_{y-2}} + \frac{ADM_{y-3}}{FM_{y-3}} + \frac{ADM_{y-4}}{FM_{y-4}}}{3} \right) \left(FDKS_{y-1} \right) + FDKSC_{y-1} \right] \tag{31}$$

(continued)

Table 1 (continued)

$$+1.2\left[\left[\left(\dfrac{\dfrac{ADM_{y-2}}{FM_{y-2}}+\dfrac{ADM_{y-3}}{FM_{y-3}}+\dfrac{ADM_{y-4}}{FM_{y-4}}}{3}\right)\left(SE_{y-1}\right)+SEC_{y-1}\right]\right.\tag{32}$$

$$+1.4\left[\left[\left(\dfrac{\dfrac{ADM_{y-2}}{FM_{y-2}}+\dfrac{ADM_{y-3}}{FM_{y-3}}+\dfrac{ADM_{y-4}}{FM_{y-4}}}{3}\right)\left(NT_{y-1}\right)+NTC_{y-1}\right]\right]\Bigg\}\tag{33}$$

$$+.25\left(LEP_{y-2}\right)\tag{34}$$

$$+.25\left(IndLandADA\right)_{y-2}\tag{35}$$

$$+\left\{.05LI\left[\delta(.05)+\delta(.10)+\delta(.15)+\delta(.20)+\delta(.25)+\delta(.30)\right]\right.\tag{36}$$

$$-.05^{2}\left\{\left[\left[\left(\dfrac{\dfrac{ADM_{y-2}}{FM_{y-2}}+\dfrac{ADM_{y-3}}{FM_{y-3}}+\dfrac{ADM_{y-4}}{FM_{y-4}}}{3}\right)\left(K_{y-1}\right)+KC_{y-1}\right]\right.\tag{37}$$

$$+\left[\left(\dfrac{\dfrac{ADM_{y-2}}{FM_{y-2}}+\dfrac{ADM_{y-3}}{FM_{y-3}}+\dfrac{ADM_{y-4}}{FM_{y-4}}}{3}\right)\left(FDKS_{y-1}\right)+FDKSC_{y-1}\right]\tag{38}$$

$$+\left[\left(\dfrac{\dfrac{ADM_{y-2}}{FM_{y-2}}+\dfrac{ADM_{y-3}}{FM_{y-3}}+\dfrac{ADM_{y-4}}{FM_{y-4}}}{3}\right)\left(SE_{y-1}\right)+SEC_{y-1}\right]\tag{39}$$

$$+\left[\left(\dfrac{\dfrac{ADM_{y-2}}{FM_{y-2}}+\dfrac{ADM_{y-3}}{FM_{y-3}}+\dfrac{ADM_{y-4}}{FM_{y-4}}}{3}\right)\left(NT_{y-1}\right)+NTC_{y-1}\right]\Bigg\}\tag{40}$$

$$-\left[\delta(.05)+2\delta(.10)+3\delta(.15)+4\delta(.20)+5\delta(.25)+6\delta(.30)\right]\Big\};\tag{41}$$

$$where:\delta(c)=\left\{\begin{array}{l}1,\dfrac{LI}{FS}\geq C\\0,else\end{array}\right\rangle\Bigg);\tag{42}$$

(continued)

Table 1 (continued)

for very sparse cost-grouping districts where there is either:

(1) Less than .5 census students per square mile in the county where the high school is located,   (43)

(2) Less than 1 formula student per square mile in the local system, and

(3) More than 15 miles between high-school attendance centers

OR

(1) More than 450 square miles in the local system,

(2) Less than .5 formula students per square mile in the local system, and   (44)

(3) More than 15 miles between high-school attendance centers.

OR

for sparse cost-grouping districts where there is either:

(1) Less than 2 census students per square mile in the county in which each high school is located,   (45)

(2) Less than 1 formula student per square mile in the local system, and

(3 More than 10 miles between each high school's attendance centers

OR

(1) Less than 1.5 formula students per square mile in the local system, and
                                                                                   (46)
(2) More than 15 miles between each high school's attendance centers.

OR

(1) Less than 1.5 formula students per square mile in the local system, and
                                                                                   (47)
(2) More than 275 square miles in the local system.

OR

(1) Less than 2 formula students per square mile in the local system, and   (48)

(2) The local system includes an area equal to 95% or more of the square miles in the largest county in which a high-school attendance center is located.

OR

for standard cost-grouping districts that do not qualify for either very sparse or sparse   (49)
grouping.

---

explained. This is an important part of the formula because it (1) shows the function of the SFM cellular information in establishing a whole system; (2) demonstrates the importance of how rules, regulations, and requirements are institutionalized; (3) illustrates how institutional organizations are dependent on and serve other institutional organizations; (4) clarifies how the various groups across departments function to implement formula terms; (5) demonstrates how rules are specified with algebraic terms; (6) explains the cost and need parts of the formula; and (7) defines a section that is utilized repeatedly in different ways throughout the larger formula. Table 1 is dependent on the SFM delivery cells, as explained in the following paragraphs.

Cells (12,14) through (12,40): Nebraska Department of Education deliveries to Components 14 through 40: The regulations and requirements upon which institutional organizations 14 through 40 are dependent are delivered in these cells from the NDE (see row 12 and columns 1 through 40 in Fig. 1). These deliveries include regulations and requirements with regard to the use of data, as well as the delivery of the databases that NDE receives from the Nebraska Department of Revenue, cell

(13,12), and from the local school district, cell (9,12). The rules, regulations, and requirements delivered will become clear below in the discussion of cells that are dependent on the deliveries for this set of cells.

Cell (14,15): Fall Membership delivery to Formula Students: The fall membership (FM) is the number of students enrolled in each grade category for the year prior (y-1) to the fall semester of the year for which state aid is being calculated. The fall membership for grade-range categories is as follows: one-half day kindergarten (Ky-1), full-day kindergarten through grade six (FDSKy-1), grades seven and eight (SEy-1), and grades nine through twelve (NTy-1) (Neb. Rev. Stat. § 79-1003(16), Supp. 2005)[2].

Cell (15,16): Formula Students delivery to Weighted Formula Students: Excluding the grade-weighting coefficients on the left side of the square brackets in parts (1) through (4) of Table 1, this section of the formula expresses the way the FM categories are adjusted to find what Nebraska law defines as formula students (FS). FS is determined as each of the grade categories is multiplied by the average ratio of the year's average daily membership (ADM) divided by the FM for the second (y-2), third (y-3), and fourth (y-4) years prior to the formula year (y0). To this product is added the number of students that the school district contracts out to other districts for the respective grade levels for the prior year. Students contracted out for the different grades are one-half-day kindergarten (KCy-1), full-day kindergarten through grade six (FDKSCy-1), grades seven and eight (SECy-1), and grades nine through twelve (NTCy-1). This specifies how the number of FS is generated (Neb. Rev. Stat. § 79-1003(18), Supp. 2005). It is delivered to weighted formula students for additional adjustments, also found in parts (1) through (4) in Table 1.

Cells (16,21) and (16,27): Weighted Formula Students delivery to Adjusted Weighted Formula Students and Aggregate Students Without Remoteness: Weighted formula students (WFS) are calculated by multiplying the grade categories in the FS term in parts (1) through (4) in Table 1 times the coefficients designated by law for weighting the different grade categories. The grade-weighting coefficients are: 0.5 for one-half-day kindergarten, 1.00 for full-day kindergarten through grade six, 1.2 for grades seven and eight, and 1.4 for grades nine through twelve (Neb. Rev. Stat. § 79-1007.01(1) (a–b), Supp. 2005). Thus, the WFS formula is parts (1) through (4) in Table 1. The calculations for weighted formula students are delivered to components 21 and 27, as indicated in Figs. 1 and 2 (they are also delivered to component 32, as indicated in cell (16,32) but that is not part of our concern here).

Cells (17,21) and (17,27): Limited English Proficiency delivery to Adjusted Weighted Students and Aggregate Students Without Remoteness: A demographic factor is added as part 5 in Fig. 1. It is the number in the year prior to the formula year of students in the local school district with limited English proficiency multiplied by 0.25 (Neb. Rev. Stat. § 79-1003(c)(*ii*), Supp. 2005). This calculation is delivered to components 21 and 27.

---

[2] All statutes cited, along with the relevant list of source laws, can be found at Nebraska legislative documents (2008) (see references).

Cells (18,21) and (18,27): Indian Land Factor delivery to Adjusted Weighted Formula Students: Another demographic factor is the Indian-land factor, which is the average daily attendance (ADA) two years prior to the formula year of students that reside on what is designated as Indian land multiplied by 0.25 (Neb. Rev. Stat. § 79-1003(c)(*i*), Supp. 2005). This is found as part 6 of Table 1.

Cell (19,21): Remoteness Factor delivery to Adjusted Weighted Formula Students: The third demographic factor is the extreme-remoteness factor, which is for school districts that have: (1) less than 200 formula students, (2) more than 600 square miles in the district, (3) less than 0.3 formula students per square mile in the district, and (4) more than 25 miles between high-school attendance centers. Districts that qualify are credited with an additional 0.125 students for each formula student (Neb. Rev. Stat. §79-1003(c)(*iv*), Supp. 2005), as indicated in parts (7) through (11) in Table 1.

Cells (20,21) and (20,27): Poverty Factor delivery to Adjusted Weighted Formula and Aggregate Students without Remoteness: The fourth demographic factor is the poverty factor, as defined in (12) through (17) in Table 1. In addition to low-income students being included in formula terms above, additional students are added to a school district's total student count according to the poverty factor. To calculate the poverty factor, either the number of children from low-income families in the district as reported by the Nebraska Department of Revenue (SFM cell 13,12) or the FS qualified for free lunch or free milk (SFM cell 9,12) is utilized, whichever is greater. That low-income student number is then decreased by the formula. The number of low-income students (LI) in the district must be at least 5% or greater of the total number of FS in the district for any additional students to be added to the student count due to the poverty factor. The function to calculate the poverty factor is calculated to increase at an increasing rate as additional percentage points above 5% are added, with the rate of increase changing with each additional 5% increment of FS. For example, if the number of low-income students is from 5 to 10% of FS, the percent the number of low-income students is of FS is multiplied by 5%; if the number of low-income students is between 10 and 15%, it is multiplied by 10%, and so forth (Neb. Rev. Stat. § 79-1003(c)(*iii*)(A–G), Supp. 2005). The formula term utilized here for the poverty factor utilizes the delta method to specify how to calculate the number of students to be added to a school district's student count, as follows: Delta and its correspondent variable (C) are combined as a function (not to indicate that they are multiplied). Examples of C with δ are $\delta(0.05)$ and $\delta(0.30)$. The conditions define that a function such as $\delta(0.15)$ is 1 or 0, depending on the ratio of LI/FS. Functions less than LI/FS are 1 and those greater than LI/FS are 0.

Cell (21,29): Adjusted Weighted Formula Students delivery to Cost Per Student Times Local Students: As clarified above, components 16, 17, 18, 19, and 21 make direct deliveries of their calculations to component 21, Adjusted Weighted Formula Students. In turn, that group aggregates those calculations to generate formula parts (1) through (17) in Table 1 (Neb. Rev. Stat. § 79-1007.01(2)(a–b), Supp. 2005). This result is generated in order for it to be utilized by component 29, Cost Per Student Times Local Students.

Cell (22,25): Excluded Total General Fund Operating Expenditures delivery to Adjusted General Fund Operating Expenditures: Each district's total general fund operating expenditures (TGFOE) for the most recently available complete data year (usually y-2) contain a series of expenditures included in the TGFOE that are deleted for calculations made by component 25, Adjusted GFOE. The expenditure items deleted are tuition paid (TP), summer school (SS), adult education (AE), transfers from other funds (TfOF), community services (CS), redemption of general fund debt service principal (GFDSP), transportation paid to other districts (TransPD), state categorical programs (StCat), retirement incentive program (RIP), and staff development assistance (SDA) (Nebraska Department of Education 2006). Excluding the sigma sign, this is shown in parts (18) through (20) of the Table 1 formula.

Cell (23,25): Transportation Allowance delivery to Adjusted General Fund Operating Expenditures: The transportation allowance for each local school district is the lesser of the following two: (1) the actual specific transportation expenditures reported by the local district (TRPT) minus transportation expenditures paid to another district (TPd), or (2) a calculated amount based on the pupil route miles transported (PRM) multiplied by $(0.405)(4.00)$ plus in-lieu-of transportation (ILT). The former (part (21)) is used if it meets the condition of being less than the latter (part (22)), and the latter is used if it meets the condition of being less than the former (Nebraska Department of Education 2006). This calculation is delivered to component 25, Adjusted General Fund Operation Expenditures.

Cell (24,25): Special Receipts delivery to Adjusted General Fund Operating Expenditures: Special receipts is determined separately for each local school district by the aggregation of the following: Tuition receipts (TR2), transportation receipts (Trans2), expenditures for special education by student age (SpEdSchAge), payment for wards of the state and wards of the court (WrdsSt&Crt), receipts for accelerated or differentiated curriculum programs (AorDCurr), and receipts from Medicare Catastrophic Coverage Act of 1988 (MCCA) (Nebraska Department of Education 2006). This sum is delivered to a number of other components, as indicated in Fig. 2 (third page); for the purposes here, the delivery of interest is to component 25, Adjusted GFOE.

Cell (25,28): Adjusted General Fund Operating Expenditures delivery to Cost Groups Cost per Student: The total general fund operating expenditures for each district are converted to adjusted general fund operating expenditures by subtracting the sums calculated by components 22, 23, and 24 (Nebraska Department of Education, 2006). These adjusted expenditures are then delivered to component 28, Cost Groups Cost Per Student.

Cell (26,28): Cost-Factor Growth delivery to Cost Groups Cost per Student: The cost-factor growth is found in parts (24) through (29) of Table 1. Parts (24) through (28) show the sum of all the districts in Nebraska of the remainder of FS minus the total of the ADM plus the tuition students (TS) for each district. That sum, in turn, is divided by the sum of the ADM plus the TS for all the districts (Neb. Rev. Stat. § 79.1007.02 (2)(a), Supp. 2005). That dividend, if it is greater than zero, is added to the sum of the following growth rates: (1) the basic allowable growth rate of expenditures by individual school districts for the formula year (BAGRy0), plus (2) the basic allowable growth rate of expenditures by individual school districts for the prior year (BAGRy-1), plus (3) one-half of any additional growth rate allowed by special action of local school boards for the formula year (0.50SBGy0), plus (4) one-half of any additional growth rate allowed by special action of school boards for the prior year (0.50SBGy1), as shown in part (29). That sum is multiplied by two and the resulting product is added to one, as designated on the left side of part 24. (Neb. Rev. Stat. § 79.1007.02(2)(b), Supp. 2005; Neb. Rev. Stat. § 79.1025, Reissue 2004; Neb. Rev. Stat. § 77-3446, Reissue 2004).

Cell (27,28): Aggregate Students Without Remoteness delivery to Cost Groups Cost per Student: Component 27 utilizes the calculations delivered from components 16, 17, 18, 19, and through 20 to find the state's aggregate total weighted students without the remoteness factor for all school districts in the state, as defined in parts (30) through (42) in Table 1. Component 27 is the same as component 21, except the remoteness factor (component 19) is not included in component 27 (Nebraska Department of Education 2006). This determines the total number of students, taken as a whole, to be used for calculation of the funds available per student.

Cell (28,29): Cost Groups Cost per Student delivery to Cost per Student Times Local Students: The databases for the cost groups cost depends on the cost grouping to which a school district belongs. The cost groupings are based on the basis of three different sets of geographical conditions. State law divides the school districts in Nebraska into three different cost groupings, which are (1) very sparse, (2) sparse, and (3) standard; and, as their names imply, these groupings are related to the geographical distribution of students across the district. The geographical density is determined by (1) census of students per square mile in the county, (2) FS per square mile in the school district, and (3) miles between high schools (see parts (43) through (49) of Table 1 for detail).

The cost per student for each cost grouping is found by dividing the numerator of parts (18) through (29) by the denominator of parts (30) through (49) in Table 1. The numerator is the sum of the adjusted GFOE (component 25) for all school districts times the growth factor (component 26). The denominator is the sum of all the ways students are counted without including the student count for remoteness (component 27). This provides a particular kind of average expenditure per child for all districts in a cost grouping (Neb. Rev. Stat. § 79-1007.02, Supp. 2005). It is referred to as the average formula cost per student for the cost grouping, and is delivered to component 29, Cost per Student Times Local Students.

Cell (29,9): Cost per Student Times Local Students delivery to Local K-12 Public School: The average formula cost per student is utilized to calculate what is called district need. This is done by multiplying the average formula cost per student delivered from component 28 times the adjusted weighted formula students of a particular school district from component 21 in order to determine each district's need for aid from the state for the part of the formula articulated in Table 1 (Neb. Rev. Stat. § 79-1007.02, Supp. 2005).

Conceptual Conclusions

The utilization of the SFM to define and explain the educational finance system of state aid to public schools allows for insights into that system and for drawing conceptual conclusions about policy, student count, cost calculations, institutional theory, and systems principles.

Nebraska School-Aid Policy Context

One of the first advantages of the SFM definition of Nebraska state aid for schools is to provide officials and citizens an opportunity to understand the parts of the system, to trace how the parts fit together, and to understand how different parts are utilized again and again in different ways throughout the school finance system. In the process, officials and citizens learn why no one understands the system or its consequences. An astute Nebraska senator stood on the floor of the Unicameral, during debate of a school finance bill, to state with regard to the education finance formula that "there are four or five people in the Western world that understand the formula, and I am not one of them." This author would say he overestimated by five because analysis had not been completed to allow anyone to gain an adequate understanding of state aid to schools in Nebraska.

Given that systems theory teaches us that systems continue to differentiate to greater levels of complexity, and, given the many complex issues in education, complexity in school finance should be expected. However, the complexity of the current formula is not necessary to determine the distribution of state aid. Additionally, such complexity inhibits understanding, discussion, and deliberation. The State of Nebraska uses computer programs that utilize the data formulated from different groups in local, state, and federal departments to determine the amount of funds that is to be paid to different school districts; but there has been no integrated algebraic formula as presented here that can be used to analyze the impact of the formula or changes in it with respect to equity, adequacy, tax burdens, and so forth – that is, to analyze for concerns that are of interest to officials, citizens, professional educators, and courts. The current system finds dollar amounts but cannot give an indication about how the various contributing parts of the computer program can be judged against the criteria of equity, adequacy, alternative allocation, and so forth.[3]

---

[3] The next analytical function that should be completed is to apply calculus to the whole formula. Such a total formula analysis would allow for the determination of distributional and incentive impacts among school districts if different aspects of the formula were to change. The calculation of the derivative of the formula would reveal the change in state funding for the district as the various aspects of the formula change. For example, what is the effect on state financing of a change in local school expenditures, or, what is the distributional effect on all other districts as local expenditures change in one district? There are numerous questions that can be answered with the first derivative. The algebraic definition found from the SFM cells provides an opportunity for partial derivatives to be used to find the kinds of rewards, incentives, and distributional effects that the structure provides for individual districts and among districts.

Throughout the 600-page Nebraska school-aid formula, the same terms and parts are repeated in many different places and ways. The same term or part may be added, subtracted, aggregated with similar terms or parts from other districts, serve in a numerator, serve in a denominator, and serve as a multiplier or multiplicand in different places in the formula. Additionally, a given term or part may be repeated more than once in another term, serving in different capacities in the other term; sometimes in both the numerator and denominator. For example, the weighted formula students in parts (1) through (4) of Table 1 are repeated in numerous mathematical capacities, as are parts (1) through (17). One reason for selecting parts (1) through (49) to demonstrate the SFM application is because those parts are utilized in so many different mathematical functions throughout the longer formula. Those parts are delivered to other components, and utilized in their calculations, and the subsequent calculations are delivered on to other components for more calculations. Parts (1) through (49) are regularly applied in new ways, which adds to its cumulative effect for the system as a whole; a cumulative causation that has been neither analyzed nor understood. It is not possible to know the final effect of such diverse treatment of terms and parts without a mathematical analysis of the algebraic expression of the formula, especially when terms or parts have direct and indirect effects. Taken together parts (1) through (49) are referred to as the *need* section of the formula. However, the need section is utilized in numerous additional ways throughout the longer formula; in the so-called resources section, equalization section, income tax allocation section, and so forth. Thus, the role played by parts (1) through (49) is much different than just to calculate school district need, and the net effect of all the direct and indirect effects of the need term is not known.

The work here is useful for demonstrating the SFM system analysis and, in particular, the analysis of the Nebraska school finance system, but the author does not intend to leave the impression that others should expect to find the same kind of finance structure for school finance in other states. Finance formula evolution has been a trend of greater differentiation among the states. Fifty years ago state school-aid formulas generally followed one of three different structures, or a combination thereof. Although educational finance textbooks try to represent state formulas as fitting into the old molds, inspection finds them not to fit. Legislative and court action, along with the ease of diverse and complicated kinds of computation due to computers, has led to great differentiation and variety from state to state.

Student Count Concerns

Three serious problems with the student count in the formula are as follows. First, the grade-weighting coefficients applied to formula students on the left side of the square brackets in parts (1) through (4) of Table 1 are generally based on the basis of tradition or power politics rather than scientific rationale. Second, other coefficients used to adjust the student count are also without scientific rationale. Third, the student count is adjusted and utilized to determine district *need* rather than to determine the payment that is needed to provide education for a child, or for a child with specific characteristics.

Generally, student-count weights "are not grounded in studies of what funding would most appropriately finance educational programs to meet the needs of pupils (i.e., what should be)" (King et al. 2003, 210). The traditions that guide the assignment of weights vary from state to state. In some states, the student weight coefficients are heavier for lower level grades than for higher ones, and school finance literature exists to support such an approach. As is clear, Nebraska weight assignments reverse that order, with full-day kindergarten through grade six weighted with a coefficient of one per student and grades nine through twelve weighted with a coefficient of 1.4 per student. No rationale is offered for such a weighting by grade level, nor for other weights applied for determining student count.

As shown in parts (1) through (4) in Table 1, the basic student count in Nebraska is based on the basis of the fall membership of the fall prior to the budget year for which the state-aid formula applies. That is contrary to the approach used by most states in the U.S. "The majority of the states base funding on pupil counts during the current year. In this approach, states provide aid on the basis of an estimate of pupil enrollment or attendance as the fiscal year begins. Subsequent adjustments reflect the actual count of students enrolled or in attendance on one or more count days" (King et al. 2003, 208). Accordingly, districts in Nebraska with an increasing trend in the number of immigrant students, for example, will fall further behind in student count because the formula count is always based on the basis of the prior year and, therefore, it never takes into account the total student body. Furthermore, the extra pupil count resulting from the limited English proficiency students does not help offset the undercounting due to growing immigrant students in a district school because it is two years behind the current budget (see part (7) in Table 1.

Additionally, Nebraska adjusts pupil membership of the prior year by the average ratio of ADM/FM for the three years prior to the prior year's FM (see parts (1) through (4)), thereby reducing the funds available to districts with higher truancy rates. This approach to student count especially penalizes poor districts with growing populations of immigrants from foreign countries who are poor and do not speak English, which is a growing trend for numerous districts in Nebraska. Immigrant student populations have high truancy rates which reduce the ADM/FM ratio, thus making such districts less able to spend the money needed to raise the ADM.

The increase in pupil membership resulting from students from Indian land should not be interpreted by the reader to mean Indian students. First, the population of Indian students in Nebraska's cities is not included in this count. Second, the pupils that qualify include children of European descent because their parents have businesses or farms on Indian reservations that they have bought or leased, or jobs that make them residents on the Indian land.

The poverty factor (parts (12) through (17) in Table 1) has very little effect on student membership because the poverty factor functions mainly to reduce the actual count of students in poverty. First, the district must have more than 5% of the total FS in poverty before any of the low-income students are counted for poverty membership. Second, as indicated in Table 1, the percent increase in membership per each additional 5% of FS is small.

Cost Calculation Concerns

As defined in Table 1, the dollar amount for the so-called need section of the school aid formula is found with the use of cost calculations. These calculations do not determine the monetary cost of need. Instead, calculations begin with what is currently being spent (TGFOE), subtract part of what is being spent (parts 18 through 23), and aggregate all districts for a state total. The result is then divided by the total number of adjusted weighted students without the inclusion of the remoteness factor students. This means that the base of *need* determination is what is being spent rather than what is needed. After stating that TGFOE should be the base for determining need, expenditures that are needed are excluded so that in the end the total amount spent by all districts is not the base. What is left (GFOE) is then increased, not by an amount to provide for a total that indicates an adequate amount of money to provide for what is needed, but, rather, by percentages (found in parts (24) through (29) in Table 1) that have nothing to do with need. Then the inadequate amount is divided by the aggregate student count in the state. Thus, the greater the need in terms of number of students, as calculated, the lower the dollar need indicated per student unit.

Any weighting that increases the student count reduces the need figure per student, given the final total expenditure figure. For example, districts with more poverty, high-school students, and students deficient in English proficiency will increase the denominator (parts 30 through 49) and thereby reduce what is indicated as the amount needed per student, without providing for the districts with the increased need. The inadequate per-student-need figure (Component 28, Cost Groups Cost per student) is then multiplied times the number of adjusted weighted formula students (Component 21) in the district to determine the defined need for each school district.

The first major mistake in the need determination process is to weight students with different characteristics or needs differently. Student weighting does not indicate the level of funding that is needed. Instead, what should be done is to use the best scientific evidence available to indicate the number of students with particular characteristics by district, and indicate the amount of funding needed by each district to adequately educate those students. This approach clarifies the real total need without all the extraneous mathematical exercises. Additionally, it calculates need in a manner so that citizens, professionals, and officials can understand, and, therefore, carry on discussions and debates as intended in a participatory democracy.

The second major mistake is the attempt to include equalization in the need section of the formula. This is done when the total expenditures of all districts are divided by the total students in all districts. Thus, since districts with a high expenditure per student are included in the numerator along with districts with a low expenditure per student, the resulting dividend for each student in low expenditure districts is raised in this part of the formula. This confuses the purpose of the need section. Equalization should not be made part of the determination of need. Need should be established in the need section and equalization elsewhere.

Contribution to Institutionalism

As Scott Fullwiler, Wolfram Elsner, and Tara Natarajan clarified in the first chapter of this volume, the SFM was innovated to provide a structure that would allow for the activation of the theory and concepts of scientific findings, general systems analysis, and institutionalism. Institutionalism has always cautioned against dependence on abstract theories formulated with a context different than the one in which the problem of interest is embedded. The importance of taking account of different contexts has grown because modern technology continually makes the world less and less homogenous. Groups, regions, and states continue to become more differentiated. From state to state, school-aid formulas have grown more different. Thus, it is not helpful to analyze them as if they all operate according to the same abstract theory in the same context. The SFM can be applied to the system in each state in order to understand it and make policy for it. This is true for the analysis of all concerns by institutionalists because they believe analysts are to base conclusions on the analysis of real-world cases, with the kind of complex detail required to complete the SFM. To offer conclusions and theories not derived from the analysis of real-world cases is not consistent with institutionalism.

An institutionalist concept exhibited in the Nebraska school-aid SFM is that the purpose of institutions is to serve other institutions and, likewise, to be served by other institutions. To visualize an institution as an independent unit is a mistake; therefore, the emphasis of SFM analysis on the delivery cell is crucial for institutional analysis. The deliveries are what keep institutions viable as well as creating a system among all components. Figs. 1 and 2 emphasize the dependence among components, emphasizing that nothing in the system exists as an independent entity.

In addition to the expression of general institutional theories, the Nebraska school-aid study uncovers concepts this author has not found in the institutionalist modeling literature reviewed. These concepts should affect the kind of modeling completed in the future by institutionalists.

First, it was documented above that social beliefs do not deliver directly to other social beliefs, rules do not deliver directly to other rules, and beliefs and rules do not deliver directly to each other. This is clear from the findings in the real-world case in the SFM demonstrated in Figs. 1 and 2. Recognition of this may help with

---

[4] Much of the legislation for equalization in the part of the formula not presented here fails because of the inclusion of *hold harmless* clauses in that legislation.

some of the confusion about institutions being rules. Institutions operate according to rules and some institutions deliver rules to other institutions. As A. Alan Schmid clarifies, rules determine which institutions are to make and deliver rules (Schmid 2004, 3). Although rules and institutions are closely related and intertwined, institutions are more than rules. Technology and institutions are also closely related and intertwined, but that does not mean that the two are the same. Institutions with the authority to do so formulate rules from belief criteria, as indicated on the left side of Fig. 2. Belief criteria do not influence or make other deliveries except through the activities of institutions.

Second, the Nebraska study confirms Wolfram Elsner's disagreement with the attempt by some to explain rule origination as the work of an individual or isolated Schumpeterian agent. Elsner reminds us of the problems with the idea of the "isolated Schumpeterian agent" (Elsner 2007, 5) and disagrees with the idea that the Schumpeterian "creative destroyer has the ideas for the rule and he/she continually explores new ideas because the mind is restless" (5). Elsner's disagreements are the following: First, the isolated Schumpeterian individual acting as a lone agent fails to take account of the fact that the design of and decisions about rules must be coordinated with a multiplicity of actors in a network of institutions located across overlapping systems (2). Second, the lone agent idea fails to recognize the different decision processes for rule innovation in different contexts (2). Third, the agent must deal with changing systems that "involve *changes of the structure of incentives* to search, explore, experiment or imitate . . ." with which the agent must deal rather than remain isolated in a fixed setting (5). Fourth, the social rule not only has to be traced back to a defined complexity but also to uncertainty problems, which have to be solved collectively (2). Fifth, institutions, as opposed to the adoption of rules by all entrepreneurs in a microcontext, "are used to solve coordination problems and thus carry new and jointly learned knowledge, however informal and tacit" (3).

The Nebraska school finance system is consistent with and, thereby, validates Elsner's reasoning. As clarified above, Nebraska education aid is a system of overlapping institutions and organizations that are coordinated by laws, court decisions, regulations, monitoring, audits, media scrutiny, and so forth. "Part of an organization is the behavior of other organizations" (Schmid 2004, 262). Changing conditions are responded to by institutional procedures as new rules are designed, challenged, lobbied by adverse interests, tested, litigated, and adopted in a dynamic setting through the transactions of components of different systems. As found in the school aid case, explicit procedures and actions are taken to prevent any actor with an entrepreneurial inkling from changing rules that are codified by the whole process. Agents (with agency power) are contained in institutional components. Too often, in economic literature, agents are defined and treated like individuals. An agent is not an individual. An agent is a person or party authorized and empowered by a principal to act in defined capacities. Agency is bestowed by the establishment of a relationship based on an understanding between persons and/or parties for an agent to act. Agents are not isolated or separate units because agency agreements are concerned with accountability, auditing, and performance. Most agents are institutional organizations (corporations, government departments, nonprofit organizations) that obtain agency status from other organizations. When persons are given agent responsibilities, they are located in an institutional organization and deal with normative criteria. Thus, social prescriptions and proscriptions called rules are not the result of self-action by agents with fixed attributes.

Third, Mark Harcourt, Geoffrey Wood, and Ian Roper recently reported the development of two groups of institutionalists with conflicting ideas about what explains behavior. One group explains behavior as being shaped by a social structure and order that is expressed in and conditioned by institutions, especially legal institutions. The other group emphasizes legislative intervention as the force shaping behavior (2007, 962). As is clear from the SFM information in Figs. 1 and 2, both explanations are correct, both are necessary to explain behavior, and neither social structure nor legislative intervention can be sustained without being integrated with and reinforced by the other.

Contribution to Systems Principles

The integration of the SFM and general systems principles has been explained elsewhere (see Hayden 2006, 51-71 and 94-106). The expression of those principles is clear in the SFM articulation of the Nebraska school-finance system – i.e. openness, feedback, evaluation, control, and so forth. The discussion here is limited to concerns about the systems principles of hierarchy and complexity.

The first concern is with recent ideas about the principle of system hierarchy that is in conflict with the findings here. Those recent ideas (which are inconsistent with original definitions about hierarchy found in systems literature) portray system hierarchy as a one-dimensional, top-down relationship. The real-world system in Figs. 1 and 2 demonstrates that is not the case. Figs. 1 and 2 demonstrate the complexity of reality. The process is not confined to top-down relationships. Rulemaking and control are crucial for establishing and maintaining hierarchy, and Figs. 1 and 2 demonstrate a real-world hierarchical system in which rulemaking and control are the consequence of integrated organizations that are sustained through a network of criteria, rules, regulations, requirements, and deliveries. Different kinds of hierarchy exist throughout the complex system in different formats, consistent with the different rules and controls.

The second concern is about complexity. Reality is complex, and the SFM assists in performing in-depth analysis of systems in order to find the complexity. Analytical failure follows when there is a commitment to simple models and abstractions that do not have a concrete base in reality. Policy failure follows from policymaking completed without a thorough understanding of the complex direct and indirect deliveries among relevant components. The SFM is especially well suited to assist in the discovery and organization of components consistent with social, economic, and ecological theory and for specifying the kinds of relationships that exist among the components to find the complexity of a system. It is also well suited for adding new components as the area of concern is expanded; that is, to add complexity.

For example, there is much more to the provision of primary and secondary education than the state public-school-aid process described above. Of importance is that a large percent of students in some districts are educated in parochial schools and those schools are not included in Figs. 1 and 2. Additionally, parochial schools coordinate some of their programs with public schools at the local level, and, as a result, are receiving public support from the state system. Depending on analytical interest, numerous different sets of components will need to be added before a full description of education in Nebraska can be achieved – component sets such as federal government programs, families, local property taxes, Bureau of Indian Affairs, entertainment industry, state tax system, markets for educational goods and services, teacher unions, ecological impacts, and so forth. The components of such concerns can be added to the SFM explained above in order to explain the larger system and the relationships defined by the cells in the larger SFM.

Appendix: Abbreviation and Symbol Reference

ADA	average daily attendance
ADM	average daily membership
AE	adult education
BAGR	basic allowable growth rate for the school district
C	correspondent variable representing the percentage in the poverty factor
CS	community services
FDKS	Fall membership of the Fall prior to the state-aid payment year of full-day kindergarten through grade six students
FDKSC	Fall membership of the Fall prior to the state-aid payment year of full-day kindergarten through grade six students contracted out
FM	Fall membership
FS	formula students
GFDSP	General Fund debt service principal
i	the individual unit in a series
ILT	in-lieu-of transportation
IndLandADA	Indian Land ADA students
K	Fall membership of the Fall prior to the state-aid payment year of kindergarten students
KC	Fall membership of the Fall prior to the state-aid payment year of kindergarten students contracted out
K-12	Kindergarten through grade twelve
LEP	Limited English proficiency students
LI	low income students. Either the (1) number of students receiving free lunch, or (2) number of low income children in the school district as reported by the Nebraska Department of Revenue, whichever of the two is greater.

MCCA	receipts from Medicare Catastrophic Coverage Act of 1988
n	the final number in a series
NDE	Nebraska Department of Education
NT	Fall membership of the Fall prior to the state-aid payment year of grades nine through twelve students
NTC	Fall membership of the Fall prior to the state-aid payment year of grades nine through twelve students contracted out
PRM	pupil route miles
RIP	retirement incentive programs
SBG	growth rate allowed by special action of school board
SDA	staff development assistance
SE	Fall membership of the Fall prior to the state-aid payment year of grades seven though eight students contracted out
SEC	Fall membership of the Fall prior to the state-aid payment year of grades seven through eight students contracted out
SFM	social fabric matrix
SpEdSchAge	special education school age
SS	summer school
StCat	state categorical programs
TEEOSA	Tax Equity and Educational Opportunities Support Act
TfOF	transfers from other schools
TGFOE	total General Fund Operating Expenses
TP	tuition paid
TPd	Transportation Paid to Another District
TRPT	Total Regular Pupil Transportation
Trans2	transportation receipts 1-1-1310-000 and 1-1-1320-000
TransPd	transportation paid to another district
TR2	tuition receipts 1-1-1210-000 and 1-1-1220-000
TS	tuition students
WrdsSt&Crt	payment for wards of the state and wards of the court
y	year
yo, y-1, y-2, y-3, y-4	year zero, year minus one, year minus two, year minus three, and year minus four respectively, with yo being the state aid payment year
δ	delta; used in delta method for the poverty factor

References

Elsner W (2007) Why meso? On 'aggregation' and 'emergence' and why and how the meso level is essential in social economics. Forum Social Econ 36(1):1–16

Harcourt M, Wood G, Roper I (2007) The importance of legislated employment protection for worker commitment in coordinated market economies. J Econ Issues 41(4):961–980

Hayden FG (1998) Normative analysis of instituted processes. In: Fayazmanesh S, MR Tool (eds) Institutionalist theory and applications: essays in honour of Paul Dale Bush, vol 2. Edward Elgar, North Hampton, MA, pp 89–107

Hayden FG (2006) Policymaking for a good society: the social fabric matrix approach to policy analysis and program evolution. Springer, New York

King RA, Swanson AD, Sweetland SR (2003) School finance: achieving standards with equity and efficiency. Allyn and Bacon, New York

Morgan DC, Hayden FG (1970) Elementary and secondary education aid: toward an optimal program for the State Government of Texas. The University of Texas at Austin, Austin

Musgrave RA (1961) Approaches to a fiscal theory of political federalism. In: Conference of Economic Research (ed) Public finances: needs, sources, and utilization. National Bureau. Princeton University Press, Princeton, NJ, pp 97–122

Nebraska Department of Education (2006) Annual financial report of Nebraska school districts 2005–2006 AFR. http://ess.nde.state.ne.us/SchoolFinance/AFR/Downloads0506/afr.xls. Accessed 18 June 2008

Nebraska Department of Education (2007) Tax equity and educational opportunities support act certification of 2006–2007 state aid. Education support services. Nebraska Department of Education, Lincoln, NE

Nebraska legislative documents, revised statutes, chapter 79: schools http://uniweb.legislature. ne.gov/legaldocs/view.php?page=index_statutes (2008) Accessed 18 June 2008

Schmid AA (2004) Conflict and cooperation: institutional and behavioral economics. Blackwell, Malden, MA

Application of the *ithink®* System Dynamics Software Program to the Social Fabric Matrix to Analyze Public School Finance Systems

Jerry L. Hoffman

Abstract State finance systems for public elementary and secondary education are a complex institution of court decisions and state statutes, working together as rules of law, agency rules and regulations, and administrative codes. The *ithink® Analyst* system dynamics software program and the social fabric matrix (SFM) were used for a public school finance lawsuit in the state of Nebraska. A model of Nebraska's education finance system, known as the Tax Equity and Educational Opportunities Support Act (TEEOSA), is constructed by integrating into the SFM the system components of belief statements, laws, rules, regulations, public finance data, and annual financial reports of public school districts, student enrollment data, and public organizations in an Excel spreadsheet. Digraphs are created using *ithink® Analyst* system dynamics program to show the flows and deliveries between and within the parts of the Nebraska education finance system. This analysis is useful in policy evaluation and development, law and rule making, and court ruling.

This chapter contains two sections. The first section will describe the key structural components of the Nebraska state aid formula as organized through the SFM. The second section demonstrates the general application of the *ithink® Analyst* to model state aid to public education as an integrated system. (This chapter does not describe or address system dynamics.)

The *ithink® Analyst* system dynamics software program and the social fabric matrix (SFM) were used for a public school finance lawsuit in the state of Nebraska. In *Nebraska Coalition for Ed. Equity v. Governor Heineman*, the plaintiffs argued that Nebraska's public education finance laws, known as the Tax Equity and Educational Opportunities Support Act (TEEOSA), do not measure the actual costs of contemporary educational standards as required by both the state and the federal government. Subsequently, the public education finance system does not provide adequate levels of public resources to support quality public kindergarten to grade

J.L. Hoffman (✉)
Nebraska State Education Association, an affiliate of National Education Association, Lincoln, NE, USA
jerry.hoffman.lincoln.ne@gmail.com

T. Natarajan et al. (eds.), *Institutional Analysis and Praxis*,
DOI 10.1007/978-0-387-88741-8_11, © Springer Science+Business Media, LLC 2009

12 schools. Nebraska state laws, therefore, violate the constitutional rights of students to equal and adequate educational opportunities. Defendants argued that Nebraska's constitution is silent on *adequate* education but only that it is *free*, and, further, public school funding is a non-justiciable political issue of the legislative branch. The Nebraska State Supreme Court agreed with the defendants (Nebraska Coalition for Ed. Equity v. Heineman 2007):

> The Nebraska Constitution commits the issue of providing free instruction to the Legislature and fails to provide judicially discernible and manageable standards for determining what level of public education the Legislature must provide. This court could not make that determination without deciding matters of educational policy in disregard of the policy and fiscal choices that the Legislature has already made…We conclude, as the district court did, that the claims therefore present nonjusticiable political questions.

America's federalist polity depends on a balance of power between the executive, legislative, and judicial branches. The legislative branch has the constitutional power to enact laws and, therefore, is the appropriate environment in which to answer political questions such as the adequacy of public school finance. The executive branch is largely responsible for the promulgation and administration of rules and regulations, which flow from laws. The role of the judicial branch is to adjudicate disputes arising from allegations of unlawful acts and the enactment of laws and promulgation of rules and regulations that violate the constitutional rights of citizens. Both the legislative and the judicial branches of government are in need of a *manageable framework* or methodology to address public education finance policy and lawmaking. How will the courts properly determine whether a law violates the constitutional rights of students to equal educational opportunities? How do publicly-elected politicians to state legislative offices negotiate legislative bills that base a state aid to public schools formula on a sound mathematical equation? What happens to each of the integrated components when new state lawmakers are delivered to public office through the democratic polity and create new public education finance laws without understanding the system dynamics of public education finance? What evaluation methodology is used by technocrats in executive branch agencies to determine if *formula needs* adequately measure the actual costs associated with delivering the qualities of *free instruction* to public school students as required by the accreditation and learning standards set by both the state and federal government? What policy analysis framework is used by academics and policy analysts to measure whether the state aid to public schools formula is delivering a sufficient level of public resources to ensure that the *free instruction* received by students between the ages of five and 21 will permit them to earn a living in a competitive labor market? What is the methodology by which the judicial branch may manage the standards required in determining if the laws governing public education finance systems are resulting in (un)equal access to educational opportunities by public school students? The *ithink® Analyst*, along with the social fabric matrix, provides a useful system dynamics methodology to lawmakers, legislative staff, public policy analysts, and court judges for analyzing public education finance systems.

A majority of public elementary and secondary education finance systems are on the basis of equalization formulae. These are complex mathematic equations that flow from laws created by, discussed among, and passed by publicly-elected state lawmakers and signed into law by state governors. The *public*, of which a majority does not have children or school-aged children, is unaware of the arcane system of public school finance. Yet, the *public* delivers income, sales, and property tax revenue to finance public education. While public school finance is arcane, the *public* is part of this system or *institution*. The institution of public finance for kindergarten through grade 12 (K-12) schools is comprised of normative beliefs, state laws, public policies, state agencies, political subdivisions, property, money, politics, mathematical formulae, individual attitudes, teachers, parents, and students. Normative belief statements are evident from state and federal constitutions, constitutional conventions, and intent language in state laws. The extent that mathematic equations, which deliver resources to pubic K-12 schools, are consistent with normative belief criteria is the focus of policy analysis using the social fabric matrix (SFM) and digraphs.

Finance of K-12 Public Education: An Integrated System

Public finance of elementary and secondary schools is an integrated system of constitutional laws and histories, court cases, state laws, policies, rules and regulations, mathematical formulae and data, money and politics. Figure 1 is the SFM of the Nebraska public finance system for elementary and secondary schools, for 2006–2007 (Hayden 2008).

Social Fabric Matrix of Nebraska State Aid for a Local K-12 Public School System, 2006–2007

The SFM is read from left-to-right; delivering components to receiving components. A cell with the number one (1) shows that a delivery is taking place. For example, social beliefs deliver criteria to institutional organizations, which deliver rules, regulations, and requirements to public K-12 school districts (Hayden 2006).

Cells 1–7, 1–8, 2–7, 2–8, 3–7, 3–8, 4–7, 4–8, 5–7, 5–8, 6–7, and 6–8 construct the normative system for public education. The social beliefs of *equity, adequacy/ sufficiency, cost efficiency, comprehensive size, consolidation, and local control* deliver requirements to the authority institutions such as the courts and the legislature. The source materials for such social beliefs include official territorial reports by commissioners of common schools, state superintendants of public instruction, constitutional conventions, and territorial legislative enactments for the period of 1860–1888. This period precedes Nebraska's official statehood in 1867 and succeeds the popular vote adopting the first state constitution in 1875. Common schools came into existence when Nebraska was a territorial government and were

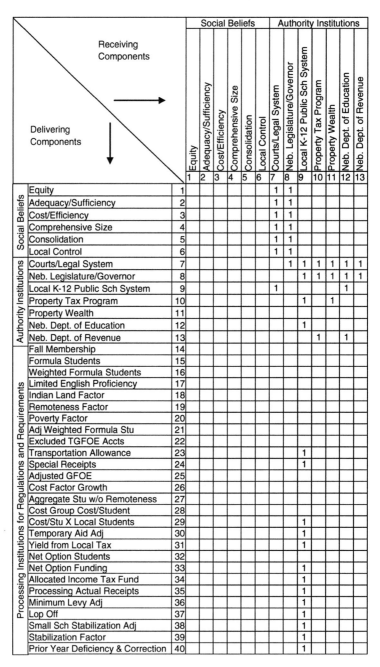

Fig. 1 Social fabric matrix of Nebraska state aid for a local K-12 public school system, 2006–2007

	Fall Membership (14)	Formula Students (15)	Weighted formula Students (16)	Limited English Proficiency (17)	Indian Land Factor (18)	Remoteness Factor (19)	Poverty Factor (20)	Adj. Weighted Formula Stu (21)	Excluded TGFOE Accts (22)	Transportation Allowance (23)	Special Receipts (24)	Adjusted GFOE (25)	Cost Factor Growth (26)	Aggregate Stu w/o Remoteness (27)	Cost Group Cost/Student (28)	Cost/Stu X Local Students (29)	Temporary Aid Adj (30)	Yield from Local Tax (31)	Net Option Students (32)	Net Option funding (33)	Allocated Income Tax Fund (34)	Other Actual Receipts (35)	Minimum Levy Adj (36)	Lop Off (37)	Small Sch Stabilization Adj (38)	Stabilization Factor (39)	Prior Year Deficiency & Correction (40)
1																											
2																											
3																											
4																											
5																											
6																											
7																											
8																											
9																											
10																		1									
11																											
12	1	1	1	1	1	1	1	1	1	1	1	1	1	1	1	1	1	1	1	1	1	1	1	1	1	1	1
13																											
14		1																									
15			1		1	1						1															
16								1						1						1							
17								1						1													
18								1						1													
19								1																			
20								1						1													
21																1											
22											1																
23											1							1							1	1	1
24											1							1				1			1	1	1
25															1												
26															1												
27															1												
28																	1			1							
29																		1							1	1	1
30																				1	1				1	1	1
31																									1	1	1
32																					1						
33																					1				1	1	1
34																									1	1	1
35																											
36																								1	1	1	1
37																										1	1
38																											1
39																											
40																									1		

Header span: Processing Institutions for Regulations and Requirements

Fig. 1 (Continued)

located in counties that had not yet established civil or municipal townships (rural) and counties that had incorporated cities (Omaha). The writings by commissioners of common schools of official territorial reports and later by state superintendants of public instruction of state reports reveal the condition of commons schools and the needed public policies to support the development of common schools for all school-aged children. The needed public policies were on the basis of the aspirations of Nebraska's earliest citizens and territorial government lawmakers that a system of free education would cause long-term improvement in the wealth, prosperity, and power of the individual, as *educated citizen,* the state (Nebraska) and the country (United States of America). That system of free education was built through local commons schools to provide every child the opportunity to expand his/her abilities (i.e., intellectual, skills, and knowledge) and therefore the political and economic capabilities of the state and the nation. The social beliefs of *equity, adequacy/sufficiency, cost efficiency, comprehensive size, consolidation, and local control* are embedded in today's public education system.

The social belief of e*quity* (cell 1–7 and 1–8) was initially referred in the territorial and state reports as u*niformity.* William E. Harvey, the first commissioner of common schools, wrote about the need for *uniformity* to establish common schools that were in financially *prosperous condition provided the Legislature will aid them* (First Annual Report of the Commissioner of Common Schools of the Territory of Nebraska to the Sixth Legislative Assembly Session 1860). *Uniformity* in tax revenue disbursement supported the *uniform* needs of commons schools such as textbooks, writing instruments, facilities, and teachers. *Uniformity* turned to *equity* with the adoption of the Nebraska state constitution in 1875. Article VIII (Education), Sect. 7 calls for the *equitable distribution of income* from the school lands fund to support a system of free education.

Adequacy/sufficiency (cells 2–7 and 2–8) is expressed in early writings specifically addressing the need to provide sufficient tax revenues to common schools. In reference to the methods for estimating resource distribution, S.D. Beals writes: "they are based on the presumption that all of the districts sustain schools; but they are not based on the supposition that ample provision is made for the accommodation of all of the children" (First annual report of the State Superintendent of Public Instruction to the Governor of Nebraska 1869). Beals introduces the notion that a system of free education is on the basis of providing *ample provision* of resources from state government. John McKenzie, Beals successor, writes in 1874 "Our school systems require years of toil and large sums of money to bring them into effective working condition" (Sixth annual report of the State Superintendent of Public Instruction to the Governor of Nebraska 1874). In general terms, a*mple* and *sustain* are early expressions of the social beliefs of *adequacy* or *sufficiency.*

Cost efficient (cells 3–7 and 3–8), *comprehensive size* (cells 4–7 and 4–8), and *consolidation* (cells 5–7 and 5–8) are introduced as social belief criteria in Nebraska around 1878. Nebraska is experiencing a rapid population settlement. The free education system of local common schools is about eighteen years old. Nebraska lawmakers consider the competing but inter-dependent public interest in free education and the private interest to maintain low tax rates on property. These belief criteria first appear officially in the writings of S. R. Thompson, McKenzie's successor, in 1878. Thompson writes: "Our school system is not benevolent, but economical. School moneys properly expended are not a gift in charity, but an investment for profit. The property of the State is made to educate the children of the State, because this is the best way to promote both the accumulation of wealth and its safe enjoyment" (Tenth Annual Report of the State Superintendent of Public Instruction to the Governor of Nebraska 1878). Common schools as economical models reflect the belief in *cost efficiency.*

Comprehensive size and *consolidation* social belief criteria are introduced by George B. Lane, Thompson's successor, in 1888. Lane writes: "While all measures for the improvement of our educational system depends primarily upon general public interest and its practical manifestation in local school affairs, it is evident that the school system itself…could be improved in the important matter of local independent school districts. There are too many small school districts, with the inevitable result of small schools, low standard, low wages and poor teachers, with poor local supervision or none at all. These evils cannot be eradicated until the petty school sovereignties are abandoned and local interest supplemented by a common and higher interest formulated by laws binding alike upon all" (Twentieth Annual Report of the State Superintendent of Public Instruction to the Governor of Nebraska 1888). Lane's report begins the movement to consolidate common schools at the state level, which is exacerbated later in the mid-twentieth century at the national level.

The social belief criterion of *local control* (cells 6–7 and 6–8) is embedded at the onset of developing the free education system of common schools. Property was the only measure of wealth in the mid-1850s. Therefore, common schools received financial resources from taxes levied on property. Common schools were encouraged to exist wherever school children lived, with walking distance from home to school being one measure for the site location of a school. The settlement of the Nebraska territory along the Missouri River westward meant that common schools were established in cities, such as Omaha, and in the rural counties where towns did not exist. Common schools were, and remain, schools *of the community.*

Cells 7–8, 7–9, 7–10, 7–11, 7–12, and 7–13 represent the *working rules* of the public education finance system based on case laws about school lands, property rights, compulsory education, taxation, and revenue. Such *working rules* guide the lawmaking processes of the Nebraska Unicameral Legislature.

Cells 8–9, 8–10, 8–11, 8–12 and 8–13 are the Nebraska state laws that set forth the public education finance system, TEEOSA. The legislative branch must enact laws to effect the constitution because constitutional language by itself is not self-legislating. Therefore, the Nebraska legislature and governor deliver the Neb. Rev. Stat. §§79-1001 to 1,033, a body of laws that define formula needs, resources, and state aid to public schools (see *formula needs – local resources = state aid below*).

Cell 12–9 is unique in that the Nebraska Department of Education (NDE) delivers, in addition to state aid to public schools, educational standards, curriculum and learning requirements, standards for the certification of teachers and education professionals, and technology and facility requirements to each public school system in Nebraska.

Such standards are presumed to be guided by the normative belief criterion of equality, as in equality in educational opportunities for each public school aged student.

Cells 12–14 to 12–40 represent the NDE's role in promulgating the rules, regulations, and requirements of the state education finance laws, managing data systems, and running the mathematical calculations of the state aid formula. The NDE annually certifies state aid to public schools on the basis of a general formulaic principle that has three main components: [educational] needs minus local resources equal state aid.

- Cells 12–14 to 12–30 are the sub-parts required to calculate the component of *formula needs*. Formula needs are calculated as {(adjusted weighted formula students (cell 12–21) times cost grouping cost per student (cell 12–28)) plus transportation allowance (cell 12–23) plus special receipts allowance (cell 12–24)] minus temporary aid adjustment factor (cell 12–30) (NDE). In 2006–2007, total formula need statewide was $2.2 billion.
- Cells 12–31 to 12–39 are the sub-parts required to calculate the component of "local resources," which is the sum of yield from local effort rate (cell 12–31) plus net option students funding (cells 12–32 and 12–33) plus allocated income tax funds (cell 12–34) plus other receipts actually received by the school district (cell 12–35) plus minimum levy adjustment (12–36) (NDE). In 2006–2007, total local resources were $1.6 million.
- Additional sub-parts of the state aid component include lop off (cell 12–37); small school stabilization factor (cell 12–38), stabilization factor (cell 12–39), and a prior year deficiency and correction (cell 12–40). In 2006–2007, total state aid to public schools statewide was $718.4 million.

Rows 14–40 contain the mathematical expressions for different parts of the state aid formula. Each row delivers specific sets of data that flow from state laws. The data are used to calculate the TEEOSA state aid formula (i.e., different parts of the needs component). What follows is for demonstration purposes only of the key sub-parts used to calculate the component of need at the public school level. The process is likened to an assembly line: fall student enrollment is the raw commodity (row 14) delivered to the state aid formula which manufactures adjusted weighted formula students (row 21) used in the production of so-called formula "needs" (rows 14–29).

- Cell 14–15: Annually each school district delivers a fall membership report to the NDE (cell 9–12) which provides a student census count for grades kindergarten (half-day and full-day) to 12 (row 14) as of the last Friday in September (NDE 2006a). Cell 14–15 is the formula used to calculate "formula students" (NDE 2006a). Fall membership is adjusted on the basis of a three-year historical ratio of average daily membership (ADM) to fall membership, which includes contracted students in grades kindergarten to 12 (NDE 2006a). Fall membership statewide is 285,546 for school year 2005–2006 (NDE 2006a). Total formula students statewide are 278, 227 for school year 2005–2006; that is,

$$\left[\left(\left(277,286 \, / \, 283,900 \right) + \left(276,787 \, / \, 284,170 \right) + \left(276,731 \, / \, 284,559 \right) \right) / \, 3 \right]$$
$$\times 285,546; or 0.964 \times 285,546.$$

Total formula students are less than fall membership but will go through a process to gain weight.

- Cell 15–16: Formula students (FS) are delivered to cell 15–16 to process "weighted formula students" (WFS). State laws assign weights to formula students in the grade ranges of half-day kindergarten (0.5), full-day kindergarten to grade six (1.0), grades seven to eight (1.2) and grades nine to twelve (1.4) (NDE 2006a). The prevailing political knowledge is that the weights represent costs associated with providing an education to students, with costs being highest in secondary grades (9–12). Without guidance from actual research, state lawmakers determined the grade level weights by political negotiation and compromise. An approximation of adjusting fall membership to formula students to derive weighted formula students is as follows: (NDE 2006a)

> FS half – day kindergarten : $5,945 \times 0.5 = 2,973$
>
> + FS full – day kindergarten to grade six : $144,931 \times 1.0 = 144,931$
>
> + FS grades seven to eight : $43,487 \times 1.2 = 52,184$
>
> + FS grades nine to twelve : $90,961 \times 1.4 = 127,345$
>
> = Total Weighted Formula Students (WFS): $372,433$

Weighted formula students are delivered to process adjusted weighted formula students to certify state aid for 2006–2007.

- Cells 16–21, 17–21, 18–21, 19–21, and 20–21: Adjusted weighted formula students flow from the calculation of weighted formula students (WFS) plus a summation of demographic factors: {limited English proficiency plus Indian land (IL) plus extreme remoteness and poverty} (NDE 2006a). As with grade weights, each demographic factor is weighted arbitrarily by state lawmakers through the political-legislative process. In the 2006–2007 certification of state aid to public schools, each demographic factor required to calculate adjusted weighted formula students was as follows: (NDE 2006b)

Weighted Formula Students : $320,971.3608$

+ Limited English Proficiency Factor : $3,886.25$ (based on $15,465$ students)

+ Free Lunch / Poverty Factor : $10,457.1555$ (based on $75,870$ students)

+ Indian Land : 234.6450 (based on 938 students)

+ Extreme Remoteness : 145.7513 (based on $1,166$ students)

= Adjusted Weighted Formula Students : $335,674$

The final step in the process of manufacturing formula needs is to multiply adjusted weighted formula students by cost grouping cost per student.

• Cell 21–28: On the basis of Nebraska state laws, public schools are segregated into three cost groupings: very sparse, sparse and standard (Nebraska Revised and §79–1007a). The formula defined in state law delivers a public school to a cost group on the basis of the requirements of student enrollment per square miles of the county in which the school is located, student enrollment per square miles of the public school district, formula students, and the distance between secondary schools. Once in a cost group the public schools total estimated general fund operating expenditures for that cost group is divided by the total adjusted weighted formula students for all public schools in the cost group. That quotient, known as the cost grouping cost per student, is multiplied by the adjusted weighted formula students, which delivers the product called *formula need*. In the 2006–2007 certification of state aid, the calculation was as follows :(Nebraska Department of Education 2006b)

Aggregate Cost Group Cost per Student : $6,047
× Adjusted Weighted Formula Students : 335,788.2532
= *Formula Need,subtotal* : $2,031,193,234.13

This exercise demonstrates that the state aid to public schools formulae receives a quantity of 284,546 statewide fall student membership (raw commodity) and manufactures a value-added quantity of adjusted weighted formula students, which in turn is used to derive a product, *formula need,* measured as a dollar cost. The SFM approach to analyzing Nebraska's public education finance formulae reveals that inconsistent values flow from one equation to the next.

For example, total weighted formula students number of 372,433, as calculated in cells 15–16, differs from the NDE quantity of 320,971.3608. Yet, the analysis uses the NDE's data for fall membership in grades kindergarten to twelve to calculate total formula students in cell 14–15 which flows into the calculation of total weighted formula students in cell 15–16. Further, the adjusted weighted formula student product in cell 16–21 is 335,674, calculated using the mathematic formula prescribed in state law with data from the NDE (Nebraska Revised and §79–1007b). The NDE uses the amount of 335,788.2532 in cell 21–28 to calculate *formula need* (NDE 2006b).

Fundamental questions flow from such inconsistencies that focus on the integrity of the public education finance system. The *ithink®* Software program is one methodology for analyzing the system dynamics of a public education finance system.

Applying *ithink®* System Dynamics to Analyze Public School Finance

The *ithink®* software program is used to develop the digraphs associated with the SFM rows 14 through 29 in Fig. 1. Digraphs are generated directly from the SFM. A digraph visually depicts (a) the complexity of the school finance system and the contextual institution of school finance, (b) the web of deliveries and flows within the institutional components of the school finance system, and (c) the state equalization formula used to provide and allocate the state resource share of public elementary and secondary schools. Further, state aid formulae are entered into the *ithink®* software program to run the mathematic equations associated with Nebraska's TEEOSA. Such analysis allows for a systems approach to public policy analysis of school finance as it relates to equity and adequacy, although this chapter does not address system dynamics.

Three levels of the public education finance system are modeled using *ithink®* (High Performance, Inc. 1990).

1. High Level Map: The high level map depicts major *processes* of the system.
2. Modeling Layer: Model *building blocks* focus on *stocks, flows, connectors, and converters. Stocks* (e.g., an institution or organization) are the basic building block which represents *anything that accumulates* (High Performance Systems 1990–1997, 15). This may include physical quantities such as money or fall student membership or non-physical qualities such as social beliefs and state statutes. *Flows* represent activities or deliveries that cause the *magnitudes of stocks* to increase or decrease (High Performance Systems 1990–1997, 15). For example, moving from fall student membership to adjusted fall membership is a flow. *Connectors* transmit information and inputs used in the *regulation of flows* (High Performance Systems 1990–1997, 16). An example is the grade level weightings used to calculate total formula students. *Converters* contain equations (High Performance Systems 1990–1997, 16). For example, the mathematic equation for calculating total formula students from fall membership is a converter. (Chapter 11 Appendix A provides the *ithink®* symbols that are used in Figs. 2–5; High Performance Systems 1990–1997, 22)
3. Equation Layer: The equations throughout the modeling layer are provided in a detailed level. *ithink®* will *run* the equations to deliver an output value such as the total *formula need.*

The SFM/digraph models of the Nebraska TEEOSA will focus only on the high level map and the modeling layer, beginning with Fig. 2, high level mapping of education finance system.

As depicted, social belief criteria (rows 1–6) are delivered to institutional organizations (rows 7–13). The institutional organizations are *processing* institutions in that rules and regulations flow to codify the *working system* of the TEEOSA state aid to public education *formula needs* (rows 14–29). A public school district,

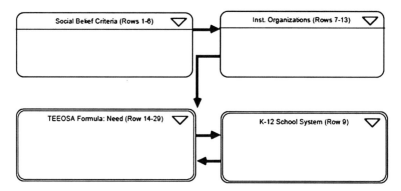

Fig. 2 High level map of education finance system

grades kindergarten to twelve, delivers data to the TEEOSA formula, such as fall
student membership, and receives a TEEOSA formula amount of state aid in the
form of money produced with state tax revenues (row 9).

The digraph in Fig. 3 provides the next level of flows and deliveries of the
education finance system. *Equity*, as a social belief criterion, is delivered to the
courts (cell 1–7) and the legislature (cell 1–8). The courts use social belief
criteria to rule on claims made in legal cases. The legislature enacts laws guided
by social beliefs. Courts intervene to rule on the constitutionality of laws relative
to social belief criterion such as *equity*, which flow from state and/or federal
constitutions (cell 7–8). This particular system dynamic, known as *working rules*,
flow to the Department of Education, the executive state agency charged with
codifying the rules and regulations of the TEEOSA education finance formula
(cells 12–14 to 12–40).

The programming sub-models for TEEOSA *formula needs* (social fabric
matrix rows 14–29) are AWFSy0 (y0 is current year, 2006–2007) and Cost Group
Cost per Student y0. *Formula need* receives input from the product of the two
programming sub-models plus previous years transportation allowance (Tran
Allowy1) plus previous years special receipts allowance (Spec Rec Allow y1).
K-12 (grades kindergarten to 12) school system (row 9) delivers Student
Enrollment to the TEEOSA formula (cell 14–15) and receives the output of the
formula in the form of State Aid y0.

Figure 4 is the digraph of the average weighted formula students programming
sub-model. This is the modeling layer of the *ithink®* software. The digraph is read
from left-to-right to illustrate the manufacturing of average weighted formula students from fall membership (raw commodity).

- Ky1 (prior year half-day kindergarten enrollment), FDKSy1 (prior year full-day
  kindergarten to grade six enrollment), SEy1 (prior year grade seven to eight
  enrollment), and NTy1 (prior year grade nine to twelve enrollment) flow into the
  Fall Membership circle or *regulator*. Each grade-level circle contains a quantity
  representing student membership. The Fall Membership regulator contains an

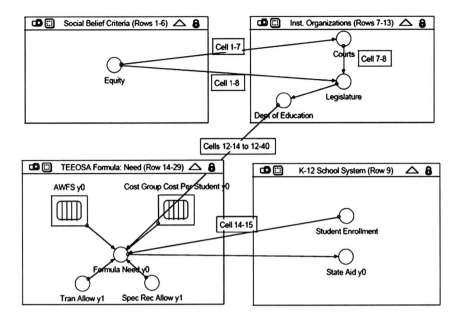

Fig. 3 Digraph of the education finance system

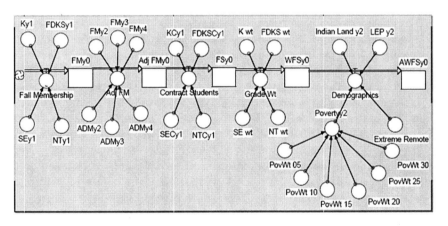

Fig. 4 Digraph of adjusted weighted formula students

equation that sums the grade-level enrollment and delivers the output to the FMy0 box or *stock* (fall membership, current year). Fall membership is 285,546 for 2005–2006. That quantity is now an input flow to calculate adjusted formula students (Adj FM).

• Fall membership (FM) is adjusted using a ratio of fall membership to average daily membership (ADM) for each of the three previous years. Of FMy2,

FMy3, FMy4, ADMy$_2$, ADMy3, and ADMy4 circles each contains a quantity that flows to the Adj FM circle, regulator, which holds the equation that produces the output to the Adj FM box or stock of 278,227. That quantity flows through the Contract Students regulator, which sums KCy1 (contracted half-day kindergarten students), FDKSCy1 (contracted full-day kindergarten to grade six students), SECy1 (contracted grade seven to eight students), and NTCy1 (contracted grade nine to twelve students). The output is FSy0, total formula students of 278,227.

- Formula students (FSy0) are an input quantity that flows to the grade weighting regulator (Grade Wt). Additional input flows include K wt (half-day kindergarten weight of 0.5), FDKS wt (full-day kindergarten to six grade weight of 1.0), SE wt (weight for grades seven to eight, 1.2), and NT wt (weight for grades nine to twelve, 1.4). The output quantity is total weighted formula students (WFSy0) of 372,433.

- Weighted formula students (WFSy0) are an input quantity delivered to the Demographics regulator. The Demographics regulator calculates the value for Adjusted Weighted Formula Students (AWFSy0) by receiving input values from Indian Land (y2 is two year old data), Limited English Proficiency factor (LEPy2), Poverty (y2 is two year old data), and Extreme Remoteness. The poverty factor (Povertyy2) is on the basis of a gradation of weights that are on the basis of the greater of two values: students qualifying for free lunch program or children living in federally-designated poverty. That value is divided by the total formula students in each public K-12 school. The percentage value receives a poverty factor weight that varies given the percentage level. For example, if poverty is less than or equal to 5%, then no weight is assigned. If poverty is greater than 5% but less than 10%, poverty factor is weighted at 0.05 (PovWt05). Poverty ranging from 10% to 15% is weighted at 0.10 (PovWt10). Poverty ranging from 15% to 20% is weighted at 0.20 (PovWt20). Poverty ranging from 20% to 25% is weighted at 0.25 (PovWt25). If poverty is greater than 25%, then the weight is 0.30 (PovWt30) (NDE 2006c). In the certification of state aid for 2006–2007, 75,870 students were participating in the free lunch program and/or living in federally designated poverty. The product of the poverty factor weights produces a quantity of 10,457.1555 students that is delivered to Povertyy2, which is the input value to the Demographics regulator. The Demographics regulator generates an output value to AWFSy0 (adjusted weighted formula students) of 335,674.

As indicated with the SFM description of the education finance system, the final step in manufacturing students to derive *formula needs* is the calculation of cost grouping cost per student.

Figure 5 is the digraph of cost grouping cost per student (CGCSy0) sub-model. The following description of cost grouping cost per student flows directly from state laws.

- The cost group regulator (Cost Group) receives quantity inflows from the following (NDE 2006a):

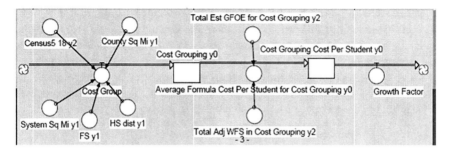

Fig. 5 Digraph of average cost group cost per student

- The census report for children five to eighteen years of age, Census5 18y2, based on two year old data.
- Square miles of the county in which the high school is located (County Sq Mi y1), based on one year old data.
- Square miles of the K-12 public school system, System Sq Mi y1, based on one year old data.
- Formula students, FS y1, for the year prior to the certification of state aid.
- Distance between high school attendance centers, measured in miles, HS dist y1, based on one year old data.

The output flow from the cost group regulator determines the cost grouping.

- Very sparse cost grouping is less than 0.5 census students per county square mile, less than 1 formula student per school district square mile, and more than 15 miles between high school attendance centers. Or more than 450 square miles in the school district, less than 0.5 formula students per school district miles, and more than 15 miles between high school attendance centers (Nebraska Revised Statutes §79–1007a).
- Spare cost grouping is less than 2 census students per county square mile, less than 1 formula student per school district square mile, and more than 10 miles between each two high school attendance centers. Or less than 1.5 formula students per public school district square mile and more than 15 miles between high school attendance centers. Or less than 1.5 formula students per public school district square mile and more than 275 square miles in the public school district. Or less than 2 formula students per square mile in the public school district and the local school district includes an area equal to 95% or more of the square miles in the largest county in which a high school attendance center is located (Nebraska Revised Statutes §79–1007a).
- Standard group is any K-12 public school district that is neither very sparse nor sparse.

That output value flows to the Average Formula Cost per Student for Grouping y0 (where y0 is 2006–2007) regulator where it receives input values from total estimated general fund operating expense for the cost group in y2, two years prior to y0, and total adjusted weighted formula students in cost grouping in y2. That quotient value of $6,047 flows to Cost Group y0. The output value, $6,047, is multiplied by adjusted weighted formula students, 335,788.2532, to deliver the product of *formula needs*: $2,031,193,234 (Nebraska Department of Education 2006c).

This layer of detail is not fully modeled at the equation layer of *ithink®*. The *ithink®* modeling layer permits a digraph presentation of the major factor processes in calculating cost grouping cost per student, as in Fig. 5.

Conclusion

Elementary and secondary education finance systems are complex. The SFM/ digraph approach to analyzing education finance systems permits the ability to both model the current system, as done in this chapter, and reform the system. A legislative policy analyst can use the SFM/digraph to model the education finance system and analyze the integrated system dynamics, flows, deliveries, and processes. Lawmakers may make more informed decisions about creating laws that change incrementally one or more of the components and factors of the education finance formulae. For example, once the current education finance system is modeled using the *ithink®* software, based on the SFM/digraph, a public policy analyst may generate various modeling scenarios. What happens to *formula need* if early childhood education were a new factor? How is average weighted formula students affected if the grade level weightings changed to more closely reflect the actual costs of providing essential educational opportunities (i.e., technology, knowledge, and skills of educators, and facilities)? Finally, the SFM/digraph provides a serious approach to evaluate education finance laws by the courts.

References

First annual report of the Commissioner of Common Schools of the Territory of Nebraska to the Sixth Legislative Assembly Session 1859–1860 (1860) Robertson & Clark. Omaha City, NE, p 5
First annual report of the State Superintendent of Public Instruction to the Governor of Nebraska, for the year ending December 31, 1869 (1869), p 63
Hayden FG (2006) Policymaking for a good society: the social fabric matrix approach to policy analysis and program evaluation. Springer, New York, pp 86–90
Hayden FG (2008) Social fabric matrix. http://cba.unl.edu/academics/economics/sfm. Accessed 14 Feb 2008
High Performance Systems (1990–1997) Getting started with the ithink software: a hands-on experience
Nebraska coalition for education equity, v. Heineman (2007) 273 Neb. 531 at 557
Nebraska Department of Education (2006) School district membership report, 2005–2006
Nebraska Department of Education (2006) Report of the tax equity and educational opportunities support act, table 4: comparison of system state aid certification information 2005/06 compared to 2006/07, p D-23

Nebraska Department of Education (2006) Tax equity and educational opportunities support act certification of 2006–2007 state aid, p 2

Nebraska Revised Statutes, §79-1007.02

Nebraska Revised Statutes, §79-1007.01

Sixth annual report of the State Superintendent of Public Instruction to the Governor of Nebraska, for the year ending December 31, 1874 (1874), p 63

Tenth annual report of the State Superintendent of Public Instruction to the Governor of Nebraska, for the year ending December 31, 1878 (1878), p 16

Twentieth annual report of the State Superintendent of Public Instruction to the Governor of Nebraska, for the year ending December 31, 1888 (1888), p 71

Ceremonial Dimensions of Market-Based Pollution Control Instruments: The Clean Air Act and the Cap-and-Trade Model*

Steven R. Bolduc

Abstract Market-based pollution control instruments represent the influence of a commitment to the principle of laissez-faire economics and the success of orthodox economics to steer public policy formation. The criteria for design and assessment of policy interventions however should not be influenced by a prior commitment to a problem-solving strategy. Rather, the inquiry guiding policy design and assessment should be guided by the recognition of social, ecological, and technological interdependence and by the discovery of evaluative criteria consistent with this interdependence.

Introduction

Economics contributes to policy debates by focusing attention on the primary analytical concepts of the discipline: costs, benefits and tradeoffs. Yet, economic efficiency as the sole evaluative criteria may not be sufficient. A necessary condition for effective policy intervention is the creation of social institutions with the capacity both to recognize relevant social, technological and ecological criteria and to implement rules and regulations consistent with these criteria. "The concern for consistency of the normative criteria is not just a deontic concern for logical completeness and consistency. It is a real-world concern of major importance. Society has lost the institutional ability to make social belief, technological, and ecological criteria consistent with each other and consistent with an instrumental flow of events and actions in its processing institutions" (Hayden 1998:102).

Increasingly, economists are expanding their analysis to consider how policies impact avenues of inquiry particularly when key stakeholders exert significant influence in research decisions. As Paul Dale Bush has made clear, "Knowledge embodied in instrumental patterns of behavior is available to the community for use

S.R. Bolduc (✉)
Minnesota State University, Moorhead, MN, USA

* Steven R. Bolduc. 2004. "Ceremonial dimensions of market-based pollution control instruments: the clean air act and the cap-and-trade model" Special Issue The Limitations of Deregulation Revisited. Guest Editors Harry M. Trebing and Edythe S. Miller. *Utilities Policy*, Volume 12, Number 3 (September): 181–191. Elsevier.

T. Natarajan et al. (eds.), *Institutional Analysis and Praxis*,
DOI 10.1007/978-0-387-88741-8_12, © Springer Science+Business Media, LLC 2009

in the problem-solving activities that sustain the life process of the community. Knowledge encapsulated within ceremonial patterns of behaviors is either effectively withheld from the problem-solving process, or, to the extent that it is permitted to be employed in the problem-solving process, the legitimacy of its use is held to the standard of ceremonial adequacy" (Bush 1983:38).

Echoing the need for a broad set of evaluative criteria, a recent National Academy of Sciences report, *Air Quality Management in the United States*, notes:

> Although the inputs of science and technology are important, they are not the sole determination of the success of an air quality management (AQM) system. Effective AQM decisions are made and implemented by elected and appointed leaders in the context of divers social, economic, and political considerations. Successful AQM requires that the input from the scientific and techno-logical communities be utilized by those leaders to produce adequate and cost-effective pollutant emission reductions for which a variety of societal consideration, including environmental jus-tice, are taken into account. The U.S. AQM system entails the promulgation of rules and regula-tions on specific types of emissions, the institution of programs that provide incentives for the creative development of new technologies, and the use of emission control technologies and systems that reduce air pollution to a sufficient degree to protect public health. *However, the effectiveness of AQM can be undermined by a breakdown in any of these components* (National Academy of Sciences 2003:28; emphasis added).

The purpose of this paper is to examine how well market-based air pollution control instruments satisfy a broad set of evaluative criteria. The suggestion is that the reli-ance on market-based solutions has hindered inquiry into policy options thereby restricting more effective – broadly considered – policy outcomes.

The structure of the paper is as follows: First, the magnitude of the environmental hazards facing policy makers is described. Second, the argument for and use of market-based air pollution controls are surveyed, using the Clean Air Act of 1970 as amended as an example of this approach. Third, the cap-and-trade model is evaluated with par-ticular emphasis upon the way in which such an approach to environmental hazards can cloud problem definition and deflect inquiry from alternate policy options. The Social Fabric Matrix (SFM) is introduced as a means both to understand the interdependence of social, technological and ecological dimensions of the life process and to identify evaluative criteria consistent with this interdependence. Lastly, recent policy interven-tions by some US states and by Canada are suggested as avenues of policy inquiry that warrant more attention at the federal tier of air quality management programs.

The core argument is that market-based pollution control instruments can be effective in encouraging innovation, but that policy outcomes could be improved with a better understanding of the government's capacity for risk management. Moreover, a market-based approach tends to undermine the legitimacy of the governance process and elevates the narrowly conceived economic evaluative criteria above the social, technological and ecological criteria necessary for effective policy, and for public support of such policy.

The Magnitude of Air Pollution Hazards and of Policy Challenges

The challenges facing air pollution policy initiatives are daunting and include public health, legal, and governance legitimacy dimensions. Stationary fuel combustion from power plants, transportation such as cars and trucks, and industrial processes emit a number of pollutants that harm human and animal health, damage ecosystems, degrade buildings surfaces and impair visibility; these impacts could be close to the source or, because of pollutant migration, could be hundreds of miles away, further complicating inquiry into the source-receptor relationships. Some air emissions, such as nitric oxide and nitrogen dioxide for example, are classified as primary pollutants since they are emitted directly into the atmosphere. Secondary pollutants result from chemical reactions between emissions and other compounds. "Control of secondary pollutants is generally more problematic than that of primary pollutants because mitigation of secondary pollutants requires identification of the precursor compounds and their sources as well as an understanding of the specific chemical reactions that results in the formation of the secondary pollutants" (National Academy of Sciences, National Research Council 2003:19).

Power plants in the United States are responsible for 11.4 million tons of sulfur dioxide (SO_2) annually which accounts for 62% of the acid rain. The plants also emit 5.2 million tons of nitric oxide and nitrogen dioxide (collectively, NO_x) annually contributing to 21% of the smog (Silverstein 2003b). Stationary fuel combustion is responsible for 87% of the SO_2 and 38% of the NO_x generated in the U.S. (National Academy of Sciences, National Research Council 2003:20). SO_2 and NO_x also react with ammonia in the atmosphere to create small particles which interfere with oxygen absorption by the lungs, contributing to a number of health problems.

In an attempt to quantify these health impacts, a November 2002 report for the Environmental Integrity Project examined 41 power plants that "emitted at least 40,000 tons of SO_2 in 2001 and had SO_2 emissions either increase or decline by less than half the national average between 1990 and 2001." From these 41 plants in 2001, they attribute between 4,800 and 5,600 premature deaths due to long-term exposure; over 3,000 hospital admission or emergency visits for pneumonia, cardiovascular problems and serious asthma; 930,000 work loss days and 111,000 asthma attacks not requiring hospitalization (Abt Associates 2002:6–10).

Coal-fired plants are also responsible for about one-third of mercury emissions and because most emissions remain close to the point of release, a regional approach to control may create hot spots of mercury concentration. Not regulated under the original Clean Air Act, mercury emissions have yet to be limited for coal plants though restrictions are in place for medical waste and garbage incinerator facilities. When it is released into the air from coal combustion, mercury combines with rainwater and collects in lakes and streams where methyl mercury is formed. This compound is bioaccumulative – i.e., concentrates in fat tissue – and is transferred up the food chain. Mercury is particularly harmful for fetuses, nursing infants, small children, and anyone with a high proportion of fish in their diet. Health impacts include lung, liver, kidney and neurological damage. Consequently, 43 states have mercury advisories warning of too much fish consumption (Silverstein 2003f).

Because of the low migration rate for mercury contamination, many have noted the inability of a cap-and-trade model to effectively protect public health against it. While average or even total mercury levels for a region may be reduced through a cap-and-trade approach, the concentration in some local hot spots may remain too high.

Quoting an EPA report, Ken Silverstein notes, "Even the EPA recognizes this: 'A cap-and-trade program raises the possibility that any particular utility may opt to purchase allowances, instead of implementing controls, and that this may result in continued mercury emissions at the previous, uncontrolled levels from that utility'" (Silverstein 2003f). Moreover, debate about current availability of effective mercury abatement technology has stymied federal rules, although Connecticut has moved forward with its own aggressive initiative. As discussed below, many states have exceeded the standards of current policy and have done so not by abandoning competition as a positive force for innovation but by strategic use of government budget and regulatory authority.

While the burning of coal contributes to the mercury contamination problem, the mining of coal continues to pose its own set of environmental problems. About one-third of coal from the Appalachia region of West Virginia, Kentucky, and eastern Tennessee is mined by "mountaintop removal." A Bush Administration proposal would "alter a rule to allow state regulators to give mining companies permission to go ahead [with such a mining technique] if they can show their efforts would preserve water quality 'to the extent possible'" (Silverstein 2004b). The advantage of the mountaintop removal technique is an access to the lower sulfur content coal just below the surface; the disadvantage is the impact from the "valley fills" of rock and soil and river, and the stream pollution and silting from run-off. Approximately 720 miles of streams have been buried and 7% of the forests of Appalachia have been cut down. Advocates of mountaintop removal mining claim the environmental benefits of low-sulfur coal and the economic benefits of land reclamation efforts outweigh costs of ecosystem damage. Opponents argue the economic benefits are minimal relative to the damage; moreover, they note that coal mining in the US occurs disproportionately in poor communities and, consequently, coal-mining practice is an environmental justice matter as well as an issue to the damage of the ecosystem.

A related environmental matter in justice, though on a global scale, is the Bush Administration's position on the Kyoto Protocol mandating a 5% reduction in CO_2 emissions below 1990 levels between 2008 and 2012. The US contributes one-quarter of the world's CO_2, the compound responsible for global warming and, consequently, has a proportionate responsibility to the world community to take the lead in reducing carbon dioxide. The impact on biodiversity is potentially severe: a recent study suggests "that more than one million species could be extinguished by 2050 if the rise in temperatures is not curtailed" (cited in Silverstein 2004c). The Administration's claim of more significant reductions through voluntary restrictions fails to provide global leadership in addressing global warming, particularly in light of the Department of Energy's estimates of a 43% increase in CO_2 emissions by US companies by 2020 (Silverstein 2003e).

In order to reduce hazards of local mercury contamination and of global warming, many have advocated greater diversification of the energy generation portfolio. To this end, nuclear power is again gaining attention despite no new facilities having been built in the US since 1979. However, the claim of nuclear power as a low cost energy source fails to account for the role of government policy in externalizing many of the costs and of managing the risk. For example, industry advocates have encouraged Congressional support for guaranteed loans to cover the high start-up capital costs of nuclear generation although similar proposals for so called "green" alternatives like geothermal or wind energy have not met with same degree of industry endorsement. In addition, the costs of exploring spent fuel storage options continue to be borne disproportionately by taxpayers while the legal battle over Yucca Mountain continues. Moreover, the 1957 Price-Anderson Act limits plant operators' liabilities risks to $9.3 billion. Nevertheless, Peter Rigby of Standard & Poors has noted, that the "industry's legacy of cost growth, technological problems, cumbersome political and regulatory oversight, and the newer risks brought about by competition and terrorism concerns may keep credit risks too high (for even federal legislation that provides loan guarantees) to overcome" (Silverstein 2003d).

The Logic of Market-Based Pollution Control Instruments

The Clean Air Act of 1970 was intended to "protect and enhance the quality of the Nation's air resources so as to promote the public health and welfare and the productive capacity of its population" (42 U.S.C. § 7401(b) as cited in NAPA 2003:9). Edmund Muskie, principal architect for the 1970 legislation, recalls:

> Three fundamental principles shaped the 1970 law. I was convinced that strict federal air pollution regulation would require a legally defensible premise. Senator Howard Baker believed that the American technological genius should be brought to bear on the air pollution problem, and that the industry should be required to apply the best technology available. Senator Thomas Eagleton asserted that the American people deserved to know when they could expect their health to be protected, and that deadlines were the only means of providing minimal assurance (1990).

The original bill created the Environmental Protection Agency and targeted carbon monoxide, nitrogen oxides, sulfur oxides, ozone, lead and particulate matter and established primary standards aimed at protecting human health and secondary standards aimed at protecting visibility and reducing damage to buildings, plants, and other aspects of public welfare (Muskie 1990). The means through which the above principles were implemented included a web of programs and, for the most part, left implementation plans to individual states. Significant amendments in 1977 and 1990 increasingly reflected the use of market-based emissions controls. For example, the 1977 amendments implemented an offset program limiting additional emissions by new stationary source polluters to the reductions achieved by the existing firms in the region. In 1979, the program was expanded with an emissions banking system that "allow" states to give credits to polluters who reduce emissions beyond the minimum needed to meet the state's plan for compliance with air quality standards" (Swaney 1987:299). Also implemented in 1979 was the "bubble" approach that measured emissions and required offsets by region rather than by the firm.

The Amendments of 1977 also implemented the dual component New Source Review (NSR) program. "The first component requires that new major sources be built with modern, cleaner equipment to minimize air pollution. The second requires that similar upgrades be installed when existing plants are modified in ways that may significantly decrease their emission" (NAPA 2003:10). As summarized in a recent GAO report, exceptions are available to firms under certain conditions, "for example, (1) a modification is considered 'routine maintenance and repair,' (2) the company agrees not to significantly increase its emissions after making a physical or operational change to its facility, or (3) the company offsets any emissions in a facility with emissions reductions achieved elsewhere within that facility" (2003a:2). The Bush Administration, in a move blocked by the US Court of Appeals, recently tried to broaden the definition of "routine maintenance and repair" to allow greater latitude in the exceptions category.

The routine maintenance clause was premised on the belief that the older coal-fired utility plants would reach the end of their operating life and be replaced with newer, more efficient combustion technology. However, "the older plants have lived on and moreover, the new ruling that favors industry will keep alive the dirtier facilities," notes Frank O'Donnell of the Clean Air Trust (Silverstein 2003c). The environmental impact of the changes in the New Source Review program are discussed below yet the issue to note here is a potential example of the concerns of utility operators maintaining disproportionate influence over the policy process relative to other stakeholders.

The use of permits reflects the ascendancy of market-based approaches to pollution control over the traditional command-and-control – both the technology-based regulations stipulating the use of particular equipment and the performance-based regulations that establishes effluent thresholds for the firms and leaves it to the firm's decisions regarding the means to achieve the goal. Yet, prior to the 1990 amendments, technology-based standards remained an essential component of the policy: firms had to demonstrate that the "best-available control technology" (BACT) was used for regulated effluents; new stationary source polluters in regions not meeting federal standards needed to demonstrate that equipment operated at the "lowest achievable emissions rate" (LAER); and existing stationary source polluters could be required to install "reasonably available control technology" (RACT) (Popp 2003:643).

The Clean Air Act Amendments of 1990 signaled the final shift from technology-based standards to market-based control instruments. For example, Title IV required permits for each ton of SO_2 emitted and a national standard, rather than the regional thresholds, was established. Choices of effluent reduction technology were left to individual firms though additional permits were granted if a firm implemented "qualifying control technologies" that would reduce SO_2 by at least 90% (Popp 2003:643).

The basic logic of the market-based approach is straight-forward: by capping the total amount of regulated effluents and establishing a market for tradable emissions permits within a region, firms able to reduce emissions at relatively low-cost will have the incentive to do so and then trade the permits, thereby allowing a spatial redistribution of emissions. Moreover, a firm might bank their permits as credit for future use thereby allowing a temporal redistribution. The effect, it is argued, is that the desired level of emissions reduction can be achieved at the lowest cost; those able to reduce emissions relatively inexpensively, through introduction of new technology for example, would have the incentive to do so in order to trade the unneeded permits. Recent compilations of the seminal articles leading to the development of market-based pollution control instruments include Tietenberg et al. (1999) and Tietenberg (2001).

However, many observers do not see the market-based pollution control instruments as necessarily generating the outcomes predicted by theoretical arguments. The suspicion stems from a simple result from General Systems Theory: one-dimensional growth of an organism leads to organism decay. For environmental systems, this means that multidimensional inquiry into ecological, social and political considerations is required. While the economists' focus on efficiency in policy analysis is of great value, a focus on monetary flows as the criteria for policy assessment falls short of the type of inquiry advocated herein. The next section elaborates on a form of structured inquiry believed to fulfill the need for broader analysis and the third section considers further the consequences of the market-based pollution control instruments.

The Elements of Valuation for Policy Assessment

The extended quote from the National Academy of Sciences identifies the importance of science and technology in the air quality management policy arena. Economists have stressed the importance of appropriate incentive structures to encourage collectively desired policy outcomes. The need to coordinate these and other strands of inquiry in a comprehensive manner has led some economists to develop approaches to a structured meta-inquiry. The aim has been to create cumulative databases for policy decision and monitoring of impacts; to integrate diverse kinds of data; to focus on scientific analysis that specifies deliveries and relationships among system components; and to provide the structure for social evaluation and institutional change.[1]

---

[1] Theories of institutional change and social valuation in the Original Institutional Economics tradition derive from the work of Thorstein Veblen, Clarence Ayres, Karl Polanyi, John R. Commons, and John Dewey. Of immediate interest are refinements by contemporary institutionalists Marc R. Tool, James Swaney, and Paul Dale Bush, and the development by F. Gregory Hayden of the means for policy evaluation and planning. In contrast to the orthodox economists' focus on a narrow conception of efficiency as the value criterion for public policy, most institutionalists identify an alternative value principle: "the continuity of human life and the noninvidious re-creation of community through the instrumental use of knowledge" (Tool 1979:300). Such a principle recognizes the complex and evolving needs of the life process in an integrated community; asserts the ongoing need for inquiry directed toward these needs; and implies the importance of participatory democracy as the means to maintain open inquiry and provide a countervailing check on the capacity of elites to capture the inquiry process (O'Hara and Tool 1998:7–8query). For an introduction to this literature the reader might begin with Hayden (1982a:637–644) and Bush (1988:1078–1086) for a concise history of the evolution of Veblen's dichotomy, and Tool (2001/1979) for an early and full treatment of a theory of social valuation. O'Hara and Tool (1998:9–15), in a volume recognizing the contributions of Paul Dale Bush, provide a concise statement of the theory of institutional change.

Criteria for evaluation are not given a priori but are the result of contextual analysis and recognition of the interdependence of the social, ecological and technological systems in the continuity of the life process. Progressive institutional adjustment requires analysis of criteria relevant to policy formation (Hayden 1995). In fact, "[a] specific standard of judgment is warranted only as long as it provides for instrumental efficiency in maintaining the causal continuity of the problem-solving process" (Bush 1988:130). Consequently, the ability of elites in government, business, or elsewhere to direct inquiry away from this continuity reflects what Thorstein Veblen identified as ceremonial patterns of behavior and results in ceremonial encapsulation – in other words, the encapsulation or capture of inquiry by vested interests to preserve the influence of vested interests. Note that this is more significant than rent-seeking behavior in that the idea of encapsulation includes more than the capture of a stream of monopoly profit. Such encapsulation might take the form of: (a) restricting innovation which can potentially diminish the power of vested interests; (b) directing inquiry towards innovation which protects and/or strengthens the source of such influence; or (c) actually replacing instrumentally warranted patterns of inquiry or action with ceremonially warranted patterns.

The Social Fabric Matrix (SFM) is an analytical tool theoretically grounded in the literature of social psychology, economics, anthropology and ecology. Using General Systems Theory as the point of departure, the SFM emphasizes flow levels and deliveries between system components as the means to understanding a real world system and allows for socioeconomic problem recognition, definition and solution by integrating qualitative and non-common denominator quantitative information (Hayden 1982a, b, 1998). The SFM provides the means through which the consequences of ceremonially warranted patterns of behavior (i.e., patterns which detract from the sustained vitality of the community at large) can better be studied. Moreover, the SFM makes explicit the gaps in delivery of social belief, technological and ecological criteria to the appropriate institutional authorities that generate and often preserve such patterns; therefore, the analyst is better able to suggest the means by which instrumentally warranted patterns of thought and action (i.e., patterns which contribute to the sustained vitality of the community at large) might be implemented. Lastly, the SFM is inherently transdisciplinary and serves to organize and direct the research needed for effective policy design and monitoring of multidimensional policy outcomes.

The SFM can be presented in either directed graph form or matrix form. The directed-graph form explicitly and visually recognizes the linkages between system components. For example, social institutions include legal systems, corporations, environmental and other special interest groups, patterns and or customs of social interaction. Note that in Fig. 1, the criteria delivery (N_B) from social beliefs to social institutions suggests that institutions must conform to social beliefs to be sustainable. Similarly, technology influences the structuring of social institutions; for example, the increased use of automobiles resulted in changes in urban planning.

The matrix form of the SFM allows the application of network analysis concepts such as reachability and centrality indices that are not part of this project

(Hayden 1982b). To "read" the matrix, note that criteria and institutional components are identified across the top of the matrix and, in the same order, down the left side. The row components are delivering to the column components, and these deliveries might include budget authority, decision criteria, environmental substances, and technology. A cell value of 1 indicates a delivery; the task of the analyst is to describe the contents and context of the delivery, and then to evaluate the system for missing deliveries (a feedback loop, for example) or missing components. Figure 1 is a generalized view, in digraph form, of how social and cultural components structure the fabric of the social system (Hayden 1998:93).

The context-specific model of the socioeconomic system as it concerns the development of the market-based pollution control instruments is presented in Fig. 2, this time the use of the matrix form rather than the digraph form. Following Hayden (1998:93–101), N_B, N_E and N_T are used to denote social belief criteria, ecological system criteria and technological criteria, respectively. The following elaborates on each of the identified cell deliveries.

Beliefs, in N_B, about the role of government in general and for technology-related policy in particular have fluctuated as national priorities have changed. However, several influences have remained, to varying degrees, relevant to policy formation. Mistrust of government intervention is well rooted in the history of US political rhetoric and government institutions. This Doctrine of the Negative State is, in part, the political analogue to the economic doctrine of laissez faire (Fine 1956). This is identified in cell [1,5] as the delivery of belief criteria to Congress. However, also firmly rooted in political discourse is the importance of a guiding

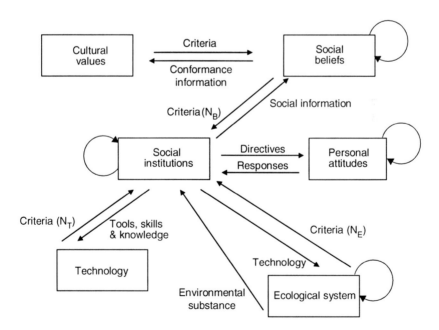

Fig. 1 Relationships among values, beliefs, attitudes, institutions, technology and the environment

			1.	2.	3.	4.	5.	6.	7.	8.	9.	10.	11.
N_B	Laissez faire	1.					1						
	Laissez innover	2.					1						
	Gov't Role: protect public health	3.					1						
	Participatory democracy	4.					1						
I_{A1}	U.S. Congress	5.						1					
	EPA	6.								1			
I_{A2}	Corporate Authorities	7.									1		
N_T	Effluent Reduction Technology	8.					1	1					
I_P	Effluent Generating Facilities	9.										1	
E	Ecological System	10.											
N_E	Health Impact Thresholds	11.					1	1					

Fig. 2 Social fabric matrix for the development of market-based pollution control instruments

role for the central government; this apparent conflict of views is evident in the Jefferson–Hamilton debates of the Constitutional Convention (Nester 1998, Chapter 1). And specific to pollution control policy, the role of the federal government is clearly affirmed in the passage of the Clean Air Act of 1970 as amended, and is indicated as the delivery of the belief criterion in cell [3,5] (see Senator Edmund Muskie's recollections quoted above).

Yet another dimension of the debates about government form and governance process is the role of participatory democracy. Peter DeLeon traces the roots of this debate within the United States by contrasting the views of James Madison and Alexis De Tocqueville, who – though both concerned about autocratic governance – each saw different resolutions to the problem (1997, Chapter 2). Madison was concerned about the undue influence from concentrations of power through factional maneuverings, and "at heart, did not trust the individual citizen to understand the requirements of government and to govern in a dispassionate manner, to overcome the 'factious spirit that has tainted our public administration'" (DeLeon 1997:22). De Tocqueville on the other hand believed the legitimacy and authority of government derives from citizen participation (Deleon 1997:27). Economists influenced by the work of John Dewey generally agree that participatory democracy is an essential element of effective problem-solving. This belief criterion is identified in cell [4,5] of Fig. 2. As discussed below, the weakness of mechanisms of participatory democracy is cited as a cause for the ascendancy of policies not consistent with the broader set of evaluative criteria.

The remaining belief criterion identified in Fig. 2 is the delivery of the principle of laissez innover in cell [2,5]. Understood as a parallel to the principle of laissez faire, the laissez innover principle identifies "technology as a self-correcting system. Temporary oversight or negative externalities will and should be corrected by technological means. Attempts to restrict the free play of technological innovation are self-defeating. Technological innovation exhibits a distinct tendency to work for the general welfare" (McDermott 1969:256). Such a view identifies technological innovation as inherently an instrumentally warranted process (i.e., necessarily "progressive" or life-improving) and fails to appreciate the role of power and influence in the policy process and in the selection of particular avenues of innovation. Similar to an adherence to the principle of laissez faire, adherence to a principle of laissez innover allows policy advocates and the public at large to abdicate the role of normative evaluation of consequences. Well-structured mechanisms of participatory democracy are the countervailing checks on such influences.

I_{A1} denotes institutional authority of the first order; in this case, the U.S. Congress and the Environmental Protection Agency are identified as the rule-making authorities. Cell [5,6] identifies the delivery of a legislative mandate and budget authority to the EPA, which in turn promulgates rules and regulations delivered to the relevant regulated firms. These firms are identified here as the institutional authorities of the second order, I_{A2}; cell [6,7] indicates the EPA's delivery of rules and regulations to the corporate authorities operating the facilities which generate regulated effluents. These corporate authorities then are empowered to establish internal operating procedures and to carry out the designated tasks; I_{P} denotes the processing facilities and this delivery is identified in [7,9]. Note that the legal structure of the corporations is identified independently of the technological process generating effluents, to explicitly distinguish the authority of management, subject to legislated obligations and prohibitions from the internal rule-making authority with respect to avenues of technological innovation.

The logic then of flow descriptions is as follows: social beliefs about the role of government and citizen participation in governance are delivered to the Congress, which in turn delivers regulatory and budget authority to the regulatory agencies. The actual content of that delivery is the complex web of legislation establishing statutory authority. With the agencies thus empowered to promulgate regulations, guidelines are delivered to the secondary rule-making authorities, i.e., the corporate authorities, which in turn establish procedures in their processing institutions. The concern of the analyst therefore is to investigate whether each of the deliveries – of budget authority, or rule-making authority, of outcome monitoring – is consistent with the ongoing welfare of the socioeconomic system at large. For example, do rules for mercury abatement effectively balance the concerns of corporate authorities over the concerns of public health for those living near a coal-fired plant?

In addition to the social beliefs (N_B) about governance process, policy-making by Congress and its regulatory agencies is also informed by ecological and technological norms. The deliveries in cells [8,5] and [8,6] represent the technological norms shaping pollution control options as legislated by Congress and implemented by the EPA. As discussed above, early pollution control policy followed predominantly a command-and-control approach, often specifying technologies to be adopted to meet mandated goals. Popp (2003) distinguishes quantitative indications of invention patterns (number of patents issued as the proxy) from the qualitative content of subsequent innovation (p. 651). "Combining data on flue gas desulfuri zation units with patent data reveals that, although the level of innovative activity fell off after the passage of the 1990 Clean Air Act, the nature of innovative activity changed" (p. 658). Prior to the 1990 amendments, innovation focused on reducing the cost of operating the scrubbers yet maintaining the 90% removal efficiency standard as required. After 1990, innovation focused on improving the efficiency of the scrubbers. The study suggests, at least for sulfur dioxide reduction, the market-based approach can alter avenues of R&D with long-term benefits for firms through lower costs of compliance and for policymakers and society at large by allowing future reductions in allowed emissions (Popp 2003:659).

An aim of the CAA of 1970, as expressed in the above quote from Senator Muskie, was the protection of public health. Policy design and subsequent assessment then requires extensive knowledge about epidemiological impacts. Abt (2002) summarizes several studies on human health impacts due to exposure to particulate matter (the result of sulfur dioxide and nitrogen oxides reacting with ammonia) that interferes with the ability of the lungs to absorb oxygen. Impacts include premature mortality, chronic respiratory illnesses, increased hospital admissions, and lost workdays. The deliveries in cells [11,5] and [11,6] represent the ecological norms (N_E), specifically health impact information, which should inform the legislative process in the Congress, the promulgation of rules and regulations at the EPA, and the subsequent assessment of outcomes from such laws, rules and regulations.

The Consequences of the Cap-and-Trade Approach for Air Pollution Control

The Social Fabric Matrix is premised on the belief that effective socioeconomic policy must be evaluated according to a broad set of criteria consistent with the ongoing vitality of the socioeconomic system. Making explicit the deliveries between system components and requiring analysts to explicate each of the deliveries for conformance with the appropriate sufficiency conditions contributes to this effort. Sufficiency conditions are numerous and do not share a common metric: utilities require regulatory stability for long-range planning; public health protection requires attention to absolute levels of source-receptor exchange, not regional averages; inquiry into new forms of power generation and new emission abatement technology requires both the delivery of the appropriate incentives and transparency of corporate influence in the innovation pipeline (Is innovation 'blocked" by vested interests whose position may be weakened by new technology?); justice concerns suggest the costs of policy intervention should not fall disproportionately on those without input in the policy process; legitimacy of the governance process requires the interests of stakeholders be considered in problem definition and the design of policy intervention.

What then are the consequences of the increased reliance on market-based control instruments? Regulated pollutants have been reduced by 70% since implementation of the Clean Air Act of 1970 (Silverstein 2003a). Since 1990, SO_2 emissions have been reduced by 32% (Abt 2002). Moreover, as noted above, firms have responded to the inventive structure of the program by focusing on innovation that lowers compliance costs for SO_2 emission. A 2003 report by the EPA reports a reduction of acidic lakes in the Adirondacks from 13% in the early 1990s to 9% and a reduction of acidic lakes in the Upper Midwest from 3% in the early 1980s to less than 1% (reported in US Newswire 2003).

However, this desirable outcome in innovation patterns must also be balanced by the spatial distribution of the SO_2 reductions to date. Total SO_2 emissions fell from 15,733,305 tons in 1990 to 10,632,613 tons in 2001; however, 16 states saw an increase in emissions with 8 experiencing more than a 20% increase. Not to be ignored is the reduction of emissions by 23 states to less than 80% of 1990 levels. Examining plant specific data, the report notes that "of 608 [specific] power plants operating in both 1990 and 2001, 285 facilities increased their emissions, and 54 decreased their SO_2 emissions by less than 15% (Abt 2002:1–6).

The spatial distribution of mercury contamination is also a concern. Even traditionally strong advocates of market-based instruments have suggested that more aggressive means are necessary to protect public health. Connecticut has taken the lead in aggressive mercury abatement by requiring coal-fired utilities to reduce mercury emission by 90% by 2008 (Silverstein 2003a). Collaboration among industry, environmentalists and lawmakers and resulting flexibility in the law suggest the antagonism between stakeholders can be overcome to achieve broad social goals.

Clarification of the "routine maintenance" clause of the New Source Review Program is necessary for regulatory stability for utilities, yet this must be balanced with public health concerns. A 2003 joint study by the Environmental Integrity Project (EIP) and the Council of State Governments/Eastern Regional Conference (CSG/ERC) estimated allowable emissions increases for the twelve state regions and for a number of pollutants. Particulate matter emission could increase by as much as 48,800 tons, or an average of 14% across the states; nitrogen oxides emissions could increase by as much as 335,000 tons, or a regional average of 14%; sulfur dioxide emissions could increase by as much as 330,000 tons from all stationary sources, or a regional average of 6% with Maine increasing 32% (EIP and CSG/ERC 2003:2).

The logic of market-based instruments inducing innovation as costs rise is sound. However, the focus on the free-market undervalues the role of government in establishing the market parameters, encouraging innovation in particular areas through targeted funding, and managing risk for high-cost capital outlays with temporally distant returns. The practical concerns of new technology development and implementation with recognized positive externalities and public good characteristics should not be left entirely to hypothesized market forces.

The technological lock-in of coal-fired plants, compounded by the fact that older plants continue to operate, can be a barrier to innovation. Moreover, regulatory uncertainty reduces planning horizons and thereby reduces attention to long-range investments in substitutes. A number of so-called "green" technologies are becoming viable but production costs remain high because of the inability to achieve economies of scale; government influence can tip the balance for products and processes nearing cost-efficient production thresholds. Geothermal heat pumps for example are very efficient, generate no emissions, and can both cool and warm a building. While the technology is currently available, high installation costs and a shortage of builders with sufficient expertise continue to slow adoption. The Power Smart Program operated by Manitoba Hydro resolves part of this barrier through a residential loan program (Spring 2003). Training subsidies for qualified builders can also provide a direct and immediate benefit. Note that this is not a case of the government picking winners and losers – a too-oft heard criticism of government intervention – but a targeted effort to remove the final barriers to marketing a tested and reliable energy alternative.

Other alternate technologies include wind power, hydrogen, and energy storage devices – each with their own implementation challenges yet also with programs to counter these challenges. Advocates for green technologies argue for incentives to diversify the energy generation portfolio with currently available technologies and to supplement research and development efforts for technologies still in the innovation pipeline. Canada has estimated the need for 2,500 megawatts of new power by 2007 yet has also proposed shutting down coal-fired plants by that year. While not abandoning the use of competitive forces in consumers' energy usage decisions, the reforms, task forces suggests, will achieve the goal by encouraging conservation and time-of-use strategies and by shifting demand to existing nuclear, hydropower, and natural gas facilities and to new emerging technologies. The task force report claims: "A process must be put in place quickly to enable the negotiation and contracting of a range of new supply capacity to address the looming supply shortfall. Private investment and risk taking should be the mainstay of the future power system, following competitive principles" (Silverstein 2004d). The risk management resources of government and clear directives with appropriate incentives can and should steer better policy outcomes. Indeed the risk management capacity of government has been essential to innovation in the private sector. As David Moss notes in his recent volume (2002), the historical record in the US: (1) "reveals risk management to have been an exceedingly flexible tool, used to address a wide range of social problems and to serve a divers set of social objectives"; (2) "reveals a remarkable degree of economic sophistication in the way leading policymakers thought about risk and the governments' role in managing it"; and (3) "helps us understand why public intervention in markets for risk was so prevalent in the United States, despite the county's reputation as being the bastion of laissez-faire" (Moss 2002:293–295).

The development of hydrogen as a reliable and efficient fuel source for autos or electricity generation remains impractical, yet dedicated research funds and political commitment can stimulate private sector efforts to commercialize the technology. The U.S. has committed nearly $2 billion over 5 years and the European Union has allocated 2.36 billion over 5 years to develop hydrogen technologies. Admittedly, the production of internal combustion engines employs millions of people and the technology lock-in is a barrier to the emergence of substitute technologies (Silverstein 2004e). Such displacement should be included as part of a comprehensive energy realignment strategy.

Renewable energy sources are also gaining attention with state government taking the lead. New York Governor George Pataki has proposed that by 2013 New York would purchase at least 25% of its energy needs from renewable sources such as wind power. By a 2001 executive order Pataki requires state agencies to purchase 10% of their electricity needs by 2005 and 20% by 2010 from renewable sources. The commitment gives private industry the incentive to continue to develop the technology and permits demand for energy from renewable sources to increase sufficiently those production efficiencies that can be realized. Chautauqua Windpower of New York estimates the 41.5 MW of wind power currently in use has avoided more than 45,000 tons of annual carbon dioxide emissions. Texas has also implemented renewable energy portfolio standards. Public support for wind power has wavered in some areas because of noise from the turbines and from television signal interference (Silverstein and Spring 2003). Consequently, as with any large-scale facility, citing concerns will exist and it is likely that these facilities will have to be in low-density population areas. However, unlike coal-fired or nuclear-powered energy plants, the downsides of the technology are not temporally or spatially disconnected; for example, the damage from coal combustion is neither readily identifiable nor readily attributable by casual observers. These factors may actually contribute to more transparency in the citing process.

A more subtle impact of relying on market-based pollution control instruments involves the threat to the legitimacy of the governance process. Political processes must be recognized as legitimate and this "legitimacy requires a social moral consensus on norms with regard to the *consequences* of social policy and with regard to the *procedures* which produce those consequences" (Hayden 1982a:634; italics in the original). The policy procedures for energy policy of the current Administration have created unnecessary antagonism between stakeholders. An August 2003 GAO report confirmed what had been widely discussed in the press: representatives and lobbyists from the petroleum, coal, nuclear, natural gas, and electricity industries dominated the National Energy Policy Development Group, chaired by Vice President Cheney (GAO 2003b).

More recently and more germane to air pollution policy specifically, a February 2004 GAO report on the process for revising the New Source Review Program notes, "A majority of the 44 state air quality officials responding to our survey believes that the December 2002 final rule will provide industry greater flexibility to modify facilities without having to install pollution control in some cases; a majority of the officials also think, however, this flexibility will come at the cost of increases in emissions and agencies workloads" (GAO 2004:6). While EPA analysis estimates the new rule will reduce emissions because firms now have some certainty with respect to plant modifications, the issue here is one of perceived legitimacy of the governance process by those closely involved with implementation and monitoring of the policy. (Note however that the EIP & CSG/ERC October 2003 report referred to above estimated increased emissions). Moreover, public support for market based programs is not strong; a 2002 survey concludes that "53% of Republicans, 69% of Independents, and 70% of Democrats oppose the [cap and trade approach of the Clear Skies Initiative proposed by the Bush Administration]." It is opposed by a majority of voters in every region of the country and is opposed by every demographic group" (reported in US Newswire 2002).

In the context of the above discussion of valuation for policy assessment, this ambiguity of public support can be interpreted as a lack of consistency between social belief criteria, ecological system criteria, and technological criteria. The informed public increasingly believes that policy is targeted to corporate needs without regard for other evaluative norms. Whether this perception is correct or not, the impact on the perceived legitimacy of the means of mechanism of governance is the same: disenfranchisement of the public from the governance process.

Conclusion

Brian Martin has suggested debates over policy issues involving complex technology can be sidetracked onto an issue of scientific debate. For example, the debates over fossil fuel usage and ozone depletion have too often been cast as a question of whether global warming is in fact now occurring. This neglects the broader policy issue; "It is quite possible to argue that fossil fuel use should be curtailed for reasons quite independent of climate change, including health impacts on coal miners, acid rain, air pollution and associated respiratory disease, promotion of the car and associated health and environmental effects, and the antidemocratic impacts of immense political and economic power of energy industries" (Martin 2000:208).

The idea of ceremonial encapsulation discussed above describes the beliefs of many observers of the policy process: industry and government elites have been driven by a one-dimensional criterion of efficiency and have neglected other criteria – ecological, social, and technological – just as crucial to the welfare of industry and society. The need to meet increased demand for power is crucial to economic growth; the need to safeguard public health is essential for a viable community. Failure to achieve either imposes costs upon society.

While the technology-based standards of the original Clean Air Act may not have generated effluent reductions at the lowest cost, the shift to market-based instruments comes at the cost of further undermining public trust in political institutions. Like much legislative activity of the early 1970s, the Clean Air Act of 1970 reflected a new balance, through creation of a new mechanism for public interest advocacy, between local government and community control on the one hand and federal government regulatory responsibility on the other (Milkis 1998). This balance should be restored in some form to assure legitimacy of ecological policies and consistency with protection of the public interest.

As discussed, several states have taken the initiative to implement stricter emissions standards or incentives for the expansion of alternate energy sources. Policy research and implementation should encourage such innovation. The public service commission (PUC) model, used on a regional basis rather than with the traditional state, can inform the creation of political institutions with the expertise to achieve this aim. Dodds and Lesser (1994) suggest alternate costs evaluations to improve PUC outcomes. However, I am advocating more extensive revisions to the breadth of analysis and use of evaluative criteria with which such commissions might be charged.

Such an approach can both address local pollution problems such as mercury emissions and help coordinate the appropriate mix of market incentives and government regulation

Policy debates that are too polarized – the use of free-market principles vs. government decree – fail to capture the full dimensions of the socioeconomic problem and the options for policy intervention. The debate should instead focus on how policy can combine the comparative advantages of each to achieve the multi-dimensional aims of society. Market-based pollution control mechanisms have the potential to encourage desired innovations and reduced emissions. However the risk management function, the capacity for government budget authority to fund the promising process and product innovation, and the role of government purchasing decisions as a means of encouraging economies of scale in the production of existing technologies must also be recognized for their potentially desirable impact on private-sector decisions. The aim is to focus the policy process on consistency of economic, social, ecological and technological norms in designing the appropriate mix of public and private actions, rather than being guided by a priori commitments to one set of options.

References

Abt Associates (2002) Particulate-related health impacts of emissions in 2001 from 41 major US power plants. Prepared for the Environmental Integrity Project/Rockefeller Family Fund. Eric Schaeffer, Project Manager. Bethesda, Abt Associates. http://64.78.32.98/pubs/PMHealthImpact2001.pdf

Bush PD (1983) An exploration of the structural characteristics of a Veblen–Ayres–Foster defined institutional domain. J Econ Issues 17(1):35–66

Bush PD (1988) A theory of institutional change. In: Tool M (ed) Evolutionary economics volume I: foundations of institutional thought. M.E. Sharpe, Armonk, NY

DeLeon P (1997) Democracy and the policy sciences. State University of New York Press, Albany

Dodds DE, Lesser JA (1994) Can utility commissions improve on environmental regulations? Land Econ 70(1):63–76

Environmental Integrity Project and the Council of State Governments/Eastern Regional Conference (2003) Reform or rollback: how EPA's changes to new source review could affect air pollution in 12 states: summary report. http://rrund.org and http://csgeast.org

Fine S (1956) Laissez faire and the general welfare state. University of Michigan Press, Ann Arbor

General Accounting Office (2003a) Clean Air Act: EPA should use available data to monitor the effects of its revisions to the New Sources Review Program. GAO-03-947 August 2003

General Accounting Office (2003b) Energy Task Force: process used to develop the national energy policy. GAO-03-894 August 2003

General Accounting Office (2004) Clean Air Act: key stakeholders' views on revisions to the New Source Review Program. GAO-04-274 February 2004

Hayden FG (1982a) Social fabric matrix: from perspective to analytical tool. J Econ Issues 16(3):637–662

Hayden FG (1982b) Organizing policy research through the social fabric matrix: a boolean digraph approach. J Econ Issues 16(4):1013–1026

Hayden FG (1995) Instrumentalist policymaking: policy criteria in a transactional context. J Econ Issues 29(2):361–384

Hayden FG (1998) Normative analysis of instituted processes. In: Fayazmanesh S, Tool M (eds) Institutional theory and applications: essays in honor of Paul Dale Bush, vol 2. Edward Elgar, Cheltenham, UK

Martin B (2000) Behind the scenes of scientific debating. Social Epistemol 14(2/3):201–209

McDermott J (1969) Technology: the opiate of the intellectuals. N Y Rev Books 31 Jul:25–35

Milkis SM (1998) Remaking government institutions in the 1970s: participatory democracy and the triumph of administrative politics. J Policy Hist 10(1):51–74

Moss DA (2002) When all else fails: government as the ultimate risk manager. Harvard University Press, Cambridge

Muskie E (1990) NEPA to CERCLA: The Clean Air Act: a commitment to public health. The Environmental Forum (January/February). http://www.cleanairtrust.org/nepa2cercla.html

National Academy of Public Administration (2003) A breath of fresh air: reviewing the New Source Review Program: summary report. Academy project Number 1965; Funded by the US EPA under contract # 68-D-01-047. http://www.napawash.org/Pubs/Fresh%20Air%20 Summary.pdf

National Academy of Sciences, National Research Council (2003) Air quality management in the United States. The National Academy Press, Washington

Nester WP (1998) A short history of American industrial policies. St. Martin's Press, New York

Popp D (2003) Pollution controls innovations and the Clean Air Act of 1990. J Policy Anal Manage 22(4):641–660

Silverstein K (2003a) Mercury rising. UtiliPoint Issue Alert 07/15/03

Silverstein K (2003b) Clean air ruling hits utilities facing suits. UtiliPoint Issue Alert 08/14/03

Silverstein K (2003c) Clean air stance may have political ramifications. UtiliPoint Issue Alert 09/09/03

Silverstein K (2003d) Nuclear power has Yucca Mountain to climb. UtiliPoint Issue Alert 10/22/03

Silverstein K (2003e) Global warming vote expected. UtiliPoint Issue Alert 10/30/03

Silverstein K (2003f) Keeping a lid on mercury. UtiliPoint Issue Alert 12/11/03

Silverstein K (2004a) Coal may shine again. UtiliPoint Issue Alert 01/13/04

Silverstein K (2004b) Mountaintop mining: an explosive subject. UtiliPoint Issue Alert 01/14/04

Silverstein K (2004c) Tougher CO_2 controls are coming. UtiliPoint Issue Alert 01/15/04

Silverstein K (2004d) Ontario serious about bold initiatives. UtiliPoint Issue Alert 01/23/04

Silverstein K (2004e) Hydrogen economy hazy. UtiliPoint Issue Alert 02/09/04

Silverstein K, Spring N (2003) The big green apple. UtiliPoint Issue Alert 07/01/03

Spring N (2003) The Rodney Dangerfield of "green" technology? UtiliPoint Issue Alert 10/01/03

Spring N (2004) Energy storage shows promise. UtiliPoint Issue Alert 01/22/04

Swaney JA (1987) Instrumental environmental institutions. J Econ Issues 21(1):295–308

Tietenberg T (2001) Emissions trading programs, volume I: Implementation and evolution, and volume II: Theory and design. Ashgate Publishing, Aldershot

Tietenberg T, Button K, Nijkamp P (1999) Environmental instruments and institutions. Edward Elgar, Northampton, MA

Tool MR (1979) The discretionary economy: a normative theory of political economy. Goodyear Publishing, Santa Monica

U S Newswire (2002) Public overwhelmingly rejects Bush 'Clear Skies' plan: favors enforcement over 'Cap and Trade' approach, says clean air trust. COMTEX News Network Inc, Washington. 29 Jul 2002

U S Newswire (2003) Report shows evidence of recovery from effects of acid rain: Cap and Trade approach credited with reversing effects of acid raid. COMTEX News Network Inc, Washington. 29 Jan 2003

Service Access Rigidities in Rural Alaska

Wayne Edwards

Abstract Access to basic services such as health care, the court system, and police protection is vital to individual and social well-being. If barriers exist that prevent people from receiving fundamental services, the quality of their lives is diminished. In the aggregation, society as a whole suffers when some of its members fail to receive services, making access barriers a prominent policy issue concerning the government at national, regional (state), and local levels.

Service availability, access, and delivery are universal problems every society faces. Resource constraints are sometimes the cause for the absence or poor provision of services. However, service rigidities do not arise solely from a lack of resources. Access rigidities do include obvious barriers like the absence of physical facilities (e.g., hospitals) and low incomes of citizens, but they also include less obvious barriers like social and family dynamics. Rigidities are often more severe in rural places, sometimes to the extent that rural community sustainability is jeopardized by service access barriers.

This chapter identifies crucial factors in service access rigidity by using a modified social fabric matrix (SFM). The components of the SFM – cultural values, societal beliefs, personal attitudes, social institutions, technology, and the natural environment – go to the core of the question of well-being and are ideally suited to identify access rigidities. Once identified, service access rigidity is quantified over geographic regions in the state of Alaska. Rigidities are found to vary not only by geography but also by service type.

Introduction

Service availability, access, and delivery are universal problems every society faces. Resource constraints are sometimes the cause for the absence or poor provision of services. However, service rigidities do not arise solely from a lack of resources.

W. Edwards
University of Alaska Anchorage, Anchorage, AK, USA

T. Natarajan et al. (eds.), *Institutional Analysis and Praxis*,
DOI 10.1007/978-0-387-88741-8_13, © Springer Science+Business Media, LLC 2009

Access rigidities include obvious barriers that are empirically observable like the absence of physical facilities (e.g., hospitals) and low incomes of citizens, but they also include less obvious barriers that are not easily measured such as social and family dynamics. Rigidities are often more severe in rural areas, sometimes to the extent that rural community sustainability is jeopardized by severe service access barriers (Edwards 2007; Edwards and Natarajan 2008).

This chapter focuses on the measurement of barriers to service access. First, an overview of the geography and demography of Alaska is presented. Second, the social fabric matrix (SFM) is used to organize the analysis of service access questions. Finally, numerical representations of service access rigidities are compared to measures of well-being. The primary result is that while measures of service access rigidities are broadly consistent with other measures in explaining geographical variation in well-being, they also reveal differences not seen in other analyses. Therefore, the access rigidity indices are useful additions to the universe of well-being measures.

Services and the Alaska Economy

Alaska is the largest state in the United States by area, but has one of the smallest populations. Even today, vast expanses of land remain unorganized by political boundaries and the overwhelming majority of communities do not lie on a connected road system, as shown in Figs. 1 and 2. Figure 1 is a map of the state showing boroughs and their names. The white areas on Fig. 1 are not defined politically. Figure 2 shows most of the borough boundaries and rural communities as defined by a recent

Fig. 1 Alaska Boroughs Map by Meghan Wilson, Institute of Social and Economic Research, University of Alaska, Anchorage

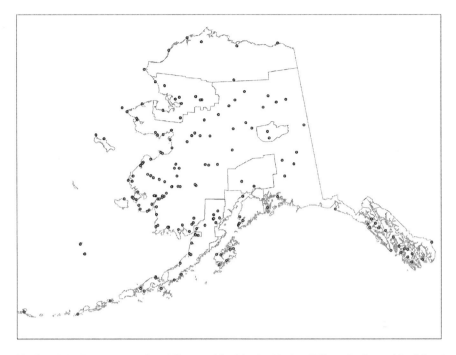

Fig. 2 Alaska Boroughs and Rural Communities Map by Meghan Wilson, Institute of Social and Economic Research, University of Alaska, Anchorage

study (Haley et al. 2007). Virtually all of the indicated rural communities lie off the scant connected road system and most lie outside of organized boroughs.

Not only does the state have vast rural areas, the state itself is quite remote – only Hawai'i is more geographically isolated from the rest of the United States than Alaska. Nevertheless, the flow of migration to and from Alaska occurs at one of the highest rates of any state (Edwards 2007; Edwards and Huskey 2008). Population demography therefore tends to be turbulent in some local Alaska communities.

Poverty, as measured by a deprivation of income, is less widespread in Alaska than in other states. For example, Alaska has had the most equitable distribution of income of any state. Alaska's Gini coefficient in 1999 was only 0.39, compared to the national average of about 0.43, and other income-based measures reveal similar results: Alaska, compared to most other states, has less poverty by income measures (Howe 2004a, b). This overarching characteristic can be found in Alaska for past several decades (Edwards and Natarajan 2007).

There are stark differences between life in rural communities and life in population centers. Rural residents face service access rigidities that urban residents do not face, and these rigidities surely reduce well-being. After all, theoretically available services have no value if they are not, in reality, available to consume (Edwards and Natarajan 2008). In addition, prices for food and energy are wildly divergent in some rural places. Recent observations indicate that food and energy prices are sometimes 500% higher in remote Alaska villages than in Alaska population centers (Simon 2009).

The argument is sometimes made that people who choose to live in rural communities are aware that access to services might be limited because of the remote nature of their residence. Even if true, this does not mean that people living in rural areas have a preference for limited services (Halpin 2008; Bryson 2007). Ultimately, questions about service delivery are social questions that must be addressed by communities and government. What services will be delivered? How will the services be delivered? Where will the services be delivered? To whom will the services be delivered? These questions are inescapable matters of public policy (Edwards and Natarajan 2007). It is crucial to know the level or severity of the rigidity in order to make public policy decisions about services.

For the purpose of this analysis, three particular categories of services are examined: health, justice, and safety. There are many other categories of services which are also important to individuals and communities (e.g., education). The reason health, justice, and safety are analyzed here is that this chapter aggregates the results of separate analyses on service access rigidities treated individually elsewhere (see Edwards 2009a, b, c). The methodology used in the analysis presented in this chapter can be extended to other service categories in Alaska or anywhere in the world.

The following discussion (adapted from Edwards and Natarajan 2007) briefly summarizes three specific categories of service access rigidities that exist in Alaska, highlighting some of the unique features of the place. These examples, while not exhaustive, are nevertheless instructive.

Health (Healthcare Access)

Access rigidities reduce healthcare consumption. In rural Alaska, the general absence of connected roads, the scarcity of physicians and nurses, and the multi-level approval procedure for statute-provided care among many rural residents (especially Natives) make service delivery difficult. Even if money is available to purchase healthcare, if the healthcare service itself is absent (or diminished), the expected transaction cannot take place. For this reason, federal mandates for healthcare of select groups of people (veterans, for example) often go unfulfilled (Bryson 2007).

Alaskans experience high morbidity rates for terminal disease, especially rural residents and Natives, indicating an apparent unfilled need for healthcare services (Statewide Library Electronic Doorway 2005). High suicide rates prevail among Alaskans, especially among young adult male Natives (Einarsson et al. 2004). Non-terminal morbidities, such as Fetal Alcohol Spectrum Disorder, are also very high in Alaska, especially in the rural population (State of Alaska 2002, 2004). Clearly, the need for improved healthcare access is great in Alaska, particularly in rural areas (Edwards 2009b).

Justice (Access to Justice)

Access rigidities to legal professionals and the court system impede resolution of disputes. Some examples include filing of restraining orders in connection with domestic abuse and violence toward women, divorce proceedings, and child support settlement enforcement (Edwards 2009c). Incidence of child abuse and neglect are often investigated and resolved through "non-police" agencies and personnel (social services, for example). Lack of non-police social service professionals makes more difficult the task of receiving justice through the court system, especially for adults in at-risk groups and children.

If affordable legal advice is not available locally, some people will make uniformed decisions about legal matters or might possibly remain outside the legal system altogether. In Alaska, the majority of the population lives near population centers and can therefore access the justice system with relative ease. Rural residents, on the other hand, are sometimes isolated from the justice system because of the literal absence of courthouses and legal professionals in rural communities. Binding rigidities that prevent access to justice remain in many rural Alaska places (Edwards and Natarajan 2007; Edwards 2009c).

Safety (Access to Police Protection)

Access rigidities to police protection increase exposure to crime (Edwards 2009a). In rural Alaska, there is a shortage of professional police officers in many places. Frequently, the only law enforcement official in a rural place is a Village Public Safety Officer and, in some places, there are no law enforcement officers at all (Roberts 2005). Reduced police protection leads to more violent crime (Anderson 2003). Victims of violent crime experience negative health outcomes (both physical and emotional) and therefore reduced well-being (DeMarban 2008).

Alaska has the highest state-level crime rates in some categories, including the highest rate of forcible rape in the country, year after year. A reduction in access rigidities to police protection might reduce crime, especially violent crime, in rural places (Edwards and Natarajan 2007).

The first step in the overall analysis toward creating an empirical measure of service access rigidity is a general organization of the categories of factors affecting the issue under consideration. It is easy to observe that, while every place has unique characteristics, most places have some characteristics in common as well. The distinction is often a matter of the level of analysis. Consider Table 1. The first column is labeled "Global Category," and the second column is labeled "Local Factor." The Global Categories are general characteristics that are relevant to most places in the world. The Local Factors are narrower characteristics and are the particular instantiations of the broader Global Category. For example, the Global Category "Availability of the service" refers literally to whether the service is

Table 1 Alaska service access rigidities.

	Rigidity	Service		
Global category	Local factor	Health	Justice	Safety
Availability of the service	Local	×	×	×
	Regional	×	×	
	Central (Anchorage, Fairbanks, Juneau)	Baseline	Baseline	Baseline
Cost	Nominal explicit	×	×	
Length of queue to receive service	Population density	×	×	×
	Administrative (in)efficiency	×	×	×
Secondary costs	Travel	×	×	
	Overnight or extended stay	×	×	
	Child care	×	×	
	Loss of work income	×	×	
	Intangibles	×	×	×
Public funding provision	Political posture of administration	×	×	×
	Group dependent	×		
Assistance available	Political posture of administration	×	×	
	Group dependent	×	×	
Qualifications to receive assistance	Income tested	×		
	Group dependent	×		
Social factors	Race	×	×	×
	Gender	×		
	Class	×		
Community factors	Political will of local government	×		×
	Effectiveness of local administration	×	×	×
	Local leadership	×		×
Family factors	Family dynamic	×	×	×
Personal factors	Personal factors	×	×	×
Jurisdiction	Jurisdiction	×		×

Source: Edwards and Natarajan (2009)

available to people in the area under consideration. This category is a relevant issue for every place in the world. If we consider a particular place, the availability of the service depends on the level of analysis or the Local Factor. In the Alaska case, three levels are identified in the Local Factor column: Local, Regional, and Central. "Local" refers to small villages of less than 1,000 people. "Regional" refers to regional centers like Bethel, Nome, Kotzebue, and Barrow. The data used in the analysis are aggregated to the Census Area level, and most (but not all) Census Areas have a regional center. "Central" refers to the three largest localities in Alaska: Anchorage, Fairbanks, and Juneau. The relevance of the Global Category might be different depending on the Local Factor.

Table 1 shows the relevance of Local Factors for each of the three service categories, Health, Justice (court system), and Safety (police protection). An "*X*" in a cell indicates that the Local Factor is a relevant consideration in the barrier or rigidity of the service category. Looking at the Global Category "Availability of the service," the Local Factor "Local" is relevant for all three service categories. This indicates that service access rigidities exist at the local level in Alaska for Health, Justice, and Safety. Therefore, in some places, especially rural ones, individuals face systematic barriers to services. At the regional level, systematic barriers to the Global Category exist only for Health, but not Justice and Safety. In other words, if individuals can reach a regional center, they will generally have access to police protection and the court system, but they might still not have access to health services. If individuals can reach Central locations, they face no systematic barriers to the Global Category.

The Local Factors are meant to be discrete in the table. For example, from the table, individuals have no systematic barrier to the Global Category "Availability of service" if they are in a "Central" place ("Central" is considered the baseline against which other places are evaluated). This statement means only that facilities exist in these places for the service to be provided. People might have other rigidities besides the mere existence of the services that keeps them from receiving it (e.g., they might not be able to afford the service). Specifically, other Global Category barriers might still exist. For example, persons living in Anchorage have many choices for healthcare facilities, but they might nevertheless not receive health care because they cannot afford to take time off from work to go to a doctor. In this example, there is no rigidity for the availability of the service, but there is a secondary cost (Global Category) issue of losing work income (Local Factor) that bars access to the service.

One important issue in Alaska that does not necessarily translate to other locations is the influence of legislation relating to Alaska Natives. Alaska Natives receive some services that non-Natives do not receive (Edwards and Natarajan 2008; Wallace 2005). A specific example is health care facilities built explicitly to serve the Native population. The influence of Native Corporations and legal provisions for Natives shows up explicitly as Local Factors for a number of Global Categories including public funding provision, assistance available, and qualifications to receive assistance. The barriers to access affecting Natives particularly show up in other categories as well, just not explicitly (e.g., social factors, community factors, and family factors).

In this analysis, Safety is assumed to be a quasi-public good (limited by congestion), Justice is assumed to be a quasi-public good (limited by explicit exclusion barriers like filing fees), and Health is assumed to be a (mostly) private good. From Table 1, it is clear that access barriers are more plentiful for the private good than they are for the quasi-public goods.

Finally, because the ultimate goal is to quantify information identified in the table, it is important to note that some categories and factors will be difficult indeed to assign values. This is particularly true of family and social factors. Some of this information can be gleaned from surveys conducted regularly in Alaska, such as the Survey of Living Conditions in the Arctic (Martin 2006). Proxies will be employed to approximate how family and personal factors create barriers to service access. In some cases, not all factors identified can be accounted for empirically.

Descriptions of Global Categories and Local Factors follow.

- *Availability of the service.* The literal availability of a service.
  - *Local.* Village Alaska outside of population centers and regional hubs.
  - *Regional.* Regional centers such as Barrow, Bethel, Nome, etc.
  - *Central (Anchorage, Fairbanks, Juneau).* The three main population centers serve as baseline instances of service availability.

- *Cost.* Transaction price of the service.
  - *Nominal Explicit.* Transaction price excluding all peripheral, incidental, and opportunity costs.

- *Length of queue to receive service.* Length of time people must wait to receive the service.
  - *Population density.* The extent to which population density affects the queue.
  - *Administrative (in)efficiency.* Paperwork barriers to receiving the service.

- *Secondary costs.* Any cost other than the nominal explicit cost.
  - *Travel.* The cost of traveling to a non-local location to receive the service.
  - *Overnight or extended stay.* Lodging and related costs when receiving a service from a non-local location.
  - *Child care.* Child care cost when a parent cannot bring a child along to receive the service.
  - *Loss of work income.* Wages that must be foregone to receive a service.
  - *Intangibles.* Costs that cannot be easily valued in dollars, such as psychological costs.

- *Public funding provision.* Level of government funding for the service.
  - *Political posture of administration (willingness to fund service).* Tendency of the current administration to fund the service.
  - *Group dependent.* Interest group funding and legislated group-dependent funding of the service. Examples of groups include veterans, Alaska Natives, etc.

- *Assistance available.* Programs available to pay all or part of the cost of the service or to provide the service for free or at a reduced price.
  - *Political posture of administration (willingness to fund service).* Tendency of the current administration to fund the assistance program.
  - *Group dependent.* Interest group facilities and legislated group-dependent facilities. Examples of groups include veterans hospitals, Alaska Native hospitals, etc.

- *Qualifications to receive assistance.* Exclusion processes in assistance programs.
  - *Income tested.* Means testing.
  - *Group dependent.* Examples of groups include veterans, Alaska Natives, etc.

- *Social factors.* Non-monetary characteristics that impede or promote service access.

- *Race*. People of different races have different experiences in receiving the service.
- *Gender*. Women and men have different experiences in receiving the service.
- *Class*. Socio-economic class. People who (households that) earn less money income face non-monetary barriers to receiving the service that people who (households that) earn more money income do not face.

- *Community factors*. Local factors having effects that vary from higher-level aggregation factors.
  - *Political will of local government*. Independent action of the local government that impedes or encourages service access for community members.
  - *Effectiveness of local administration*. Independent action of the local administrators that impedes or encourages service access for community members.
  - *Local leadership*. Independent action of a local leader or institution that impedes or encourages service access for community members.

- *Family factors*. Factors occurring at the family level of measurement.
  - *Family dynamic*. Any attribute that impedes or encourages consumption of the service at the family level. For example, male dominance favors service consumption by males and discourages service consumption by females.

- *Personal factors*. Personality of the individuals that makes them more or less likely to receive the service.

- *Jurisdiction*. Confusion of authority and / or responsibility of local, state, federal, Native or other institutions.

The Social Fabric Matrix

Before operationalizing content into a measure, it is imperative to organize and process it in an easily understood format. Gregory F. Hayden's SFM (Hayden 2006) is well suited to the material and issues presented in this chapter and it provides greater structure than the description offered in Table 1 alone. Concerned with the narrow and superficial analysis sometimes used in economic inquiry, Hayden developed a cross-disciplinary methodology to "allow for the convergence and integration of conceptual frameworks in instrumental philosophy, general systems analysis, Boolean algebra, social system analysis, ecology, policy analysis, and geobased data systems" (Hayden 2006:73). The SFM is particularly useful in articulating relevant connections in complex situations (Hayden 1982).

Hayden suggested six main components that must be identified and integrated in order to understand a problem, including cultural values, societal beliefs, personal attitudes, social institutions, technology, and the natural environment. Table 2 presents a reorganizing of the content of Table 1 into the SFM framework. The same

Table 2 Alaska service access rigidities in the social fabric matrix:

		Local service availability 1	Local service availability 2	Regional service availability 1	Regional service availability 2	Central service availability	Nominal explicit cost	Population density queue	Administrative (in)efficiency queue	Travel cost	Cost of extended stay	Child care cost	Loss of work income
		D01	E01	D02	E02	D03	D04	F01	D05	D06	D07	D08	D09
Local service availability 1	D01						110	111	111	110	110	110	110
Local service availability 2	E01	110					110						
Regional service availability 1	D02	111							110	110	110	110	110
Regional service availability 2	E02			110									
Central service availability	D03	111		111					110	110	110	110	110
Nominal explicit cost	D04												
Population density queue	F01	111		111		111							
Administrative (in)efficiency queue	D05									110	110	110	110
Travel cost	D06												
Cost of extended stay	D07												
Child care cost	D08												
Loss of work income	D09												
Intangible costs	D10												
Political willingness to fund service	B01	111								110	110	110	110
Group dependent service funding	D11	100		100									
Political willingness to fund assistance programs	B02	110											
Group dependent assistance	D12	110		100									
Income tested assistance	D13	110											
Race	F02	111											
Gender	F03	100											
Class	D14	100											
Political will of local government	D15	101											
Effectiveness of local administration	D16	111											
Local leadership	C01	101											
Family dynamic	A01												
Individual dynamic	C02												
Jurisdiction	D17	111	111	111	111	111							

SFM category legend. *A* Cultural values; *B* societal beliefs; *C* personal attitudes; *D* social institutions;

Intangible costs	Political willingness to fund service	Group dependent service funding	Political willingness to fund assistance programs	Group dependent assistance	Income tested assistance	Race	Gender	Class	Political will of local government	Effectiveness of local administration	Local leadership	Family dynamic	Individual dynamic	Jurisdiction
D10	B01	D11	B02	D12	D13	F02	F03	D14	D15	D16	C01	A01	C02	D17
111														101
										110				
111														101
111														
												111	111	
111														
110														
110														
110														
110														
110														
110														
					110									
110														
110														
111														
111														
111														
	111		110											
	111		110						111	111				
111														
111														

E technology; *F* the natural environment. Cell legend: $f(i,j,k) = $ (health, justice, safety) categories appear in both the rows and the columns. Two concepts are emphasized in the SFM framework: flows and deliveries (Hayden 2006:85). As described in the methodology chapters of this book and by many other authors, the matrix indicates where a row category makes a delivery to the column category. Because three different types of services are analyzed here, each cell in Table 2 is coded for individual services, as in (1).

$$f(i,j,k) = (\text{health}, \text{justice}, \text{safety}). \tag{1}$$

Deliveries are coded as "1" and the absence of a delivery is coded as "0." Therefore, a cell coded (110) indicates that the row factor delivers to the column factor for health and justice, but not for safety. Cells where no substantial deliveries occur are left entirely blank.

While every cell indicating a delivery has unique and valuable information, there are two groups that are of particular interest. The first is the differences in how service availability is affected by social institutions vs. technology. The second is the vast array of deliveries into intangible costs.

Technology has made a dramatic difference in healthcare delivery in rural Alaska (Berman and Fenaughty 2005). Even though many rural places in Alaska do not have physical healthcare facilities, most do have high-speed internet service via satellite communications. This technology allows for teleconferencing between patients and medical professionals in different locations, expediting some services. Local service availability as a technology factor (E01), therefore, delivers into local service availability as a social institution (D01) in the SFM. The technology aspect of service availability also delivers into nominal explicit cost of the service (D04) where a physical facility might exist, whereas the social institution aspect of service availability does not. These sorts of distinctions are made abundantly clear by use of the SFM.

Intangible costs (D10) are a dominant force in the SFM. Of the 27 characteristics analyzed in the SFM, seventeen of them make deliveries into intangible costs. Intangible costs are often neglected in empirical analysis because their objective measures are absent. The SFM indicates that it would be a serious oversight not to take into account the non-monetary costs of service access barriers. In the indices that are created from the information in the SFM, proxies must be used to represent intangible costs because they are such a large part of the total social cost of service access rigidities.

The SFM informs the creation of indices. Following Hayden's paradigm, the data points and weights afforded individual components of an index are determined by the interrelation of the categories. The final information included in an index is limited by the availability of data. Nevertheless, the SFM helps to identify which data are relevant.

Access Rigidity Index

Condensing information on access rigidities into a singular expression is convenient and useful for empirical analysis. Following the example of the Human

Development Index (Fukuda-Parr and Kumar 2003:245–253), access rigidity indices for regions (Census Areas) in Alaska are created. There are two broad categories of indexes: those measuring the *absence* or *deprivation* of a characteristic and those measuring the *presence* or *capability* of a characteristic. In the former case, the general equation is

$$Z_j = \left(\frac{1}{I} \left(\sum_i^I X_i^\alpha \right) \right)^{\frac{1}{I}},$$ (2)

and the latter equation is

$$Z_j = \left(\sum_i (\omega_i)(X_i)^{1-\varepsilon} \right)^{\frac{1}{1-\varepsilon}}.$$ (3)

In (2), Z is the measured index calculated over "*I*" components (*X*) for a particular place "*j*." The weighting factor, α, gives larger importance in the index to larger numbers. Therefore, this index is useful in measuring a rigidity that exists – the absence of access. A higher index number indicates more difficulty in receiving the service.

In (3), Z is the measured index calculated over "I" components (*X*) for a particular place "*j*." The nominal weighting factor is ω for each component. In addition to ω, each component is also weighted by "$1-\varepsilon$," effectively penalizing smaller numbers. In (3), therefore, a smaller index number indicates a greater difficulty (barrier) in receiving the service in question.

Each component, *X*, is calculated either as an incidence percentage or as a deviation from goalpost boundaries. As in Fukuda-Parr and Kumar (2003:247), deviation calculations are

$$X_i^{calc} = \left[\frac{X_i - X^{low}}{X^{high} - X^{low}} \right].$$ (4)

The high and low goalpost values are determined on a case-by-case basis and usually reflect observed maximum and minimum values.

Preliminary estimates of service access rigidity indices for each Census Area in Alaska are presented in Table 3. Each of these numbers measures the presence of a rigidity. Therefore, a higher number indicates greater difficulty in receiving the given service in the indicated Census Area. Space limitations prevent a detailed exposition of the calculation of the indices here (complete discussions appear in Edwards 2009a, b, c). In general, components are identified using the SFM. Data are gathered from primary sources including the Alaska Division of Community Advocacy (http://www.commerce.state.ak.us/dca/commdb/CF_COMDB.htm), Alaska Court System (http://www.state.ak.us/courts), the Justice Center at the University of Alaska Anchorage (justice.uaa.alaska.edu), and other state and federal agencies. Table 3 presents an index of access rigidity for each of the three categories of services discussed, as well as a composite index of the three, which is a simple average of the health, justice, and safety indices. Two other measures of economic well-being,

Table 3 Service access rigidities indices (c. 2000)

Region (census area)	Median income[a]	Composite index[b]	Health index[c]	Justice index[c]	Safety index[c]	Percent in poverty[d]
Aleutians East	47,875	0.677	0.525	0.714	0.794	8.5
Aleutians West	61,406	0.777	0.650	0.857	0.825	12.6
Anchorage	55,546	0.000	0.000	0.000	0.000	6.1
Bethel	35,701	0.280	0.225	0.286	0.330	6.7
Bristol Bay	52,167	0.364	0.250	0.429	0.414	22.2
Denali	53,654	0.383	0.255	0.429	0.465	5.9
Dillingham	43,079	0.442	0.325	0.429	0.571	4.8
Fairbanks North Star	49,076	0.113	0.195	0.000	0.143	17.9
Haines	40,772	0.350	0.335	0.429	0.286	7.0
Juneau	62,034	0.042	0.125	0.000	0.000	10.2
Kenai Peninsula	46,397	0.086	0.115	0.143	0.000	5.8
Ketchikan Gateway	51,344	0.304	0.340	0.429	0.143	8.9
Kodiak Island	54,636	0.339	0.650	0.143	0.225	7.2
Lake and Peninsula	36,442	0.502	0.505	0.429	0.571	17.3
Matanuska-Susitna	51,221	0.033	0.100	0.000	0.000	8.8
Nome	41,250	0.245	0.305	0.143	0.286	17.3
North Slope	63,173	0.394	0.315	0.143	0.725	7.8
Northwest Arctic	45,976	0.421	0.355	0.143	0.765	15.5
Prince of Wales-Outer Ketchikan	40,636	0.345	0.320	0.429	0.286	14.5
Sitka	51,901	0.208	0.285	0.143	0.195	6.8
Skagway-Hoonah-Angoon	40,879	0.418	0.275	0.429	0.550	7.8
Southeast Fairbanks	38,778	0.360	0.365	0.429	0.286	17.3
Valdez-Cordova	48,734	0.330	0.375	0.286	0.330	7.8
Wade Hampton	30,184	0.420	0.455	0.429	0.375	28.8
Wrangell-Petersburg	46,434	0.349	0.315	0.286	0.445	8.3
Yakutat	46,786	0.505	0.655	0.432	0.429	8.5
Yukon-Koyukuk	28,666	0.543	0.485	0.429	0.714	18.1
Mean	46,842	0.342	0.337	0.313	0.376	11.42
Standard Deviation	8,900	0.184	0.166	0.214	0.252	5.99

[a]Real (99) dollars household income. *Source*: US Bureau of the Census; Alaska Economic Trends; ISER
[b]Simple average of health, justice, and safety indices
[c]Author's preliminary calculations – see Edwards (2009a, b, c) for details
[d]Edwards and Natarajan (2008)

median income and the percent of households in poverty, are also presented in the table for comparison. The Anchorage Census Area is considered the baseline index so that the value of the Anchorage indices are all zero. The indices for all other areas of the state, then, represent relative rigidities compared to the largest urban area in Alaska. See Fig. 3 for a map of the Census Areas in Alaska.

Consider first the Composite Index. The areas most like Anchorage – the ones with the lowest measured access rigidities – are population centers like Juneau,

Fig. 3 Alaska Census Areas. *Source*: Jones and Shattuck (2000:17)

Fairbanks, Kenai Peninsula, and Matanuska-Susitna. Areas with the highest measured access rigidities are the most remote, are off the connected road system, and have no major regional hub such as Aleutians West at 0.777, Aleutians East at 0.677, and Yukon-Koyukuk at 0.543. These results are broadly consistent with the expectation that services are more difficult to receive the more remote is the place.

Individual service access indices reveal that, in some places, different services are harder to come by than others. For example, the Composite Index for Kodiak is 0.339, which is roughly the average observed rigidity. However, both the Safety and Justice indices are below their state averages in Kodiak, while the Health Index is substantially higher than its state average. In Denali, the Health Index is relatively low while the Justice and Safety Indices are relatively high. Substantial heterogeneity in service access rigidity is observed throughout the state across both geography and service type.

Table 4 organizes the data from Table 3 into rankings in order to compare more easily compare the different measures. Median Income is ranked from the highest income to the lowest, Percent in Poverty is ranked from the lowest to the highest poverty level, and the access rigidity indices are ranked from the lowest measured rigidity to the highest. In each case, a lower rank number is preferred (less measured poverty, higher measured income, less measured service access rigidity). North Slope is ranked first for median income and ninth for poverty, but 18th for service access rigidity by the composite measure. Conversely, Fairbanks North Star is ranked fifth for the composite service access rigidity but 24th for poverty and 11th for median income. In other areas, the rankings are more even. Sitka, for example, is ranked in the top half of the rankings by all measures and Wade Hampton is in the bottom half of the rankings by all measures.

A closer look at the individual service access indices shows that, for the most part, they move together. At the same time, there is enough variation to demonstrate that a separate accounting for specific service access rigidities is productive.

Table 4 Ranks of service access rigidities indices (c. 2000)

Region (census area)	Median income	Composite index	Health index	Justice index	Safety index	Percent in poverty
Aleutians East	13	26	24	26	26	13
Aleutians West	3	27	26	27	27	18
Anchorage	4	1	1	2.5	2.5	4
Bethel	25	8	6	12	13.5	5
Bristol Bay	7	16	7	19	16	26
Denali	6	17	8	19	19	3
Dillingham	18	22	15	19	21.5	1
Fairbanks North Star	11	5	5	2.5	5.5	24
Haines	21	14	16	19	10.5	7
Juneau	2	3	4	1.5	2.5	17
Kenai Peninsula	16	4	3	7.5	2.5	2
Ketchikan Gateway	9	9	17	19	5.5	16
Kodiak Island	5	11	25	7.5	8	8
Lake and Peninsula	24	23	23	19	21.5	23
Matanuska-Susitna	10	2	2	2.5	2.5	15
Nome	19	7	11	7.5	10.5	21
North Slope	1	18	13	7.5	24	9
Northwest Arctic	17	21	18	7.5	25	20
Prince of Wales- Outer Ketchikan	22	12	14	19	10.5	19
Sitka	8	6	10	7.5	7	6
Skagway-Hoonah- Angoon	20	19	9	19	20	11
Southeast Fairbanks	23	15	19	19	10.5	22
Valdez-Cordova	12	10	20	12	13.5	10
Wade Hampton	26	20	21	19	15	27
Wrangell-Petersburg	15	13	12	12	18	12
Yakutat	14	24	27	25	17	14
Yukon-Koyukuk	27	25	22	19	23	25

These differences in the separate indices might prove useful in explaining the complex dynamics of some observed economic decisions in Alaska. For example, there are extremely high rates of both in- and out-migration in some of the Census Areas in Alaska that are difficult to account for on the basis of common economic measures such as jobs, poverty, and income (Edwards 2007). Perhaps part of the explanation is due to regional amenities or barriers to some amenities like healthcare, justice, and safety.

Conclusion

Basic services like healthcare, justice, and safety are necessary for any society to thrive. In many localities in the U. S. and abroad, some people have difficulty accessing these vital services because of a wide variety of barriers. Barriers that prevent people from receiving fundamental services diminish the quality of their lives. In the aggregation, society as a whole suffers when some of its members do not have ready access to healthcare, justice, and safety.

The analysis related in this chapter makes use of Hayden's SFM to organize and assess the presence of service access rigidities that exist in Alaska. The SFM made the creation of empirical measures for the rigidities possible. The empirical measures in the form of indices show the relative difficulty in receiving basic services across Alaska. While, in general, more remote places have greater barriers to receiving analyzed services than urban places, important differences exist from place to place and service to service.

Ultimately, the indices created through the application of the SFM to the question of service access in Alaska can be used in empirical evaluation of social and economic questions. For example, no empirical consensus has been reached on the determinants of migration in Alaska (Edwards and Huskey 2008). The indices presented in this chapter, or similar indices, could be used as independent variables in regression analysis of migration. While a large part of the reason a person moves from one place to the next is often employment, another part of the decision is likely local amenities. Service access rigidity indices can be used to proxy for (the absence of) local amenities.

Reference

Anderson C (2003) Millions of crimes go unreported. A news article posted on the CBS News Web site 10 Mar 2003. http://www.cbsnews.com

Berman M, Fenaughty A (2005) Technology and managed care: patient benefits of telemedicine in a rural health care network. Health Econ 14(6):559–573

Bryson G (2007) VA's health services nonexistent in the bush. Anchorage Daily News, published on-line 1 Dec 2007 at http://adn.com

DeMarban A (2008) Slowly, Western Alaska starts to break silence on sexual abuse. Anchorage Daily News, published on-line 22 Jan 2008 at http://adn.com

Edwards Wayne (2007) Small moves in a big place: migration as a preference signal. Polar Geogr 30(3 and 4):139–152

Edwards W (2009a) Crime prevention in limited access areas. Manuscript, University of Alaska, Anchorage, AK

Edwards W (2009b) Health barriers in Alaska communities. Manuscript, University of Alaska, Anchorage, AK

Edwards W (2009c) Obstacles to justice in rural environments. Manuscript, University of Alaska, Anchorage, AK

Edwards W, Huskey L (2008) Search with an external opportunity: an experimental exploration of the Todaro Paradox. Ann Reg Sci 42(4):807–819

Edwards W, Natarajan T (2007) Rigidities, living conditions, and institutions in the Far North. Forum Soc Econ 36(2):63–72

Edwards W, Natarajan T (2008) ANCSA and ANILCA: capabilities failure? Native Stud Rev 17(2):69–97

Edwards W, Natarajan T (2009) Rural society and barriers to well-being. Journal of Northern Studies 3(1), forthcoming.

Einarsson N et al (2004) Arctic human development report. Stefansson Arctic Institute, Reykjavik

Fukuda-Parr S, Shiva Kumar AK (2003) A technical note: calculating the human development indices. Chapter 2.9 in Readings in Human Development. Oxford University Press, New York

Haley S et al (2007) Executive summary of vital business enterprises for rural Alaska: what works? Pamphlet. University of Alaska, Institute of Social and Economics Research, Anchorage, AK

Halpin J (2008) Villages plead for resources to fight crime. Anchorage Daily News, published on-line 29 Jan 2008 at http://adn.com

Hayden FG (1982) Social fabric matrix: from perspective to analytical tool. J Econ Issues 16(3):637–662

Hayden FG (2006) Policymaking for a good society: the social fabric matrix approach to policy analysis and program evaluation. Springer, New York

Howe L (2004a) Alaska income distribution and poverty over time: the effect of the permanent fund dividend. Draft manuscript, Institute of Social and Economic Research, University of Alaska, Anchorage, AK

Howe L (2004b) Alaska settlement patterns. Draft Manuscript, Institute of Social and Economic Research, University of Alaska, Anchorage, AK

Jones EJ, Shattuck K (2000) Alaska Bureau of Vital Statistics, 1999 Annual Report. Alaska Department of Health and Social Services, Division of Public Health, Bureau of Vital Statistics, Juneau, Alaska

Martin S (2006) Stylized facts of migration in Alaska. Manuscript, Institute of Social and Economic Research, University of Alaska, Anchorage, AK

Roberts J (2005) Improving public safety in rural Alaska: a review of past studies. Alaska Justice Forum 21(4):1–8

Simon M (2009) In rural Alaska villages, families struggle to survive. CNN.com. Accessed 9 Feb 2009

State of Alaska (2002) Alaska Health Profiles Online Annual Report 2000. Prepared by the State of Alaska Health and Social Services Department. http://www.hss.state.ak.us. Accessed 30 Aug 2005

State of Alaska (2004) Healthy Alaska 2010 indicators. Prepared by the Alaska Bureau of Vital Statistics. http://www.hss.state.ak.us/dph/bvs. Accessed 30 Aug 2005

Statewide Library Electronic Doorway (2005) FAQ Alaska – frequently asked questions about Alaska: Alaska native Claims Settlement Act. http://sled.alaska.edu/akfaq/akancsa.html. Retrieved 16 June 2005

Wallace S (2005) ANWR: the great divide. Smithsonian 36(7):48–56

Indian Agriculture in a Liberalized Landscape: The Interlocking of Science, Trade Liberalization, and State Policy

Tara Natarajan

Abstract Mainstream macroeconomic policy in India has sought to alleviate rural poverty and food insecurity by expanding agricultural production, providing agricultural credit through a national agricultural banking system, programs of employment generation to alleviate income poverty, and some state-level midday meal schemes at schools. The green revolution was introduced in the late sixties, making India food self-sufficient at the national level. Even as the country accumulated buffer stocks of food, problems of hunger and starvation nevertheless persisted at the individual, household, village, and regional levels. Beginning in the late nineteen eighties, India gradually began to adopt market friendly policies. The economic crisis in 1991 set India on a path of fast track liberalization and structural adjustment resulting in comprehensive initiatives by the Government to promote the industrialization of agriculture. The government has opened up contract farming, food processing, horticulture, value added agricultural products, export crops, and biotechnology, and has allowed private corporations to invest in agriculture. This rapid industrialization is a transformative process. The social fabric matrix approach demonstrates this process where trade liberalization, scientific research, agricultural policy, and the ideology of neo-liberalism are interlocking agents shaping the contemporary industrialization of agriculture in India today. Thus, in the context of a liberalizing India, the concept of transformation replaces the term development and helps to focus our attention on a detailed understanding of the interactive institutional process of change in agriculture. The question continues to be whether or not the contemporary expansion of the agrarian sector through industrialization has served in preventing the ever-present problem of endemic hunger that nearly 320 million Indians still face.

T. Natarajan (✉)
Saint Michael's College, Burlington, VT, USA

T. Natarajan et al. (eds.), *Institutional Analysis and Praxis*,
DOI 10.1007/978-0-387-88741-8_14, © Springer Science+Business Media, LLC 2009

Introduction

Conventional economics views poverty primarily as income poverty. Concomitantly in the case of rural poverty, mainstream policy seeks to alleviate the same from the perspective of employment generation, creating incomes, and finding ways to make agriculture profitable. The plethora of work across the social sciences in development and poverty studies since the early 1980s particularly that of Dreze and Sen [(1981, 1989, 2001), Chambers et al. (1982), Chambers (1995), Yunus (1998)] have made an irrefutable case against the conventional view of poverty and in favor of a multidimensional perspective in both theory and praxis. Sen has argued that it is essential to measure poverty as capability deprivation rather than as a lowness of income. While an increase in income is a strong contributor to alleviating poverty, it is only one aspect of the complex condition and it is in fact creating and enhancing well-being and not just the alleviation of income poverty that should be in focus; therefore, one must look for non-income factors that interact in creating deprivation and vulnerabilities.

Chambers work based on area studies illustrates how poor people's needs differ from those assumed for them by professionals. In his article entitled "Poverty and livelihoods: whose reality counts" he

> ...explores how professionals' universal, reductionist, and standardized views of poverty differ from the views of the poor themselves. ... In the new understandings of poverty, wealth as an objective is replaced by wellbeing and "employment" in jobs by livelihood. Chambers (1995:173)

Mohammed Yunus who established the Grameen Bank, a micro credit institution, argues for self-employment supported by credit, as opposed to generating wage employment, as the solution to the problem of poverty (1998). Under certain conditions he argues that wage employment can perpetuate poverty in the short and medium term because a job may keep a person poor if their earnings do not satisfy their basic needs. Yunus (1998:58) explains, "...the removal or reduction of poverty entails a continuous process of wealth or asset creation, so that the asset-base of a poor family, particularly their access to productive assets from which they can generate additional income and wealth, becomes stronger at each economic cycle...". Yunus points to the fact that in conventional development strategy, it is the wealthy within a nation or multinationals who own power plants, financial institutions, telecommunications infrastructure, etc. and they serve their own interests before they serve those of the poor. He thus calls for a radical rethinking and decentralization of credit by incorporating the concept of not only financial returns but also social returns (Yunus 1998). Mohammed Yunus and the Grameen Bank were awarded the Nobel Peace Prize in 2006 for their efforts to create economic and social development from below (Nobel Prize 2006).

This chapter describes through evidence how conventional growth economics has been operationalized in the case of rural development policy and agriculture in India both historically and also in the contemporary context of neo liberal policies of liberalization. The analysis reveals the interlocking of trade liberalization, agricultural scientific research, agricultural policy in India, and the ideology of neo-liberalism that have been instrumental agents in shaping the industrialization of agriculture in India. The green revolution was introduced in the late sixties, making India food self sufficient at the macro level. Nevertheless, at the individual, household, village and regional levels, problems of hunger and starvation persisted in many places in India. Nearly 320 million Indians, who account for one-third of the estimated 840 million hungry across the world, face the violent threat of hunger on a persistent basis.[1] It is therefore critical to examine if the contemporary expansion of the agrarian sector through industrialization has served in preventing the continuing problem of endemic hunger.

A Survey of India's Agrarian Development Strategy

India became independent from British colonialism in 1947. The first Prime Minister of a free India Pandit Jawaharlal Nehru was the chief architect of what came to be known as "Nehruvian Socialism". India, not unlike most post-colonial countries of the world, favored an economic strategy of state-directed economic development, thereby giving rise to a "mixed economy". (Patnaik and Chandrasekhar 1998; Bajpai and Sachs 1997). This strategy was characterized by economic planning, with a large role for the public sector in key industries like steel, power, coal, oil, banks, and other financial institutions and extensive state regulation of the economy. Bajpai and Sachs (1997) argue that the historical context of the new post-colonial nations' state led industrialization (SLI) was a defensive reaction against the capitalist "First World" which included both governments and multinational enterprises. Thus, "... neither inflows of foreign capital nor a development strategy based on free trade seemed a sensible approach to national economic development for fragile, newly independent states in what seemed to be an essentially hostile world" (Bajpai and Sachs 1997:137). Bajpai and Sachs (1997) argue that while the choice of SLI can be justified in the post-colonial historical context it shows that the performance of closed state-led economies in terms of growth rates was very poor.[2]

The post-independence strategy of state directed economic development in India was characterized by 5-year plans, the centerpiece of India's model of a mixed economy under the direction of the celebrated planning theoretician C.P. Mahalanobis. The plans in general contained detailed output targets for both agriculture and industry. Public sector investment, also considered as plan expenditure, was closely and effectively controlled (Little 2002). Each plan however has a core focus and the first 5-year plan while small and essentially an amalgam of existing

---

[1]Joseph 2006.

[2]See Bajpai and Sachs (1997) in which they present a moving average of average growth for four always closed and eight always open economies between 1965 and 1985 as evidence to argue that open economies grew much faster than closed economies.

investment projects was also aptly dubbed the agricultural plan. However, starting in the mid 1980s India began to modernize and move towards integrating itself into a global market economy. The economic crisis of 1991 forced India to adopt the program of liberalization and structural adjustment of its macro economy. Thus within a span of 60 years in post independent India, the method of achieving economic growth has swung from a highly interventionist state led strategy to a radically liberalized market economy.

Agriculture has always occupied a central place in the Indian economy and society. It contributed to 35% of the GDP in 1984 and 17.5% in 2006 which is still a sizable contribution compared to approximately 11.3% in China for 2007 (Central Intelligence Agency 2009; World Bank 2008a, b). Population below the poverty line in rural areas was 30.2% compared to 24.7% in the urban areas for the year 1999–2000 (World Bank 2005). The fact that poverty resides predominantly in rural India has played an important role historically in India's approach to agricultural development and rural poverty alleviation initiatives. Issues of food security, hunger, and rural poverty have been treated primarily as matters of production and distribution at the regional and macro level and from the perspective of income and resource poverty at the micro level. In addition, the Indian government created a massive agricultural banking sector that refinances and provides a wide variety of loans and assistance to farmers down to the village level. Broadly speaking, however, the Indian state has approached agricultural development and rural poverty alleviation largely by modernizing agricultural production through science, technology, and more recently via industrialization and trade liberalization.

Agricultural development has always been viewed as being critical for economic development of the entire economy. For instance, Foster and Rosenzweig (2008) argue that advances in agricultural productivity increase welfare by lowering the cost of food, releasing persons to engage in non-farm activities that produce goods and services and enrich lives. Therefore, one of the chief concerns in 1960s India was to increase agricultural production and productivity. Modern scientific knowledge and technology were thus introduced to Indian agriculture through the "green revolution." Funded by the Ford Foundation a team of plant breeders and agricultural scientists primarily from the United States introduced new high-yielding agricultural technologies to India and other South Asian rice growing regions such as Sri Lanka, Thailand, Indonesia, and Vietnam. In India, the green revolution technology was introduced to rice fields in the south and wheat fields in the north of the country. This technology primarily comprised of high yielding seed varieties (HYVs) which require new inputs such as assured and well controlled irrigation water in hot dry areas along with fertilizers and pesticides to complement the HYVs. Much has been written and researched on the impact of the green revolution in India. Most prominent are the long term longitudinal comparative studies at the village level that have been conducted in the rice growing state of Tamil Nadu, southern India, Sri Lanka, and other areas of South Asia.[3] The aim of introducing

---

[3]For further reading on longitudinal and village level studies on the impact of the green revolution see Farmer (1977, 1979), Harriss (1982), Harriss-White (2004) Hazell and Ramaswamy (1991).

green revolution was to make India food self sufficient. Ganguly (2003) notes that for instance in 1978–1979 India recorded grain production output of 131 million tons which established India as one of the world's biggest agricultural producers, making India an exporter of food grains at that time. However, the relative success or failure of green revolution technology is a heavily debated topic. The content of the debates ranges from issues of socio-economic consequences of the new technology, negative environmental impacts, and high costs associated with such technology resulting in the exclusion of poorer farmers. B.H. Farmer argues that whatever maybe the economic, social, and political consequences of this technology, the basic problems of production associated with green revolution are by no means solved. He argues that production problems arise because of the suitability of such technology to specific agro ecological conditions only, the inadequate appreciation of the variability in agriculture and the fact that technology has not sufficiently overcome problems set by the natural environment (Farmer 1979). Since the green revolution in the sixties, India has initiated similar "revolutions" in dairy, fisheries, and oil seeds popularly known as the "white, blue and yellow revolutions" respectively (Sharma 2003). These "revolutions" demonstrate the ways in which scientific knowledge and state policy have combined to produce and shape agricultural development in India.

While the green revolution arguably made India a net exporter of food grains, it has not solved the problems of chronic hunger and undernourishment in the country.[4] In order to address these issues, the government of India, began intervening in food markets and initiated food for education and health programs in addition to employment oriented programs with an aim to alleviate poverty and increase food security of the poor. The public distribution system (PDS) was established in the early 1950s with an aim to target the poor and protect them from food-price inflation. The effectiveness and cost of the PDS program in India has been much criticized and many argue that the access of the poor to the PDS is still very limited. Other direct interventions and programs include midday meal schemes for children in government run schools. Most notable are those in the states of Tamil Nadu, Gujarat, Kerala, and to an extent in Orissa and Madhya Pradesh. Recent programs such as the Sampoorna Grameen Rozgar Yojana (SGRY) launched in 2001 aimed at providing food and employment to people below the poverty line in rural areas. More recently the National Rural Employment Guarantee Scheme (NRGS) was launched in 2005 that provides one hundred "man days" of employment to every adult in a family in rural India. The government has also intervened in food markets by providing subsidized inputs and controlling prices, and has restricted internal and external trade in agricultural commodities (Srinivasan 2000).

Despite a variety of interventions in food distribution, according to the World Bank (2005), the prevalence of undernourishment in India between 1990 and1992 was 46.7% and between 2000 and 2002 it was 44.9% of the population. Sen (2002)

---

[4]See Dreze (2003), Sen (2003), Sen and Patnaik in Joseph (2006).

argues that deprivation, regular malnutrition, and endemic hunger are common especially for landless rural laborers, whose entitlement to food in the market economy of India rests on their ability to sell labor in a tight labor market and buy food in exchange thus making the relative price of food high quite often. According to Sen

> India's 'self-sufficiency' in food has to be assessed in the light of the limited purchasing power of the Indian masses. ... There has been no great 'shortage' in the market – no 'crisis' to deal with – but at least a third of the rural population has regularly – and quietly – gone to bed hungry and malnourished. The government has been able to ignore this endemic hunger because that hunger has neither led to a run on the market, and chaos, nor grown into an acute famine with people dying of starvation. Persistent orderly hunger does not upset the system. (Sen 2002:33)

Despite calls for a direct focus on hunger in social policy, India has forged towards establishing a path for achieving high economic growth potential. Arguments that suggest a causal link between high rates of economic growth and reduction in poverty, dominate the discourse. For example Srinivasan (2000) contends that

> ... Indian GNP per capita averaged about 1.5% during 1950–80 and the poverty head – count ratio fluctuated between 42% and 62% with no trend. It then doubled to about 3.6% per capita until the macroeconomic crisis in 1991 after which radical economic reforms ensued and GNP per capita has averaged at 4% per capita until 1998 and poverty has declined to about 35% in 1997. ... A decomposition of reduction in poverty into contributions due to growth and redistribution suggests that growth accounted for 80% of the decline in the poverty ratio over a 40 year period since the mid-1950s and almost 100% since 1970. (Srinivasan 2000:281)

India's penchant for creating economic growth can be seen clearly in the neo liberal strategies which were adopted pursuant to the 1991 economic crisis in exchange for loans exceeding $5 billion from the International Monetary Fund.[5] India also borrowed long term development loans under the World Bank's structural adjustment programs that stress liberalization of markets, promote export oriented growth strategies, and decidedly oppose state-sponsored industrialization.[6] According to Sen (2002:162) such a pattern of development will have the effect of excluding ambitious programs of social services which according to him have been "...sadly unimaginative and breathtakingly conservative" to begin with. In the case of agriculture the outward oriented approach has resulted in its industrialization with focus on agro food processing and exports of value added agricultural products.

---

[5]India suffered a severe macroeconomic and balance of payment crisis in the early 1990s. The consolidated gross fiscal deficit of the central and state governments in fiscal year 1990–1991 was as a high as 9.4% of GDP. With a GDP growth of 1.3%, an inflation rate over 10%, and by the summer of 1991 with foreign exchange reserves plummeting to below 2 weeks' worth of imports, India was on the verge of bankruptcy (Bhagwati 1993).

[6]See Sen (2002), Kothari and Minogue (2002), Patnaik and Chandrasekhar (1998).

Economic Reforms and the New National Outlook on Agriculture

The economic crisis of 1991 set India on a process of fast track liberalization and structural adjustment program which removed internal and external barriers to trade, deregulated industry, moved towards freeing the food grains market and reducing food subsidies, as well as privatized and opened up the financial markets.[7]

With over 110 million farmers and workers, Indian agriculture is the largest private sector enterprise contributing to nearly 25% of the country's gross domestic product. The agricultural sector produces over 51 major crops besides providing raw material to Indian agro-based industries. Nearly one-seventh of the country's total export earnings accrue from agricultural sector.

From a macro perspective, agricultural production is said to have been resilient in the last few decades. India has emerged as the second largest producer of rice, wheat, groundnut, fruits, and vegetables in the world (Indian Development Report 2004). Patnaik and Chandrasekhar (1998) state that while India's food grain production has grown steadily around 2.5% per year which is a little higher than population growth, the 1990s have experienced some striking changes in food grain production. They state that over the periods 1990–1991 and 1996–1997, which are considered to have been good agricultural years, the growth of food grain production dropped to 1.4% which is distinctly lower than population growth rates. They cite two major causes for a drop in food grain production. They are (1) a shift in land use towards the production of a variety of non-food commercial crops and emphasis on export agriculture such as prawn fisheries, sunflower, and orchard crops and (2) a drastic decline in public investment in agriculture. While the 1990s saw a boost in private gross capital formation, Patnaik and Chandrasekhar (1998) contend that this investment occurred in nontraditional export agriculture. According to them, the years between 1990 and 1991 and 1996 and 1997 saw a sharp decline in land use for coarse grains and a concomitant shift towards using land for export crops like sunflower and even rice.

India's agricultural trade policy in the year of liberalization is said to have been dualistic. Exports of some plantation crops and a few commercial crops were free from export restrictions, but export of essential commodities, particularly food products, were subject to bans and quotas. India's comparative advantage measured in terms of different measures of protection is considered to be high for rice, fruits and vegetables, as well as meat and marine products (Gulati 1998). As a result of dismantling Quantitative Restrictions on imports as per World Trade Organization (WTO) agreement on agriculture, commodity-wise strategies and arrangements are being formulated for protecting the grower from adverse impacts of undue price

---

[7] I am grateful to Dr. Sunder Ramaswamy, President Monterey Institute of International Studies and Fredrick C. Dirks Professor of Economics Middlebury College for his input to the section on economic reforms in India.

fluctuations in world markets and for promoting exports. Import duties on manufactured commodities used in agriculture are being rationalized. In order to promote agricultural exports, the Government of India ear marked 41 agricultural export zones spread over 17 states entailing an investment of approximately $273 million. A projected export target of more than $714 million during the next 5 years is likely to be achieved and a substantial amount of direct and indirect employment is predicted to be generated as result of these zones (ibid). The optimism regarding the projected targets is on the basis of the diversified nature of agriculture consisting of a large variety of crops, fruits, vegetables, and a flourishing dairy sector, and India is among the world leaders in output of many products. India recently made a significant breakthrough in food grains exports by being ranked as the sixth major exporter of wheat and in rice exports next to Thailand and ahead of Vietnam. The government has also liberalized the exports of pulses with the view that it would encourage farmers to produce more as they would get remunerative prices.[8] Among agro-based industry products, cotton yarn and fabrics are the single largest foreign exchange earner. Export of marine products was at $1,214 million and tea and coffee exports were at $228.17 million[9] (SISI 2005).

The concern to liberalize agriculture, legitimate albeit, has resulted in exclusive attention paid by researchers and policy analysts to the subject of "slowness" of agrarian reforms, thereby overshadowing the ongoing revolutionary changes being experienced by agriculture as a direct result of trade and industry liberalization. The era of trade liberalization has seen comprehensive initiatives by the Government, which has launched programs to promote the development of food processing industries both for the domestic and export markets. The government has employed a strategy based on dynamic comparative advantage[10] which is on the basis of the argument that gains from trade can arise because of (a) technical efficiency, (b) new trading opportunities, (c) improvements due to learning, adoption of better farm practices, and newer technologies. The Ministry of Agriculture has set up an inter-Ministerial Task Force which has recommended the promotion of direct marketing and contract farming. It has also advocated the development of agricultural markets in private and cooperative sectors, expansion of future trading to cover all agricultural products, and use of information technology to provide market-led extension services to farmers (TIDCO 2004a).

---

[8]Pulses are defined by the Food and Agricultural Organization of the United Nations (FAO) as annual leguminous crops solely harvested for the dry grain, yielding from 1 to 12 grains or seeds. Pulses are used for food and animal feed. Pulses are important food crop due to their high protein and essential amino acid content and for playing a key role in crop rotation due to their nitrogen fixing ability. (http://en.wikipedia.org/wiki/Pulse_(legume))

[9]Based on such arguments, many have advocated deregulating and liberalizing agriculture. However, it must be noted that even amongst those who advocate deregulating and liberalizing agriculture, many academics and policy makers in India have questioned the ad hoc nature of many of the reform decisions in agriculture particularly that of decontrolling input prices and relaxing import controls (Gulati 2002).

[10]I am grateful to Clifford Poirot for his thorough and insightful comments on this issue that appeared in paper I presented at the AFIT meetings in 2006.

Along with opening up the market place for trade and industry, economic liberalization has also opened up the space of ideas and discourses in which the private sector and both corporate and agricultural scientific research centers now have an active role. The latter primarily comprises of agricultural scientific research centers and universities, which are influential in shaping agrarian India.[11] Agricultural research centers consist of domestically rooted private research institutes, public–private partnerships, international research agencies operating in various Indian locations, and also publicly funded extension-type research centers connected to agricultural universities or relevant departments in universities.

In addition to research centers, economic liberalization has allowed a variety of private companies both domestic and international, to actively involve themselves in agricultural production, distribution, and food retail. Private companies such as Pepsi co, a key player in Indian agribusiness, are not only introducing new products and market opportunities but are also introducing new production arrangements such as contract farming (TIDCO 2004a). Furthermore agribusinesses are also forging links with cutting edge business management universities which are in turn spreading these new ideas to farmers through agricultural research and extension. The entry of corporate agriculture into agriculture in India is a distinctly new phenomenon of the 1990s, a result of the rapidly growing food processing industry and biotechnology (Gulati 2002).

Couched in a particular ideology,[12] liberalization of trade, industry, and finance, privatization, and agrarian policy in India are unequivocally transforming the agrarian landscape in India.

The significance of the more amorphous and uneven changes, as a result of a liberalized economy, is arguably a historical marker akin to that of the green revolution of the sixties, with the important distinction that the ongoing change is not being caused by a cohesive singular factor. Economic reforms in India coincided with globalization, creating a dynamic new economy in India, thereby interlocking domestic structural changes and global market opportunities. The food market in particular began to experience globally induced changes and new markets have opened up in processed foods and pre-prepared packaged foods, simultaneously facilitated by the spread of super market chains in Indian metropolitan areas. The demand for the production of certain exportable food and non-food crops, as well as the inflow of foreign finance capital into agriculture particularly ventures in agro processing, necessarily alters land use and production arrangements. Functional

---

[11] Note that agricultural scientific research agencies are by no means uniquely post liberalization phenomena. They have been an active part of agricultural research in India, particularly since the green revolution. The current climate of liberalization and the government's active role in making agriculture an industrialized sector has certainly made agricultural research and crop breeding a key part of the ongoing changes India.

[12] Harriss-White (2004) refers to Shaffer (1984) to explain the overlapping of politics in the policy process. Also see Hayden (1989, 1992, 1993, 2006) to understand the treatment of interlocking relationships in the policy process.

and personal distribution of income in the agrarian and non-agrarian sector change as factor use, production, and ownership arrangements are bound to change.[13]

Development often connotes a particular form of positive change in conventional economics, where the nature and process of change are often conceived of narrowly, in a depoliticized manner, becoming akin to modernization as the end product of change. However, what is required is an analysis of the "production" of development. This can be achieved by recognizing the notion of agency, defined as a network of institutions and actors that through their actions and interactions "produce" development.[14] An important theoretical argument therefore emerges from this chapter that in the context of a liberalizing India, the concept of transformation replaces the term development and helps to re-focus our attention on a detailed understanding of the interactive institutional process of change in agriculture. Agency of transformation is thus brought into direct focus. This helps us to understand outcomes and beneficiaries better because agency, agenda, and outcomes of this process are inextricably linked and are now spoken about in explicit terms.

The next section provides details regarding the actions, policies, and the interactions between the various agents who have been identified as being instrumental in the current transformation of agrarian India. These interlocking relationships among agricultural research centers, state agricultural policies, and agri-businesses are described in the specific case of the state of Tamil Nadu in southern India. Tamil Nadu, primarily a rice growing region was chosen because of the prevalence of the rigidities posed by seasonality and also because it was one of the states influenced significantly by the green revolution in the 1960s. Today Tamil Nadu is in the forefront of pushing agro based industries.[15]

Interlocking Institutional Relationships: Shaping and Deploying the Agrarian Development Agenda

The first part of this section uses government policy documents, specifically the National Agricultural Policy announced in July of 2000 to glean (1) the recent position of the Government of India on agriculture, approximately a decade after liberalization, (2) its view on agricultural performance, status, needs, and proposals for reforms, and(3) critically evaluate the meaning of agricultural reforms as articulated by the government. The second part of this section discusses the role of the

---

[13] See Ray (1998) for a theoretical explanation of the concepts of functional and personal distribution of income. For a critique and discussion of the effects of commercialized agriculture in India see Bhalla in Chadha and Sharma (1997).

[14] See Kothari and Minogue (2002).

[15] The author conducts field studies in dry land areas of Tamil Nadu and Andhra Pradesh in southern India. Specifically, she conducted field research in a dry land district of Tamil Nadu in 1999–2000 and continues to collaborate with her long time field collaborator Dr. Arivudai Nambi who resides in Chennai, Tamil Nadu.

private sector in agriculture, i.e., private corporations and agricultural scientific research centers. Together these two parts reveal interlocking relationships between the institutional agents, who are key players in shaping agriculture in India's liberalized market economy. The liberalized market economy, the institutional agency of transformation, provides both the ideological landscape and new institutional policy framework, now given the legitimacy and procedural clarity through specific capital friendly policies.

Current National Agricultural Policy: The case of Tamil Nadu

The government's policy statement begins with promises of food security, fair prices, infrastructure, land reforms, sustainable agriculture, and biodiversity, however, with the specific focus being food processing and value added products. It also articulates its concern over rural poverty and the importance of maintaining the goal of food security, both of which it hopes to address through the promotion of international trade in agricultural commodities with the use of ecologically sustainable practices and biotechnology. Broad, rife with internal contradictions, replete with arguably vacuous goals the government speaks to every conceivable stake holder and agenda in agriculture. In its statement regarding the goal of agrarian reforms it reads, "The establishment of an agrarian economy which ensures food security to India's billion people, raw materials for its expanding industrial base and exports, and a fair and equitable reward system for the farming community for what they provide to the society, will be the mainstay of reforms in the agriculture sector" (TIDCO 2004b:1).

The Government echoes the commonly accepted sentiment that agriculture has become a relatively unrewarding profession and attributes this to "unfavorable price regime and low value addition" (TIDCO 2004b:2). It goes on to say that

> the national agricultural policy seeks to actualize the vast untapped growth in Indian agriculture, strengthen rural infrastructure to support faster agricultural development, promote value addition, accelerate growth of agro business, create employment in rural areas, secure fair standard of living for the farmers and agricultural workers and their families, discourage migration to urban areas, and face the challenges arising out of economic liberalization and globalization. (TIDCO 2004b:2)

The policy statement makes commitments towards rapid growth rate in the agricultural sector on the basis of efficient resource use and conserving biodiversity, growth that will be equitably and regionally distributed, growth that is demand driven, caters to domestic markets, and maximizes from exports of agricultural products while keeping the growth technologically, ecologically, and economically sustainable and socially acceptable. The five point general statement on agriculture is followed by detailed sections on sustainable agriculture, food, and nutritional security. Its statement on sustainable agriculture makes the reclamation of degraded and fallow lands a priority and emphasizes its commitment to conserving soil and water. It is crucial to note here that the government seeks to achieve many of its conservation goals through the use of bio-technology for "...evolving plants that would be low in water usage and are pest resistant." (TIDCO 2004b:2) This sentence is immediately followed by its commitment to the conservation of bio-resources, traditional knowledge, and organic farming while also developing the processing of food for medicinal purposes (TIDCO 2004b:3).

An entire section of this policy document is devoted to "food and nutritional security." It is not difficult to notice the overt contradiction between the title of this section and the points following it which discuss with great fervor the special efforts being made towards developing agro based industries, both rain fed and irrigated horticultural crops, tubers, and plantation crops. The only consistent message in the national agricultural policy document is with respect to expanding agro based industries as a way of creating new agro industrial jobs to combat the negative income effect generated by population growth.

The government has also made a commitment to research and extension linkages particularly with a view to creating "farmer responsibility." It stresses the need for decentralized extension systems in which the corporate sector features as one of the examples of decentralized institutions along with *Krishi Vigyan Kendra's* (KVKs), nongovernmental organizations (NGOs), and cooperatives.

Spice a bi-monthly publication of The National Institute of Agricultural Extension Management called MANAGE, an organization of the Ministry of Agriculture, government of India, devoted its March (2003) volume to "successful cases of contract farming." It opens with "The government of India's National Agricultural policy envisages that private sector participation will be promoted through contract farming and leasing arrangements to allow accelerated technology transfer, capital inflow and assured markets for crop production, especially oilseeds, cotton and horticultural crops." (Spice 2003:1) Contract farming is proposed as an arrangement that will provide an assured market for farmers produce. The lack of markets and market access for sellers of farm output has been a major bottleneck and a risk factor.

> Contract farming is defined as a system of production and supply of agricultural/ horticultural produce under forward contracts between producers/ suppliers and buyers. The essence of such an arrangement is the commitment of the producer/ seller to provide an agricultural commodity of a certain type, at a time and price, and in the quantity required by a known and committed buyer. (Spice 2003:1)

Such an arrangement involved a predetermined price, stipulated quality, and quantity of the product which would be produced in a certain land size and would be harvested and delivered to the contractor. The contractor in return supplies the farmer with selected inputs, including technical advice. The terms of such contractual arrangements differ across crops, contracting agency, farmers, and required inputs. Contracting arrangements are being practiced by a few Indian companies such as Hindustan Lever Ltd, the Indian subsidiary of Uni Lever Ltd and also Pepsi Foods Ltd. Pepsi Foods Ltd installed a $5 million tomato processing plant in Punjab on the basis of contract farming arrangements. According to MANAGE (2003:2) "The PepsiCo's model of contract farming, measured in terms of new options for farmers, productivity increases, and the introduction of modern technology, has been an unparalleled success." It goes on to note that one of the important factors in PepsiCo's success is the strategic partnership of the company with local bodies like the Punjab Agricultural University (PAU) and Punjab Agro Industries Corporation Ltd. (PAIC) speaking about the interlocking nature of agency and agenda among corporations, state, and agricultural research. PepsiCo has since then expanded to Basmati rice, chillies, peanuts, and potatoes. What is being pushed is

> to establish an agrarian economy that ensures food and nutrition security to a population of over a billion, raw material for its expanding industrial base, surpluses for exports, and a fair and rewarding system for the farming community, 'commitment driven' contract farming is no doubt a viable alternate farming model, which provides assured and reliable input service to farmers and desired farm produce to the contracting firms. (Spice 2003:6)

Tamil Nadu which is a rice growing state in southern India as noted previously was one of the states influenced by the green revolution and today is in the forefront of industrializing its agrarian areas by focusing on value added agriculture. They have focused on the development of horticulture, free trade zones, export processing zones, food processing industrial estates, and food parks since liberalization. This "thrust" towards certain exports related to food processing is in keeping with the national policy articulated in various national documents of the Ministry of Food Processing Industry (MFPI). According to the MFPI (2000) "…food processing and agro industries have been accorded high priority with a number of important incentives." The Ministry asserts that "Food processing is one of the thrust areas identified for exports. Free trade zones (FTZ) and export processing zones (EPZ) have been set up with all infrastructure." Post harvest infrastructure, establishment of food processing industrial estates or food parks, and cold storage infrastructural facilities have been identified as sectoral priorities by the national government.

The extent of the government's commitment to exports, processed foods, and agricultural value added products is evident in the creation of the new ministry of food processing in 1988. The MFPI is the nodal agency of the Government of India for processed foods and is responsible for developing a strong and vibrant food processing sector with the following stated goals:

- Stimulating demand for appropriate processed foods.
- Achieving maximum value addition and by-product utilization.
- Creating increased job opportunities, particularly in rural areas.
- Enabling farmers to reap the benefits of modern technology.
- Creating surpluses for exports.

In the era of economic liberalization where private, public, and co-operative sectors are to play their rightful role in development of the food processing sector, the Ministry acts as a catalyst for bringing in greater investment into this sector, guiding and helping the industry in a proper direction, encouraging exports, and creating a conducive environment for the healthy growth of the food processing industry. Within this overall objective, the Ministry aims at the following:

- Better utilization and value addition of agricultural produce for enhancement of income of farmers.
- Minimizing wastage at all stages in the food processing chain by the development of infrastructure for storage, transportation, and processing of agro-food produce.
- Induction of modern technology into the food processing industries from both domestic and external sources.
- Maximum utilization of agricultural residues and by-products of the primary agricultural produce and also of the processing industry.
- Encouraging R&D in food processing for product and process development and improved packaging.
- Providing policy support, promotional initiatives, and physical facilities to promote value added exports. (Ministry of Food Processing Industries 2000)

TIDCO (2004a) has a detailed and comprehensive policy document on contract/corporate sector farming under the title, "Tamil Nadu for the development of fruits and vegetables". The state government publicizes multiple goals such as rural industrialization, high quality food for consumers, reduction in post-harvest losses, increased exports, and employment generation in its agenda to industrialize agriculture. On the basis of the comparative advantages of the state such as its agro-climatic conditions it encourages certain horticultural and plantation crops. The state of Tamil Nadu strongly supports the entry of the corporate sector into farming and believes that "corporate bodies are in a position to achieve commercial objectives better than individual entrepreneurs" and are therefore promoting "...schemes to persuade entrepreneurs to float companies with the primary goal of running agricultural farms" (TIDCO 2004a:14). The state also believes that "a direct result of corporate farming will be to provide employment to graduates turned out by agricultural universities to lend a professional touch to farm management" (TIDCO 2004a:15).

The state has enacted new policies that directly move forward the agenda of industrializing agriculture. An *exemption* from the land ceiling act which prohibits holding or acquiring any land in excess of ceiling area under Sec. 37-A of the Tamil Nadu Land Reform (Fixation of Ceiling on Land) Act 1961 has been made with a view to promoting any entity that is in the business of value addition. The Government of India has developed guidelines for leasing or purchasing recently degraded forest lands, reserved forests, as well as other forests, which can now be acquired for the development of plantations as public–private partnerships or joint ventures. In addition, cultivable waste land or "poramboke" land now owned by the government will be made available for developing agro based industry (TIDCO 2004a). The state government has also granted a "capital subsidy" to the tune of 20% of fixed assets subject to a ceiling of $50,000. The most significant policy is the "pollution clearance charge" which grants an exemption from payment to the Tamil Nadu Pollution Control Board, which is levied per annum. The state lists those industries involved in the production of fruits and vegetables that will be awarded industry status for express purpose of availing of concessions or incentive subsidies.

In the case of India, what liberalization has meant for agriculture is the development of agro industries, food processing, contract farming, increasing production for the export market, and widespread development of horticulture among other changes. While the aforementioned impact of economy wide reforms on the agricultural sector varies vastly by region, it does not obviate the general trend, namely industrializing agriculture whose main goal is that of commercialization with outlets in both domestic and international markets and thus creating new revenue opportunities for states.

Agricultural Research and the Private Sector

Scientific research foundations now have a significant role to play in agriculture, particularly plant breeding. The International Crop Research Institute for the Semi Arid Tropics (ICRISAT) is one such organization in Patancheru, a semi arid district in the state of Andhra Pradesh in southern India. As a nonpolitical and non-profit research organization that aims to serve the poorest of the poor through science, ICRISAT conducts agricultural research and extension in various semi-arid regions of the world. It belongs to the Alliance of Future Harvest Centers and is supported by the Consultative Group on International Agricultural Research (CGIAR). CGIAR is a strategic alliance of international organizations, governments, and private organizations that support the mission of mobilizing science to benefit the poor. Financed by member contributions, two-thirds of its funding is from industrial countries, specifically the members of the Development Assistance Committee of the Organization for Economic Cooperation and Development (OECD). They work in the areas of agro-ecosystems, biotechnology, and plant improvement in addition to institutions, markets, and policy impact analyses. (ICRISAT 2009)

On the domestic front, there are institutes that conduct similar research and directly influence farming. M.S. Swaminathan Research Foundation (MSSRF) in Chennai, India, is a pertinent example of "private sector intellect" in agricultural research where science and social science are combined, particularly to conduct agricultural extension work. MSSRF conducts research in agricultural science and technology, has overlapping interests with domestic and global agri-businesses, publicizes its commitment to biodiversity and sustainability, and interlocks with state level policy making in agriculture, an agenda that, as we have seen, is currently on the basis of the demands and opportunities afforded by global markets and a liberalized economy.

Investments in research and development in agriculture have been shown to yield high economic returns (Gulati 2002). He points to several studies which show that public research and extension together account for half the growth in total factor productivity in Indian agriculture in the post green revolution period. Expenditure on research as a proportion of agricultural GDP in India is said to be as low as 0.3% as compared to 0.7% for developing countries as a group. Several academics and policymakers are also explicitly calling for Indian agricultural research to associate itself with business and industry and "benefit" from "public–private" partnerships in agriculture.

As noted earlier MSSRF located in Chennai, India is one of the leading domestically grown private agricultural research institutes, a non-profit trust. The basic mandate of MSSRF is to "…impart a pro-nature, pro-poor and pro-women orientation to a job-led economic growth strategy in rural areas through harnessing science and technology for environmentally sustainable and socially equitable development." (http://www.mssrf.org/).

MSSRF focuses largely on regional agrarian development and conducts research in the following areas:

• Coastal Systems
• Biodiversity
• Biotechnology
• Eco technology
• Food Security Information, Education, and Communication

The foundation's vision and approach is best understood through the founder M.S. Swaminathan's public speeches, the institute's publications, their research workshops, and seminars. The foundation is committed to science and technology as a vehicle for achieving sustainable food security, nutritional adequacy, and poverty alleviation.

Swaminathan was one of the key players in the implementation of green revolution in the 1960s, which is often claimed to have lead India onto the path of achieving national level food security. However, Swaminathan now speaks about the fatigue of green revolution, as well as the growing damage to the ecological foundations essential for sustainable food security caused by green revolution crops. He now criticizes the basic green revolution farming system of rice-wheat rotation which, he argues, has led to the displacement of grain fodder legumes capable of enriching the soil. "What is now happening is best described as land and water mining and not farming." He thus calls for an "ever green revolution," i.e., "improvement of production in perpetuity without associated social or ecological harm" which he argues is vital for safeguarding food security (Swaminathan 2001:12). He believes in "…the power of blending traditional practices with frontier technologies." As a plant breeder he firmly believes that India must not condemn advances in the breeding of transgenic crops as it will not be in the interest of sustainable food and nutritional security. He believes that India's explosive population makes the case to produce "…more crop per unit of land and per every drop of water." (Swaminathan 2003:5). MSSRF defines sustainable food security as "physical, economic, social and ecological access to balanced diets and safe drinking water, so as to enable every individual to lead a productive and healthy life in perpetuity." In his talk entitled "Science and Our Agricultural Future," Swaminathan speaks of the necessity of fostering bonds of partnership between universities and industries by encouraging industrial research parks like those that surround leading research universities in the United States (Swaminathan 2003). This call for scientific partnerships that would encourage participatory research with farming families to develop location specific technologies is on the basis of the belief that there is a critical triangle to be served by science in providing food and nutritional security, and alleviating poverty while being environmentally and ecologically sustainable (Singh 2001). The inherent contradictions notwithstanding, there are needs for substantial commitment from the state governments by way of complementary public sector investments for the foundation to achieve any of their goals.

The body of work and ideas spanned by MSSRF and other policy oriented extension research institutes speak to every possible view point and stake holder. At least in the case of the state of Tamil Nadu, this current trend is intimately tied to what Harriss-White calls Tamil Nadu's "garden state" (Harriss-White 2004). The work of institutes such as the MSSRF in part is in keeping with the national agricultural policy and its agenda but also informs and directs agricultural policy particularly at the state level. Publications of "The Central Marine Fisheries Research Institute," "Aquaculture Authority News," "Indian Council of Agricultural Research: A science and technology newsletter," "Directorate of Oilseeds Research," and "Syngenta" on the benefits of mapping the rice genome, are but a few examples of the influence of science, technology, and trade in shaping agriculture in India today.

Dry land or semi arid regions in rural India face peculiar rigidities that stem from their heavy dependence on monsoon rains. In addition to promoting a commercialized strategy particularly in dry land agriculture, scientific research on developing pest resistant and more productive varieties of dry land crops has been conducted extensively in the semi arid tropics. Research in agricultural science and technology has tried to find answers to enable the semi arid tropics to better cope with seasonal rigidities and thereby alleviate dry land poverty in rural India. Just as green revolution was focused on semi arid regions, today's strategy of commercialized diversification in crop production is being considered as the way out of dry land rigidities.

Figure 1 is a modified diagraph of the interactive institutional flows that are the key actors and processes in the industrialization of agriculture in India. The diagraph is a visual representation of what has been explained in the section "Interlocking Institutional Relationships: Shaping and Deploying the Agrarian Development Agenda." The governments' position is one of adopting a growth led strategy to expand the agrarian sector, take advantage of trade liberalization, create agro based industries, and enter into production arrangements such as contract farming using both domestic and foreign investments. Harriss-White's labeling of Tamil Nadu's agrarian policies as one that is creating a "garden state" could not be more accurate. Agribusiness corporations clearly have an interest and an active role in shaping the landscape. From the point of view of revenues that could ensue from corporate investments in agriculture, the development of the agro industrial sector is a priority sector as far as state governments such as that of Tamil Nadu are concerned. Making agriculture profitable at the regional and macro level through a clearly neo-liberal strategy is therefore a well entrenched practice in India.

Table 1 is a social fabric matrix (SFM) that lists the social beliefs, institutions, technology, and environmental components that have been identified in this paper as

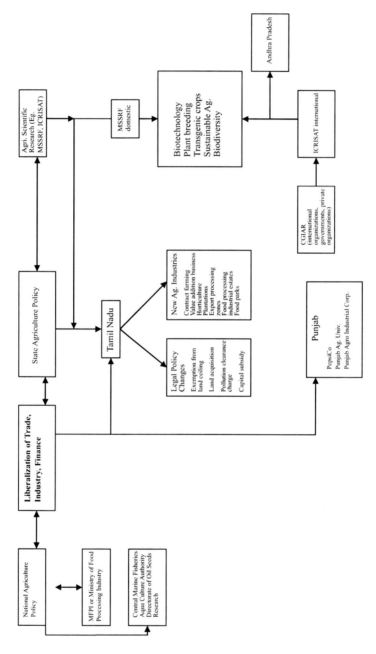

Fig. 1 Network of Institutions: Interlocking of Science, Liberalization, and State Policy

being part of creating an industrialized transformation of agrarian India. The cells that contain "one (1)" are indicative of a significant flow between the delivering and receiving components. The SFM shows societal beliefs such as the ideology of neo-liberalism, belief in market expansion, and economic growth that have created associative and regulative institutions[16] of liberalization, and national and state agricultural policies. The cluster of deliveries among various institutions is depicted as the diagraph in Fig. 1 which shows the interlocking relationships among agricultural scientific research, trade, and agricultural policy in India. The SFM contains two ecological components namely sustainable agriculture and biodiversity that have been stated as important goals of national and state agricultural policies. MSSRF also states these among their goals. This SFM has introduced negative deliveries among institutions I 07, 10, 12, 13, 15, 18, 19, 21, 22, 23, 26, and 27 to argue about potential negative impact on the ecologically based goals. The paper also argues that the stated policy goals that seek to industrialize agriculture and create sustainable agriculture that is pro poor and maintaining biodiversity as seen in the TIDCO, MFPI, and MSSRF documents are internally and mutually contradictory. Lastly the SFM situates the following question in context: how does the strategy of industrializing agriculture seek to address the very real and violent threat of hunger and malnutrition that millions of poor in India suffer from even today?

Rural "development"?

With growth rates ranging between 8.4 and 9.2% between 2003 and 2007, India has been one of the fastest growing economies in the nineties and into the turn of the century (World Bank 2008a, b). However, eminent economists and policy makers have been trying to get public attention and action on the existence of endemic hunger, rising starvation, and the worst malnutrition in the face of baffling accumulations of food stocks and rapid economic growth (Dreze 2003 and Sen 2003). At a public hearing on hunger and the right to food, speaking about food policy in India, Sen (2003:3) asserted "We are evidently determined to maintain, at heavy cost, India's unenviable combination of having the worst undernourishment in the world and the largest of unused food stocks on the globe."

About 320 million Indians reportedly go to bed hungry, representing a third of the estimated 840 million hungry in the world. Minority groups such as the Adivasis in areas such as Rajasthan and Jharkhand experience this chronic hunger disproportionately, with some 90% of 1,000 households surveyed being chronically hungry, 37% of rural households falling below the poverty line, and 80% of rural households showing calorie deficit.

> There is need for more explicit analysis of the effects of public policies on the different classes, and in particular on the extreme underdogs of society who, along with their deprivations

---

[16] See Table 1 in Chap. 9 in this volume by Parto and Regmi (2009).

Table 1 Systems Interactions and Impacts of the Industrialization of Indian Agriculture

		Neoliberalism, market opportunity and expansion	Economics growth	science and technology for poor (pro poor policies)	Privatization, liberalization	National agricultural policy	MFPI	State agricultural policy	Legal policy changes (I05–08)	Exemption from land ceiling	Land acquisition	Pollution clearance charge	Capital subsidy	New ag industries (I10–I16)
		B01	B02	B03	I01	I02	I03	I04	I04	I05	I06	I07	I08	I09
Neoliberalism, market opportunity and expansion	B01		1		1	1	1	1						
Economics growth	B02				1	1	1			1				1
science and technology for poor (pro poor policies)	B03		1			1		1						
Privatization, liberalization	I01	1	1	1		1	1	1	1					1
National agricultural policy	I02	1	1	1	1		1	1	1					1
MFPI	I03	1			1	1		1	1					1
State agricultural policy	I04	1	1	1	1	1	1		1	1	1	1	1	1
Legal policy changes (I05–08)	I04	1	1		1	1	1	1		1	1	1	1	1
Exemption from land ceiling	I05					1								1
Land acquisition	I06					1								1
Pollution clearance charge	I07					1								1
Capital subsidy	I08													1
New ag industries (I10–I16)	I09		1			1		1	1					
Contract farming	I10		1											
Value addition	I11		1											
Horticulture	I12		1											
Plantations	I13		1											
Export processing zones	I14		1											
Food processing industrial estates	I15		1											
Food parks	I16		1			1								
Central marine fisheries research	I17						1	1						1
Aquaculture authority	I18						1	1						1
Directorate of oil seeds research	I19						1	1						1
MSSRF,ICRISAT	I20		1	1				1						1
Biotechnology	T21						1	1	1					1
Plant breeding	T22						1	1	1					1
Transgenic crops	T23						1	1	1					1
Sustainable age	E24			1										
Biodiversity	E25			1										
Pepsico	I26	1	1		1		1	1						1
Syngenta, Monsanto	I27	1	1	1	1	1	1	1	1					1

SFM category legend. B societal beliefs; *I* institutions; *T* technology; *E* environment

	I10	I11	I12	I13	I14	I15	I16	I17	I18	I19	I20	I21	I22	I23	E24	E25	I26	I27
Contract farming																		
Valueaddition																		
Horticulture																		
Plantations																		
Export processing zones																		
Food processing industrial estates																		
Foodparks																		
Central marine fisheries research																		
Aquaculture authority																		
Directorate of oil seeds research																		
MSSRF,ICRISAT																		
Biotechnology																		
Plant breeding																		
Transgeniccrops																		
Sustainableag																		
Biodiversity																		
Pepsico																		
Syngenta. Monsanto																		

I10	I11	I12	I13	I14	I15	I16	I17	I18	I19	I20	I21	I22	I23	E24	E25	I26	I27
		1					1	1	1	1	1	1	1	1	1		
1	1	1	1	1	1	1					1	1				1	1
1	1	1	1	1	1	1	1	1	1						1		
1	1	1	1	1	1	1										1	1
1	1	1	1	1	1	1			1							1	1
1	1	1	1	1	1	1					1		1			1	1
		1														1	
1	1	1	1	1	1	1										1	
1	1	1	1	1	1	1								-1	-1		
1	1	1	1	1	1	1											
1	1	1	1	1	1	1			1								
1		1	1	1	1	1								-1	-1		
1		1	1	1	1	1											
1		1	1	1	1	1								-1	-1		
1	1	1	1													1	
1	1		1	1		1								-1	-1		
1	1		1			1								-1		1	
		1	1	1	1		1								-1		
	1		1	1		1								-1	-1		
1	1	1	1	1	1									-1	-1		
											1	1	1	1	1		1
		1	1				1	1	1	1		1		-1	-1	1	1
		1	1						1	1				-1	-1	1	1
		1	1	1	1				1	1				-1	-1	1	1
															1		
														1			
1	1	1	1	1	1	1								-1	-1		
										1	1	1	1	-1	-1		

(particularly low income, bad health care, inadequate opportunities of schooling), are also remarkably underfed and undernourished. (Sen 2003:4)

Ultimately the question of poverty, in this case rural poverty, is multidimensional and resides deeply at the local, household, and individual level. Growth led strategies could certainly serve and address needs of a certain form of development at the national, state, and regional level. However, relief from persistent hunger, endemic hunger, malnutrition, and food security at the individual level is a matter that goes beyond income poverty. Social poverty, powerlessness, and structures that create conditions for exclusion and marginalization of vast groups of rural poor in India cannot be addressed through the creation of market opportunities afforded by comparative advantage in food processing. Current agricultural policy and agrarian change in India needs to be directly focused on proactive social reforms, land reforms, and the creation of socioeconomic conditions that focus on non-income aspects of poverty, broadly speaking what Dreze and Sen (1989) call capability enhancing. Empowerment at both the individual and social level is not achieved or sustained solely by economic opportunities. People have to be able to participate in those economic opportunities and it is all those aspects of poverty unrelated to income that create and deepen conditions of non-participation for the poor and disenfranchised in India.

However, does a purely global market driven strategy have answers to long standing and growing problems of the vulnerable and marginalized in India? Ownership of finance capital and production arrangements will inevitably create income and opportunities afforded by these structures, ensuing relationships, and flows of income. The agency of the poor does not seem to have a central place in the current transformation of agrarian India because the focus is on finding opportunities to make agriculture profitable at the regional and macro level through agro based industries. How does this liberalized agrarian landscape directly address the needs of the rural poor in India?

These questions are raised with the aim of arguing for an agrarian policy framework that focuses on creating rural, local self dependent rural communities where livelihoods, hunger, rural poverty, food distribution, and security are the central concerns. What this paper also demonstrates is that in general a framework needs to be developed that situates state policy in a liberalized market environment. More specifically this paper calls for a framework for conducting impact analyses of agrarian industrialization on rural populations with an ultimate interest in analyzing its effect on poverty and sustainable development.

Abbreviations

CGIAR	Consultative Group on International Agricultural Research
EPZ	Export processing zones
FTZ	Free trade zones
HYVs	High yielding seed varieties
ICRISAT	International Crop Research Institute for the Semi Arid Tropics

KVKs	Krishi Vigyan Kendras
MSSRF	M.S. Swaminathan Research Foundation
NGOs	Nongovernmental organizations
NRGS	National rural employment guarantee scheme
PAIC	Punjab Agro Industries Corporation Ltd
PAU	Punjab Agricultural University
PDS	The public distribution system
SGRY	Sampoorna Grameen Rozgar Yojana
SLI	State led industrialization
WTO	World Trade Organization

References

Bajpai N, Sachs JD (1997) India's economic reforms: some lessons from East Asia. J Int Trade Econ Dev 6(2):135–164

Bhagwati J (1993) India in transition. Clarendon, New York

Bhalla GS (1997) Structural adjustment and the agricultural sector in India. In: Chadha GK, Sharma AN, Indian Society of Labor Economics (eds) Growth, employment and poverty. Sangham Books Ltd, London

Chambers R (1995) Poverty and livelihoods: whose reality counts? Environ Urban 7(1):173–204

Chambers R, Longhurst R, Arnold P (1982) Seasonal dimensions to rural poverty. Pinter Press, London

CIA (2009) http://www.cia.gov/library/publications/the-world-factbook/geos/ch.html#Econ

Dreze J (2003) Hunger amidst plenty. http://www.indiatogether.org/2003/dec/pov-foodsec.htm

Dreze J, Sen A (1981) Poverty and famine: an essay on entitlement and deprivation. Clarendon, Oxford

Dreze J, Sen A (1989) Hunger and public action. Clarendon, Oxford

Dreze J, Sen A (2001) India: economic development and social opportunity. Clarendon, Oxford

Farmer BH (ed) (1977) Green revolution?: technology and change in rice growing areas of Tamil Nadu and Sri Lanka. Westview Press, Boulder

Farmer BH (1979) The 'green revolution' in South Asian ricefields: environment and production. J Dev Stud 15(4):304–319

Foster AD, Rosenzweig MR (2008) Economic development and the decline of agricultural employment. In: Paul Schultz T, John S (eds) Handbook of development economics, vol 4. North-Holland, Amsterdam, pp 3051–3083

Ganguly S (2003) http://www.indiaonestop.com/Greenrevolution.htm

Gulati A (1998) Indian agriculture in an open economy. In: Ahluwalia IJ, Little IMD (eds) India's economic reforms and development. New Delhi, Oxford

Gulati A (2002) Economic reforms and the rural sector in India. Econ Dev South Asia 2:38–56 Elgar Reference Collection

Harriss J (1982) Capitalism and peasant farming: agrarian structure and ideology in northern Tamil Nadu. Oxford University Press, Bombay

Harriss-White B (2004) Policy and the agricultural development agenda. In: Barbara H-W, Jankarajan S (eds) Rural India facing the 21st century. Anthem Press, London

Hayden GF (1989) General systems analysis. Survey of Methodologies for Valuing Externalities and Public Goods

Hayden GF (1993) Institutionalist policy making. In: Tool MR (ed) Institutional economics: theory, method, policy. Kluwer, Dordrecht

Hayden GF (2006) Policymaking for a good society: the social fabric matrix approach to policy analysis and program evaluation. Springer, Berlin

Hazell PBR, Ramaswamy C (1991) The green revolution reconsidered: the impact of high-yielding rice varieties in South India. John Hopkins Press, Baltimore, MD Published for IFPRI

ICRISAT (2009) http://www.icrisat.org/index.htm; http://www.cgiar.org/who/members/funding. html; http://www.cgiar.org/

Joseph A (2006) "Covering the Republic of Hunger" in India Together. http://www.indiatogether. org/2006/jan/ajo-hunger.htm. Accessed Feb 1 2008

Kothari U, Minogue M (2002) Critical perspectives on development: an introduction. In: Uma K, Martin M (eds) Development theory and practice: critical perspectives. Palgrave, Basingtoke

Little IMD (2002) The strategy of Indian development. The Economic Development of South Asia, vol 1. Elgar Reference Collection

Ministry of Food Processing Industries (2000) New Delhi. http://mofpi.nic.in/aboutus/goals.htm; http://mofpi.nic.in/policies/index.htm. Accessed 1 Mar 2007

Nobel Prize (2006) http://nobelprize.org/nobel_prizes/peace/laureates/2006/press.html

Parto S, Regmi A (2009) Microcredit and reconstruction in Afghanistan: an institutionalist critique of imported development. In: Natarajan E, Fullwiler S (eds) Institutional analysis and praxis: the social fabric matrix approach. Springer, Berlin

Patnaik P, Chandrasekhar CP (1998) India: *dirigisme*, structural adjustment, and the radical alternative. In: Dean B, Epstein GA, Robert P (eds) Globalization and progressive economic policy. Cambridge University Press, Cambridge

Ray D (1998) Development economics. Princeton University Press, Princeton

Sen AK (2002) How is India doing. The Economic Development of South Asia, vol 1. Elgar Reference Collection

Sen AK (2003) Hunger in India. Address made at a public hearing on hunger and the right to food, Delhi University, 10 Jan 2003

Sharma A (2003) India. In: WTO agreement on agriculture: the implementation experience – developing country case studies. Food and Agricultural Organization of the United Nations, Rome. http://www.fao.org/docrep/005/Y4632E/y4632e0f.htm#fnB54#fnB54. Accessed 1 Mar 2008

Singh RB (2001) Special address on "Science for sustainable food security, nutritional adequacy, and poverty alleviation in the Asia-Pacific region." MSSRF-FAO Expert Consultation. 25–28 June 2001, Chennai, India

Small Industries Services Institute (2005) Agro processing industries: problems and potential. SISI, Chennai

Spice (2003) Contract farming venture in India: a few successful cases. In: The National Institute of Agricultural Extension Management (MANAGE), vol 1, No. 4. Ministry of Agriculture, Government of India

Srinivasan TN (2000) Poverty and undernutrition in South Asia. Food Policy 25:269–282

Swaminathan MS (2001) Enhancing farm productivity in perpetuity: twenty steps to sustainable food security. A special address in the proceedings of MSSRF-FAO expert consultation on science for sustainable food security, nutritional adequacy, and poverty alleviation in the Asia-Pacific region, Chennai, India, 25–28 June 2001

Swaminathan MS (2003) Science and our agricultural future. An inter-disciplinary dialogue on biotechnology for food, health, nutrition and water security, M.S. Swaminathan Research Foundation, Chennai, 9–12 Jan 2003

TIDCO (2004a) Contract/corporate sector farming policy: Tamil Nadu for the development of fruits and vegetables. http://www.tidco.com/tn_policies/contract_farming.asp. Accessed on 1 Mar 2005

TIDCO (2004b) National Agricultural Policy. http://www.tidco.com/india_policies/other_sect_ GOI_policies/National_agricultural_policy1. Accessed 1 Mar 2005

World Bank (2005) http://devdata.worldbank.org/wdi2005/index2.htm

World Bank (2008) http://web.worldbank.org

World Bank (2008) http://devdata.worldbank.org/AAG/ind_aag.pdf

Yunus M (Fall 1998) Poverty alleviation: is economics any help? Lessons from the Grameen Bank experience. J Int Aff 52:339–352

Implementation of Analytical Devices and the Interactive Social Fabric Matrix Website

Tristan Markwell

Abstract Analytical tools and techniques for the social fabric matrix (SFM) are introduced. A website is detailed which will allow collaborative work with researchers around the world. Associated with this is a tool to standardize the creation and editing of SFM displays. A tool to analyze and produce summary statistics for the special case of a symmetric common-denominator SFM is presented and detailed. Mathematical results from graph and matrix theory are employed. A prior result is presented and paired with a tool to enable automatic calculation of feedback potential within a system, and necessary caveats and limitations are laid out. A set of assumptions is laid out that allows the stability of a system to be determined using intermediate matrix theory, and the most restrictive assumption is relaxed.

Introduction

The social fabric matrix (SFM) is a powerful analytical tool (Hayden 2005). However, the greatest weakness of the tool is that the SFM itself lacks a robust set of supporting analytical tools or techniques to assist in creating information and informing policy judgments. This chapter introduces a website, programs, and mathematical results that should assist in making the results match the level of complexity of the problems being studied.

The first section discusses the value of the ability to work and learn collaboratively using the SFM. A website and an accompanying program are introduced to facilitate this task. The website allows for broad participation and for sharing and modification of SFMs, facilitating collaboration on and revision of research into problems using a SFM framework. The program standardizing the layout, formatting, and editing of SFMs to empower that communication is presented.

The next section introduces a solution to a lack of adequate analytical tools for a specific type of SFM problem. When an SFM is symmetric and reflects a single

T. Markwell (✉)
Providence Health & Services, Portland, OR, USA

T. Natarajan et al. (eds.), *Institutional Analysis and Praxis*,
DOI 10.1007/978-0-387-88741-8_15, © Springer Science+Business Media, LLC 2009

type of delivery, it is possible to examine the extent to which the elements interact. This has been done before, but a program and its underlying logic are presented to make what was once a very burdensome process almost trivial, which should expand its usefulness for analysis.

The final section enhances analysis of SFM problems by bringing some more advanced mathematical results to light. Boolean graph theory has been used with SFMs in the past to discuss the extent to which subsystems can influence one another, allowing insight into the feedback nature of systems. This approach is reintroduced along with a program to generate these results very easily. In addition, linear algebra, or matrix theory, is used to describe results helpful for finding positive feedback in SFM systems. The general contours and outcomes of this approach are laid out, with results presented under a number of assumptions that could be relaxed with additional analysis. However, the final assumptions are broad enough to support the basic structure of essentially any SFM problem, regardless of size or complexity.

Standards for and Collaboration in SFM Research: The SFM Web Site

Clarence Ayres discovered that technology is the combination of tools, skills, and knowledge; therefore, the kind and quality of the tool element influences the kind, quality, and expression of skills and knowledge (Ayres 1944/1978). Seymour Melman went further to discover the importance of work tasks and job demand. He concluded from his studies that if tasks are too complex and job demand too heavy with regard to a technology, productivity is constrained. Thus, work tasks need to be designed to enhance the work experience (Melman 1983: 131–133). Richard Nelson emphasized that technology itself, especially social technology, is dependent on the collection of procedures called *routine*, which is worked out as intra-organizational interactions in production processes (Nelson 2005: 155–162). This is also the case for those working in the world of science with the need for the application of well-developed research techniques that are dependent on well-defined routine. "By far the greater part of modern scientific research, including research done at universities, is in fields where practical application is central in the definition of a field" (Nelson 2005: 245–249).

Consistent with the conclusions of Ayres, Melman, and Nelson, the author has taken steps to develop further the technical routine of the SFM by programming Microsoft Excel to allow for easier and more complete use and manipulation of the SFM as new research or changing reality calls for changes in the matrix's components. The ease of the user interface should make it the preferred way to create and edit SFMs for research or presentations. In addition, the sharing of SFMs is enabled by the use of a new website, which should allow collaboration across universities and even continents.

The website http://cba.unl.edu/academics/economics/sfm/ is publicly available and collaborative. Anyone can upload or download any documents to or from the site. This enables as broad use by the research community as can be desired.

Fig. 1 SFM website

Figure 1 illustrates the website's format and organization. The documents are grouped in bundles of up to three: the required SFM Boolean matrix file, a file explaining the deliveries indicated on the SFM, and a diagram detailing the digraph view of the SFM. Procedures for uploading and modifying files are clearly documented in a PDF file labeled "SFM Site Instructions."

All this potential of the website for collaboration is aided and strengthened by a feature designed by the author, i.e., the SFM Editor. This Microsoft Excel document and the associated program standardize the presentation of SFM information. It allows the creation of SFMs of essentially any size and organizes the elements or components of the SFM in two ways: it numbers them for easy reference with the program itself as well as with collaborators; and it groups them into categories of components so that the data is ordered conceptually for greater understanding. In addition, it handles all the formatting so the user can focus on simply inputting the information. At the time of writing, the SFM Editor available on the website is version 1.0; as needed or desired improvements occur, the program will be updated. Accompanying the Editor are the SFM Editor Instructions, which give a full explanation of the use of the program.

A Special Problem: Symmetric Common-Denominator Matrix: The Case of Corporate Directorship Interlock

It would greatly simplify the policymaking and analytic tasks associated with using the SFM if all deliveries could be put in the same terms; i.e. a common denominator. Different policies could be evaluated simply on the basis of which maximizes the flow of some desirable delivery to one or more relevant nodes. However, this is generally antithetical to the idea of the SFM, which was created "[t]o fulfill the need for modeling transactional complexity" (Hayden 2005: 28). Though "various groups have proposed various indicators to serve as the single measure or common denominator function….[e]ach of these have failed to meet such an impossible standard" (ibid: 71). Using the money value of products as an example, "[e]qual dollar cost figures that show equal expenditures for flu vaccinations and cigarettes do not indicate the same value or the same burden" (ibid). Clearly, one should not expect many problems to lend themselves to such reduction.

However, there are some cases where the SFM approach will result in a matrix with a natural (rather than imposed) common denominator. The best example is the study of interlocking directorships of corporations (Hayden et al. 2002). The special relevance of this topic is due to the fact that "today the most powerful social and economic institution is the network made up of translocked corporate organizations" (ibid: 672). Of special interest are corporate chains of four boards of directors, with a common director serving as the link in the chain. These blocs are of sufficient size to "effectively coordinate plans and decisions" (ibid: 673).

In practical application, these blocs can be difficult to find, organize, and summarize because of the potential volume of the problem. Due to the math, as the number of corporations increases, the number of potential power blocs can increase more than exponentially. At the time the problem was investigated, "[n]either an exact mathematical algorithm nor computer program exist[ed] for finding the power blocs" (ibid: 681). That is no longer the case, as the description below will demonstrate. Such a development can, among other things, allow for the study of interlock over time (ibid: 697).

Following convention, the information about interlocking directorships can be presented in an SFM (or, if ideologically helpful, in a subset of an SFM) that simply measures whether or not two corporations share one or more directors. This is basically a simple adjacency matrix, which will by the nature of sharing necessarily be symmetric. A value of 1 is used to indicate one or more shared directors. The diagonal is by definition not set to 1. This is the appropriate convention because the search for chains of interlocking directorships does not require the use of the (trivial) fact that each corporation shares directors with itself. A simple example of the format is given in Fig.2.

There are several ways to conceptualize the search for power blocs. One is to look at each firm, list all of the interlocks (all possible "two-blocs"), then for each of those list all of the interlocks for the second corporation to form all possible "three-blocs," and then once more to find all of the power blocs. This method tends to "over-search" and leads to many duplicate power blocs, which must be weeded out (ibid: 681–682).

The alternative, which is somewhat more systematic, is to start by conceptualizing the set of "potential" power blocs, i.e., all the unique groupings of four of the corporations being considered (to make sure the groups are unique, one could stipulate that the corporations be in numeric or alphabetical order). In each of the groupings, the total number of interlocks is considered. If the number is less than 3, or if

	A	B	C	D	E	F	G	H	I	J	
1	Corporate		Corporation								
2	Interlock	A	B	C	D	E	F	G	H		
3		A		1							
4		B	1				1		1		
5		C								1	
6		D		1			1				
7		E				1			1	1	
8		F		1			1				
9		G					1			1	
10		H			1				1		
11											

(Corporation label appears vertically on left of rows A–H)

Fig. 2 Adjacency matrix

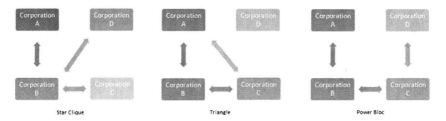

Fig. 3 Possibilities with three interlocks

any corporation has no interlocks, the group cannot be a power bloc. If the number is more than 3, the group must be a power bloc. If the number of interlocks is exactly 3, there are three possibilities, depicted in Fig.3: either all three interlocks involve a common corporation, in which case the group is a "star clique" (ibid: 703); three corporations are mutually interlocked, forming a triangle that excludes the fourth; or they form a power bloc (these alternatives are mutually exclusive). These five conditions could be generalized into a single condition involving minimally sufficient conditions, but the number of computations is similar and the condition is less intuitive. One of the added benefits of performing the determination in steps is that for lower density matrices the (negative) status of many of the potential power blocs becomes clear partway through the process, which will allow savings in computing time.

The author has developed a template in Microsoft Excel that allows the automatic and relatively quick discovery of all power blocs in an interlock matrix as well as the calculation of several summary statistics useful in describing the relative strength of each corporation (see ibid: 677–680). The template contains a macro that automatically searches for all unique blocs and lists them for the user along

(1) Corporation No. & Name	(2) Total Power Blocs Involved	(3) Rank Order of Col 2	(4) Number of Corps Reached	(5) Rank Order of Col 4	(6) Col. 2 Divided by Col. 4	(7) Rank Order of Col. 6	(8) Sum of Cols. 2, 4 & 6	(9) Rank Order of Col. 8	(10) Sum of Cols. 3, 5, & 7	(11) Rank Order of Col. 10
A	2	7	4	7	0.5	7	6.5	7	21	7
B	5	2	5	5	1	2	11	3	9	3
C	1	8	3	8	0.33333333	8	4.33333333	8	24	8
D	4	4	6	2	0.66666667	4	10.6666667	4	10	4
E	8	1	7	1	1.14285714	1	16.1428571	1	3	1
F	4	4	6	2	0.66666667	4	10.6666667	4	10	4
G	5	2	6	2	0.83333333	3	11.8333333	2	7	2
H	3	6	5	5	0.6	6	8.6	6	17	6

Fig. 4 Summary information

	A	B	C	D
1	Corporation 1	Corporation 2	Corporation 3	Corporation 4
2	A	B	D	E
3	A	B	E	F
4	B	D	E	F
5	B	D	E	G
6	B	E	F	G
7	C	E	G	H
8	D	E	G	H
9	E	F	G	H
10				

Fig. 5 Power bloc list

with a tabular summary and a matrix giving the number of power blocs shared by pairs of corporations. The summary, which is given on the second tab and displayed in Fig. 4, gives several measures of the strength or degree to which the corporation is embedded in the corporate network, along with rankings. The three main measures are the total number of power blocs in which the corporation is involved, the total number of other corporations reached through power blocs, and the ratio of these two figures, which represents the average density of the corporation's linkages (ibid: 691). In addition, as an attempt to aggregate these measures, a sum of the three values explained above and a sum of the ranks for each of the three measures are presented. This information can be extremely useful for finding or confirming the identity of the key corporations in the interlocks, but must not displace the overall understanding of the interlock as a holistic system for coordination of decisions. The forest (system of interlocking directorships) cannot be fully described by the properties of the trees (the individual corporations).

The third and fourth tabs of the workbook (shown in Figs. 5 and 6) also contain useful information by looking at the interlocks in a different way. The third tab lists all the power blocs by the corporations involved. It can serve as a quick reference in order to demonstrate the connectedness of a system. The fourth tab lists the number of shared power blocs for each pair of corporations, which can serve to pinpoint the key linkages or directors that empower the network.

	A	B	C	D	E	F	G	H	I	J	K
1	Corporate Interlock		Corporation								
2			A	B	C	D	E	F	G	H	
3	Corporation	A			2		1	2	1		
4		B		2			3	5	3	2	
5		C					1		1	1	
6		D		1	3		4	1	2	1	
7		E		2	5	1	4	4	5	3	
8		F		1	3		1	4	2	1	
9		G			2	1	2	5	2		3
10		H				1	1	3	1	3	
11											

Fig. 6 Power bloc sharing

The program was designed for ease of use, flexibility, and speed of computation. All that is necessary is to paste the matrix into the first sheet (in a symmetric format), run the macro "blocs," and answer three straightforward questions about the format of the adjacency matrix. The program is available as 4blocs.xlt on the website http://cba.unl.edu/academics/economics/sfm/.

Contributions from Mathematics: The Case of Positive Feedback and System Stability

The SFM seems to beg for serious mathematical analysis, notwithstanding the danger of losing sight of the qualitative and holistic aspects of the approach. Part of the mathematical attractiveness is that the SFM approach is simultaneously presented as a matrix and a directed graph, and as such it sparks imagination on two fronts. The work below focuses on measures relating to feedback within and stability of systems.

Graph Theory

With a directed graph, one of the most natural questions that arise is whether every node can be reached by every other node, or whether some nodes are inaccessible to others. In general, this process is often presented in terms of a road map, and whether there are one-way bridges or dead-end streets that would prevent someone from legally driving from any point in the city to any other point (Ore 1990: 65–66). In the context of SFM problems, this can be thought of as whether deliveries from any given element of the matrix can have an impact on some other specified element. This is an important question in terms of system feedback, as explained below.

To fully explore the direct and indirect influences that elements of an SFM can have on other elements, some manipulation is necessary. The analysis is simplest by considering a straightforward SFM with Boolean entries representing deliveries. The SFM can be thought of as an adjacency matrix (not necessarily symmetric), denoted simply by **A**. Using standard results and notation from linear algebra, $(\mathbf{A} + \mathbf{I})^m$, where **I** represents the identity matrix of the same size as **A**, gives the number of paths from the row element to the column element in m moves (deliveries) or less. More fundamentally, these calculations can be done in Boolean fashion, such that all positive numbers are given the value 1, which gives a representation of which elements can be "reached" by other elements in a certain number of moves. Eventually, this "reachability" matrix stabilizes to give the total list of which elements can influence which other elements (Razavi 1983: 222).

One property of a (final/stable) reachability matrix is that if each of two elements can reach the other, then their reach is the same; i.e., they have the same capacity to reach and be reached by all the other elements of the system. This fact allows the elements to be arranged in groups of mutual reach. The reachability matrix can then be "condensed" into a matrix showing the reach of these groups by using the row/column of any one element of each group to represent the whole (since they all contain the same information) and removing the rows and columns of all the other elements of the group (Razavi 1983: 227).

Before explaining the usefulness of these condensation matrices, a word regarding a methodological hazard of this procedure should be given. The danger of the grouping involved in the formation of condensation matrices is that it is purely based on the empirics of the flows in the SFM under consideration and is not based on the coherence of the group as a mental construct. However, this warning aside, the condensation matrix gives an overview of the SFM by explaining the ability of groups of elements to impact one another. This makes it particularly useful to measure the degree of feedback within a system. As "[n]egative feedback… leads to the convergence of system behavior toward some goal" (Hayden 2005: 58), a lack of feedback can put the "downstream" elements in danger because the "upstream" elements are not responsive to their ability to manage what is being delivered.

There are two possibilities for a condensation matrix: either it has one element, representing the entire SFM, or it has multiple groups. In the former case, any element has the potential to (directly or indirectly) impact any other element. In the latter, the incidence of "0" in a cell means that the group associated with the row is unable to give feedback to the group associated with the column, making the deliveries from the column group unresponsive to the row group.

The usefulness of this analysis should be qualified. Just because groups of mutually reachable elements exist does not mean that those groups are stable subsystems. It is possible that the feedback is unrelated to one or more of the (potentially many) types of deliveries from other elements. It is also possible that though there is feedback, the feedback is of a positive nature, which tends to be destructive. Both of these are "false negatives," where the analysis does not indicate a problem where one exists. Because of this, the method described is best used to identify areas where feedback is definitely missing, making this a useful but partial tool in the analysis of systems. More in-depth approaches to discerning the nature of the feedback will be discussed in the next section.

	A	B	C	D	E	F	G	H	I	J	K	L	M	N
1	Condensation Matrix											Elt. #	Element Name	Grp. #
2			Rec. Group #									1	Legal Tender Laws	1
3			1	2	3	4	5	6	7	8		2	Federal Reserve Act	1
4		1	1	1	0	1	1	0	1	1		3	US Courts/Legal System	1
5	Del. Group #	2	0	1	0	0	0	0	0	0		4	Federal Reserve Banks	2
6		3	0	0	1	0	0	0	0	0		5	Board of Governors	3
7		4	0	0	0	1	0	0	0	0		6	FOMC	1
8		5	0	0	0	0	1	0	0	0		7	Banks	4
9		6	0	0	1	1	0	1	0	0		8	Open Market Desk	5
10		7	0	1	0	0	1	0	1	1		9	Treasury	6
11		8	0	0	0	0	1	0	0	1		10	Primary Dealers	7
12												11	Congress	8
13														

Fig. 7 Sample condensation matrix based on Hayden (2006: 126)

Because this method requires substantial and somewhat complicated computational work to complete, the author has created a program in Microsoft Excel that uses SFMs in the standard SFM Editor format described above and calculates and displays both the reachability matrix and the condensation matrix, along with the definition of all of the groups in the latter. All the user needs to do is paste the entire standard SFM page into the first tab of the book and run the macro ReachCondense. The workbook is available on http://cba.unl.edu/academics/economics/sfm/ as ReachCondense.xls. An example of the output is presented in Fig.7.

Matrix Theory

Moving beyond the identification of missing feedback structures, it would be very helpful to be able as well to identify systems characterized by positive feedback. This is because "[p]ositive feedback systems...tend to be unstable since a change in the original level of the system provides an input for further change in the same direction" (Hayden 2005: 58). However, for this work, positive feedback systems need to be carefully defined. Cases that might casually be described as positive feedback, but where the end result is simply greater than the initial disturbance, are not included, because although there is magnification of the disturbance, the magnification is self-limiting. A simple example of this would be the neoclassical/Keynesian concept of a government-purchases multiplier, assuming that the marginal propensity to consume is less than 1 (Mankiw 2007: 283–285). The positive feedback under consideration, the kind that exhibits real danger of instability or self-destructiveness, doesn't have that same limitation on the level of feedback. Instead, a disturbance in flows encourages larger and larger (in magnitude) disturbances that can quickly overwhelm elements of a system.

Matrix theory/linear algebra offers some insights on how this identification might be done. Flows can easily be analyzed in the matrix format with greater descriptive power than when dealing simply with a Boolean digraph/matrix. When information about the sensitivity of the flows is added to our knowledge set, conclusions about overall system sensitivity are relatively easy to derive. It is important to remember that due to any number of possible eccentricities within a system, which are ignored here, the following should be considered necessary (but not always sufficient) conditions for stability.

The following analysis makes several assumptions that could be relaxed with more in-depth treatment. The first is that all the deliveries from one element of the matrix to another can be described by determinate functions, although the exact form does not have to be known. The second is that the functions (at least approximately) depend only on the level of the deliveries and are not sensitive to the stock of some deliverable. The third is that the functions are smooth to the extent that a local linear approximation is reasonable. The fourth is that all deliveries occur with roughly the same frequency. The fifth and most problematic is that the SFM involves only one type of delivery. Obviously, this last assumption is the one that most needs to be relaxed, as it seriously limits our ability to tackle real-world problems.

Within the bounds of these assumptions, we can conceptualize a matrix $\mathbf{F}$ giving the levels of delivery from the element associated with the row to the element associated with the column as functions of the flow in to the row element. Again, we do not need to know the exact functional form. From this matrix, we can construct the matrix $\mathbf{f}$ where each cell is given by the partial derivative of the corresponding cell in $\mathbf{F}$ with respect to the level of delivery to the row element of the SFM. Using this notation, $\mathbf{f}$ essentially gives the sensitivity of the deliveries in $\mathbf{F}$ in terms of changes in the deliveries to any of the elements. Using $\mathbf{dx}$ to represent a vector giving the change in the flow level to each of the elements of the SFM, and using $\mathbf{D}$ to represent a vector of arbitrary potential shocks to the elements of the system (theoretically these could be thought of as external or due to the normal operation of a dynamic system), the system can be represented as

$$\mathbf{dx}_t = \mathbf{f} \cdot \mathbf{dx}_{t-1}, \mathbf{dx}_0 = \mathbf{D}. \tag{15.1}$$

The condition for stability is that at some point the flows stop increasing or decreasing. Otherwise, the continued change in the flow level would either overwhelm (in the case of an increase) or cut off (in the case of a decrease) the receiving elements. Thus, the condition for stability is that

$$\lim_{t \to \infty} \mathbf{dx} = \mathbf{0}. \tag{15.2}$$

It is clear from (2) that this is equivalent to requiring that

$$\lim_{t \to \infty} (\mathbf{f})^t \cdot \mathbf{D} = \mathbf{0}. \tag{15.3}$$

or more simply

$$\lim_{t \to \infty} (\mathbf{f})^t = \mathbf{0}. \tag{15.4}$$

Hence, it becomes crucial to find whether the sensitivity matrix $\mathbf{f}$ will tend toward the zero matrix under repeated multiplication.

Fortunately, there is a very simple way to test this condition, given a bit of understanding about matrices. Many important properties of a square matrix can be described by the eigenvalues. The eigenvalues of $\mathbf{f}$ are the collection of scalars λ that enable the equation

$$\mathbf{f}\mathbf{y} = \lambda\mathbf{y} \tag{15.5}$$

to hold for some vector $\mathbf{y}$ (Anton and Rorres 2000: 338). For any sensitivity matrix $\mathbf{f}$ describing relationships among the n elements in a system, n eigenvalues $\lambda_1, \lambda_2, ..., \lambda_n$ will exist, along with n associated eigenvectors $\mathbf{y}_1, \mathbf{y}_2, ..., \mathbf{y}_3$. This is not the appropriate place for a thorough introduction to the topic; however, it is sufficient to note that some eigenvalues may have the same value, and if so, their associated eigenvectors may or may not be linearly independent (the implications of this will be discussed later) (ibid: 353). In addition, eigenvalues (and eigenvectors), even for matrices made up of real numbers, can be complex, i.e. of the form $a + b \cdot i$, where

$$i = \sqrt{-1}. \tag{15.6}$$

Most basic statistical packages and even some websites can calculate eigenvalues quickly and easily, so no more than minimal linear algebra experience is required to use the results presented below.

Given the above background, the condition for stability can be stated simply: the sensitivity matrix $\mathbf{f}$ meets the mathematical conditions for stability if and only if each of its eigenvalues is within the unit circle in the complex plane. If the eigenvalues are real, then this condition means they must be less than 1 in absolute value; if the eigenvalue is a complex number of the form $a + b \cdot i$, then the condition requires that

$$\sqrt{a^2 + b^2} < 1. \tag{15.7}$$

Stability at the boundaries of these conditions is somewhat more complicated and will not be discussed.

The justification of this result is made much easier if all the eigenvectors are linearly independent (they together span the entire real n-space). Given this, the matrix $\mathbf{f}$ can be rewritten as $\mathbf{PAP}^{-1}$, where $\mathbf{P}$ represents a square matrix formed by concatenating all of the eigenvectors of $\mathbf{f}$, and $\mathbf{A}$ is a matrix consisting completely of zeros except for the main diagonal, where each of the n entries represents one of the eigenvalues of $\mathbf{f}$: $\lambda_1, \lambda_2, ..., \lambda_n$ (ibid: 347–349). In this case,

$$\lim_{t \to \infty} \left(\mathbf{PAP}^{-1} \right)^t = \lim_{t \to \infty} \mathbf{PA}^t \mathbf{P}^{-1} \tag{15.8}$$

As $\mathbf{P}$ and $\mathbf{P}^{-1}$ are finite, nonzero matrices, the behavior of $\mathbf{A}^t$ determines the limit. The t-th power of a diagonal matrix is simply the same diagonal matrix with each entry raised to the t-th power (ibid: 354). Thus, the condition is equivalent to the n simple conditions

$$\lim_{t \to \infty} \lambda_i^t = 0; \ i = 1, 2, \ldots, n \tag{15.9}$$

Clearly this is equivalent to

$$\left| \lambda_i \right| < 1 \tag{15.10}$$

as anything outside of the unit circle would be driven away from the origin by repeated self-multiplication.

The justification is somewhat less clear when the matrix cannot be diagonalized, as none of the above work can be replicated. However, the result still holds, as the following general but less intuitive explanation will show. If

$$\lim_{t \to \infty} \left(\mathbf{f} \right)^t = \mathbf{0}, \tag{15.11}$$

then as t increases it brings $(\mathbf{f})^t$ closer to the zero matrix, which has n eigenvalues of 0. Thus, stability requires that the eigenvalues of $(\mathbf{f})^t$ all tend toward zero as t increases without bound. However, it is easily demonstrated that if λ is an eigenvalue of $\mathbf{f}$ then λ^t is an eigenvalue of $(\mathbf{f})^t$ (ibid: 343). Thus, as t increases without bound, it must be the case that λ^t gets arbitrarily close to 0 for each eigenvalue λ of $\mathbf{f}$. This, however, is the same condition as in the diagonalizable case presented above; thus, mathematical stability is equivalent to (10) for each i.

As stated above, the most problematic assumption made in the above work is the requirement that the SFM under consideration only have one type of delivery. Although most of the rest of the assumptions are "close enough" to make the eigenvalue approach useful, this restriction would fatally hamper its applicability to real-world policy problems. Fortunately, this assumption can be relaxed without much trouble at all.

Assume now a system of n elements where m different deliveries flow between the elements, with the other previous assumptions still holding. For maximum generality, assume that the level of flow of each type of delivery to each element can in turn affect the flow of each delivery to each element from that element. That is, each of the nm flows into an element can affect each of the nm flows being delivered by that element. This can all be represented by a matrix $\mathbf{\Phi}$ with nm rows and nm columns, better conceptualized as an $m \times m$ matrix, where each entry is "block" – an $n \times n$ matrix. Each of these $n \times n$ submatrices, as above, describes the sensitivity of the flow from the row element to the column element; however, the sensitivity of the flow needs to be more carefully defined. More fully, let us denote entries in $\mathbf{\Phi}$ with the convention $\phi_{i,j,k,l}$, with i and j between 1 and n; and k

$$\begin{bmatrix} \begin{bmatrix} \varphi_{1,1,1,1} & \cdots & \varphi_{1,n,1,1} \\ \vdots & \ddots & \vdots \\ \varphi_{n,1,1,1} & \cdots & \varphi_{n,n,1,1} \end{bmatrix} & \cdots & \begin{bmatrix} \varphi_{1,1,1,m} & \cdots & \varphi_{1,n,1,m} \\ \vdots & \ddots & \vdots \\ \varphi_{n,1,1,m} & \cdots & \varphi_{n,n,1,m} \end{bmatrix} \\ \vdots & \ddots & \vdots \\ \begin{bmatrix} \varphi_{1,1,m,1} & \cdots & \varphi_{1,n,m,1} \\ \vdots & \ddots & \vdots \\ \varphi_{n,1,m,1} & \cdots & \varphi_{n,n,m,1} \end{bmatrix} & \cdots & \begin{bmatrix} \varphi_{1,1,m,m} & \cdots & \varphi_{1,n,m,m} \\ \vdots & \ddots & \vdots \\ \varphi_{n,1,m,m} & \cdots & \varphi_{n,n,m,m} \end{bmatrix} \end{bmatrix}$$

Fig. 8 Schematic of Φ

and l between 1 and m, both inclusive. In terms of the matrix, $\phi_{i,j,k,l}$ represents the entry in the i-th row and j-th column of the submatrix in the k-th block row and l-th block column of the overall $m \times m$ block matrix (Fig. 8 should help the reader visualize Φ). In terms of the system, $\phi_{i,j,k,l}$ represents the sensitivity of the i element's flow of delivery l to element j with respect to the overall flow of delivery k to the element i. This allows the full flexibility discussed earlier so this approach can apply to essentially any system.

In addition, the vector of initial disturbances needs to be modified. As there are n elements with m categories each available for perturbation, there must be nm elements. In keeping with the rest of the setup, define Δ as the disturbance vector and conceptualize as a "stack" of m vectors, each with n entries. The g-th entry in the h-th n-vector represents the level of initial disturbance in delivery h to element g. Also, let δx denote the $nm \times 1$ vector (set up in the same order as Δ) which gives the change in the overall flow level of each delivery to each element at an arbitrary time. With this notation set up, the system operating with the disturbance can be represented by the equations $\delta x_t = \Phi \delta x_{t-1}$, $\delta x_0 = \Delta$.

Certainly, changing the system so that one has to deal with matrices within matrices can make the problem more intimidating. However, once the problem is set up, Φ is just a matrix with nm rows and nm columns and can be treated like any other matrix. Because of this, all of the above results still hold. Thus, for a system represented in an SFM, the system is stable if and only if each of the nm eigenvalues λ of Π lies within the unit circle of the complex plane. This is no trivial computational task (for an SFM with 40 elements and 25 kinds of deliveries, there are 1,000 eigenvalues), but all that is required is processing power.

It might seem strange that such a simple result can tell so much about the stability of a socioecological system. However, at the point of the calculations, the complicated work has already been done by scientists in measuring the effects of the flows on the various system components. Once these data are collected, the SFM powerfully organizes this material and allows the manipulation that enables the system to be studied holistically. Again, this result was developed by making several assumptions and does not reflect all of the complexity of the systems it describes, but it should serve as a useful tool in studying the stability/sustainability of a system.

Conclusion

The SFM approach is still largely underutilized. The vast majority of policy decisions are still being made without a holistic look at the likely consequences on the socioecological context and a complex theoretic model and set of formal tools. Hopefully, as the SFM approach becomes more robust and the output becomes increasingly sophisticated, its use at all levels of policymaking will increase.

The work above should make clear that with regard to the potential analytic utility and power of the SFM, the surface is just being scratched. The use of the standard SFM website and formatting tools should allow greater and easier collaboration than in the past. Individuals inside and outside of academia, and in any location, can work together on a single problem simply. Also, there is now a location where the interested policy scientist could go to become acquainted with the use of the SFM in real-world problems. In addition, the Editor should allow for simpler manipulation and adjustment of the SFM, making it easier to respond to changes in the knowledge base.

The work with corporate interlock and power blocs is surely representative of many other potential "special cases" of SFM analysis. Just as the linkages between corporate directorships reveal the reach and collusive potential of the corporations involved, so other algorithms can allow for the development of indicators for other types of problem. Also, now that time-series analysis of corporate interlock is feasible, the construction of a "database for trends, comparisons, and statistical analysis" should be possible (Hayden et al. 2002: 697).

The very simple nature of the SFM as a Boolean digraph means that the possibilities for general analytic results from either graph theory or matrix theory are essentially limitless. The examples presented above have to do with positive feedback and system stability. However, the robustness of these results could be expanded and assumptions relaxed.

In addition, there are many other areas where more mathematical focus is needed, such as the impact of the different clocks in system time (see Hayden 2005: 156–158) on the outcomes. This is an exciting field of study to approach mathematically because there is relatively little that has been formally explored and integrated into the literature on the SFM. Further work would certainly increase the descriptive and analytical power, the amount and quality of collaborative research, and thus the relevance of the SFM approach.

Acknowledgement The author would like to thank Dr. F. Gregory Hayden for his guidance on integrating mathematics and the SFM, and Roger A. Simonsen and Derek J. Augustine for building and maintaining the SFM website.

References

Anton H, Rorres C (2000) Elementary linear algebra: applications version. Wiley, New York

Ayres CE (1944/1978) The theory of economic progress: a study of the fundamentals of economic development and cultural change. New Issues Press, Kalamazoo, MI

Hayden FG (2005) Policymaking for a good society: the social fabric matrix approach to policy analysis and program evaluation. Springer, New York

Hayden FG, Wood KR, Kaya A (2002) The use of power blocs of integrated corporate directorships to articulate a power structure: case study and research recommendations. J Econ Issues 36(3):671–706

Mankiw NG (2007) Macroeconomics, 6th edn. Worth, New York

Melman S (1983) Profits without production. Knopf, New York

Nelson RR (2005) Technology, institutions, and economic growth. Harvard University Press, Cambridge

Ore O (1990) Graphs and their uses. Mathematical Association of America, Washington

Razavi MB (1983) Modeling an Islamic economic system: an interaction delivery matrix and Boolean digraph approach. Dissertation, Universityof Nebraska

Conclusion

The Impact of the Social Fabric Matrix in Analysis and Policy Advice

Richard V. Adkisson

Abstract The social fabric matrix (SFM) has been used in policy analysis for some 25 years. Several examples of SFM analysis are included within this volume. This chapter looks at these and other works and asks two simple questions. First, has the SFM shown itself to be a useful tool for policy analysis? Second, has SFM-based research and policy advice exercised real-world policy influence? Several examples are used to demonstrate that the answer to both of these questions is a qualified yes. The SFM fills an important role in the policy analysis toolbox and has in some cases had significant but hard won influence on actual policy.

Introduction

A quarter of a century has passed since the social fabric matrix (SFM) was introduced (Hayden 2006). Many of the chapters of this volume demonstrate its usefulness in analyzing socioeconomic problems. It is a tool that matches the theory, philosophy, and methodology of applied institutional economics. It has achieved a respectable level of acceptance within segments of the academic community where holistic/systems thinking is encouraged. However, it is sometimes the case that great academic ideas and tools lose some of their shine when applied to real-world problems. Is this the case with the SFM? Can the SFM extend the policy influence of economics generally and evolutionary-institutionalist economics particularly? Has the SFM had significant policy influence? This chapter examines the SFM's usefulness and influence as a tool for applied policy analysis.

Before directly addressing the SFM question, a brief overview of the general policy value of economics is in order.

R.V. Adkisson
Wells Fargo Professor of Economics and International Business, New Mexico State University, Las Cruces, NM, USA

T. Natarajan et al. (eds.), *Institutional Analysis and Praxis*,
DOI 10.1007/978-0-387-88741-8_16, © Springer Science+Business Media, LLC 2009

Economics and Economists in the Policy Realm

When one considers that all, or nearly all, policy decisions have economic
aspects to them, it is easy to see why economists are involved in policy analysis.
Approximately 12% of Ph.D. economists are employed by various governmental
entities and thus clearly in position to influence public policy. No doubt this
understates the degree to which economists are involved in policy. For example,
approximately 60% of Ph.D. economists are employed in colleges and universities, where their duties are primarily academic, yet many of them `regularly do
policy work for government and other entities with policy influence (Woodbury
2000). Still, the reputation of economists, and therefore economics, in the policy
realm is checkered at best.

According to Nelson "the worlds of applied policy economics and of academic
economics have been diverging for some time" (1987:85). His conclusion is based
on a historical survey of policy economics beginning with the progressive era of the
early twentieth century. It is not clear that the situation has changed in the two
decades since this history was written. Nelson writes that "economists tend to view
their proper professional role in the governing process as that of experts separate
from politics, value judgments, and other subjective and normative factors" (loc.
cit.:49–50). It seems that economists often assume they know the answers and like
to ignore (real-world) things that clutter their analysis.

Economists come to their distaste for policy clutter honestly. In many ways, they
are socialized to avoid it (Colander and Klamer 1987; Colander 2005). Standard,
though abstract, economic models often suggest clear policy answers but the
answers tend to be the same regardless of the problem: find a market solution; don't
regulate anything; government can only make things worse. To push an agenda
other than that suggested by economic rationality would be misguided. When they
look away from reality to draw policy conclusions, they are simply honoring the
notion of scientific objectivity. Unfortunately, this sense of honor can limit
economists' policy influence.

Nelson proposes several steps that could be taken (to increase policy influence)
by economists. "A first step would be to accept the fact that in many areas of policy
it is probably necessary to be an entrepreneur and advocate for specific economic
policies" (1987:85). The second step

> "would be to do what is possible to develop the types of knowledge and skills needed to
> assume this role (advocate) more effectively" (1987:86). This would require economists to
> "invest greater effort in improving writing skills, facility in reasoning by analogy, com-
> mand of institutional details, knowledge of legal processes and reasoning, and political
> awareness and savvy. They might need to devote more time and effort to investigations of
> history, law, politics and institutions, and their bearing on the economic topics of policy
> concern" (Nelson 1987:86).

Nelson is suggesting that economists adopt an advocacy role. While overly simplistic economics-based recommendations do not hold up well in policy debates, the
good and useful things economists have to say (concern for efficiency, the reality of

trade-offs, etc.) need to be expressed. To advocate is to give economic analysis a louder voice among the many competing interests shaping a policy decision. Still, as mentioned above, to do so would be a big step for many professional economists. By training, most academics are ingrained with the notion that one should remain objective in one's advice giving. One should simply do the analysis and let the facts/analyses speak for themselves. This positivist bias is especially strong among those educated in economics, mathematics, and science (Morçöl 2001).

Recognizing that economists are sometimes less effective than they could be in the policy arena, Aaron (1992) asked a legislator, a presidential advisor, and a journalist what economists might do differently to make themselves more useful in the policy realm. The answers he received did not paint too clear a picture but neither were they inconsistent with Nelson's analysis. The legislator, Lee Hamilton, said economists should "express their ideas on important policy issues clearly and simply, without jargon" while not oversimplifying. He continues by saying that "one of the most useful roles an economist can perform is to remind policymakers that the economy is complex, that we must be keenly aware of the unintended consequences of our actions" (Hamilton 1992:61).

The White House advisor made five suggestions for policy effectiveness. Most of these apply specifically to macroeconomic policy and to economists employed directly by the White House. The general advice seems to reduce to this. "Economists must go beyond theoretical frameworks and lists of possible alternatives, and have the courage to make recommendations based on sound economic judgments, leaving it to others to insert political considerations" (Eizenstat 1992:71). In other words, others involved in the policy process are not bashful in making their cases; economists should be bolder in making their case.

The journalist expressed a different concern. In their eagerness to benefit from media exposure and consulting fees, some of the best minds of the profession are self-allocating to the mundane and losing credibility. "The best of our graduate faculty are beginning to show up more often as authors of court briefs or newspaper opinion columns than of articles in the *American Economic Review*. That might be good for communication, but lousy for the credibility and future of the profession" (Weinstein 2000:73). He continues, "the distinction between a scholar's work and scholarly work is becoming blurred. More is at stake than a mere loss of innocence if the profession's leading lights can no longer be, well, trusted to tell all. Where once scholars served as reliable authorities, they now serve as advocates" (Weinstein 2000:76). This concern agrees with Krugman's (1994) discussion of policy entrepreneurs. Seeing things happening in Brazil, Farria (2001) referred to this phenomenon as the consultancy disease. Similarly, Woodbury suggests that economists "may risk irrelevance if we take a purely academic stance, we risk seeing our work misinterpreted and used in ways that the original research does not support when we wander into the minefield of policy" (Woodbury 2000:418).

Perhaps the comment below sums up the self-limiting policy role of economics and economists:

[N]oneconomists seek guidance to the redress of specific economic problems. Here there has been a marked failure across all mainstream strains of thought. It lies in their common belief in the irrelevance – worse, the impotence – of "policy," which is to say the useless-ness of political (governmental) powers to affect the outcome of economic dynamics. This attitude represents more than a distancing of economics from the disorderliness of politics or a frustration with the difficulties of applying "scientifically" exact economic remedies. It is an *abdication from the moral obligations* of a discipline that would have not raison d'être if social malfunctions did not exist in the portion of society we call "the economy" (Heilbroner and Milberg 1995:94, emphasis added).

Several generalizations are possible, based on the works mentioned above.

- Economics and economists have a useful and important role to play in policy analysis but their influence has not been as strong or useful as it could be.
- To have greater impact on policy, economists must become more active advocates of their policy perspectives. However, care must be taken that their advocacy be based on generally agreed upon economic principles rather than ideology (or personal self-interest).
- The tools of academic discourse are useful in exploring the frontiers of eco-nomic knowledge, but policy recommendations, while consistent with academic findings, should be clearly and simply expressed.
- Economists need to incorporate a broader perspective into their recommenda-tions and recognize the political and other forces at work in policy decisions.
- Economics and economists have little reason to exist in a perfect, problem-free world.

The Social Fabric Matrix as a Policy Tool

The SFM was developed less to illustrate how the economy works than as a tool to find out how the economy works. Certainly original institutionalist theory and instrumen-talist/pragmatist philosophy informed the creation of the SFM and continues to guide many SFM users. Given the theory behind the matrix, SFM users must seriously con-sider the interdependence of cultural values, societal beliefs, personal attitudes, social institutions, technology, and the ecological system as they conduct their analysis (Hayden 2006:8). Still, even with its strong philosophical and theoretical moorings, SFM analysis does not anticipate any particular economic patterns or behavior prior to conducting analysis. In a review of Hayden's 2006 book, Peach put it this way:

The role of the SFM is to help organize the process of analysis so that the experts from many disciplines understand the big picture, to ensure that nothing gets lost, and to design a research program focused on issues that matter. Recognizing which issues are important is critical (Peach 2006:1168).

Another review suggested that "Hayden might be called a complexifier" (Gould 2007:399). Perhaps the most enthusiastic endorsement came from Elsner who wrote, "the SFM in fact may serve as the future methodology not only for complex heterodox economic analyses but also for policy evaluation in order to make policy more consistent with the complexity of reality" (Elsner 2007:200).

Along with the other work presented in this volume, the example below shows how the SFM can be used to reveal the workings of real-world economies. The following example might be loosely classified as an industrial organization example.

The SFM and the Case of the Private Central Planning Core

Industrial organization scholars are often concerned with industrial concentration. The major concern is that oligopolistic and monopolistic structures give firms power over price and thus cause markets to allocate resources inefficiently. Generally, the focus is on concentration within particular industries. Original institutionalists are equally concerned about concentrations of economic power but don't limit their analyses to disruptions of market decision making. Putting it more broadly, "to possess economic power is to be able to exercise significant control of the decisionmaking process" (Klein 1987:1341). In a world of horizontally and vertically integrated corporate business organization where the economic size of single corporations can dwarf those of many countries of the world, it is hard to accept that having influence over prices is the only way economic power is expressed particularly if there is a means for seemingly independent corporations to coordinate their plans with one another.

Munkirs (1985) examined the national economy and identified a "central planning core" (CPC) of corporations knitted together in web of interlocking directorships. The existence of the CPC tightens the network of contacts and facilitates information flows between corporations. This structure expands the power of core corporations by allowing the coordination of decision making and planning across corporations and industries, presumably matching decisions to the desires of the CPC. The CPC is the modern corporate equivalent of the good old boy networks of simpler times.

Using the SFM and the mathematics of graph theory, Hayden and Stephenson (1992) undertook the task of finding the State of Nebraska's CPC and its ties to the state's flagship university, The University of Nebraska. There were many prior assumptions about centers of power within Nebraska but no one had clearly identified them before this study. In the spirit of the following statement, Hayden and Stephenson let the data speak for themselves:

> The SFM approach does not prejudge where the center lies. In Nebraska, the CPC included corporations involved in banking, insurance, communications, food processing, equipment production, investment, transportation, and so forth. The SFM method determines the central core and the degree of reachability to the core, rather than forcing investigators to hypothesize the core (Hayden and Stephenson 1992:76).

Another purpose of Hayden and Stephenson's work was to test (for the Nebraska case) Veblen's (1957 [1918]) hypotheses about the influence of business/pecuniary interests in the academy. Finding also that the University was closely integrated into Nebraska's CPC, they conclude the following.

> Corporate influence no longer obtrudes itself *from outside* into the university. It has become *internalized* within the university as academic administrators become active participants in the central planning core. Thus, the pecuniary logic now dominates *from within* the institution of higher learning (Hayden and Stephenson 1992:77; emphases in original).

Using the SFM and related techniques, Hayden and Stephenson identified Nebraska's central planning core, showed that it was more concentrated than previously thought, identified a hierarchy within the core (degree of connectedness), and tied the core to the state's flagship university. Building on this research,Stephenson and Rakow (1993) examined the position of women in the CPC. Stephenson and Hayden (1995) applied similar analysis to the national economy and were thus able to compare the level of power concentration in Nebraska to that in the nation (Nebraska's CPC being somewhat more concentrated than the national CPC). But does this work have policy relevance?

Suppose that a state legislature is operating under the assumptions that corporations in the state, regardless of whether they dominate their own industry, operate independently in their business decisions, and that the flagship university operates independently of the worldly concerns of business. Now suppose that the legislature is considering a change in the corporate tax structure, funding of a new university program, or setting procurement policies for the state. In the first instance, the legislature might turn to the university to provide an analysis of the impacts of the tax change, assuming that the analysis will be objective. In the second case, legislators might assume that the program, perhaps supported by business, is designed to serve the broader public social good. In the third case, legislators might require that in-state companies be favored in the procurement process, assuming that competition among the "independent" companies will result in fair pricing. If the real world matches the assumptions, things should go well, but what if the assumptions are wrong?

The SFM-based analysis described above reveals a different world, at least in the Nebraska[1] case. While the analysis doesn't prove that corporations are conspiring with one another or that the integrity of the university has been compromised, it does reveal a structure that makes such things possible. Knowing of the existence of the CPC and its connections to the university would, at a minimum, allow and encourage policymakers to ask appropriate questions as policy changes are considered. For example, if the university analysis indicates that a reduction of the corporate tax will increase state revenues and boost the state economy substantially, a wise legislator might ask that the analysis be reviewed by another independent analyst before factoring the impact study into a decision. Likewise, knowing of the interconnectedness of local corporations might cause them to drop the policy of favoring in-state companies.

The Influence of SFM-Based Policy Analysis

The example above suggests that the SFM and the open-systems approach can be useful tools for policy analysis. Several examples are provided in this volume, and others are available. For example, Groeneweyen and Beije (1989) used the SFM

---

[1]There is nothing in the analysis to suggest that Nebraska is a special case. It just happens that it was chosen for analysis.

approach to analyze the French communication industry. Meister (1990) looked at U.S. federal farm policy. Hayden (2004, 2005) studied Polish hog production. Hayden and Fullwiler (2001), Hayden (2002), and Hayden et al. (2002) looked at various issues related to the proposed location of a low-level radioactive waste dump in north central Nebraska. All of the work mentioned above contributed to the body of academic knowledge, but has SFM analysis had significant policy influence?

As suggested earlier in this chapter, the gap between academic research and policy influence is often difficult to bridge. Equally, it may be difficult to know when the gap has been crossed and when it hasn't. The connection is not always clear. Sometimes extensive reports are written and ignored. At other times the slightest suggestion can result in policy changes. And, who knows how many policy-makers continue to hear and respond to the faint whispers of their old professors as they go about their daily routines?

Hayden suggests that his work with Bolduc (2000) represents the SFM-based research that had the most policy influence to date (personal communication).

The SFM and the Case of Low-Level Radioactive Waste

In 1980 the Federal Low-Level Radioactive Waste Policy Act was passed. The Act moved the responsibility for low-level radioactive waste disposal to the states and suggested that states organize regional waste disposal compacts. In 1983, Nebraska joined a pact with Kansas, Oklahoma, Louisiana, and Arkansas. Unsatisfied with the rate of progress, the Act was amended in 1986 to impose progress and enforce requirements. Eventually, it was concluded that Nebraska should host the waste site for the compact, and in 1989 Boyd County was selected as the final site. Boyd County is a rural county along Nebraska's northern border with South Dakota.[2] At the time it was chosen, the county had a population of about 2,800 people scattered over 540 square miles.

Hayden and Bolduc (2000) identified several problems with the legislation but their analysis focused primarily on the financial feasibility. Two major factors drove them to the conclusion that the compact was caught up in a "financial death cycle" (p. 274). "The combination of declining waste volume, increasing facility costs, and the contractual requirement that disposal fees be sufficient to cover unit costs has resulted in estimated disposal fees for the CIC [Central Interstate Low-Level Radioactive Waste Compact] facility much higher than industry norms" (p. 263). Previous estimates set the maximum charge that compacts could charge (and survive) at $250 per cubic foot of waste (p. 274).

Hayden and Bolduc used the SFM and associated digraph to sort out the details of the cost-plus contract governing the development of the contract. Development funds were borrowed from large waste producers with the understanding that interest

---

[2] http://www.geocities.com/~daburton/LLRW/Neb-Chronology2.html.

would accrue during development and construction and the costs would be paid out of operating revenue after the site opened. Given the cost-plus structure of the contract, these costs accrued rather quickly, providing substantial profits to the developer but threatening the financial viability of the project. Having used the SFM/digraph to sort out the contract, the revealed equations were modeled in a system dynamics model so that cost/revenue projections could be made. Hayden and Bolduc estimated that the compact would have to charge $18,500 per cubic foot to cover contractual costs (p. 274). After much ado, the Hayden and Bolduc estimates were accepted. Nebraska withdrew from the compact in 1999, and the waste site was never built.[3]

It is worth noting that advocacy also played a major role in exerting the policy influence just discussed. Hayden was a member of the Commission overseeing the project and worked closely with political decision makers throughout the process. He was called to task by many who didn't like the report's findings. For example, site supporters quietly hired a high-level consulting firm to scrutinize the study (personal communication). Hayden even had his intelligence publically questioned. The Vice President of U.S. Ecology, the firm developing the facility reportedly said "I can't see in any realistic way how any intelligent person could come up with that conclusion" (Anderson 1997). The advocacy was not short lived either. Several years were invested in this project.

The SFM and School Funding

Another project currently underway is yet to have specific policy influence but has shown great promise. Hayden (2007), Hoffman and Hayden (2007), and Hoffman (this volume) have been unraveling the intricacies of K-12 education financing in Nebraska. As in many states, a Nebraska School District's state funding is determined by a formula. In Nebraska's case (and probably in other states) the formula has been incrementally changed over the years. Nebraska's 1976–1977 school finance formula could be expressed as one continuous algebraic formulation of one page. The 2006–2007 formula requires some 600 pages when fully expressed, though an abridged version of 138 pages is available (Hayden 2007). As with the contracts in the radioactive waste case above, the SFM was used to sort out the scattered details of the funding formula as they had been expressed in various pieces of legislation. A digraph was created to represent the system, and a system dynamics model incorporating the formula was developed. The driving force behind this research is a series of lawsuits challenging the equity and adequacy in educational funding.

Hoffman and Hayden (2007) conclude that that the best response to the complexity and inadequacy of the formula is to scrap it and start again by creating a new set of funding rules that clearly meet current social norms. Advocacy of this

---

[3]For a popular account of the struggle over the waste site, see Cragin (2007).

position has inspired serious consideration of the proposal to rethink school funding, but active opposition (favoring instead further incremental change) has also arisen and slowed the reform process (Walton 2007).

The two cases above provide some important lessons about using the SFM effectively to impact policy decisions. First, the SFM is one important tool in a larger tool chest of analytical tools. In both the waste and education cases, the SFM/digraph was used to reveal the reality of very complex systems that were non-obvious prior to SFM analysis. Later it was necessary to bring in the tools of mathematics, system dynamics, and computer modeling to bring the project to life. Second, substantial intellectual resources and time were (and are still being) devoted to the analysis and advocacy in each case. Third, advocacy, supported by analysis, is not universally welcomed. Opposition will arise to any suggestion of change. Finally, the analysts involved were in regular contact with influential policy makers throughout the research process and often relied on their support when opposition arose.

Economics and the SFM Approach – Toward More Effective Policy Analysis: Conclusions

This chapter began with an overview of economics and economists in the policy realm. Several criticisms were apparent. Economists need to advocate for policy, but advocacy needs to agree with sound principles rather than ideology. Economists need to express themselves clearly to policy audiences. Economists need a broader perspective. The final question here is, does the SFM help in these regards? The answer is a qualified yes.

As discussed above, the SFM is moored to original institutional economic theory, a system-oriented theory that guides inquiry but doesn't dictate particular results. The SFM invites the analyst to find reality. In the radioactive waste example, good social decisions could not be made until the reality of the cost-plus contracts were revealed by the SFM. The reality was a "financial death cycle that resulted when analysis and democracy [were] excluded from policy and decision making" (Hayden and Bolduc 2000:275). Likewise, the school financing issue cannot be adequately addressed until the reality of the current system is understood. Using the SFM, advocacy can be backed with knowledge and understanding rather than ideology and private interests.

Reality is not always simple. Perhaps that is why the reviewer suggested that Hayden is a "complexifier" (Gould 2007:399). Still, SFM analysis provides several levels of communication. The SFM can be studied. The digraph provides a visual map of the system revealed in the SFM. The equations provide the necessary detail. The system dynamic models provide another level of communication and, ultimately, the results can be expressed in simple terms as in the case of the $18,500 per cubic foot disposal fee or the fact that it requires 600 pages of equations to express the school funding formula.

It should certainly be clear that the SFM invites analysts to take a broader perspective. Cultural values, beliefs, attitudes, technology, the environment, and institutions of all sorts are, by definition of the SFM process, incorporated into the analysis. Thus if legislative approval is necessary, it can be incorporated into the model. If conflicting beliefs are at work, they will be revealed. Certainly SFM analysis reveals a complex world, but it also brings order to the complexity and richness to the analysis.

Certainly, incorporating the SFM into policy analysis addresses many of the deficiencies discussed above. Still, one must take care in assigning its policy value. Just as just math, just theory, just econometrics, just data, etc. do not provide a complete toolbox for economic analysis, neither does the SFM. Yet it is of great value, particularly in identifying systems that are not otherwise obvious, but its value grows when it is combined with other analytical tools. In the examples used here, the tools were extensive study of documents, legal analysis, mathematics, system dynamic modeling, clear and detailed writing, and *ithink* computer software (see also Tristan Markwell this volume). As Gill puts it, "the final configuration of the matrix is less important than the process underlying its construction. Through building the matrix, the analyst will derive relevant insights into the cause of the problem under investigation" (Gill 1996, p.173). Revelation of the complex system feeding the complex problem in the frame of proper theory and its corresponding methodology is a major first step toward problem resolution.

References

Aaron HJ. Symposium on economists as policy advocates. J Econ Perspect. 1992;6:5960.
Anderson J (1997) Waste-site study raises cost issues: US ecology disputes prediction of doom. Omaha World Herald June 24
Colander D. The making of an economist redux. J Econ Perspect. 2005;19:175198.
Colander D, Klamer A. The making of an economist. J Econ Perspect. 1987;1:95111.
Cragin S. Nuclear Nebraska: the remarkable story of the little county that couldn't be bought. New York: American Management Association; 2007.
Eizenstat SE. Economists and White House decisions. J Econ Perspect. 1992;6:6571.
Elsner W. Policymaking for a good society: the social fabric matrix approach to policy analysis and program evaluation (book review). Intervention. J Econ. 2007;4:20003.
Faria JR. Rent seeking in academia: the consultancy disease. Am Econ. 2001;45:6974.
Gill R. An integrated social fabric matrix/system dynamics approach to policy analysis. SystDyn Rev. 1996;12:167181.
Gould AE. Policymaking for a good society: the social fabric matrix approach to policy analysis and program evaluation (book review). Soc Sci J. 2007;44:399401.
Groeneweyen J, Beije PR. The French communication industry defined and analyzed through the social fabric matrix, the *Filière*approach, and network analysis. J Econ Issues. 1989;23:105974.
Hamilton LH. Economists as public policy advisers. J Econ Perspect. 1992;6:6164.
Hayden FG. Policymaking network of the iron-triangle subgovernment for licensing hazardous waste facilities. J Econ Issues. 2002;36:47784.
Hayden FG. Network consequences due to oligopolists and oligopsonists in the hog industry, pollution from hog production, and the failure to regulate ecological criteria. J Econ Issues. 2004;38:48391.

Hayden FG. Combining equity and the precautionary principle: examples drawn from hog production in Poland. J Econ Issues. 2005;39:35764.

Hayden FG. Policymaking for a good society: the social fabric matrix approach to policy analysis and program evaluation. New York: Springer; 2006.

Hayden FG (2007) Nebraska stateaid formula for a local K-12 public school system, 2006–2007. Department of Economics working paper, University of Nebraska, Lincoln

Hayden FG, Bolduc SR. Contracts and costs in a corporate/government system dynamics model: a United States case. In: Elsner W, Groenewegen J, editors. Industrial policies after 2000. Boston: Kluwer; 2000.

Hayden FG, Fullwiler ST. Analysis of the financial assurance plan in the license application for a low-level radioactive wastedisposal facility. J Econ Issues. 2001;35:37383.

Hayden FG, Stephenson K. Overlap of organizations: corporate transorganization and Veblen's thesis on higher education. J Econ Issues. 1992;26:5385.

Hayden FG, Wood KR, Kaya A. The use of power blocs of integrated corporate directorships to articulate a power structure: case study and research recommendations. J Econ Issues. 2002;36:617705.

Heilbroner R, Milberg W. The crisis of vision in modern economic thought. Cambridge: Cambridge University Press; 1995.

Hoffman JL, Hayden FG. Using the social fabric matrix to analyze institutional rules relative to adequacy in education funding. J Econ Issues. 2007;41:359367.

Klein PA. Power and economic performance: the institutionalist view. J Econ Issues. 1987;21:134177.

Krugman P. Peddling prosperity: economic sense and nonsense in the age of diminished expectations. New York/London: Norton; 1994.

Meister BA. Analysis of federal farm policy using the social fabric matrix. J Econ Issues. 1990;24:189224.

Morçöl G. Positivist beliefs among policy professionals: an empirical investigation. Policy Sci. 2001;34:381401.

Munkirs JR. The transformation of American capitalism: from competitive market structures to central private sector planning. New York: M.E. Sharpe; 1985.

Nelson RH. The economics profession and the making of public policy. J Econ Lit. 1987;25:4991.

Peach JT. Policymaking for a good society: the social fabric matrix approach to policy analysis and program evaluation (book review). J Econ Issues. 2006;40:116869.

Stephenson K, Hayden FG. Comparison of the corporate decision networks of Nebraska and the United States. J Econ Issues. 1995;29:84369.

Stephenson K, Rakow S. Female representation in U.S. centralized private planning: the case of overlapping directorships. J Econ Issues. 1993;27:45970.

Veblen T (1957[1918]) The higher learning in America: a memorandum on the conduct of universities by business men. First American Century Series Edition. Hill and Wang, New York

Walton D (2007) Analysis illustrates complexity of state aid to schools formula. Lincoln Journal Star July 27, Lincoln

Weinstein M. Economists and the media. J Econ Perspect. 1992;6:73770.

Woodbury SA. Economics, economists, and public policy. Q Rev Econ Finance. 2000;40:417430.

Index

Breinigsville, PA USA
28 September 2009
R3748200001B/R37482PG224659BVX5B/5/P

9 780387 887401